ISBN 978-0-282-49534-3
PIBN 10853681

1 MONTH OF
FREE
READING

at

www.ForgottenBooks.com

By purchasing this book you are eligible for one month membership to ForgottenBooks.com, giving you unlimited access to our entire collection of over 1,000,000 titles via our web site and mobile apps.

To claim your free month visit:

www.forgottenbooks.com/free853681

English
Français
Deutsche
Italiano
Español
Português

www.forgottenbooks.com

Mythology Photography **Fiction** Fishing Christianity **Art** Cooking Essays Buddhism Freemasonry Medicine **Biology** Music **Ancient Egypt** Evolution Carpentry Physics Dance Geology **Mathematics** Fitness Shakespeare **Folklore** Yoga Marketing **Confidence** Immortality Biographies Poetry **Psychology** Witchcraft Electronics Chemistry History **Law** Accounting **Philosophy** Anthropology Alchemy Drama Quantum Mechanics Atheism Sexual Health **Ancient History** **Entrepreneurship** Languages Sport Paleontology Needlework Islam **Metaphysics** Investment Archaeology Parenting Statistics Criminology **Motivational**

THE ROMANCE OF BIBLE CHRONOLOGY.

THE

ROMANCE OF
BIBLE CHRONOLOGY

An Exposition of the meaning, and a Demonstration
of the Truth, of every Chronological statement
contained in the Hebrew Text of the
Old Testament.

VOLUME I.

THE TREATISE.

BY THE

REV. MARTIN ÁNSTEY, B.D., M.A. (London).

MARSHALL BROTHERS, LTD.,
LONDON, EDINBURGH AND NEW YORK.
1913.

Dedication.

To my dear Friend

REV. G. CAMPBELL MORGAN, D.D.

to whose inspiring Lectures on

"THE DIVINE LIBRARY IN HUMAN HISTORY"

I trace the inception of these pages, and whose intimate knowledge and unrivalled exposition of the Written Word makes audible in human ears the Living Voice of the Living God,

I DEDICATE THIS BOOK.

THE AUTHOR.

October 3rd, 1913.

FOREWORD.

By Rev. G. Campbell Morgan, D.D.

It is with pleasure, and yet with reluctance, that I have consented to preface this book with any words of mine.

The reluctance is due to the fact that the work is so lucidly done, that any setting forth of the method or purpose by way of introduction would be a work of supererogation.

The pleasure results from the fact that the book is the outcome of our survey of the Historic movement in the redeeming activity of God as seen in the Old Testament, in the Westminster Bible School. While I was giving lectures on that subject, it was my good fortune to have the co-operation of Mr. Martin Anstey, in a series of lectures on these dates. My work was that of sweeping over large areas, and largely ignoring dates. He gave his attention to these, and the result is the present volume, which is invaluable to the Bible Teacher, on account of its completeness and detailed accuracy.

Bible study is the study of the Bible. There are many methods and departments ; none is without value ; all of them, when done thoroughly rather than superficially, tend to the deepening of conviction as to the accuracy of the records.

In no case is this more marked than in departments which are incidental rather than essential.

If, in such a matter as that of dates—which seems to be purely incidental, and is of such a general nature that few have taken the trouble to pay particular attention to it—the method of careful study shows that these apparently incidental references are nevertheless accurate and harmonious, then a testimony full of value is borne to the integrity of the writings.

To this work Mr. Anstey has given himself, with great care, and much scholarship. The results are full of fascination, and are almost startling in their revelation of the harmony of the Biblical scheme.

The method has been that of independent study of the writings themselves, with an open mind, and determination to hide nothing, and to explain nothing away.

The careful and patient student is the only person who will be able to appreciate the value of this work ; and all such will come to its study with thankfulness to the Author ; and having minds equally open and honest, will be able to verify or correct. In this process I venture to affirm that the corrections will be few, and the verification constant.

Westminster Chapel,
Buckingham Gate, S.W.,
October 11th, 1913.

ὁ τολμῶν τὶ παραλάσσειν τῶν γεγραμμένων ἀπ᾽ ἀργης, οὐκ ἐν ὅδῳ ἀληθείας ἵσταται.

He who attempts to alter any part of the Scriptures, from indolence or incapacity, stands not in the path of Truth.

Epiphanius Against Heresies, Book I.

PREFACE BY THE AUTHOR.

THE Studies embodied in the following pages have been undertaken with a view to ascertaining and exhibiting the exact chronological relation of every dated event recorded in the Old Testament. The object of the writer is the production of a Standard Chronology, which shall accurately represent the exact date at which each event took place, so far as this can be ascertained from the statements contained in the text itself.

No other dates are given. All merely approximate or estimated dates are omitted as inexact. All merely probable or conjectural dates, inferred from speculative reconstructions of the historical situation, and not guaranteed by the words of the text, are rejected as unverifiable. All dates certainly known, but derived from other sources—such as profane history and modern discovery—are excluded from the Chapters on the Chronology of the Old Testament. They appear only in the Chapters on Comparative Chronology and in the Chronological Tables (Vol. II). The Chronology adopted in these pages is supported by Josephus, but does not lean upon him. It is, to some extent, confirmed by the results of modern discovery, as tabulated in the Guides to the Babylonian, Assyrian, and Egyptian Antiquities published by the Authorities of the British Museum, but it stands upon its own foundation, and is dependent upon none of them.

Chronology is a branch of History. As such it is governed by the laws which determine the validity of the results reached by the process of scientific investigation and historical enquiry. It is also a branch of Applied Mathematics, and Mathematics is an exact Science. In a truly scientific Chronology there is no room for any date which is not demonstrably true. This view of the limits of the subject accounts for the absence of the note of interrogation (?) after any date in the Chronological Tables, and for the somewhat dogmatic or Euclidian tone in which the conclusions reached by this method are expressed. Like Mathematics, Chronology has its axioms, its postulates, and its definitions, of which the most important and the most fundamental is the trustworthiness of the testimony of honest, capable, and contemporary witnesses, like that of the men whose testimony is preserved in the Records of the Old Testament.

9

CONTENTS.

VOLUME I.—THE TREATISE.

INTRODUCTION.

PERIOD I.—THE PATRIARCHS—*Genesis*.

PERIOD II.—THE THEOCRACY—*Exodus to* 1 *Samuel* 7.

CONTENTS.

INTRODUCTION.

CHAPTER I.—SCOPE, METHOD, STANDPOINT AND SOURCES.

THE *purpose* of the present work is to construct a Standard Chronology of the period covered by the writings of the Old Testament.

In addition to the Hebrew Massoretic Text of the Old Testament, there are many other sources affording data for the construction of a Chronology of this period, of which the principal may be classified as follows :—

1. Other Texts and Versions such as (1) the Septuagint (LXX) or Greek Version of the Old Testament, and (2) the Samaritan Pentateuch.

2. Ancient Literary Remains, such as those fragments of Sanchoniathon of Phœnicia, Berosus of Chaldea, and Manetho of Egypt, which have come down to us ; the national traditions of Persian History preserved in the writings of the Persian poet, Firdusi ; the books of the Old Testament Apocrypha ; the works of the Jewish Historian Josephus, and the Talmudic Tract, *Sedar Olam.*

3. Ancient Monumental Inscriptions upon Rocks, Temples, Palaces, Cylinders, Bricks, Steles and Tablets, and writings upon Papyrus Rolls, brought to light by modern discoveries in recent times.

4. The Classic Literature of Greece and Rome.

5. Astronomical Observations and Calculations, especially eclipses of the Sun, eclipses of the Moon, and the risings of Sirius the dog-star with the Sun.

6. The works of Ancient and Modern Chronologers.

The results obtained from any one of these several sources must, if true, be consistent with the results obtained from each of the other sources.

The aim of the present work is to make an exhaustive critical examination of the data contained in the first of these several sources only, and to develop and construct therefrom a Standard Chronology of the events of the Old Testament, so far as this can be obtained from the chronological data which lie embedded in the Hebrew Massoretic Text of the Old Testament, and independently of any help which may be derived from any other source.

The results thus obtained will be compared at every stage with those obtained from the data afforded by the other sources named above, but whilst the data afforded by the Hebrew Text of the Old Testament are made the subject of an exhaustive critical examination, every step in the series being scientifically investigated and rigorously established in accordance with the recognized laws of historical evidence, the data afforded by these other sources are not thus dealt with, but are left over for investigation by other workers in these several branches of chronological enquiry and research.

The establishment of a Standard Chronology of the Hebrew Text of the Old Testament is a first requisite for the correct interpretation of the results obtained from other departments of chronological study, as, without this, no true and sure comparison can be made between the dates given in the Old Testament and those obtained from other sources.

The *Method* adopted is that of accurate observation and scientific historical induction. Each recorded fact is accepted on the authority of the text which contains it. Each book in the Old Testament is carefully examined, and every chronological statement contained therein is carefully noted down. After thus collecting all the relevant statements of the text, and making a complete induction of all the facts, a chronological scheme is constructed, in which every dated event in the Old Testament is duly charted down in its proper place. There is no selecting of certain facts to the exclusion of certain other facts. There is no attempt to reconcile apparently discrepant statements by conjectural emendations of the text. The scheme is not bent to meet the exigencies of any particular theory, but all the statements that bear upon the subject of Chronology are brought together and interpreted in relation to each other in such a way as to form one complete harmonious table of events in which the whole of the relevant facts contained in the Old Testament are exhibited and explained in the light of the time relations which obtain between them.

An attempt is made to exhibit the results thus obtained to the eye, by means of Diagrams, Charts, Tables and other forms of graphic representation, clearness of apprehension being regarded as equally important with accuracy and precision of statement, in any adequate and satisfactory presentation of this somewhat intricate and difficult subject. In this way an endeavour is made to secure a result which shall be at once both Scriptural and scholarly, and at the same time easy to understand.

The present essay deals only with the Hebrew Text of the Old Testament in the form in which it has reached us from the hands of the Massoretes. That Text has an origin and a history, and our view of its origin may perhaps influence us in our estimate of its value and its authority. Into the question of the authorship, the date, and the composition of the various books of the Old Testament, the integrity of the Text, and the various sources from which it has been derived, the present writer does not now enter. In like manner, all questions relating to the preservation and transmission of the Text are left untouched, the sole aim of the writer being to ascertain and to elicit from the Text as it stands the chronological scheme which lies embodied therein. The authenticity of the records, and the accuracy of the Text in its present state of preservation, is taken for granted. The results obtained from this study will be authoritative within the limits of the authority accorded to the text itself. The materials afforded by the Text are dealt with in accordance with the requirements of modern scientific method. Care has been taken to secure for each step in the Chronology the value of historic proof or demonstration, so that each subsequent induction may proceed upon an assured scientific foundation.

The authority to be accorded to the results obtained from the six other sources named above is that of corroborating or conflicting witnesses, not that of the verdict of a jury, and not that of the pronouncement of a Judge.

The results obtained from the testimony of these other witnesses may be *compared* with those obtained from the Old Testament Record, but they must not be erected into a Standard of established Truth, and used to *correct* the testimony of the principal witness.

(1) *Other Texts and Versions.*

1. The Septuagint (LXX) is a translation of the Hebrew Scriptures of the Old Testament into Hellenistic Greek. It was made at Alexandria in Egypt, a portion at a time, the Pentateuch being the portion translated first. The translation of the entire work occupied some 70 years (B.C. 250–180). It was commenced in the reign of Ptolemy II, Philadelphus, King of Egypt (B.C. 284–247). It was translated by Alexandrian, not Palestinian Jews, and was the work of a number of independent translators, or groups of translators, separated from each other by considerable intervals of time. It was the work of a number of men who had none of that almost superstitious veneration for the letter of Scripture, which characterized the Jews of Palestine. A Palestinian Jew would never dare to add to, to take from, or to alter a single letter of the Original. The translators of the LXX, on the contrary, are notorious for their Hellenizing, or their modernizing tendencies, their desire to simplify and to clear up difficulties, their practice of altering the text in order to remove what they regarded as apparent contradictions, and, generally, their endeavour to adapt their version to the prevailing notions of the age, in such a way as to commend it to the learning and the culture of the time. Hence the centenary additions to the lives of the Patriarchs in order to bring the Chronology into closer accord with the notions of antiquity that prevailed in Egypt at that time. Like the modern critic, the LXX translator did not hesitate to " correct " the record, and to " emend " the Text, in order to make it speak what he thought it ought to say.

2. The Samaritan Pentateuch is a venerable document written in the very ancient pointed Hebrew Script, which appears to have been in use (1) in the time of the Moabite Stone which dates from the 9th Century B.C. (2) in the time of the Siloam Inscription, which dates from the 7th Century B.C., and (3) in the time of the Maccabees, *i.e.*, in the 2nd Century B.C. The Manuscript, which is of great age, is preserved in the Sanctuary of the Samaritan Community at Nablous (Shechem). It modifies the Hebrew Text in accordance with the notions prevailing amongst the descendants of the mixed population introduced into Samaria by the Kings of Assyria, from Sargon (2 Kings 17 [24]) in the 8th Century B.C. to " the great and noble Asnapper " (Ezra 4 [10]) probably Ashurbanipal, in the 7th Century B.C. It alters " Ebal " to " Gerizim " in Deuteronomy 27 [4], bears traces of a narrowing, rather than a broadening outlook, and represents the tendencies that prevailed amongst the Samaritans in the 9th to the 2nd Centuries B.C. If it is not so old as the LXX, the constructor of the Text may have had before him both the Hebrew

Original and the Greek LXX Version, and may have picked his own way, selecting now from the one, and now from the other, in accordance with his own predilections and his own point of view.   But it is more than probable that the Samaritan Pentateuch is much older than the LXX, and that it was translated from Hebrew into Samaritan about the time of Hezekiah in the 8th Century B.C.   (See *The Samaritan Pentateuch and Modern Criticism,* by J. Iverach Munro, M.A., 1911).

The tendency of the modern mind, which is imbued with Greek rather than with Hebrew ideals, is to over-estimate the authority of the LXX as compared with the Hebrew.   Many scholars look upon it as a translation of a different Hebrew Text from that preserved in our Hebrew Bibles, but the variations are all easily accounted for as adaptations of the Original Hebrew to meet the views of the Hellenized Jews of Alexandria.   The differences in the order of the books, the various omissions and the many additions, show that the point of view has been changed, and though the framework and the main substance of the LXX is the same as that of the Hebrew, the modifications are sufficient to indicate that we are reading a translation of *the same original* produced in the new world of Greek culture, rather than the translation of *a different original* produced in the old world of Hebrew religion.   The patriarchal Chronology of the LXX can be explained from the Hebrew on the principle that the translators of the LXX desired to lengthen the Chronology and to graduate the length of the lives of those who lived after the Flood, so as to make the shortening of human life gradual and continuous, instead of sudden and abrupt.   The Samaritan patriarchal Chronology can be explained from the Hebrew.   The constructor of the scheme lengthens the Chronology of the Patriarchs after the Flood, and graduates the length of the lives of the patriarchs throughout the entire list, both before and after the Flood, with this curious result, that with the exception of (1) Enoch, (2) Cainan, whose life exceeds that of his father by only five years, and (3) Reu, whose age at death is the same as that of his father, every one of the Patriarchs, from Adam to Abraham, is made to die a few years younger than his father.   This explains why the Chronology of the years before the Flood is reduced by 349 years.   Could anything be more manifestly artificial ?   The LXX and the Samaritan Pentateuch may take their place in the witness box, but there is no room for them on the bench.

(2) *Ancient Literary Remains.*

Of ancient literary remains outside the classical literature of Greece and Rome, but little has been preserved.   A collection of these, known as Cory's Ancient Fragments, was made and published by Isaac Preston Cory in 1832.

1. *Sanchoniathon* is said to have written a *History of Phœnicia*, and to have flourished in the reign of Semiramis, the Queen of Assyria, the wife of Ninus, and, with him, the mythical founder of Nineveh.   She lived B.C. 2000, or according to others, B.C. 1200.   Sanchoniathon was quoted by Porphyry (b. A.D. 233) the opponent of Christianity, in his attack on the

writings of Moses. Porphyry says, Sanchoniathon was a contemporary of Gideon, B.C. 1339. His writings were translated into Greek by Philo Byblius in the reign of Hadrian (A.D. 76–130). Philo was a native of Byblos, a maritime city on the coast of Phœnicia. He had a considerable reputation for honesty, but some scholars believe his work to be a forgery ; others believe that he was himself deceived by a forger. According to Philo Byblius, Sanchoniathon was a native of Berytus in Phœnicia. His *Phœnician History* may be regarded as one of the most authentic memorials of the events which took place before the Flood, to be met with in heathen literature. It begins with a legendary cosmogony. It relates how the first two mortals were begotten by the Wind (Spirit) and his wife Baau (Darkness). It refers to the Fall, the production of fire, the invention of huts and clothing, the origin of the arts of agriculture, hunting, fishing and navigation, and the beginnings of human civilization. Sanchoniathon gives a curious account of the descendants of the line of Cain. His history of the descendants of the line of Seth reads like an idolatrous version of the record in Genesis. The whole system of Sanchoniathon is a confused, unintelligible jargon, culled from (1) the mythologies of Egypt and Greece, and (2) a corrupt tradition of the narrative in Genesis. It may well have been forged by Porphyry, or by Philo Byblius, in order to prop the sinking cause of Paganism, and to retard the rapid spread of Christianity in the 2nd and 3rd Centuries of the Christian Era. Sanchoniathon is said to have written, also, a history of the Serpent, to which he attributed a Divine nature. These fragments of Sanchoniathon, or Philo Byblius, or whoever the author was, have been preserved to us in the writings of Eusebius.

2. *Berosus* was a Chaldean priest of Belus, at Babylon. He lived in the time of Alexander the Great (B.C. 356–323). About B.C. 268, he wrote in the Greek language a history of Babylonia from the creation, down to his own time. Only fragments of his work remain. These have been preserved to us in the pages of Apollodorus (B.C. 144), Polyhistor (B.C. 88), Abydenus (B.C. 60), Josephus (A.D. 37–103), Africanus (A.D. 220), and Eusebius (A.D. 265–340), who give varying accounts of those parts of Berosus' work which they quote. Berosus obtained the materials for his history from the archives of the temple of Belus at Babylon. His story of the creation of the world, of the ten generations before the Flood, and the ten generations after it, correspond somewhat with the Mosaic narrative in Genesis. The first man, Alorus, was a Babylonian. The tenth, Xisuthrus, corresponds to Noah, in whose reign Berosus places the great Deluge. The ten Kings before the Flood occupy a period of 120 Sari (Hebrew עשׂר = ten, a decad) or 1,200 years, each containing 360 days, a total therefore of 432,000 *days*, which the Chaldeans in after years magnified into 432,000 *years* in order to enhance their antiquity. In the reign of the first King, Alorus, an intelligent animal called Oannes came out of the Red Sea, and appeared near Babylonia in the form of a fish with a man's head under the fish's head, and a man's feet which came out of the fish's tail. This is Berosus' account of Noah, who appears again under the name of Xisuthrus, whilst Alorus, the Nimrod of Genesis and the founder of Babylon, is placed at the top of the Dynasty of ten Kings, of which Xisuthrus, or Noah, is the tenth. Xisuthrus builds a

B

vessel, takes into it his family, and all kinds of animals and birds, and when the waters are abated, birds are sent out from the vessel three times, quite after the manner of the Biblical Noah.   Mankind starts from Armenia, and journeys toward the plain of Shinar, following the course of the Euphrates. There, Nimrod, aspiring to the universal sovereignty of the world, builds the Tower and the City of Babel.   The builders are dispersed, and the Tower is destroyed.   There is a reference to Abraham, and a detailed account of the reigns of the Kings of Babylon from Nabopollasar, who overthrew the Empire of Assyria, to Nebuchadnezzar and his destruction of the Temple at Jerusalem.   Berosus also mentions Evil Merodachus, Neriglissoorus, Laborosoarchodus, and Nabonnedus, in the 17th year of whose reign, at the end of the Seventy Years during which Jerusalem was in a state of desolation, Cyrus came out of Persia with a great army and took Babylon.

3. *Manetho*, of Sebennytus in Egypt, was a learned Egyptian priest. At the request of Ptolemy Philadelphus, King of Egypt (B.C. 284–247), he wrote, in the Greek language, about the year B.C. 258, a work on *Egyptian Antiquities*, deriving his materials from ancient records in the possession of the Egyptian priests.   The work itself is lost, but portions of it are preserved in Josephus, Africanus, and Eusebius.   It contains a list of the 31 dynasties of the Kings of Egypt, from Menes, the first King, with whom the civilization of Egypt takes its rise, to the conquest of Egypt by Cambyses (B.C. 529–521).   Its value for historical and chronological purposes is problematical, for (1) the accounts of the work handed down to us by Africanus and Eusebius contain contradictions in almost every dynasty, (2) the lists are incomplete, and (3) we have no means of ascertaining which of the dynasties are consecutive, or successive, and which are co-existent, or contemporary.

4. The Persian Epic Poet, *Firdusi* (A.D. 931–1020) was born at Khorassan. He wrote the history of Persia in verse, from the earliest times down to A.D. 632. This is not Chronology.   It is not even history.   It is a poetic rendering of the legendary national traditions of Persia.   The uncritical nature of the poet, and the unhistorical character of his work, may be gathered from the fact that the reigns of the first four Kings of the second, or Kaianian dynasty, are reckoned as follows :—

1. Kai Kobad	.. 120	years.
2. Kai Kaoos	.. 150	,,
3. Kai Khoosroo	.. 60	,,
4. Lohrasp	.. 120	,,

The unique value of Firdusi's poem arises from the fact that it gathers up and preserves the national Persian tradition of the Chronology of the period between Darius Hystaspes and Alexander the Great (B.C. 485–331), just as the Talmudic Tract, *Sedar Olam* gathers up and preserves the national Jewish tradition of the chronology of the same period.

The Chronology of this period has never yet been accurately deteimined. The received Chronology, though universally accepted, is dependent on the list of the Kings, and the number of years assigned to them in Ptolemy's Canon.   Ptolemy (A.D. 70–161) was a great constructive genius.   He was the author of the Ptolemaic System of Astronomy. He was one of the founders of the Science of Geography. But in Chronology he was only a late compiler and contriver, not an original witness, and not a contemporary historian, for he lived in the 2nd Century after Christ. He is the only authority for the Chronology of this period. He is not corroborated. He is contradicted, both by the Persian National Traditions preserved in *Firdusi*, by the Jewish National Traditions preserved in the *Sedar Olam*, and by the writings of *Josephus*.

It has always been held to be unsafe to differ from Ptolemy, and for this reason. His Canon, or List of Reigns, is the only thread by which the last year of Darius Hystaspes, B.C. 485, is connected with the first year of Alexander the Great, thus :—

PERSIAN KINGS AS GIVEN IN PTOLEMY'S CANON.

PERSIAN KINGS.	REIGNS.	NABONNASSARIAN ERA.	B.C.	
			CONNUM-ERARY.	JULIAN.
Cyrus	reigned 9 yrs. from	210	538	538
Cambyses	,, 8 ,, ,,	219	529	529
Darius I. Hystaspes ...	,, 36 ,, ,,	227	521	521
Xerxes	,, 21 ,, ,,	263	485	486
Artaxerxes I.				
Longimanus	,, 41 ,, ,,	284	464	465
Darius II. Nothus ...	,, 19 ,, ,,	325	423	424
Artaxerxes II. Mnemon	,, 46 , ,,	344	404	405
Artaxerxes III. Ochus ...	,, 21 ,, ,,	390	358	359
Arogus or Arses... ...	,, 2 ,, ,,	411	337	338
Darius III. Codomannus	,, 4 ,, ,,	413	335	336
Alexander the Great ...	,, — ,, ,,	417	331	332
	207			

From this 207 years of the Medo-Persian Empire, we must deduct the first two years of the Co-Rexship of Cyrus with Darius the Mede. This leaves seven years to Cyrus as sole King, the first of which, B.C. 536, is " the first year of Cyrus, King of Persia" (2 Chron. 36 ^{22}), in which he made his proclamation giving the Jews liberty to return to Jerusalem. That leaves 205 years for the duration of the Persian Empire proper.

In Ptolemy's Table of the Persian Kings, all the Julian years from Xerxes to Alexander the Great inclusive are connumerary. Therefore each requires to be raised a unit higher to give the Julian years in which their reigns began. Ptolemy reckons by the vague Egyptian year of 365 days. The Julian year is exactly 365¼ days. Had Ptolemy never written, profane Chronology must have remained to this day in a state of ambiguity and confusion, utterly unintelligible and useless, nor would it have been possible to have ascertained from the writings of the Greeks or from any other source, except from Scripture itself, the true connection between sacred Chronology and profane, in any one single instance, before the dissolution of the Persian Empire in the

1st year of Alexander the Great.   Ptolemy had no means of accurately determining the Chronology of this period, so he made the best use of the materials he had, and contrived to *make* a Chronology.   He was a great astronomer, a great astrologer, a great geographer, and a great constructor of synthetic systems.   But he did not possess sufficient data to enable him to fill the gaps, or to fix the dates of the Chronology of this period, so he had to resort to the calculation of eclipses.   In this way then, not by historical evidence or testimony, but by the method of astronomical calculation, and the conjectural identification of recorded with calculated eclipses, the Chronology of this period of the world's history has been fixed by Ptolemy, since when, through Eusebius and Jerome, it has won its way to universal acceptance.   It is contradicted (1) by the national traditions of Persia, (2) by the national traditions of the Jews, (3) by the testimony of Josephus, and (4) by the conflicting evidence of such well-authenticated events as the Conference of Solon with Crœsus, and the flight of Themistocles to the court of Artaxerxes Longimanus, which make the accepted Chronology impossible. But the human mind cannot rest in a state of perpetual doubt.   There was this one system elaborated by Ptolemy.   There was no other except that given in the prophecies of Daniel.   Hence, whilst the Ptolemaic astronomy was overthrown by Copernicus in the 16th Century, the reign of the Ptolemaic Chronology remains to this day.   There is one, and only one alternative.   The prophecy of Daniel 9 [24-27] fixes the period between the going forth of the commandment to return and to build Jerusalem (in the first year of Cyrus) to the cutting off of the Messiah (in the year A.D. 30) as a period of 483 years. If this be the true Chronology of the period from the 1st year of Cyrus to the Crucifixion, it leaves only 123 years instead of the 205 given in Ptolemy's Canon, for the duration of the Persian Empire.

	Daniel.		Ptolemy.	
Persian Empire (Cyrus to Alexander the Great)	123 years		205 years	
Greek Empire (Alexander the Great to A.D. 1)	331	,,	331	,,
	454	,,	536	,,
A.D. 1 to the Crucifixion, A.D. 30 ..	29	,,	29	,,
	483	,,	565	,,

a difference of 82 years.

Consequently the received or Ptolemaic Chronology, now universally accepted, must be abridged by these 82 years.   The error of Ptolemy has probably been made through his having assigned too many years, and perhaps too many Kings, to the latter part of the period of the Persian Empire, in the scheme which he made out from various conflicting data.

We have to choose between the Heathen Astrologer and the Hebrew Prophet.

Other interpretations have been given of the date of " the going forth of the commandment to return and to build Jerusalem " (Dan. 9 [25]).

Bishop Lloyd, the author of the Bible Dates in the margin of the Authorized

Version, reckons the 483 years from the leave given to Nehemiah to rebuild the walls of Jerusalem in the 20th year of Artaxerxes, whom he identifies with Artaxerxes Longimanus (Neh. 2 [1]), and to make the fulfilment fit the prophecy on the erroneous Ptolemaic reckoning of the Chronology he has to curtail the interval by reckoning in years of 360 days each.

Dr. Prideaux reckons the 483 years from the date of Ezra's return in the 7th year of Artaxerxes (Longimanus), Ezra 7 [1-28].

Scaliger reckoned the 70 weeks of Daniel as commencing in the 4th year of Darius Nothus, B.C. 420, and ending at the destruction of Jerusalem, A.D. 70.

Others have reckoned the 483 years from the going forth of the commandment in the 2nd year of Darius Hystaspes (B.C. 519) to build the Temple (Ezra 4 [24], 5 [1]—6 [15]).

But the true point of departure for the 70 weeks, and therefore for the 483 years also, is unquestionably the 1st year of Cyrus (Dan. 9, 2 Chron. 36 [20-23], Ezra 1 [1-4], Isa. 44 [28], 45 [1-4. 13]), and no other epoch would ever have been suggested but for the fact that the count of the years was lost, and wrongly restored from Ptolemy's conjectural astronomical calculations.

It would be far better to abandon the Ptolemaic Chronology and fit the events into the 483 years of the Hebrew prophecy.

The one great fundamental fact to be remembered is the fact that modern Chronology rests upon the calculations of Ptolemy as published in his Canon or List of Reigns. And since the foundation of Greek Conjectural Computation Chronology, upon which Ptolemy's Canon rests, is unstable, the superstructure is likewise insecure. Ptolemy may be called as a witness. He cannot be allowed to arbitrate as a Judge. He cannot take the place of a Court of Final Appeal. He cannot be erected into a standard by which to correct the Chronology of the text of the Old Testament.

5. The Books of the *Old Testament Apocrypha* are useful as showing the interpretation put upon the books of the Old Testament in later times, but they are not authoritative. The 1st Book of Esdras is useful as showing how the writer interpreted the narrative of Ezra. Sir Isaac Newton says " I take the Book of Esdras to be the best interpreter of the Book of Ezra." The view which makes the succession of the Kings of Persia mentioned after Cyrus in Ezra 4, (1) Darius Hystaspes, (2) Ahasuerus (=Xerxes), (3) Artaxerxes (= Longimanus) is the view now held by many modern Biblical scholars.

In Esdras 3 [1-2], 2 [30], cp. Ezra 4 [5], the Ahasuerus of Esther is identified with Darius Hystaspes. This identification is adopted by Archbishop Ussher and by Bishop Lloyd (Esther 1 [1] A.V. Margin), the date there given (B.C. 521) being that of the accession of Darius Hystaspes. See Ussher's Annals, *sub anno mundi* 3484. Ussher identifies the Ahasuerus of Esther with the Artaxerxes of Ezra 7 [1]—Neh. 13 [6], and also with Darius Hystaspes, Ezra 6 [14] (translate Darius *even* Artaxerxes). There is every reason to believe that this double identification is correct.

The 2nd Book of Esdras is of no value for chronological purposes. In the book of *Tobit*, Cyaxeres the Mede, who with Nebuchadnezzar's father (also called Nebuchodonossor) took Nineveh, is identified with Ahasuerus. In *Bel and the Dragon*, Darius the Mede, the predecessor of Cyrus, is identified with Astyages.

There is great confusion between the use of the names Cyaxeres and Astyages. As Sir Isaac Newton says : " Herodotus hath inverted the order of the Kings Astyages and Cyaxeres, making Cyaxeres to be the son and successor of Phraortes, and the father and predecessor of Astyages, whereas according to Xenophon the order of succession of the Kings of Media is (1) Phraortes, (2) Astyages, (3) Cyaxeres, (4) Darius the Mede, after which comes (5) Cyrus the Great, the founder of the Persian Empire." The testimony of these various authorities is perplexing and confusing. They must all be called as witnesses, but in no case can they be looked upon as authorities to be accepted in preference to the text of the Old Testament.

6. *Flavius Josephus* (A.D. 37–103), the famous historian of the Jews, was a cultured Jew, a Pharisee, and a man of good family. He went to Rome, A.D. 63, and when the Jewish war broke out he led the Jews of Galilee against the Romans. Eventually he surrendered. His life was spared, but he was put in chains for three years. He gained the favour of Vespasian, and later on that of Titus, to whom he urged his countrymen to surrender. After the fall of Jerusalem he lived as a Roman pensioner till his death, A.D. 103. His three great standard works are (1) *The Antiquities of the Jews* (published A.D. 93), a history of the Jewish people from the Creation to the time of Nero, without exception the most valuable record of ancient history next to that of the Old Testament, on which it is almost entirely dependent as far as the history related in the Old Testament goes. (2) The *Wars of the Jews* (published A.D. 75), the story of the destruction of Jerusalem by Titus, A.D. 70. (3) *Contra Apion* (written A.D. 93), an appendix to his *Antiquities*, and a defence of his statements in that work respecting the very great antiquity of the Jewish nation.

These three great works contain most valuable chronological materials, but the figures given are not reliable. They are not always self-consistent, in some cases they have been carelessly copied, and in others they have been " corrected " by his Hellenistic editors in order to bring them into accord with those of the LXX. Apart from this it must be admitted that Chronology was not a strong point with Josephus, and Chronology being but a secondary object with him, he was not always over careful in his calculations. His original figure for the years from Adam to the Flood was probably 1656, the same as in the Hebrew Text, but his Hellenistic editors have (1) " corrected " his ages of the Patriarchs, making the six centenary additions in accordance with the figures of the LXX, and then (2) " corrected " the total by turning the one thousand of the number 1656 into a figure 2, thus making it 2656, whereas the correct addition of the figures as altered would be 2256. For the period from Shem to Terah's 70th year the number given is 292 years, the same as the Hebrew Text, but the numbers assigned to the Patriarchs have again been " corrected " by his editors by means of the centenary additions of the LXX, and consequently when totalled up they amount to 993 instead of 292. The consequence is that the Chronology of

Josephus in its present state is a mass of confusion.   Nevertheless, his *history* is that of a historian of the first rank, and since his account of the closing years of the Persian Empire agrees with that of the National Persian Traditions incorporated in the poem of Firdusi, and with that of the National Jewish Traditions preserved in the *Sedar Olam*, he stands as a witness against the longer Persian Chronology of Ptolemy, now universally accepted, and for the shorter Chronology of the Prophet Daniel.

Josephus' account of the monarchs of the Persian Empire is as follows :—

1. Cyrus.
2. Cambyses = Artaxerxes of Ezra 4$^{7-23}$.
3. Darius Hystaspes.   2nd year, Temple foundation laid.
                       9th year, Temple finished.
4. Xerxes = Artaxerxes of Ezra 7^{1}–8^{36}.
                       25th year, Nehemiah came to Jerusalem.
                       28th year, Walls of Jerusalem finished.
5. Cyrus (son of Xerxes), called by the Greeks Artaxerxes, and identified with the Ahasuerus of Esther.
6. Darius the last King, a contemporary of Jaddua and Alexander the Great.

Altogether Josephus gives only six monarchs instead of Ptolemy's ten, of which six monarchs the last is contemporary with Jaddua, the son of Johannan, the son of Joiada.   So that Jaddua was contemporary with Alexander the Great, and Jaddua's father (or his uncle), the son of Joiada, was contemporary with Nehemiah, who chased him (Neh. 13^{28}).   Consequently from Nehemiah and the son of Joiada, whom he chased, to Alexander the Great, is only one generation.   But Ptolemy makes it 100 years, or, if the Artaxerxes of Nehemiah is correctly identified with Darius Hystaspes, 150 years.

We may reject the *Chronology* of Josephus, but his succession of the High Priests, and the Kings of Persia is good evidence against the list given by Ptolemy, and in favour of the shorter Chronology of the prophet Daniel, and the Book of Nehemiah.

7. The *Sedar Olam Rabbah, i.e.*, " The Large Chronicle of the World," commonly called the " Larger Chronicon," is a Jewish Talmudic Tract, containing the Chronology of the world as reckoned by the Jews.   It treats of Scripture times, and is continued down to the reign of Hadrian (A.D. 76-138).   The author is said to have been Rabbi Jose ben Chaliptha, who flourished a little after the beginning of the 2nd Century after Christ, and was Master to Rabbi Judah Hakkodesh, who composed the Mishna.   Others say it dates from A.D. 832, and that it was certainly written after the Babylonian Talmud, as it contains many fables taken from thence.

The *Sedar Olam Zeutah, i.e.*, " Small Chronicle of the World," commonly called the " Lesser Chronicle," is said to have been written A.D. 1123.   It is a short chronicle of the events of history from the beginning of the world to the year A.D. 522.

Both contain the Jewish tradition respecting the duration of the Persian

Empire. This tradition is " that in the last year of Darius Hystaspes, the prophets Haggai, Zechariah and Malachi died, that thereon the spirit of prophecy ceased from among the Children of Israel, and that this was the obsignation or sealing up of vision and prophecy spoken of by the prophet Daniel (Dan. 9 ^{24}). The same tradition tells us that the Kingdom of the Persians ceased also the same year, for they will have it that this was the Darius whom Alexander the Great conquered, and that the whole continuance of the Persian Empire was only 52 years, which they reckon thus :—

Darius the Median reigned	1 year
Cyrus	3 years
Cambyses (whom they identify with the Ahasuerus who married Esther)	16 ,,
Darius (whom they will have to be the son of Esther) 32	,,
Total 52	,,

This last Darius, they say, w; s the Artaxerxes who sent Ezra and Nehemiah to Jerusalem to restore the state of the Jews, for they tell us that Artaxerxes among the Persians was the common name for their Kings, as that of Pharoah was among the Egyptians."

Now we may say with Dr. Prideaux in his *Historical Connection of the Old and New Testaments*, published in 1858, from which the above extract is taken, that " this shows how ill they have been acquainted with the affairs of the Persian Empire," and that " their countryman, Josephus, in the account which he gives of those times, seems to have been but very little better informed concerning them," or, *we may draw the contrary conclusion*, that Josephus knew the history of his own country better than Ptolemy.

How long *did* the Persian Empire last ? We may ask the Persians themselves, and if we do they will tell us that they have no records of the period, these having been all swept away by the Greek and Mohammedan Invasions. But they have certain vague, floating, national traditions, cast into an epic poem by Firdusi, and from these we learn that the succession of the Persian Monarchs was as follows : (1) Darius Hystaspes, (2) Artaxerxes Longimanus, (3) Queen Homai the mother of Darius Nothus, (4) Darius Nothus the bastard son of Artaxerxes Longimanus, and (5) Darius, who was conquered by Alexander the Great. All the Kings between these two Dariuses they omit.

Or again we may ask the Jews, and if we do they will tell us that the Persian Empire lasted only 52 years, from the first of Cyrus to the first of Alexander the Great. We may go to Ptolemy, and if we do he will determine the length of the period and make out a list of kings for us by means of astronomical calculations and conjectural identifications of recorded with calculated eclipses, and then we shall get a Persian Empire lasting 205 years. But if we take the account given in Nehemiah, and the years specified by the prophet Daniel, we shall find that the Persian Empire continued for a period of 123 years.

The Jews shortened it to 52 years. " Some of them," says Sir Isaac

Newton, " took Herod for the Messiah, and were thence called Herodians. They seem to have grounded their opinion on the 70 weeks, which they reckoned from the first year of Cyrus. But afterwards, in applying the prophecy to Theudas and Judas of Galilee, and at length to Bar Cochab, they seem to have shortened the reign of the Kingdom of Persia." This explains why the Jews underestimated the duration of the Persian Empire, and it shows that originally they reckoned about 123 years. Now,

> From 1st year Cyrus, to 1st year Alexander the Great = 123 years
> From 1st year Alexander the Great to Herod (B.C. 331–4) .. .. = 327 „
> From 1st year Cyrus, to the birth of Christ .. .. = 450 „

If, then, the wise men from the East had heard of Daniel's prophecy, and had kept an accurate account of the years, and if the Jews of Palestine were also expecting the Messiah at the very time when He was born (B.C. 4) on the ground that it was then within 33 years of the 483 predicted in Daniel for His appearance, and therefore now time for Him to be born, this would indicate that they reckoned the time between the 1st year of Cyrus and the birth of Christ as a period of 450 years. And since the 327 years (B.C. 331 to B.C. 4) from Alexander the Great to the birth of Christ were in all probability accurately computed by the Greeks, for they began their reckoning by Olympiads within 60 years of Alexander's death, it leaves exactly these 123 years for the duration of the Persian Empire, and abridges the accepted Ptolemaic Chronology by 82 years, for 205–123 = 82, which is the exact year expressed for these events in the Chronology of the Old Testament, as developed in these pages, for Cyrus' 1st year is shown to be the year AN. HOM. 3589, whence 3589 + 483 = 4071 (inclusive reckoning), for the Crucifixion, and as Christ was about 30 years of age when He began His ministry, and His ministry lasted three years, He was born AN. HOM. 4038, or exactly 450 years after the 1st year of Cyrus, Christ having been born four years before the commencement of the Christian Era. But 450 years before the actual date of the birth of Christ is B.C. 454. The true date of the 1st year of Cyrus is therefore B.C. 454, not B.C. 536, which makes the Chronology of this period 82 years too long.

It may be objected that in the Battle of Marathon, which was fought B.C. 490, Darius Hystaspes was defeated by the Greeks, and that the Greek Chronology, which was reckoned by Olympiads from B.C. 776 onward, cannot be at fault to the extent of 82 years. But that is just the very point in dispute. The Greeks did not make a single calculation in Olympiads, nor had they any accurate chronological records till sixty years after the death of Alexander the Great. All that goes before that is guess work, and computation by generations, and other contrivances, not the testimony of contemporary records.

The *Sedar Olam*, therefore, may be called as a witness, and it is not to be ruled out of court by any objections raised by the Greeks, but it must be called as a witness only, not as arbitrator or Judge.

(3) *Ancient Monumental Inscriptions.*

Ancient Monumental Inscriptions upon rocks, temples, palaces, cylinders, bricks, steles, and tablets, and writings upon papyrus rolls, brought to light by modern discovery in recent times, constitute one of the most valuable sources affording data, not for the correction of Biblical data, but for the construction of a Chronology of their own, for the period covered by the writings of the Old Testament. The witnesses are exceedingly numerous, and when they are rightly interpreted, they may be regarded as authentic, though of course errors may be graven upon the rock, or written upon ancient papyrus rolls, quite as readily as upon Hebrew manuscripts. In no case can it be allowed that recent discoveries either have made, or can make good a claim to the infallibility which modern scholarship denies to Pope and Bible alike. The Monuments themselves may, and do, sometimes err. They may, and sometimes they do, chronicle the lying vanities of ambitious tyrants. They may be incorrectly deciphered, incorrectly interpreted, or incorrectly construed, in relation to other events.

It is a matter of fundamental importance, and it cannot be too emphatically pointed out, that the interpretation at present put upon the Chronology of the monuments is predetermined by the assumption on the part of the interpreter of the validity of the accepted Ptolemaic Chronology.

Should it be proved that that Chronology is overstated by 82 years, the monuments would bear exactly the same witness to the truth of the revised Chronology as they now bear to the truth of the Ptolemaic dates. The Ptolemaic Chronology is assumed by the interpreter of the testimony of the Monuments as one of his premises. It is therefore bound to come out in his conclusion, but it is not thereby proved to be true.

An illustration will make the matter clear. The Sayce-Cowley Aramaic Papyri discovered at Assuan in 1904, and published in 1906 by Robert Mond, are dated quite confidently and quite absolutely from 471 or 470 to 411. Papyrus A bears date " the 14th (15 ?) year of Xerxes." This is interpreted as meaning, and is quite definitely declared to be, the year B.C. 471 or 470. Now in Ptolemy's Canon the date of Xerxes is given as the equivalent of B.C. 485. His 14th year will therefore be B.C. 471, and his 15th B.C. 470.

Again in the *Drei Aramaische Papyrus Urkunden aus Elephantiné* (Three Aramaic Papyrus Documents from Elephantiné), published by Prof. Sachau, of Berlin, in 1907, the date given in the original is " the month of Marcheschwan in the 17th year of Darius." This is interpreted as referring to Darius Nothus, whose date is given in Ptolemy's Canon (allowing for the fact that Ptolemy's year is one of 365 days only) as B.C. 424. His 17th year will therefore be 408 or possibly 407. With this interpretation, derived solely from Ptolemy's Canon, the document is forthwith dated B.C. 408–407.

In both cases the interpreters have assumed that the Chronology of Ptolemy's Canon is the truth, and they are ready, without more ado, to interpret or to correct the dates given in Nehemiah in the light of these " modern discoveries." For Prof. Sachau proceeds at once to draw chronological inferences from the fact that "Delajah and Schelemjah, the sons of Sanaballat, the Pekah of Samaria" are mentioned in lines 29, 30, and, in his comment on these lines, he exclaims, "Have then the Jews of Elephantiné obtained no knowledge whatever of Nehemiah and his great national work? Or had so much grass grown over the contention with Sanballat since the return of Nehemiah to Babylon somewhere about the year B.C. 433, that the Jewish community at Elephantiné believed themselves able to disregard these things?"

The assumption of the truth of Ptolemy's Canon is of course perfectly legitimate, so long as it is remembered that it *is* an assumption, and not a conclusion. But if any attempt is made to fix the date of Nehemiah from references to the sons of Sanballat in the Sachau documents, the argument is invalid. It moves in a circle. It first assumes the truth of the Ptolemaic, Chronology, and then uses a deduction from that assumption to prove the truth of it. It is correcting the Hebrew Text of Nehemiah by Ptolemy using the testimony of one witness (Ptolemy) to *adjudicate* against the testimony of the other (the Hebrew Text of Nehemiah), when the whole point at issue is which of these two witnesses is to be believed. It is not therefore correct to say that the date of Nehemiah is fixed by these modern discoveries at Assuan, apart altogether from the question raised by Prof. Margoliouth as to whether they may not be forgeries. All the facts contained in the Assuan documents can be fitted into the revised Chronology necessitated by the Hebrew Text, as easily as, if not indeed more easily than, they have been fitted into the received Chronology of Ptolemy. It is of primary importance to remember that the whole point in dispute is as to the truth of one or the other of two conflicting witnesses, the Hebrew Old Testament and Ptolemy. It is absurd to attempt to adjudicate upon the matter by first *assuming* the truth of one witness, and then on the basis of that *assumption* pronouncing judgment against the other.

Similarly the dates assigned by modern scholars to the Monuments of Egypt go back far beyond the year of the creation of Adam as fixed by the Hebrew Text of the Old Testament, 4038 years before the actual birth of Christ, i.e., in the year B.C. 4042. These Monumental dates rest upon a basis of hypothesis and conjecture, and involve the assumption of the truth of the testimony of the witness Manetho. But since one witness cannot be used to correct another, Manetho and the dates derived from the assumption of the truth of his testimony cannot be used to prove the incorrectness of the chronological statements of the Old Testament.

All sources must be used, and all witnesses must be heard, but it must be remembered that the witness of the Old Testament is not confuted by an interpretation of the testimony of Monumental Inscriptions which depends for its validity on the truth of the conflicting testimony of Manetho.

Moreover the whole trend of the results of recent discovery in the realm of Biblical Archæology has been toward the establishment of the Text of the Old Testament as an unimpeachable witness to the truth. The Stele of Khammurabi, the Tel-El-Amarna Tablets, the Moabite Stone, the Behistun Inscription, Babylonian and Assyrian and Egyptian Monumental Records.

The Assyrian Eponym Canon, the discoveries of Layard, George Smith, and Sir H. Rawlinson, and all the more recent discoveries of our own time, *when rightly interpreted*, point in the same direction.

(4) *Classic Literature of Greece and Rome.*

The Classic Literature of Greece and Rome is the prime source of our information respecting the Chronology of the civilized world.

Of the principal Greek and Roman *Historians*, who may be regarded as authentic witnesses to the facts of contemporary history, as distinguished from mere *Chronologers* or *Compilers* of dates, whose writings stand on an entirely different footing, the following are worthy of special mention:—

I. *Greek Historians.*

1. *Herodotus*, the "Father of History" (B.C. 484–424), born at Halicarnassus, author of the world-famous "history" of the Persian War of Invasion from the first expedition of Mardonius, son-in-law and General of Darius Hystaspes, to the discomfiture of the vast fleet and army of Xerxes. Translated by George Rawlinson.

2. *Thucydides* (B.C. 471–401 or 396), author of the *History of the Peloponnesian War*, one of the greatest monuments of antiquity. Translated by Benjamin Jowett.

3. *Xenophon* (B.C. 430–c. 357), the essayist, historian, and military leader who was appointed General of the 10,000 Greeks, who joined the expedition of the Persian Prince Cyrus the younger against his brother Artaxerxes Mnemon, and were defeated at Cunaxa (B.C. 401). Xenophon was the author of (1) the *Anabasis*, an account of this expedition, (2) the *Cyropædia*, a historical romance of the education and training of Cyrus the Great, (3) the *Hellenica*, a history of contemporary events in Greece, and (4) the *Memorabilia* or *Reminiscences of Socrates*.

4. *Polybius* (B.C. 204–122), one of the 1,000 hostages carried off by the Romans after the Conquest of Macedonia, B.C. 168. He became acquainted with Scipio Africanus, and wrote a history of Greece and Rome for the period (B.C. 220–146).

5. *Dionysius* of Halicarnassus (B.C. 70–6), essayist, critic and historian. He lived at Rome for 20 years (B.C. 30–10), where he amassed materials for his *Romaike Archaiologia*, a history of Rome from the early times down to the first Punic War.

6. *Strabo* (B.C. 63–A.D. 21), the world-famous geographer, born at Amasia in Pontus, Asia Minor. He was educated at Rome. He travelled from Armenia to Etruria, and from the shores of the Euxine to the borders of Ethiopia. The fourth book of his celebrated *Geography* is devoted to Gaul, Britain and Ireland. He also wrote *Historical Memoirs* and a *Continuation of Polybius*, but these are both lost.

7 *Diodorus Siculus* (fl. A.D. 8), a native of Sicily. Hence his name Siculus. A historian of the time of Julius Cæsar and Augustus. He travelled widely in Asia and Europe, and devoted 30 years to the writing of a Universal History of the World down to Cæsar's Gallic Wars. Only 15 of his 40 books, with some fragments, have survived.

8. *Plutarch* (A.D. 50–120), the most attractive and the most widely read of all the Greek writers. He lectured at Rome during the reign of Domitian. His famous *Parallel Lives of Greek and Roman Writers*, 46 in all, are universally known and admired. His essays and his biographies breathe a fine moral tone. They inspired some of Shakespeare's greatest plays, and much of the noblest literature of modern times.

9. *Arrian* (2nd Century A.D.), served in the Roman army under Hadrian, and was Prefect of Cappadocia, A.D. 135. He sat at the feet of Epictetus, and composed a treatise on moral philosophy. His most important works are (1) his *History of Alexander the Great*, (2) an account of India, and (3) a description of the coasts of the Euxine. He also wrote on military subjects and on the chase.

10. *Lucian* (A.D. 120–200), a humorous writer, born at Samosata on the Euphrates, in Syria. He practised as an advocate at Antioch, travelled through Greece, Italy and Gaul, and was appointed Procurator of part of Greece. He ridicules the religion and the philosophy of the age, and gives a graphic account of contemporary social life. He wrote the *Dialogues of the Gods*, the *Sale of Philosophers*, *Timon*, and other works. His famous *Dialogues of the Dead* are intended to show the emptiness of all that seems most precious to mankind.

11. *Dion Cassius* (b. A.D. 155), the "last of the old historians" who knew the laws of historic writing. He was born at Nicea, and was the son of a Roman Senator, but his mother was a Greek. Dion Cassius himself became a Roman Senator, and was appointed Governor of Pergamos and Smyrna. He composed a history of Rome from the time of Aeneas to his own day.

12. *Appian* (2nd Century A.D.), a Greek of Alexandria. He wrote in Greek a valuable history of Rome. He was contemporary with Trajan, Hadrian and Antoninus Pius. He deals with the history of each of the nations that was conquered by Rome, and of the civil war which preceded the downfall of the Republic. He preserves the statements of earlier authors whose works are now lost.

II. *Roman Historians.*

1. *Cicero* (B.C. 106–43), orator, statesman, philosopher, and man of letters. He was Consul, B.C. 63. He foiled the Catiline conspiracy. He was exiled and recalled. He supported Pompey against Cæsar. After the overthrow of Pompey, Cæsar received

him as a friend. He then lived in literary retirement and wrote his great works. After Cæsar's death he delivered his philippics against Antony, and was proscribed and put to death by Antony's soldiers. His *De Amicitia, De Officiis,* and *De Senectute* awaken thought and form pleasant reading.

2. *Julius Cæsar* (B.C. 100-44), general, triumvir, dictator, and man of letters. In nine years (B.C. 58-49) he proved his great military genius by subduing Gaul, Germany, Britain, and most of Western Europe to the Roman yoke. In B.C. 55 and again in B.C. 52 he invaded Britain, from which he retired, virtually discomfited. Cæsar espoused the cause of Democracy, Pompey that of Aristocracy. In January, B.C. 49, Cæsar crossed the Rubicon. He drove Pompey out of Italy, and in B.C. 48 he defeated him at Pharsalia, and was appointed dictator. Coins were struck bearing his effigy, and the title Imperator was made a permanent addition to his name. With the assistance of the Greek Astronomer Sosigenes, he reformed the Calendar, and introduced the Julian year, which began on January 1st (A.U.C. 709 = B.C. 45), the first year of the Julian Era. The Julian year consisted of exactly 365¼ days ; the first three years contained 365 days, and another day, making 366, was added for every fourth year. The Julian year remained in use till December 22nd, 1582, when the year was again reformed by Pope Gregory XIII, assisted by the mathematician Clavius, and for the Roman World that day became January 1st, 1583. The Gregorian year was not introduced into England till September 3rd, 1752, which day became September 14th by Act of Parliament. The Gregorian year drops the additional leap year day every century (A.D. 1700, 1800, 1900, etc.), except when it is divisible by four (A.D. 2000). Julius Cæsar was about to embark on a great career of states- manlike economic and political reorganization when he was assassinated by Brutus on the Ides of March, A.U.C. 710 = B.C. 44.

3. *Sallust* (B.C. 86-34), a member of the Roman Senate. Expelled for immorality. An adherent of Julius Cæsar. Appointed Governor of Numidia. He wrote the history of the *Catiline Conspiracy,* and the *War with Jugurtha.*

4. *Livy* (B.C. 59-A.D. 17), lived at Rome at the Court of his patron and friend Augustus. He wrote 142 books of *Annales,* a history of Rome, of which, however, only 35 remain.

5. *Cornelius Nepos* (1st Century B.C.), a native of Verona, and a friend of Cicero. He wrote *De Viris Illustribus.* Only a fragment of it remains, and the authorship of this is disputed.

6. *Tacitus* (A.D. 54-117), an eminent Roman historian. Appointed quaestor, tribune, prætor, and *consul suffectus.* His *De Situ Moribus et Populis Germaniae* is our earliest source of information respecting the Teutons. His *Historiae,* covering the period A.D. 68-96, and his *Annales* covering the period A.D. 14-68, are

historic works of first rate importance. They give a terrible picture of the decay of imperial Rome.

7. *Suetonius* (born c. A.D. 70), a Roman advocate, and private secretary to the Emperor Hadrian. His *Lives of the Twelve Cæsars* is valuable for its anecdotes, which illustrate the character of the Emperors.

It is through the Greeks that we have received our knowledge of the history of the great Empires and civilizations of the East. Even Sanchoniathon and Berosus and Manetho, have all come to us through the Greeks. It was the Greeks who created the framework of the Chronology of the civilized ages of the past, and fitted into it all the facts of history, which have reached us through them. Apart from the Bible, the vague floating national traditions of the Persians and the later Jews, and the direct results of modern exploration, all our chronological knowledge reaches us through Greek spectacles. Here as everywhere else it is " thy sons O Zion against thy sons, O Greece " (Zech. 9 [13]). It is Nehemiah and Daniel against Ptolemy and Eratosthenes. It is Hebraic Chronology against Hellenic Chronology. And here the Greek has stolen a march upon the Hebrew, for he has stolen his Old Testament and forced his own Greek Chronology into the Hebrew record, Hellenizing the ages of the Hebrew Patriarchs in the Greek LXX.

Are we then to accept the testimony of the Greek as correcting or anti-quating the testimony of the Hebrew ? By no means. Let the Greek be heard as a witness, but let him not presume to pronounce sentence as a Judge. Clinton's *Fasti Hellenici* is perhaps the most valuable treatise on Chronology ever produced. But it is not infallible. Clinton's standard is Ptolemy's Canon ; Sayce's standard is the Monuments. But neither of these sources is competent to correct the Hebrew Old Testament, which must be placed in the witness-box alongside of them, not in the dock, to be sentenced by them.

To begin at the beginning, the point of departure for Greek Chronology, the 1st Olympiad, B.C. 776, upon which everything else depends, rests upon no firmer foundation than that of tradition and computation by conjecture.

The opening sentence of Clinton's Tables reveals the basis upon which he builds. He says : " The first Olympiad is placed by Censorinus in the 1014th year before the Consulship of Ulpius and Pontianus, A.D. 238 = B.C. 776. Solinus attests that the 207th Olympiad fell within the Consulship of Gallus and Verannius. These were Consuls A.D. 49, and if the 207th Games were celebrated in July, A.D. 49, 206 Olympiads, or 824 years had elapsed, and the first games were celebrated in July 776."

But Censorinus wrote his *De Die Natali*, A.D. 238, and Solinus also belongs to the 3rd Century A.D. They are not, therefore, contemporary witnesses, and we do not know how far their computations were derived from hypothesis and conjecture, or how far they rest upon a basis of objective fact. Never-theless, this point has been made the first link in the chain of the centuries, a chain flung out to float in the air, or attached, not to the solid staple of fixed fact, but only to the rotten ring of computation and conjecture. The Canon of Ptolemy rests upon this calculation. Eusebius (A.D. 264-349) adopted it, and set the example of making Scripture dates fit into the years of the Greek Era. Eusebius is based upon Manetho (3rd Century B.C.), Berosus (3rd Century B.C.), Abydenus (2nd Century B.C.), Polyhistor (1st Century B.C.), Josephus (A.D. 37–103), Cephalion (1st Century A.D.), Africanus (3rd Century B.C.), and other sources now lost. Eusebius' Chronology was contained in his " Chronicon." This was translated by Jerome, and has been followed by all subsequent writers down to the present day.

The one infallible connecting link between sacred and profane Chronology is given in Jeremiah 25 [1.] " The fourth year of Jehoiakim, which was the first year of Nebuchadnezzar." If the events of history had been numbered forward from this point to the birth of Christ, or back from Christ to it, we should have had a perfectly complete and satisfactory Chronology. But they were not. The distance between the 1st year of Nebuchadnezzar and the birth of Christ was not known. It has been fixed by conjecture, with the assistance of Ptolemy. Clinton fixes it at B.C. 606, Sayce at B.C. 604, and from this date, thus fixed, Chronologers reckon back to Adam and on to Christ. The distance between the 1st year of Nebuchadnezzar and the birth of Christ has not been measured by the annals or chronicles of any well-attested dated events. It was originally fixed by Ptolemy, by means of computation and conjecture, and recorded events have been fitted into the interval by computing Chronologers as far as the fictitious framework would allow.

The opening sentence of Sir Isaac Newton's Introduction to his *Short Chronicle from the first memory of things in Europe to the Conquest of Persia by Alexander the Great*, shows how entirely fluid and indeterminate were those first years of Grecian history.

" The Greek Antiquities," says Newton, " are full of poetic fictions, because the Greeks wrote nothing in prose before the conquest of Asia by Cyrus the Persian."

The uncertainty as to the epoch of the foundation of Rome and the Era which dates from that event, is just as great as the uncertainty as to the beginnings of the history of Greece. The following is a list of the dates that have been sanctioned by various writers :—

	B.C.
Varro, Tacitus, Plutarch, Dion, Aulus Gellius, Censorinus, etc.	753
Cato, Dionysius of Halicarnassus, Solinus, Eusebius, etc. ..	752
Livy, Cicero, Pliny and Velleius Paterculus .. .. 753 or	752
Polybius	751
Fabius Pictor and Diodorus Siculus	747
L. Cincius	728

A margin of 25 years.

These uncertainties in Greek and Roman Chronology, and the late and purely conjectural character of the foundation upon which they rest, show how impossible it is for us to erect the Chronology of the classic literature of Greece and Rome into a standard by which to correct the Chronology of the Hebrew Old Testament.

Nearly all the great Empires of the East seem to have thrown the origin of their dated history back into the 8th Century.

						B.C.
Babylon (Nabonassarean Era)	..	..	..	..	..	747
Greece (1st Olympiad)	..	..	..	..	..	776
Rome (Foundation of the City)	..	..	..	..	..	753
Lydia	..	..	..	..	..	716
China	..	..	..	..	..	781
Media	..	..	..	..	..	711

It may be of interest to add the following remarks respecting the origin of the Vulgar Christian Era :—

It was not until the year A.D. 532 that the Christian Era was invented by Dionysius Exiguus, a Scythian by birth, and a Roman Abbot. He flourished in the reign of Justinian (A.D. 527–565). He was unwilling to connect his cycles of dates with the era of the impious tyrant and persecutor Diocletian, which began with the year A.D. 284, but chose rather to date the times of the years from the incarnation of our Lord Jesus Christ " to the end that the commencement of our hope might be better known to us and that the cause of man's restoration, namely, our Redeemer's passion, might appear with clearer evidence." The year following that in which Dionysius Exiguus wrote these words to Bishop Petronius was the year 248 of the Diocletian Era. Hence the new Era of the Incarnation as it was then reckoned was 284 + 248 = A.D. 532. Dionysius abhorred the memory of Diocletian with good reason, for in the 1st year of his reign, from which the Diocletian Era begins, he caused a number of Christians who were celebrating Holy Communion in a cave to be buried alive there. The Diocletian Era was, from this fact, sometimes called the Era of the Martyrs.

Dionysius reckoned the year of our Lord's birth to be the year A.U.C. 753, according to Varro's computation, i.e., the year 45 of the Julian Era. Dionysius obtained this date from Luke's statements that " John the Baptist began his ministry in the 15th year of the reign of Tiberius," and that " Jesus was beginning to be about 30 years of age " (Luke 3 $^{1-2\,3}$). Tiberius succeeded Augustus, August 19th, A.U.C. 767. Therefore his 15th year was A.U.C. 782. Subtract the assumed year of the Nativity, 753, and the remainder is 29 years complete, or 30 current.

But according to Matthew, Christ was born before the death of Herod, that is, according to the computation of the Chronologers, before 749. Hence the year of the Incarnation, the year A.D. 1, was fixed four years too late, and to remedy this we have to express the true date of our Lord's birth by saying that He was born B.C. 4. It was subsequently discovered that the source of the error lay, not with the Evangelists, Matthew or Luke, but in the fact that Tiberius began to reign as colleague or partner with Augustus some years before Augustus died, and that the length of his reign after Augustus' death was not 26 years, but 22. In this way the difficulties were cleared up. The Era of the Incarnation was allowed to remain and the birth of Christ was set down as having occurred in the year B.C. 4.

C

(5) *Astronomical Observations and Calculations.*

Astronomical Observations and Calculations are regarded by many Chronologers as the surest and most unerring data for fixing the dates of various events. Eclipses can be calculated both backward and forward. They are distinguished from each other by the time when, and the place where, they can be seen, the duration of the eclipse, and the quantity or number of digits eclipsed. They have therefore been regarded as a means of correcting and determining the dates of the events at which they have occurred, and the results thus obtained have been invested with a kind of quasi-infallibility. The date of our Lord's birth is fixed by means of an eclipse of the moon recorded by Josephus as having occurred shortly before Herod's death.

Tables of eclipses have been furnished by Chronologers and Astronomers from B.C. 753 to A.D. 70, and a list of 44 of the most remarkable of these (25 eclipses of the sun, and 19 eclipses of the moon) is given in Hales' *New Analysis of Chronology*. The most celebrated of these eclipses is that known as the " Eclipse of Thales," from the fact that Thales foretold the year in which it would happen. It has been used by Chronologers to adjust the various Eras and the Chronologies of Assyria, Babylon, Media, Lydia, Scythia and Greece. But it has proved an apple of discord. Five several eclipses, occurring at as many different dates, have been identified by different astronomers as the one in question. The eclipse is described by Herodotus as occurring in the sixth year of the war between the Medes and the Lydians, on the river Halys, when during an obstinate battle the day suddenly became night. Both armies ceased fighting, a treaty of peace was arranged, and confirmed by a marriage compact.

This " Eclipse of Thales " thus described by Herodotus has been identified with the following five distinct astronomically calculated eclipses of the sun :—

(1) On July 30, B.C. 607—By Calvisius.
(2) ,, May 17 ,, 603— ,, Costard, Montucla and Kennedy.
(3) ,, Sept. 19 ,, 601— ,, Ussher.
(4) ,, July 9 ,, 597— ,, Petavius, Marsham, Bouhier and Larcher.
(5) ,, May 28 ,, 585— ,, Pliny, Scaliger, Newton, Ferguson, Vignoles and Jackson.

It will be seen from the above that there are many sources of error which must be allowed for, before attaching to the chronological result arrived at the infallibility which belongs to a mathematical calculation.

There may be errors of observation on the part of the historian, errors of calculation on the part of the astronomer, and errors of identification on the part of the Chronologer, who may wrongly conclude that the dated eclipse calculated by the astronomer is one and the same with the eclipse described by the historian. The mistake of investing these astronomically determined chronological dates with the infallibility of a mathematical calculation, is that of assuming that the strength of the chain is that of its *strongest* link, instead of that of its *weakest* link. The astronomical calculations may be infallibly correct, and demonstrably accurate to the tick of the clock, but that only fixes the infallibility of one link in the chain, the strength and security of which cannot be transferred to the other links, or to the result as a whole. We cannot, therefore, obtain from Astronomical Observations and Calculations the material we need to enable us to use them as a standard by which to test the truth of the Chronological Statements of the Old Testament. Like the testimony of the Monuments, and all the other witnesses, the testimony of Astronomy must be heard and adjudged upon ; it must not presume to adjudge upon the testimony of other witnesses.

(6) *Ancient and Modern Chronologers.*

The works of ancient and modern Chronologers are of great help in enabling us to correlate the testimony derived from all the various sources from which evidence can be secured.

But Chronologers are not infallible ; sometimes they arrive at differing and contradictory conclusions, sometimes they follow each other like a flock of sheep, each adopting the conclusions reached by his predecessor ; sometimes they are dominated by a scheme or plan into which they endeavour to fit the facts, and in this endeavour the facts are sometimes distorted. The millenary schemes of Ussher (that prince of Chronologers), and of the early Christian fathers, the septenary scheme of R. G. Faussett, developed in his most excellent and valuable work on the *Symmetry of Time*, the hypothetical Chronology of modern Assyriologists and Egyptologists, constructed in such a way that it can be made to fit in with their interpretation of the testimony of the Monuments, the determination of dates by Ptolemy's method of fitting the facts into his scheme of calculated eclipses, are all instances of the danger of bending the facts in order to make them fit the theory of the constructor. The only safe and true method of Chronology is to take into consideration the whole of the facts, weigh them one and all as evidence is weighed in a Court of Law, and to draw only such conclusions as may be warranted by the laws of evidence or testimony, or historic proof.

A brief notice of the principal works of some of the more important Chronologers will serve as a fitting introduction to our own investigations. They may be classified as follows :—(1) Early Greek and Latin Chronologers, (2) Early Christian Chronologers, (3) Byzantine Chronologers, (4) The Great Armenian Chronologer, Abul-Faragus, (5) Modern Chronologers.

I. *Early Greek and Latin Chronologers*, from the 5th Century B.C. to the Christian Era.

1. *Hellanicus* (b. B.C. 496), a Greek logographer. He drew up a chronological list of the priestesses of Juno at Argos. He constructed his Chronology on the principle of allowing so many years to each priestess, or so many priestesses to a century.

3. *Ephorus* (4th Century B.C.), was a disciple of Isocrates (B.C. 436–338). He was the first Greek who attempted the composition of a universal history. He begins with the return of the Heraclidae into Peloponnesus (B.C. 1103) and ends with the 20th year of Philip of Macedon, the father of Alexander the Great.

3. *Timaeus Siculus* (B.C. 260) wrote a history of Sicily, his native country. He was the first to use the Greek Olympiads as the basis of Chronology. As he wrote in the 129th Olympiad, B.C. 260, the preceding 128 Olympiads are not contemporary chronicles, but chronological computations. Timaeus instituted a comparison between the number of successive Ephors and Kings at Sparta, Archons at Athens, and Priestesses at Argos, arranging them into his chronological scheme of Olympiads. He brought the history down to his own time, and where he left off Polybius (B.C. 204–122) began.

4. *Eratosthenes* (b. B.C. 276) has been called the " Father of Chronology," and it is worth noting that his method was the method of *conjecture*, not the method of *testimony*. He was a native of Cyrene, a man of letters under the Ptolemies of Egypt, and keeper of the famous library at Alexandria in the reign of Ptolemy IV. Euergetes (B.C. 246–221). He discovered the obliquity of the ecliptic, and wrote some important works on mathematical geography and on the constellations. He made the first scientific measurement of the earth, but his result was one sixth too large. He made the parallel of Rhodes, in ancient astronomy what the meridian of Greenwich is to us. His *Chronographia* is an exact scheme of general Chronology. He wrote about 100 years after Alexander the Great, and arrived at his chronological conclusions by reckoning about 30 or 40 years to each generation or succession of Kings, Ephors or Priestesses, and thus greatly exaggerated the antiquity of the events of Greek history.

5. *Apollodorus* (2nd Century B.C.) followed the lines laid down by Eratosthenes. He wrote a metrical chronicle of events from the fall of Troy to his own day.

6. *Ptolemy*, the author of Ptolemy's Canon (or Claudius Ptolemaeus to give him his full name), deserves a more extended notice. He was the originator of the Ptolemaic System of Astronomy, so called because it was collected from his works. The main idea of this system or theory of the Universe was that the earth was stationary, and that all the heavenly bodies rotated round it in circles at a uniform rate. It was displaced by the Copernican system in the 16th Century.

Ptolemy flourished in Egypt in the 2nd Century A.D., during the reigns of Hadrian and Antoninus Pius. He was an astronomer and a geographer. His *Geographia*, a work in eight books, was illustrated by a map of the world, and 26 other maps. He was the first to attempt to reduce the study of geography to a scientific basis. He took Ferro in the Canaries as the westernmost part of the world, placed it nearly 7° too far east, and calculated his longitudes from it, whilst his latitudes were reckoned from Rhodes.

Ptolemy was born at Pelusium in Egypt. The date of his birth is generally given as A.D. 70, and he survived Antoninus Pius, who died A.D. 161. This would make him 91 years of age. But the Arabians say he died at the age of 78, in which case he must have been born later than A.D. 70. He recorded observations at Alexandria between A.D. 125 and 140. The authentic details of the circumstances of his life are extremely few. The following particulars are gleaned from *Ptolemy's Tebrabiblos or Quadripartite, being four books on the influence of the Stars*, by J. M. Ashmand (pubd. 1822). Ptolemy was looked upon by the Greeks as being a man most wise and most divine on account of his great learning. He was a man of truly regal mind. He corrected Hipparchus' Catalogue of the fixed stars, and formed tables for the calculation and regulation of the motions of the sun, moon and planets. He collected the scattered and detached observations of Aristotle, Hipparchus, Posidonius and others on the economy of the world, and digested them into a system which he set forth in his Μεγάλη Σύνταξις, the *Great System*, or *Great Construction*, a work divided into thirteen books, and called after him the Ptolemaic system. All his astronomical works are founded on the hypothesis that the earth is at rest in the centre of the universe. Round the earth the heavenly bodies, stars and planets move in solid orbs, whose motions are all directed by one *primum mobile*, or first mover, of which he discourses at large in the *Great System*. He also treats in the same work of the motions of the sun, moon and planets, gives tables for finding their situations, latitude, longitude, and motions. He treats of eclipses, and the method of computing them. He discourses of the fixed stars, of which he furnishes a catalogue with their magnitudes, latitudes, and longitudes.

Ptolemy's Order, false as it was, enabled observers to give a plausible account of the motions of the sun and moon, to foretell eclipses, and to improve geography. It represented the actual phenomena of the heavens, as they really appear to a spectator on the earth.

In the year A.D. 827, the *Great System* was translated by the Arabians into their own language, and by them its contents were made known to Europe. Through them it came to be known as the "Al Magest" (The Great Work). In Latin it became "Magna Constructio" and in English "The Great System," "The Ptolemaic System," or "The Great Construction."

Ptolemy was not so much an author as a practical astronomer. His *Geographia* is not a treatise on Geography, but an exposition of principles and directions for the construction of a map. Ptolemy's Canon is simply a Canon or List of Kings, with the years of their reigns. It is not accompanied by any explanatory treatise. It is generally regarded as the most precious Monument of ancient Chronology. In it he uses the Egyptian Vague, or Calendar year, of exactly 365 days. By this means, his New Year's Day works back, and occurs one day earlier every four years, and the year B.C. 521 (the Julian year of 365¼ days) contained the New Year's Day of two of the Egyptian Vague, or Calendar years of Ptolemy's Canon, one on January 1st, and the other on December 31st. They are the years 227 and 228 of Ptolemy's Nabonassarean Era. Ptolemy gives to each king the whole of the year in which his predecessor dies. This year is his *first year*. Cyrus diêd, and Cambyses began to reign in the year B.C. 529. But the whole of that year is given to Cambyses and is reckoned as his *first* year. In the same way Ptolemy took no account of the short reigns of less than a year. These odd months were included in the year of the preceding or the following king.

Ptolemy terminates his Canon at the reign of Antoninus Pius, in which he lived. It was continued by Theon, his successor in the chair of astronomy in Alexandria, and later on by other writers. Ptolemy's fixed point of departure is the New Moon on the 1st day of the 1st month (Thoth) of the first year of the Era of Nabonassar.

In view of the incomparable importance of Ptolemy's Canon as the basis upon which alone the determination of the date of the commencement of our own universally accepted Vulgar Era, the Common Christian Era, depends, the list is here reproduced entire. It is taken from the British Museum Copy of the *Tables Chronologiques des Regnes de C. Ptolemaeus, Theon, etc., par M. L'Abbé Halma* (published in Paris, 1819).

PTOLEMY'S CANON.

Table of Reigns.

YEARS OF THE REIGNS BEFORE ALEXANDER INCLUDING HIS OWN.

Nabonassar	..	.. 14	14	Mesesimordae ..	.. 4	59
Nadius	..	.. 2	16	Second Interregnum ..	8	67
Chinzar and Poros	..	5	21	Asaridin ..	.. 13	80
Iloulaius	..	.. 5	26	Saosdouchin ..	.. 20	100
Mardocempad	..	.. 12	38	Cinilanadan ..	.. 22	122
Arcean	..	.. 5	43	Nabopollassar	.. 21	143
First Interregnum	..	2	45	Nabocolassar ..	.. 43	186
Bilib	..	.. 3	48	Iloaroudam ..	.. 2	188
Aparanad	..	.. 6	54	Nericasolassar	.. 4	192
Rhegebel	..	.. 1	55	Nabonad	 17	209

PERSIAN KINGS.

Cyrus	..	.. 9	218	Artaxerxes II ..	.. 46	389
Cambyses	..	.. 8	226	Ochus ..	.. 21	410
Darius I	..	.. 36	262	Arogus ..	.. 2	412
Xerxes	..	.. 21	283	Darius III ..	.. 4	416
Artaxerxes I	..	.. 41	324	Alexander of Macedon ..	8	424
Darius II	..	.. 19	343			

YEARS OF THE MACEDONIAN KINGS AFTER ALEXANDER'S DEATH.

Philip	..	..	.. 7	7	Ptolemy Epiphanes	.. 24	143
Alexander II	..	.. 12	19	,, Philometor	.. 35	178
Ptolemy Lagus	.. 20	39	,, Euergetes	.. 29	207
,, Philadelphus	38	77	,, Soter	.. 36	243
,, Euergetes	.. 25	102	Dionysius the Younger	29	272
,, Philopator	.. 17	119	Cleopatra	 22	294

ROMAN EMPERORS.

Augustus	..	43	337	Titus ..	 3	404
Tiberius ..	..	22	359	Domitian	 15	419
Caius	 4	363	Nerva ..	 1	420
Claudius	.. 14	377	Trajan ..	 19	439
Nero	 14	391	Adrian	.. 21	460
Vespasian	 10	401	Aelius Antoninus	.. 23	483

The following is the list of Ptolemy's works :—

1. Ἡ Μεγάλη Σύνταξις = Magna Constructio = Almagest = The Great System of Astronomy. This was his great master-piece. It is a treatise on Astronomy, containing all the principles of the Ptolemaic system.

2. Τετράβιβλος = Quadripartite. A treatise in four books on the influence of the stars. A thoroughly pagan treatise on Astrology.

3. Καρπός or Centiloquy, or Book of a hundred aphorisms; a fifth book containing the fruit of the former four, and a kind of supplement to them. As an example of the aphorisms, we may quote the following, "Love and hatred lessen the most important, as they magnify the most trivial things."

4. *A Treatise on the Signification of the Fixed Stars.* A daily calendar of the risings and settings of the stars, and the weather produced thereby.

5. *The Geographia.*

6. *The Canon or Table of Reigns* given above.

Ptolemy's Canon is described in the article on "Chronology," in the *Encyclopædia Britannica,* 11th Edition, as "the only authentic source of the history of Assyria and Babylonia before the recent discoveries at Nineveh." This expresses the view now held by most modern scholars, but we must not overlook the fact that the authenticity here ascribed to it belongs equally to the Biblical Record. It is frequently said that the Assyrian List of Eponyms confirms the Assyrian part of the Canon of Ptolemy, and that this ought to give us confidence in the rest of the Canon. True, but wherever the Assyrian List of Eponyms confirms the Assyrian part of the Canon of Ptolemy, it confirms also the Assyrian part of the Biblical Record of the Old Testament. It is strange that scholars do not see this. Still more strange that since the Canon of Ptolemy agrees with the Assyrian Eponym list in those parts in which the Biblical Record also agrees with it, they should regard this as proof of the authenticity of the Canon of Ptolemy, but not as proof of the authenticity of the Biblical Record, which they immediately proceed to correct by the Canon of Ptolemy, in those later parts, in which there is no Assyrian Record, and by the Assyrian Eponym List, in those earlier parts of which there is no record in the Canon of Ptolemy. If agreement with the Assyrian Records authenticates Ptolemy's Canon it authenticates the Biblical Record also. The three records are in agreement wherever they all meet together. The Biblical Record does not positively disagree with the Assyrian Record, but there is a period for which there are no Assyrian Records, for the contemporary Assyrian records, from the 14th year of Amaziah (B.C. 833) to the 35th of Uzziah (B.C. 772), are a blank. According to Willis J. Beecher this is a period of 61 years, during which the only Assyrian Records are those of the 10 years' reign of Shalmanezer III (IV), a net blank of 51 years between the two Assyrian Kings, Ramman-nirari III and Asshur-daan III. The Assyrian Records omit these 51 years, consequently we must either omit 51 years of the history contained in the Biblical Record, or else add 51 years to the Assyrian Record, for the events of the Biblical and the Assyrian Records synchronize both before and after.

As Ptolemy's Canon does not begin till B.C. 747, or 25 years after the close of this period of 51 years, it is illegitimate to say that the agreement between the Assyrian Eponym Canon and Ptolemy's Canon at a later period must lead us to pass sentence in favour of the Assyrian Records and against the Biblical Records, at an earlier period, for at that later period there is the same agreement between the Assyrian Eponym Canon and the Biblical Records that there is between the Assyrian Eponym Canon and Ptolemy's Canon.

The real explanation of the difference between the Assyrian Records and the Biblical Records is probably this : Assyria was overtaken by some disaster, and the 51 names were either lost by accident, or destroyed by design. The longer Chronology of the Biblical Records is supported (1) by the Biblical accounts of the events which took place during these 51 years, (2) by the long numbers given in Josephus, (3) by the synchronism of the Egyptian date of the Invasion of Shishak, in Rehoboam's time, with the Biblical date B.C. 978, and not with the Assyrian date B.C. 927, and (4) by the explanation given by Georgius Syncellus (c. A.D. 800), in his *Historia Chronographia*, of the reason why Ptolemy commenced his Canon in the year B.C. 747, and did not include in it the earlier period in which the discrepancy of 51 years occurs, *viz.*, that the Assyrian Records for that period had been tampered with. He says : " Nabonassar, King of Babylon, having collected the acts of his predecessors, destroyed them in order that the computation of the reigns of the Assyrian Kings might be made from himself." It is most probable that Assyria was overtaken by some unknown disaster just after the time of the powerful monarch Ramman-nirari III, at the beginning of the blank period of 51 years. For in his time we find the Assyrians taking tribute from the whole region of the Mediterranean, Judah alone excepted, whilst at the end of the blank period, in the reign of Asshur-daan III, we find that their power over this region had been lost, and that they were now engaged in a desperate struggle to regain it.

The fact is (1) the Biblical, the Assyrian and the Ptolemaic Records are all agreed with regard to a certain central period; (2) the Biblical and the Assyrian Records do not agree at an earlier period unless we admit a break of 51 years, but there the Ptolemaic Record has not begun. On the other hand (3) the Biblical Record (as interpreted by the present writer) and the Ptolemaic Record do not agree with regard to a later period, but there the Assyrian Record has ceased. Any conclusion drawn from these premises to the effect that since the chronological data of Ptolemy are confirmed by the Assyrian Chronology our verdict must be pronounced against the Scriptural system, is absolutely unwarranted. The authenticity of the Canon of Ptolemy is established, by its agreement with the Assyrian Eponym Canon, just so far as the authenticity of the Biblical Record is established by its agreement with the Assyrian Eponym Canon, but no further. The point in dispute between Ptolemy's Canon and the Biblical Record lies, not in the Assyrian but in the Persian Period.

One other fact must be borne in mind. Ptolemy is not like the Greek and Latin historians, such as Herodotus and Tacitus, bearing witness to the truth of contemporary events. He belongs to the 2nd Century A.D., and the point in dispute refers to his figures for the period of the Persian Empire some 500 years before. He writes no history. He merely gives a list of names and figures. He is not a historian vouching for the truth of facts of which he has personal knowledge, but the contriver of a scheme filling up gaps in the history he has received, and dating events by means of astronomical computations. Such testimony cannot for one moment be compared with the continuous records of contemporary witnesses like Ezra, Nehemiah and Daniel.

To the list of these six early Greek authors must be added the name of the Latin writer Censorinus.

> 7. *Censorinus* (A.D. 238) wrote his work *De die Natali* in the year A.D. 238. Like Ptolemy he was a compiler of dates and a calculator of Eras. He fixed the date of the last Sothic period before his own time, as that covered by the years B.C. 1321–A.D. 139. This calculation is used by Egyptologers in dating the reign of Merenptah, the Pharaoh of the Exodus. The passage is one of first rate importance. It is therefore given in full. Censorinus says :—

" The Egyptians in the formation of their great year had no regard to the moon. In Greece the Egyptian year is called ' cynical ' (doglike), in Latin ' canicular " because it commences with the rising of the Canicular or dogstar (Sirius), to which is fixed the first day of the month which the Egyptians call Thoth. Their civil year had but 365 days without any intercalation. Thus with the Egyptians the space of four years is shorter by one day than the space of four natural years, and a complete synchronism is only established at the end of 1461 years " (Chapter XVIII).

" But of these Eras the beginnings always take place on the first day

of the month which is called Thoth among the Egyptians, a day which
this present year (A.D. 238) corresponds to the VIIth day of the Kalends
of July (June 25), whilst 100 years ago this same day corresponded
to the XIIth day of the Kalends of August (July 21) at which time
the dogstar is wont to rise in Egypt " (Chapter XXI).

This information is used by Egyptologers in translating the Egyptian
Vague year of 365 days into the Julian year of $365\frac{1}{4}$ days. Taking together
the somewhat doubtful testimony of Manetho and the calculations of modern
Astronomers, based on the information given by Censorinus, they are able
to arrive at a date for the reign of Merenptah, the Pharaoh of the Exodus.
But the validity of the result obtained is dependent upon the truth of a considerable number of assumptions, and cannot be regarded as anything but
hypothetical or tentative.

Another calculation by Censorinus of still more fundamental importance
is his determination of the date of the 1st Olympiad. This he places in the
1014th year before the consulship of Ulpius and Pontianus, A.D. 238. Of these
1014 years, 238 belong to the present Era A.D. This leaves 776 for the number
of years before the commencement of the present era, and accordingly the
1st Olympiad is dated B.C. 776.

The fragment is here given in full. It is taken from *Cory's Ancient
Fragments.*

> " I will not treat of that interval of time which Varro calls historic ;
> for he divides the times into three parts. The first from the beginning
> of mankind to the former cataclysm. The second, which extends to
> the 1st Olympiad, is denominated Mythic, because in it the fabulous
> achievements are said to have happened. The third, which extends
> from the 1st Olympiad to ourselves, is called historic, because the
> actions which have been performed in it are related in authentic history.
>
> " The first period, whether it had a beginning, or whether it always
> was, certainly it is impossible to know the number of its years. Neither
> is the second period accurately determined, yet it is believed to contain
> about 1600 years, but from the former cataclysm, which they call that
> of Ogyges, to the reign of Inarchus, about 400 years, and from thence
> to the 1st Olympiad, something more than 400 ; of which alone, inas-
> much as they are the last years of the Mythic period, and next within
> memory, certain writers have attempted more accurately to determine
> the number. Thus Sosibius writes that they were 395 ; Eratosthenes 407 ;
> Timaeus 417 ; Orethres 164. Many others also have different opinions,
> the very discrepancy of which shows the uncertainty in which it is
> involved.
>
> " Concerning the third interval, there was also some disagreement
> among different writers, though it is confined within a period of only
> six or seven years. Varro has, however, examined the obscurity in
> which it is involved, and comparing with his usual sagacity the chronicles
> and annals of different states, calculating the intervals wanted, or to be
> added by reckoning them backwards, has at length arrived at the truth,

and brought it to light. So that not only a determinate number of years, but even of days can be set forth.

"According to which calculations, unless I am greatly deceived, the present year, whose name and title is that of the consulships of Ulpius and Pontianus, is from the 1st Olympiad the 1014th, reckoning from the summer, at which time of the year the Olympic games are celebrated ; but from the foundation of Rome it is the 991st ; but this is from the Palalia (April 21st), from which the years, *ab urbe condita*, are reckoned. But of those years which are called the Julian years, it is the 283rd, reckoning from the Kalends of January, from which day of the year Julius Cæsar ordered the beginning of the year to be reckoned. But of those years which are called the Augustan it is the 265th, reckoning also from the Kalends of January of that year, in which, upon the 16th of the Kalends of February (Feb. 15th) the son of the Divine Julius Cæsar was saluted Emperor and Augustus, on the motion of Numatius Plaucus, by the Senate and the rest of the citizens in the consulship of himself for the 7th time, and M. Vipsanus Agrippa.

"But the Egyptians, who two years before had been reduced under the dominion of the Roman people, reckon 268 Augustan years : for by the Egyptians in like manner as by ourselves, certain years are recorded, and they call their era the Era of Nabonnagarius, and their years are calculated from the first year of his reign, of which years the present is the 986th.

"The Philippic years also are used among them, and are calculated from the death of Alexander the Great, and from thence to the present time 562 years have elapsed. But the beginning of these years are always reckoned from the first day of that month which is called by the Egyptians Thoth, which happened this year upon the 7th of the Kalends of July (25th of June), for a hundred years ago from the present year of the consulship of Ulpius and Brutius the same fell upon the 12th of the Kalends of August (21st July), on which day Canicula regularly rises in Egypt. Whence we know that of this great year which was before mentioned under the name of Solar Canicular or Trieteris, by which it is commonly called, the present current year must be the 100th.

"I have been careful in pointing out the commencement of all these years, lest anyone should not be aware of the customs in this respect, which are not less various than the opinions of the philosophers. It is commenced by some with the New Sun, that is at the Winter Solstice, by many at the Summer Solstice ; others again reckon from the Vernal, or from the Autumnal Equinox. Some also begin the year from the rising or the setting of Vergilia (Pleiades), but many from the rising of the Dogstar."

Hence the year B.C. 776, thus determined by Censorinus, has been made the pivot upon which Chronology has been made to depend. The scheme or framework being determined beforehand, all that remained was to make the facts fit into the space allotted to them, and all dates, both sacred and profane, have been made to conform to the requirements of the scheme.

Eusebius accepted this basis, and adapted the Chronology of the Old Testament to it, and he and Jerome, who translated his work into Latin, are followed by all subsequent writers. They all adopt the principle, though they differ somewhat in their application of it. Eusebius identifies the year B.C. 776 with the 49th of Uzziah. Elsewhere he copies Julius Africanus and identifies it with the 1st year of Ahaz. Syncellus identifies it with the 45th year of Uzziah. Clinton says it was in reality the 33rd year of Uzziah. But the method adopted is the same, and through Eusebius the Era has passed into the works of all subsequent writers, and thus the space of time between the first of Cyrus as Sole Rex and the year of our Lord A.D. 1, has been fixed beforehand, as a space of 536 years instead of 454, as it is by Daniel. The important thing to note is that this fixing of the dates is not based on con-temporary-testimony like that of Jeremiah 25 [1], in which we are distinctly told that the 4th year of Jehoiakim was the 1st year of Nebuchadnezzar, but is arrived at by a process of computation worked out 1,000 years after the event, and resting ultimately upon the shadowy calculations of Eratosthenes and Timaeus, who obtain their data by multiplying the number of Ephors, Kings, Archons or Priestesses by the number of years which they imagined each of these various officers would be likely to have occupied these several posts.

II. *The Early Christian Chronologers.*

1. *Theophilus of Antioch* (3rd Century A.D.) was one of the great luminaries of the Early Christian Church, and the founder of the historical school of Antiochian Theology, which was opposed to the allegorical school of Clement and Origen of Alexandria. According to *Abulfaragi*, he reckoned 5197 years from the Creation to the Era of the Seleucidae, B.C. 312, which gives the date of Creation as B.C. 5509, in accordance with the longer reckoning of the LXX. But he reckons 330 years from the Creation of Adam to the birth of Seth, and he omits the two years after the Flood.

2. *Julius Africanus* (c. A.D. 220–230), ambassador to Elagabolus, A.D. 218. He rebuilt his native town, Emmaus, A.D. 222, and died A.D. 232. He was the author of *Pentabiblos*, a system of Chronology begin-ning with the Creation of Adam, which he dated B.C. 5500, in accordance with the reckoning of the LXX. He omits the two years after the Flood, a very common error, and he calculates the *death* of Peleg, whose name he interprets as signifying a great fundamental *division* of time, at precisely 3,000 years from the Creation. Other millenary systems usually make it 3,000 years to the 130th year of Peleg, his age at the birth of his son Reu, according to the figures of the LXX.

3. *Clement of Alexandria* (3rd Century A.D.) was a disciple of Pantaenus, the founder of the famous catechetical school at

THE ROMANCE OF BIBLE CHRONOLOGY.

Alexandria, and the teacher of Origen. He was a widely-read scholar, familiar with the whole body of classic literature, and with the books of the Old and New Testaments. He was the founder of the allegorical school of Biblical Interpretation, and the author of some able defences of Christianity against the absurdities and immoralities of pagan theology. The four works of his that have come down to us are (1) *An Admonition to the Gentiles*, (2) *The Paedagogue*, (3) *Stromata*, and (4) *Who is the rich man that is saved*? Amongst his lost works the most important, known to us only through fragmentary paraphrases in other authors, was his great work entitled *Hypotyposes i.e.*, Types or *Adumbrations*.

4. *Eusebius* (A.D. 265–340) was the Father of Ecclesiastical history, and the most learned man of his age. In his *Ecclesiastical History* he traces the history of the Christian Church from the birth of Christ to the year 324. His *Preparatio Evangelica* and his *Demonstratio Evangelica* still exist in an imperfect form. Of his *Chronicon*, the treatise in which he elaborates his Chronology, we have fragments in Greek, and a translation into Latin by Jerome. The name of Eusebius is one of first rate importance in the history of Chronology. It was Eusebius who first adopted the hypothetical Era of the Greek Olympiads, and assuming its truth, equated the years there given to the annals of the Old Testament, thus creating an error of 82 years according to the present writer's interpretation of the Hebrew Records, by placing the 1st Olympiad 82 years higher than the truth, and adapting the events of history to the Chronology thus framed, instead of adapting the framework of the Chronology to the events. The importance of Eusebius lies in the fact that the example which he set, and the figures which he gave, have been followed ever since.

5. *Epiphanius* (A.D. 310–402) was born in Palestine. He became Bishop of Constantia, in the Island of Cyprus, in the year A.D. 367. He was a good theologian, an accurate scholar, and a great linguist. His *Refutation of all Heresies* was a standard defence of Christianity against all forms of Pagan, Gnostic and Arian error. It is from the first book of his work *Against Heresies* that the motto of the present work has been taken, as an indication of the writer's belief that any departure from the methods of exact science, and any alteration of the Massoretic Text, or any variation from the words of the Hebrew Verity can only lead us *away* from the Truth. Epiphanius accused Aquila, first a Pagan, then a Christian, and finally a renegade Jew, of wresting Scripture in his translation of the Old Testament into Greek (published A.D. 128) in order to invalidate its testimonies concerning Christ.

6. *Ephraem Syrus* (A.D. 325–378), a Syrian theologian, born at Nisibis. He retired to Edessa, where he lived in retirement. He wrote

in Syriac, but his works have been translated into Greek and Latin. He adopted the Chronology of the LXX. and accused the Jews of having subtracted 600 years from the generations of Adam, Seth, etc., in order that their own books might not convict them of the fact that Christ had already come, He having been predicted to appear for the deliverance of mankind after 5,500 years. In this Ephraem was wrong, for it was the Greek Translators of the LXX. text who added the six centuries to the Chronology of the Hebrew Text, and not *vice versa*. The " prediction " alluded to was the almost universal tradition of the Jews that the world would last for 7,000 years, and as man was made on the sixth day, and fell by sin, so the Messiah would come to redeem the world in the sixth millennium, AN. HOM. 5000 to 6000, and the date of the Creation according to the LXX. was B.C. 5508.

7. *Jerome* (A.D. 340–420), called in Greek Hieronymus, was one of the most learned scholars of the Early Christian Church. He studied Hebrew, and spent some years in a cave at Bethlehem, where he lived a celibate life, and devoted himself to the work of translating the Old Testament into Latin, his version, the Latin Vulgate (A.D. 397), being regarded as authoritative, or Canonical in the Roman Catholic Church ever since the Council of Trent, A.D. 1545–1563. His other writings included his *De Viris Illustribus*, and his *Dialogi contra Pelagianos* and his translation into Latin of Eusebius' *Chronicon*, which thus determined the Chronology of Western Europe, till the time of Bede, Eusebius being followed by all sorts of authors right down to the present day.

III. *Byzantine Chronologers.* These are contained in the *Corpus Scriptorum Historiae Byzantinae*, a collection of works by various authors, the three principal of which are the works of Georgius Syncellus, and Johannes Malalas, and the *Chronicon Paschale*.

1. *Georgius Syncellus* (A.D. 792), Monk and Historian. His *Chronographia* contains a most valuable account of the Chronology of the Byzantine School of learning in the Centuries between the Early Christian Fathers and the Revival of Learning in modern times, led, in the department of Chronology, by Scaliger. Syncellus has given us two very valuable Canons, or lists of Kings, (1) *The Astronomical Canon* which he entitles " The Years from Nabonassar—according to the astronomical Canon." This is precisely Ptolemy's Canon from the first year of Nabonassar to the last year of Alexander the Great. (2) The *Ecclesiastical Canon*, which he entitles " The years from Salmonasar, who is also Nabonassar according to the Ecclesiastical reckoning, up to Cyrus, and thence to Alexander of Macedon."

2. *Johannes Malalas* or Malelas (9th Century A.D.), another Byzantine historian, writes another *Chronographia*.

3. The *Chronicon Paschale* also belongs to this group.

IV. *The Great Armenian Chronologer—Abulfaragus, Abulfaragi, Abul-Faraj, Gregory or Bar-Hebraeus* (A.D. 1226–1266).

This celebrated historian, whose real name was Gregorius Bar-Hebraeus, wrote a Compendium of Universal History from the Creation of the World to A.D. 1273, entitled *The History of the Dynasties*. Abulfaragus was an Armenian Jew. He was brought up as a physician. After his conversion he settled in Tripoli, and became the first Bishop of Guba (1246) and afterwards Bishop of Aleppo. Although he was a leader of the Jacobite sect of Christians in Syria, he was much admired by Mohammedan, Jewish and Christian writers. He was at once the most learned, the most accurate, and the most faithful historian of all the Syrian writers. His history of the world contains valuable information respecting the Saracens, the Tartar Mongols, and the Conquest of Ghenghis-Khan. Around his name there has sprung up an extensive literature, the titles of which occupy many pages in the Catalogue of the British Museum. To Abulfaragi we owe the most correct adjustment of the Saracen Dynasty.

V. *Modern Chronologers.*

Of these the number is legion. We select only a few of the more important. Most of them are mentioned in the article on " Chronology " in the *Encyclopædia Britannica* (11th edition).

1. *Joseph Scaliger* (A.D. 1540–1609) was born at Agen in France. He studied at the University of Paris, and was a man of exceptional genius, and consummate scholarship. He was converted to Protestantism, and lectured at Geneva. His writings mark the rise of a new era in historical criticism. His monumental work *De Emendatione Temporum* (published A.D. 1596) laid the foundations of the science of modern Chronology. He was distinguished by the brilliancy of his genius and the extent of his erudition. He invented the Julian period of 7980 years from B.C. 4714 to A.D. 3266, formed by the multiplication of the cycles of the sun 28 years, the moon 19 years, and the indiction 15 years. In its first year the cycle of the sun was 1, of the moon 1, and of the indiction 1. The three cycles will not so correspond again till the end of the cycle. The Julian period has no relation to the Julian *year* or the Julian *Era*, both of which take their names from Julius Cæsar. The Julian *period* is named after the family name of Scaliger, his father's name being Julius Cæsar Scaliger. Joseph Scaliger discovered the cause of the precession of the Equinoxes. He interpreted the prophecy of Daniel's 70 weeks .as ending at the destruction of Jerusalem, A.D. 70, and conse-

quently as commencing B.C. 420 in the 4th year of Darius Nothus. He inserted the 5 years omitted by the Jews, to make up the 430 years from Abraham's migration into Canaan to the Exodus.

2. *Sethus Calvisius* (A.D. 1603) was the author of an important work, which he called the *Opus Chronologicum*.

3. *Dionysius Petavius* (Denis Petau, b. A.D. 1583) was a Chronologer of the first rank. He was born at Orleans, and published in 1627 his great work *De doctrina temporum*, in 1630 a continuation of the same, and in 1633-4 an abridgment of it, entitled *Rationarum Temporum*. Petavius was a Catholic, and his system is used principally in the Romish Church. He was learned in languages, deeply read in universal history, a capable mathematician, an astronomer equal to the calculation of eclipses, a man of indefatigable industry and patience, and a consummate Chronologer. He exposed the errors of the ingenious and fanciful scheme of his rival Scaliger. He adhered to the *Hebrew Verity* and reprobated any and every " emendation " of, or departure from, the Massoretic Text. He entered the following useful caveat against the substitution of chronological hypotheses and unverifiable conjectures for the patient unravelling of the meaning of the Text, in which alone is to be found the testimony of the ancients, the only true basis of scientific Chronology. " As nothing is more easy, so nothing is less tolerable, than to transfer to the most ancient writers the fault of our own error and unskilfulness ; on the contrary, nothing is more prudent and more desirable than to attribute very much to the authority and fidelity of the ancients ; and not to recede therefrom, except where we are admonished and convinced by the clearest and plainly necessary indications of truth."

4. *James Ussher* (A.D. 1581-1656), Archbishop of Armagh, was born at Dublin, and educated at Trinity College. He took holy orders in 1601, and soon acquired a reputation as a powerful preacher, both in Dublin and London. In 1607 he became Professor of Divinity at Trinity College, Dublin. He rose by his transcendent merits, and became in 1625 Archbishop of Armagh, and in 1634 Primate of all Ireland. His greatest work is the *Annales Veteris et Novi Testamenti* (1650-1654), translated in 1658 as *The Annals of the world . . . to the beginning of the Emperor Vespasian's Reign*. Ussher was a profound scholar, and one of the brightest luminaries of the Church of Ireland. He was a munificent patron of Oriental Literature. To him, we owe the publication of the *Samaritan Pentateuch*. He always admitted the liability of both the Old Testament and the New to the errors of copyists, but he adhered very closely to the Massoretic Text of the Old Testament, and was enabled thereby to construct a system of Chronology which has held its own to this day. His dates were;

revised by Wm. Lloyd, Bishop of St. Asaph (subsequently Bishop of Worcester), and published by him in the margin of his *Holy Bible with Chronological Dates and Index.* " Lloyd's Bible " (published 1701) is thus the first Bible published with marginal dates.

The principal improvement of Ussher is the correction of the age of Terah at the birth of Abraham, from 70 years to 130. He dates the creation of the world in the year B.C. 4004, a remarkable astronomical epoch which La Place described as " one in which the great axis of the earth's orbit coincided with the line of the equinoxes, and consequently when the true and mean equinoxes were united." His principal errors were his misinterpretation of " the 480th year " in 1 Kings 6[1], and his misdating of the accession of Uzziah in the 15th instead of in the 27th year of Jeroboam II. His system has prevailed principally in the British Empire, and amongst the Reformed Churches of the Continent, as that of Petavius has prevailed amongst divines of the Church of Rome. Ussher is not infallible, but he thoroughly deserved the universal esteem which his chronological achievements secured for him.

5. *Philippe Lobbe* (fl. 1651) is the author of a treatise entitled *Regia Epitome Historiae Sacrae et profanae.*

6. Beveridge (fl. 1669) was a mathematical genius. In his *Institutionum Chronologicarum libri duo,* he gives rules for adjusting the *Julian Period* and the *Mohammedan Hegeira* to the Christian Era.

7. *Sir John Marsham* (fl. 1672), was the author of the *Chronicus Canon Egyptiacus Ebraicus et Graecus,* a learned, acute, and ingenious, but unsuccessful attempt to reconcile the comparative Chronologies of Egyptian, Hebrew, Phœnician, and Greek antiquities. He steers a middle course between Petavius and Ussher. He followed Josephus, and was himself followed by Sir Isaac Newton in identifying the famous Egyptian King Sesostris with the Sesac, or Shishak, who plundered the Temple in the reign of Rehoboam.

8. *Paul Pezron* (fl. 1687), is the author of a chronological work entitled *L'Antiquité des temps rétablié et défendu,* published in 1687. Four years later he published a *Défense* of the same.

9. *Henry Dodwell* (fl. 1701) wrote a treatise on technical Chronology entitled *De Veteribus Graicorum Romanorumque cyclis.*

10. *Sir Isaac Newton* (1642–1727), the illustrious natural philosopher, was born at Woolsthrope Manor in Lincolnshire. He was the greatest mathematician of modern times. He discovered the binomial theorem, and the method of fluxions, and in 1666 the contemplation of the fall of an apple led to his greatest discovery of all, that of the law of gravitation. The following year he discovered the composite nature of light. He held the Chair of Mathematics at Cambridge for 33 years. In 1699 he became Master of the Mint. He represented his University

D

in Parliament, and was elected President of the Royal Society, a post which he occupied for 24 years. He was knighted in 1705. He lived to his eightieth year, and was buried in Westminster Abbey. Bishop Burnet described him as the " whitest soul he ever knew." Sir Isaac Newton made a hobby of Chronology, and became an ardent student of the subject during the last 30 years of his life. He read widely, and thought deeply on the problems of early Chronology, and came to the conclusion that the Greeks and the Latins, no less than the Babylonians, the Assyrians and the Egyptians, had greatly exaggerated their antiquity, from motives of national vanity. In his great work *The Chronology of Ancient Kingdoms Amended*, which was published posthumously in 1728, the year after his death, he endeavoured to construct a system on new bases, independent of the Greek Chronologers, whose unsatisfactory method of reckoning by generations, reigns and successions he exposed, laying bare the foundations on which their Chronology rested, and thereby overthrowing the elementary dates of Greek, Latin and Egyptian Chronology. He reduced the date of the taking of Troy from B.C. 1183 to 904. He followed Sir John Marshall in identifying Sesostris with Shishak, whose date he thus reduced from B.C. 1300 to 965. Newton cites Thucydides and Socrates, the musician Terpander, and the Olympic disk of Lycurgus, he uses his calculation of the precession of the equinoxes since the time of Hipparcus, and he substitutes a reckoning of 20 years each instead of 33 for the succession of the Kings of Sparta. Newton cannot be said to have established his point, but he has certainly destroyed the possibility of regarding the Chronology of the Greeks as a stable foundation for any system of Chronology that can be used as a standard by which to judge, and correct, the testimony of the Old Testament. Yet this conjectural Chronology of the Greeks is the foundation upon which the Canon of Ptolemy rests, and the Canon of Ptolemy is the only obstacle in the way of the establishment of the Chronology of the Old Testament.

11. *Alphonse des Vignolles* (fl. 1738), has written a very valuable treatise on Chronology entitled the *Chronologie de l'histoire Sainte*. Des Vignolles, Jackson, and Hales are the main advocates of a return to the longer Patriarchal Chronology based on the LXX. in preference to the shorter Patriarchal Chronology given in the Hebrew Text, which was adopted by Scaliger, Petavius and Ussher at an earlier date, and subsequently by Clinton. Canon Rawlinson, and most Egyptologists adopt the longer Chronology, or demand a still earlier date for the rise of civilization in Egypt, but the entire weight of their argument rests upon their interpretation of the testimony of Manetho and Berosus, and the astronomical calculations by which it is supported.

12. *N. Leuglet Dufresnoy* (fl. 1744) is the author of some very carefully compiled dates, entitled *Tablettes chronologiques de
l'histoire universelle.*

13. *The Benedictine Congregation of Saint Maur* published in 1750,
in one large quarto volume, their elaborate treatise *L'Art de
verifier les dates.* This was subsequently enlarged into 38
octavo volumes published between 1818 & 1831.

14. *John Jackson* (fl. 1752), the author of *Chronological Antiquities,*
and a disciple of the acute and learned Vossius, is the first
English Chronologer of the modern school to break away from
the sure ground of the Hebrew Text, hitherto accepted by
Scaliger, Petavius and Ussher alike, and to adopt the longer
Chronology of the Greek LXX. His work is distinguished
by learning and ingenuity. It reveals a spirit of adventure,
and a love of change, and abounds in ingenious criticisms and
"conjectural emendations" of the received systems. His
fundamental error is his introduction of the 130 years of the
interpolated Second Cainan, between Arphaxad and Salah,
from the LXX. version of Gen. 11 [13,] where alone it is to be found.
He also adopted the common error that Terah was 70 years
old at the birth of Abraham, though Ussher had proved that
he was 130. He took a step in the right direction in rejecting
Ussher's interpretation of the length of the period from the
Exodus to the 4th year of Solomon in 1 Kings 6 [1,] and substituted 579 years instead of 480. It should have been 594
years. He critically determined his fundamental date B.C. 586
for the destruction of the Temple.

15. *John Kennedy* (fl. 1752) was the Rector of Bradley in Derbyshire.
His system is based on the Hebrew Text, of which he has made
a special study from the point of view of astronomy. His
*New method of stating and explaining the Scripture Chronology
upon Mosaic Astronomical principles, mediums and data, as
laid down in the Pentateuch* develops the astronomical principles
followed by Moses, and demonstrates their superiority to
modern methods of intercalation from the Metonic and the
Callipic cycles to the Julian and the Gregorian rectifications
of the length of the year. He translates Hebrew technical terms
like *Tekuphath Hasshanah* = The Vernal or the Autumnal Equinox,
explains that Moses always *measures* time by *solar* years, and
always *computes* time by *lunar* years. He shows how time
is measured by the Hebrew Shanah or year, consisting of an
annual revolution of the earth round the sun, containing the
whole of the four seasons, and therefore always invariable, and
how the *Mognadim* (translated seasons), the sacred feasts of the
Jews (Passover, Pentecost and Tabernacles), are pinned down
to this solar year. His exposition of the story of the flood
shows that Noah was exactly 365 days in the ark, and explains
Moses' method of computing in terms of the months of the lunar

year, whilst measuring time in terms of the solar year. In his great work *Physiological Chronology*, a bulky quarto volume of 750 pages, he dates the creation B.C. 4007. He postulates the infallibility of the Hebrew Text, which he says "has never been corrupted in the article of Chronology by Jew or Pagan, by chance or design. It is not more certain that there is a sun and moon in the heavens than it is that not a single error of the press, or of a Jewish transcriber, has crept into the present copies of the Hebrew Massoretic Text, to give the least interruption to its chronological series of years." Kennedy's view of the infallibility of the Hebrew Massoretic Text, coupled with his feeling of certainty with regard to the results obtained from his mathematically exact astronomical calculations, accounts for the dogmatic tone which characterizes his works. This note of infallibility is very annoying to modern scholars, who rejoice in the larger liberty afforded by the method of hypothesis and conjecture !

16. *John Blair* (fl. 1754) takes rank with the most painstaking and accurate Chronologers of modern times. He published his *Chronology and History of the World* first in 1754, and subsequently prepared a new edition very much enlarged. This was published in 1857. He adopts the method of tabulation, and aims at precision of statement and accuracy in his results.

17. *Principal Playfair* of St. Andrews, Scotland (fl. 1784), has given us in his *System of Chronology* a technical and a historical treatise which may be regarded as an improvement on *Blair's Chronology*. He begins with an account of the principles of the science, and carefully defines his terms.

18. *A. H. L. Heeren* (fl. 1799) is the author of a work in German entitled a *Handbuch der Geschichte der Staaten des Alterthums*. It was published in 1799, and is characterized by those qualities of comprehensiveness, thoroughness, and modernity of standpoint which we look for in works by German writers.

19. *G. G. Bredow* (fl. 1803) has given us another German *vade mecum* on the subject, entitled a *Handbuch der alten Geschichte, Geographie, und Chronologie*. It was published in 1803, and contains his *Historische Tabellen*.

20. *Wm. Hales* (fl. 1809) one of the ablest and best of our modern Chronologers. The fulness, variety, and sustained interest of his treatment of the subject in the four octavo volumes of his *New Analysis of Chronology and Geography, History and Prophecy*, is altogether beyond praise. This was published in 1809–1814. His object is a comprehensive treatment of the whole subject in all its branches, on principles at once both Scriptural and scientific. He gives an interesting account of the elements of technical Chronology, a review of the history of Chronology, and some valuable rules for "chronologizing." His Chronology of the Old Testament treats of the period from

Adam to Herod the Great. His Chronology of the New Testament treats of the period from Herod the Great to the destruction of Jerusalem, to which is appended an exposition of the prophecies of Daniel and Revelation, in reference to the prophetic history of the Church. In his final volume he surveys the entire field of profane Chronology, including the remains of Sanchoniathon, Berosus, Manetho, and the important historical works of Ctesias, Herodotus, the Persian historian Mirkhond, Ptolemy, Abulfaragus, and Syncellus. He follows *Jackson* in adopting the longer Chronology of the LXX., but "judiciously" rejects the Second Cainan. His date for the Creation is B.C. 5411. He has a decidedly modern note, and in his treatment of Scripture he tempers reverence with intelligence, and lowers the "superstitious veneration of the Hebrew Verity or supposed immaculate purity of the Massoretic editions of the Hebrew Text to the proper level of rational respect." His reasons for rejecting the shorter Hebrew Chronology and adopting in preference the longer Greek Chronology of the LXX. are subjective and inconclusive. His work contains a very large quantity of useful chronological material, including many valuable Tables.

21. *C. G. Zumpt* (fl. 1819) is the author of the *Annales Veterum Regnorum.*

22. *Buret de Longchamps* (fl. 1821) has left us some valuable *Tableaux Historiques Chronologiques et Géographiques.*

23. *Henry Fynes Clinton* (fl. 1824) is perhaps the ablest, the soundest, and the most complete and satisfactory of all our modern Chronologers. His *Fasti Hellenici* (1824–1834), his *Fasti Romani* (1845–1850), and his *Epitomes* of these two elaborate works (1851–1853) are absolutely indispensable to anyone who desires to make an exhaustive study of the subject. His reasoning is clear, his authorities are numerous, and his tone is moderate. His three large quarto volumes of the *Fasti Hellenici* alone are a library in themselves. His Chronology contains perhaps fewer errors than that of any of his predecessors. He determines the Joshua-Judges "Chasm" (20 years instead of 13) and the Samuel "Chasm" (32 years instead of 20) by means of a subjective estimate, or conjecture, instead of by inference from the data contained in the Text, and for the Persian and Greek period from Cyrus to Christ, he adopts the figures of the Canon of Ptolemy instead of those of the prophet Daniel. Like most other Chronologers, he does not understand the Scripture method of recording the lengths of the reigns of the Kings of Israel and Judah. He is to be blamed for his assertion that the figures given in the Books of Kings and Chronicles are sometimes "corrupt" and to be rejected. But apart from these errors, which make his Era for the Creation B.C. 4138, just 96 years too long, he is a most worthy and a most judicious guide.

24. *Christian Ludwig Ideler* (fl. 1825) has produced in his *Handbuch der Mathematischen und technischen Chronologie* a most valuable treatment of a recondite subject. His researches into the construction of the calendars used by all the different nations of antiquity, have opened up a mine of useful information. His *Lehrbuch der Chronologie*, published in 1831, is a smaller handbook upon the same subject.

25. *M. L'Abbé Halma* (fl. 1819) makes considerable use of Ideler in his great work, *Tables Chronologiques des Regnes de C. Ptolemaeus*. This was published in Paris in 1819, and is an admirable account of Ptolemy's Canon, which he describes as "the most precious Monument of ancient Chronology."

26. *Sir Harris Nicholas* (fl. 1833) is the author of a valuable *Chronology of History* (published in 1833).

27. *Edward Greswell* (fl. 1852) has left us three large and important works on technical Chronology. (1) *Fasti Temporis Catholici* (1852), (2) *Origines Kalendariae Italicae* (1854) and (3) *Origines Kalendariae Hellenicae* (1862)

28. *B. B. Woodward & W. L. R. Cates* (fl. 1872) published in 1892 a most valuable *Encyclopædia of Chronology*.

29. *J. C. Macdonald* (fl. 1897) has collected in his *Chronologies and Calendars* some interesting curiosities of Chronology.

30. *David Ross Fotheringham* (fl. 1906) has written a useful little handbook on the *Chronology of the Old Testament*.

Other works of equal importance are omitted for lack of space, or because they deal only with some one special aspect of the subject, but room must be found for the bare mention of (1) *Benjamin Marshall's Chronological Tables* (1713). Marshall was the literary executor of Bishop Lloyd, whom he closely followed. (2) *Dr. Humphrey Prideaux's Historical Connection of the Old and New Testaments*. The 1858 edition, revised by J. Talboys Wheeler, contains a valuable account of Rabbinic authorities on Chronology, by Dr. McCaul. (3) *Schrader's Cuneiform Inscriptions and the Old Testament*, a Monumental work, but unfair to the Hebrew Records. (4) *Sir Edward Denny's Seventy Weeks of Daniel ;* he is the first to explain the principle of *Anno Dei* reckonings. (5) *Palmoni* an essay written to prove that every date in the Bible is a fictitious construction, having less relation to objective fact than to the exercise of the mythopoetic faculty as applied to numbers. (6) *Henry Browne's Ordo Saeculorum*, an excellent Chronology of the Holy Scripture, working backwards from Christ to Adam, and eliciting the mystical qualities of the numbers of the years employed in the Divine Administration of the times and seasons. (7) *Lumen's* startling redatement of the days of Nehemiah in his *Prince of Judah*. (8) *Sir Robert Anderson's Coming Prince*. (9) *Canon Girdlestone's* excellent little 77 page *Outlines of Bible Chronology*. (10) *Charles Foster Kent's Historical Bible*, which construes the Chronology in accordance with the Higher Critical theory of the origin of the Text, and last, but not least, two works of surpassing merit. (11) *Willis Judson Beecher's Dated Events of the Old Testament* (1907), and (12) *The Companion Bible*, published by the Oxford University Press.

CHAPTER II.   THE TRUSTWORTHINESS OF TESTIMONY

THE Science of History stands upon a different basis from that of the Science of Nature. In all matters relating to the facts and events of past history there is one and only one kind of proof possible, and that is, not deductive proof, as in Mathematics, and not inductive proof of the·kind which is admissible in the Natural Sciences, but legal, evidential, or historical proof, of the kind required in a Court of Law.

If a man denies a mathematical truth, that truth can be demonstrated in such a way as to compel belief. If for example, a man denies that two and two make four, or that the three angles of a triangle are equal to two right angles, it is not the propositions that become of doubtful validity, but the competence or the sanity of the man who denies them.

Or again, if he denies that oxygen and hydrogen under certain given conditions combine to form water, he can be taken into a chemical laboratory, in which the fact is verified, and ocular demonstration of its truth is given so as to again compel belief.

But when we come to the sifting of evidence, and the proof of the truth of events belonging to the past, the case is essentially different. If a man denies that there ever was such a person as Alfred the Great, or William the Conqueror, or Napoleon, or Jesus Christ, Moses, Abraham, or Adam, the only kind of proof which it is possible to adduce in support of the fact of the past existence of these persons is that of evidence, or testimony. The lawyer " proves " his case by calling his witnesses ; the historian by adducing Monumental, documentary, or other evidence.

The trustworthiness of testimony is the fundamental postulate of all history. If this be called in question it is impossible to proceed a single step in the Science of History. But some testimony is not trustworthy, and it is the business of the historian, or the Chronologer, to sift the evidence, to probe the character of the witness, and to test the trustworthiness of the testimony given. For the prosecution of this task certain rules have been laid down which define the limits within which testimony may be regarded as worthy of acceptance and belief.

A credible witness is one who is at once both honest, capable and contemporary.

Take the case of Alfred the Great and the cakes, which he is said to have spoiled. The story may be true, or it may not, but in any case it cannot be *proved*. For when the records are searched, and the evidence is examined, it is found that there is no document, no witness, no testimony of any kind in support of the truth of the story until we come to that of the Welsh historian, Aser, who was not only not contemporary with the event, but did not live till some two centuries later. It is, of course, quite possible that the story may have been preserved by tradition without embellishment or exaggeration, and without any other kind of departure from the truth, but the lack of contemporary evidence or testimony must ever prevent its taking rank as an assured historic fact.

With the writers of the New Testament the case is entirely different. They were honest and capable men. They were also contemporary with the events which they record. When the Books of the New Testament were finally accorded a place in the Sacred Volume, the rule by which they were judged was, whether they were written by an Apostle, or by a companion of one of the Apostles, that is by one who was contemporary with the events narrated. The Apostles base the trustworthiness of their testimony upon the fact that they had themselves *seen* and *heard* the things which they record. " That which we have heard, which we have seen with our eyes, which we have looked upon, and our hands have handled of the Word of Life. . . . . that which we have seen and heard declare we unto you " (1 John 1 [1. 3]). " And he that saw it bare record, and his record is true " (John 19 [35]). " We cannot but speak the things which we have seen and heard " (Acts 4 [20]). Great stress was laid upon the fact that in order to be an Apostle at all, a man must be a contemporary of our Lord, and an eye-witness of the Resurrection : " Wherefore of these men which have companied with us all the time that the Lord Jesus went in and out among us . . . . . must one be ordained to be a witness with us of the Resurrection " Acts 1 [21. 22]).

It was on this fact also that St. Paul, who (as far as we know) never saw our Lord in the days of His humiliation, based his claim to apostleship : " Am not I an Apostle ? Have not I seen the Lord ? " (1 Cor. 9 [1]).

In like manner the writers of the remaining books of the New Testament, the companions of the Apostles, laid great stress on the fact that they also obtained the facts which they record from the lips of men who were " eye-witnesses and ministers of the Word " (Luke 1 [2]). The required conditions are all fulfilled. The truth of the testimony of the writers is " proved " in the only way in which any recorded fact of past history can be " proved " at all. But the " proof " is not of such a nature as to compel belief. For belief is ultimately an act of the will, a revelation of personality, and a disclosure of presuppositions held in the mind, which make the evidence produced acceptable or inconclusive.

The events recorded in the Old Testament are more distant, but the Canons of Credibility applied to the New Testament are equally valid for the Old. The remoteness of the events does not exempt them from the requirements of honesty, capacity and contemporaneity in the writer, but we must not expect the same amount of evidence or proof in respect of the records of antiquity that we do in respect of the history of modern times.

It is reasonable to attach a higher value to the testimony handed down from generation to generation in ancient times than to that of our own days, in respect of which a more rigorous demand for documentary evidence may be pressed.

According to the text of the Old Testament, Adam was for 243 years contemporary with Methuselah. Methuselah for 98 years was contemporary with Shem, and Shem for 150 years was contemporary with Abraham. The period from Adam to Abraham is bridged over by a chain of evidence or testimony containing only two intermediate links. This may be compared with the testimony preserved by tradition from the time of a man's great-grandfather, through his grandfather and his father to his own generation.

The time of Abraham was an age of advanced civilization. The men of his day lived in a world that teemed with schools and libraries and books. The state of education in the age of Abraham, says Professor A. H. Sayce, was quite equal to that of the common people in our own country in the middle of last Century. The period of written or documentary evidence dates from before the time of Abraham. The family records were doubtless kept and handed down from Abraham, Isaac and Jacob to Joseph, whose " coffin," that is ark or chest (Gen. 50 [26], cp. Ex. 40 [20], 2 Chron. 24 [11], where the same word is thus translated) may well have contained other relics and heirlooms beside the bones of Joseph.

In a conversation with a friend, the present writer, in claiming authenticity for the chronological records of the early chapters of Genesis, was met by the objection—" At any rate there were no Registrars of Births and Deaths in those days," to which he replied, "That is just exactly what the fifth chapter of Genesis is." It might have been copied from the fly leaf of an old Patriarchal family Bible, or genealogical family chart. The family records that are preserved in these days are little else but records of births, marriages and deaths, but they go back farther than any other records in the family chest.

Moses was the literary executor of Joseph, and the custodian of the heirlooms of antiquity preserved by the chosen race. He was an authentic reporter of evidence, and the Book of Genesis bears indications of being an original work, incorporating other authentic writings older than itself. From the Exodus to the end of the Old Testament history, which reaches its conclusion in the Books of Nehemiah and Malachi, all the writers were either original witnesses of the events to which their testimony is borne, or else they obtained their facts from authentic contemporary records.

The fact that all the writers of the Old Testament were aided by Divine Inspiration gives a *double* sanction, and a supernatural authority to their writings. As mere human witnesses, and altogether apart from Divine Inspiration, their evidence would be valid for the periods on which they wrote.

The testimony they bear is one and undivided, it is continuous and uninterrupted from the Patriarchal period to the Theocratic ; from that to the Monarchic, the period of the Captivity, the Return, the Scribes, the Talmudists, and the Massoretes, the writings of the Old Testament have been handed down in one continuous, unbroken line of succession, until the time of their publication in the printed Hebrew Bibles of the present day. They are therefore worthy of acceptance as the work of honest, capable and contemporary witnesses, whose testimony has been faithfully preserved, and duly accredited to each succeeding generation, right down to, and including, our own.

CHAPTER III.   CANONS OF CREDIBILITY.

THE Hebrew Records of the Old Testament possess, from the very earliest times, a definite historical character, in marked contrast with those of other nations.   The antiquities of the Greeks are full of poetic fictions.   They wrote nothing in prose till after the conquest of Asia by Cyrus.   " Their own times," says Sir Isaac Newton, in his *Chronology of Ancient Kingdoms Amended*, " were divided into three parts.   Those before the Flood of *Ogyges* they called ' Unknown,' because they had no history of them.   Those between the Flood of Ogyges and the 1st Olympiad they called ' Fabulous,' because it was full of fables.   Those subsequent to the 1st Olympiad, B.C. 776, they called historical, but they had no Chronology of the times preceding the Persian Empire," except in so far as they subsequently constructed one by means of inference and conjecture.   The antiquities of all other nations are likewise lost in the mists of early legend, myth and fable.   The religious systems of Greece and Rome, Egypt and India, Persia and other nations of the East, did not even postulate a historical basis.   The farther back we trace their past history, the more obscure and uncertain it becomes.

With the Hebrew Records the case is quite different.   The history of the race begins with an epoch which is quite definite, and the record of the first 2369 years, the period covered by the Book of Genesis, is stated with such minute accuracy and precision, that for those who accept the Hebrew Text there is no possible alternative to that of Ussher, as shown in the margin of the Authorised Version of our English Bibles.   The chronological record is accurately continued, and may be definitely traced through the succeeding Centuries.   It is only when we reach the latest records of Ezra and Nehemiah that chronological difficulties become acute, and only after the close of the Canon that the count of the years is altogether lost.

The annals of the Hebrew nation are authentic narratives by contemporary writers.   The Biblical Record is the Record of the redeeming activity of God.   This Record is embedded in a human history, but it is a miraculous history throughout.

It is not only a history of the external events of the life of men.   In its primary significance it is a history of God, and of His activity within the realm of human history.   Hence, none but men informed by the Spirit of God could write it, and only by faith in the truth of the Revelation can we ever hope to be able to understand it.   The essence of Revelation is redemption, and redemption is a deed of God, done, as it were, within the veil, yet manifesting itself to us in the Revelation given in Holy Scripture, as a Divine movement in human history.

We trace the history in one unbroken line, from the Creation of Adam to the Crucifixion.   Bible Chronology is an exact science.   It is not built upon hypothesis and conjecture.   It rests ultimately upon evidence, or testimony, but it does occasionally require the use of the method of scientific historic induction.

The historical character of the Old Testament has been vigorously assailed, from the rise of historical criticism, which owed its origin to that great master spirit, Niebuhr, down to the present day ; but the supposed parallelism between the early records of other nations, with their prodigies, and miracles, and Divine appearances, their myths and legends, and fictitious personages, does not really exist. Accurate historical investigation establishes the authenticity of the facts, and the reality of the persons presented to us in the writings of the Old Testament, so far as these can be tested by the application of the laws of history or the Canons of historic Truth.

These Canons are of universal applicability. They are aptly formulated by George Rawlinson in his Bampton Lecture for 1859, on " The Historical Evidences of the Truth of Scripture Records." They may be briefly summarized as follows :—

Canon I. When the record which we possess of an event is the writing of a contemporary, supposing that he is a credible witness, and had means of observing the fact to which he testifies, the fact is to be accepted as possessing the first, or highest degree of credibility. Such evidence is on a par with that of witnesses in a Court of Justice.

Canon II. When the event recorded is one which the writer may reasonably be supposed to have obtained directly from those who witnessed it, we should accept it as probably true, unless it be in itself very improbable. Such evidence possesses the second degree of historical credibility.

Canon III. When the event recorded is removed considerably from the age of the recorder of it, and there is no reason to believe that he obtained it from a contemporary writing, but the probable source of his information was oral tradition ; still, if the event be one of great importance, and of public notoriety, if it affected the national life, or prosperity—especially if it be of a nature to have been at once commemorated by the establishment of any rite or practice—then it has a claim to belief as probably true, at least in its general outline. This, however, is the third, and a comparatively low degree of historical credibility.

Canon IV. When the traditions of one race are corroborated by the traditions of another . . . the event which has this double testimony, obtains thereby a high amount of probability, and, if not very unlikely in itself, thoroughly deserves acceptance.

Canon V. Direct records, such as those which proceed from the agents in the occurrences, public inscribed Monuments such as have frequently been set up by Governments and Kings, state papers, such as those contained in the Books of Ezra and Esther, autobiographies and memoirs, deserve the very highest degree of credit, and are the best and most authentic sources of history.

Canon VI. Indirect records, embodying the result of personal enquiry and research, are to be placed on a much lower footing, and must be judged by the opportunity, the competency, and the veracity of their composers.

Canon VII. The cumulative evidence of two or more independent witnesses to the same event, increases the probability of the event, not in an arithmetical, but in a geometrical ratio. " At the mouth of two or three witnesses " the word to which such witness is borne is " established " (Deut. 19[15].)

Canon Rawlinson enters a caveat against the exaltation into a Canon of historical truth, of the false assumption now almost universally prevalent, of " the inviolability of the chain of finite causes, and the impossibility of miracles." Events are not self-caused, and self-sustained, possessing powers that lie beyond the control of the Divine Will, and working by their own inherent power of self-determination, or necessity. They take place either mediately, in obedience to the Laws of Nature, which are simply so many expressions of the will of God, or else immediately, as a result of the direct, immediate act of God, in which case they are described as miraculous, or supernatural. The sacred records themselves are the proof of the miraculous events contained in them. The principles of historical criticism do not force us to reject them, but compel us to accept them as true.

The same great and important truth is excellently expressed by H. F. Clinton in his great work *Fasti Hellenici*, in which he says : " The history of the Israelites is the history of miraculous interpositions. Their passage out of Egypt was miraculous. Their prosperous and adverse fortunes in that land, their servitudes, and their deliverances, their conquests and their captivities, were all miraculous. The entire history, from the call of Abraham to the building of the second Temple, was a series of miracles. It is so much the object of the sacred historians to describe these, that little else is recorded. The ordinary events and transactions, which constitute the civil history of other states, are either very briefly told, or omitted altogether ; the incidental mention of these facts being always subordinate to the main design registering the extraordinary manifestations of Divine power. For these reasons, the history of the Hebrews cannot be treated like the history of any other nation ; and he who should attempt to write their history, divesting it of its miraculous character, would find himself without materials. Conformably with this spirit, there are no historians in the Sacred Volume of the period in which miraculous intervention was withdrawn. After the declaration by the mouth of Malachi, that a messenger should be sent to prepare the way, the next event recorded by any inspired writer, is the birth of that messenger. But of the interval of 400 years between the promise and the completion, no account is given. And this period of more than 400 years between Malachi and the Baptist is properly the only portion in the whole long series of ages from the birth of Abraham to the Christian Era which is capable of being treated like the history of any other nation."

And now, having defined the scope of the subject, and explained the true method of treatment to be employed in dealing with it, and the standpoint from which it ought to be viewed, or the standard by which our decisions with respect to it, ought to be governed, we are able to commence our own study of the *Romance of Bible Chronology*, claiming only on behalf of the Hebrew Text, this one great primary element of common justice, *the right to be heard*, without being struck on the mouth, or shut out of court, or " emended " or " corrected," or otherwise inhibited by fallible witnesses whose testimony has no more right to be regarded as valid than that of the Hebrew Text of the Old Testament itself.

PERIOD I. THE PATRIARCHS—*Genesis.*

CHAPTER IV. THE ANTE-DILUVIAN PATRIARCHS—FROM ADAM TO NOAH.

(AN. HOM. 1–1056.)

THE opening verse of Genesis speaks of the Creation of the heavens, and the earth, in the undefined beginning. From this point we may date the origin of the world, but not the origin of man. For the second verse tells of a catastrophe—the earth *became* a ruin, and a desolation. The Hebrew verb הָיָה (hâyâh = to be) here translated *was*, signifies not only " to' be " but also " to become," " to take place," " to come to pass." When a Hebrew writer makes a simple affirmation, or merely predicates the existence of anything, the verb הָיָה is *never expressed.* Where it *is* expressed it must always be translated by our verb to *become*, never by the verb *to be*, if we desire to convey the exact shade of the meaning of the Original. The words תֹהוּ וָבֹהוּ (tohû va-bohû), translated in the A.V. " without form and void " and in the R.V. " waste and void " should be rendered *tohû*, a ruin, and *bohû*, a desolation. They do not represent the state of the heavens and the earth as they were created by God. They represent only the state of the *earth* as it afterwards *became*—" a ruin and a desolation." This interpretation is confirmed by the words of Isaiah 45 [18], " He created it not *tohû* (a ruin) : He formed it to be inhabited (habitable, not desolate)." This excludes the rendering of Gen. 1 [2] in the A.V. and the R.V. as decisively as the Hebrew of Gen. 1 [2] requires the rendering of *hàyàh* by the word " became " instead of the word " was," or better still " had·become," the separation of the *Vav* from the verb being the Hebrew method of indicating the pluperfect tense.

The noble Cathedral, once a perfect work of art, with its crowds of devout worshippers, becomes, with the lapse of ages, a dilapidated *ruin*. Forsaken by those who once frequented its hallowed courts, it becomes a *desolation*. Similarly the words of Gen. 1 [2], " And the earth became without form and void " are intended to convey to us the fact that the cosmos, once a beautiful and perfect whole, *became* a " ruin " and a " desolation." What the cause of this catastrophe was, we are not told, though some speculative interpreters have connected it with the fall of Satan. We know neither the cause, nor the time, nor the manner in which the calamitous change took place. There is no point of contact between the Hebrew *tohû* "ruin" and the Greek conception of *chaos*, the primeval, shapeless, raw material out of which the world was formed. Genesis 1 [2] does not describe a stage in the process of the creation, but a disaster which befell the created earth ; the original creation of the heavens, and the earth, is chronicled in Gen. 1 [1]. The next verse, Gen. 1 [2], is a statement of the disorder, the ruin, and the state of desolation into which the earth subsequently fell. What follows in Gen. 1 $^{3\cdot31}$ is the story of the restoration of a lost order by the creative word of God. Between the creation of the heavens and the earth " in the beginning " (Gen. 1 ^{1}) and the catastrophe by which they became a " ruin " and a " desolation " (Gen.1 ^{2}) we place those countless ages required by the geologist for the formation of the various strata of the earth's crust, and the fossil remains embedded therein.

The length of time described by the Hebrew word *Yom* = day, as used in this chapter, cannot be definitely determined. The word itself is frequently used to express a long period, an entire Era. The time occupied by the whole process of the six days' work is referred to in Genesis 2 ^{4} as " the *day* that the Lord God made the heavens and the earth." The use of the expression " and evening came and morning came—day one " (Gen. 1 ^{5}; repeated Gen. 1 $^{8\cdot13\cdot19\cdot23\cdot31}$) seems to suggest a literal day as measured by the revolution of the earth on its axis, but it cannot be said to be proved that the writer is not here using the words " evening and morning " in a figurative sense, for the commencement and the completion of whatever period he intended to mark by his use of the word " day." In the same verse (Gen. 1 ^{5}) the word " day " is used to mark a still briefer period, viz. that portion of the day when it is light.

The attempt to parcel out the six days' work into the six geological Eras, to which they somewhat roughly, but by no means accurately correspond, cannot be regarded as a satisfactory explanation of the writer's intention and meaning. There may be certain analogies between the order of Creation as described in the first chapter of Genesis, and the order of the formation of the various strata of the crust of the earth as read by the geologist, and in the order of the occurrence of the fossil remains which are found embedded in the stratified layers of the earth's crust, for God's works are all of a piece ; but there are also great and manifest divergencies, and these are so great, and so manifest that the two series cannot be said to run absolutely parallel with each other, or to perfectly correspond. The natural interpretation of the narrative, to one who recognizes the greatness of the power of God, is that which understands the chapter as a record of the creation of the world in six literal days ; but it cannot be denied that the word " day " may have been used by the writer in a figurative sense, and intended by him to indicate a more extended period corresponding to a geological Era of time.

The creation of Adam took place on the sixth day after the creation of light. Whether this sixth day is to be interpreted as the sixth literal day, as measured by the space of time required for the revolution of the earth upon its own axis, or as a sixth geological Era, must remain uncertain, as there is nothing in the Hebrew Text to decide between the more precise and the more extended connotation of the term.

Similarly the question discussed by Ussher in his *Annals of the Old and New Testaments*, by Kennedy in his *New Method of Scripture Chronology*, by R. G. Faussett in his *Symmetry of Time*, and many other writers, as to the exact month, day and hour at which the first year of the life of Adam began, whether at the autumnal or at the vernal Equinox, cannot be decisively determined.

The following considerations make it appear probable that the original point of departure for the year was the autumnal Equinox, and that this was changed at the Exodus by Divine command, to the vernal Equinox, at all events, as far as the Hebrew people were concerned, whilst other nations may have continued to reckon their New Year's Day from the autumnal Equinox, or may have invented Eras of their own. We know that the later Jews Hellenized their calendar, introducing the principle of intercalation, and using the Greek Metonic cycle of 19 years for this purpose, instead of adhering to the Mosaic principle of direct observation, and eschewing astronomical calculations altogether.

(1) The order of the " evening and the morning " which formed the first day suggests by analogy the propriety of making the year also commence in the autumn.

(2) The autumnal season of harvest, when the fruits of the earth were ripe, seems to be the most appropriate time of the year for the appearance of man on the earth which had been specially prepared for him.

(3) The change of " the first month of the year " to Abib or Nisan occurring at the spring of the year (Exodus 12 ^{2}, 13 ^{4}, Deut. 16 ^{1}) suggests that up to that time the first month of the year was the month which followed immediately upon the Autumnal Equinox. This fixing of Abib or Nisan as the first month of the year may, however, have been a return to the original mode of reckoning from the Creation and a rejection of the Egyptian method of reckoning by the Vague calendar year of exactly 365 days.

But it is not till we reach the fifth chapter of Genesis that we meet with our first definite chronological datum, and here we find a complete list of the ante-diluvian patriarchs. The list is as follows. We adopt the term *Anno Hominis* rather than *Anno Mundi*, for, as we have seen, the *world* was created " in the beginning." This was ages before the creation of Adam, the true starting point of every Chronology. Ussher's date, B.C. 4004, should be removed from Gen. 1 ^{1}, and placed at Gen. 1 ^{26}, or Gen. 5 ^{1}.

The Ante-diluvian Patriarchs : From the Creation to the Flood.

ANNO HOMINIS.

    0. Adam created (Gen. 5 [1]).

 130. Age of Adam at birth of Seth (Gen. 5 [3]).

 130. Seth born.

 105. Add age of Seth at birth of Enos (Gen. 5 [6]).

 235. Enos born.

  90. Add age of Enos at birth of Cainan (Gen. 5 [9]).

 325. Cainan born.

  70. Add age of Cainan at birth of Mahalaleel (Gen. 5 [12]).

 395. Mahalaleel born.

  65. Add age of Mahalaleel at birth of Jared (Gen. 5 [15]).

 460. Jared born.

 162. Add age of Jared at birth of Enoch (Gen. 5 [18]).

 622. Enoch born.

  65. Add age of Enoch at birth of Methuselah (Gen. 5 [21]).

 687. Methuselah born.

 187. Add age of Methuselah at birth of Lamech (Gen. 5 [25]).

 874. Lamech born.

 182. Add age of Lamech at birth of Noah (Gen. 5 [28]).

1056. Noah born.

 600. Add age of Noah at the Flood (Gen. 7 [6]).

AN. HOM. 1656. The Flood.

The design of this genealogical list is to give a Chronology of the period from Adam to the Flood. The line chosen is the line of Noah the preserver of the race, the line of the promised Messiah the Redeemer of the race. It must not be assumed that the son named in each generation is either always or generally the eldest son of his father. This is not stated, it is not suggested, it is not implied. Certainly Seth is not the eldest son of Adam, nor is Shem the eldest son of Noah, though he is mentioned in this list (Gen. 5 [32]) before his eldest brother Japheth (Gen. 10 [21]). Moses selects from the genealogical family records only those entries which relate to the chosen people, and those other races who are brought into contact with them in the course of their later history. The line of Noah, Abraham, Isaac and Jacob is selected because to them was given the promise of the " Seed," in whom all the nations of the earth are to be blessed. The theme of the Old Testament is the Redeemer. All its selections are governed, and all its omissions are explained, by this fact.

That the interest of the recorder of these Tables was chronological, may be inferred from the careful attention which he has paid to the subject of Chronology, and the very precise nature, and chronological form of the statements made respecting the ages of each of the Patriarchs. It may also be inferred from the fact that though he gives the descendants of the line of Cain, he attaches no Chronology to that line ; his chronological purpose

E

is served if the succession of events is accurately and fully recorded along the one line of succession which he adopts as his chronological Era.

The number of the years of the life of each of the Patriarchs is mentioned, in addition to the years before and after the birth of the son named, probably in order to show by this double statement that however extraordinary the length of the life of the Patriarch, there is no mistake about the accuracy of the figures. There is no reason to doubt the fact that our first fathers were endowed with a better physical frame, which enabled them to live a longer life than the men of the present day. The attempt to interpret the names of these men as the eponymous names of tribes or dynasties, or to give the word "year" a different signification from that which it ordinarily bears, or to discount the narrative as mythical, and the personages named in it as fictitious, is a fallacy induced by a presumed, but false analogy between the Biblical narrative and the legendary accounts of the origins of other nations, or by the gratuitous assumption that as things are to-day, so they always have been, and always will be. We have the same authority for believing that Adam was 930 when he died, that we have for believing that Joseph was 30 when he stood before Pharoah, and 110 when he died.

The narrative nowhere states, and it must not be understood to imply, that each succeeding Patriarch was born on the very day on which his father attained the age named at his birth. As the purpose of the list is chronological, it must be interpreted to mean that the fractions of a year which are not mentioned are included in the age of the father. Moses intended his calculations to be both accurate and complete. He reckons by complete years, and gives the whole of the year in which the son is born to the age of the father at his son's birth. This is proved by the two instances of Methuselah and Noah. Methuselah's age at death is stated to have been 969 years (Gen. 5 [27]) but he was only 968 years, 1 month and 17 days old, plus whatever fraction of the year of his birth was included in the 65th year of his father Enoch, when the Flood began. Noah's age when the Flood was upon the earth is given as 600 years (Gen. 7 [6]), but it was only on the 17th day of the 2nd month of his 600th year that the fountains of the deep were broken up (Gen. 7 [11]). These statements are given by Moses in order to explain the technical principles on which the Chronology is built. Those who make them into "discrepancies" are self-convicted, (1) of an error of interpretation, and (2) of attributing to the author the mistake which has been made by themselves.

Moses' tables of the Patriarchs, like Ptolemy's Canon of Kings, are constructed on astronomical principles. The numbers taken collectively constitute an uninterrupted series of true, tropical solar years, and register with astronomic accuracy the number of solar revolutions from the creation of Adam to the death of Joseph, which no Chronologer who accepts the statements of the Hebrew Text can make either one year more, or one year less, than 2369. Adam lived 930 years. The first year of his life runs parallel with the year Anno Hominis 1. The year in which he died runs parallel with AN. HOM. 930. Seth was born in the 130th year of Adam's life, the year AN. HOM. 130. It is not suggested that the Patriarchs were all born at the autumnal Equinox, or all on the same day of the same month of the year. The years are integral, and take no account of fractions. The year of Seth's birth is reckoned to Adam. The 131st year of Adam's life, the year AN. HOM. 131, is reckoned as the 1st year of the life of Seth. Hence, we may safely conclude that Moses' reckoning of years is inclusive, and Noah is said to be 600 years old at the beginning, and not at the end of his 600th year.

The numbers given in this genealogical list are characterized by the strictest regard for accuracy and precision. This is confirmed by the fact that since Ussher, no Chronologer who has adopted the numbers given in the Hebrew Text as the basis of his calculation, has ever failed to fix the Flood in the year AN. HOM. 1656, and the death of Joseph in the year AN. HOM. 2369.

CHAPTER V. THE NOAH-SHEM CONNECTION.

(Noah's age at the birth of Shem = 502 years).

AN. HOM. 1056–1558.

THE early Chronology of the Hebrew Scriptures is contained in a series of connected statements, each covering a definite period. Between each of these definite periods is an apparent chasm, or want of connection. A closer and more attentive study reveals the fact that the connecting link between the several periods is always supplied, but it has to be diligently sought for. The five apparent chasms at which the continuity of the chronological record appears to be broken off are as follows :—

1. The Noah-Shem connection, which determines the exact age of Noah at the birth of Shem, viz. 502 years.

2. The Terah-Abraham connection, which determines the exact age of Terah at the birth of Abraham, viz. 130 years.

3. The Joseph-Moses connection, which determines the exact number of years which elapsed between the death of Joseph, with which the Chronology of the book of Genesis ends (Gen. 50 [26]), and the birth of Moses, with which the Chronology of the book of Exodus begins (Exodus 7 [7]), viz. 64 years.

4. The Joshua-Judges connection, which determines the number of years that elapsed during the administration of Joshua and the Elders that overlived him, between the division of the land at the end of the Seven Years' War of Conquest, with which the Chronology of the Book of Joshua ends (Joshua 14 [7, 10] with Numbers 10 [11, 12], 13 [17, 20]), and the oppression of Cushan-Rishathaim of Mesopotamia, with which the Chronology of the Book of Judges begins (Judges 3 [8]), viz. 13 years.

5. The Eli-Saul connection, which determines the number of years that elapsed between the death of Eli and the beginning of the reign of Saul, viz. 20 years. This is given in the summary of 1 Samuel 7 [2].

These breaks in the consecutive statements of the Chronology are made good in various ways. The discussion of them will occupy five separate chapters of this work. They form a series of chronological problems of increasing difficulty, but it will always be found, on closer inspection, that the materials for forming an exact Chronology are always given, so that we are never left to hypothesis or conjecture, and never have to fall back upon the statements of Josephus or other external testimony.

In this chapter we have to deal with the Noah-Shem connection, i.e. to ascertain the age of Noah at the birth of Shem. The problem is solved by the inclusion of an intermediate date, the epoch of the Flood, from which we reckon back to the birth of Noah, and on to the age of Shem at the birth of his son Arphaxad.

The two statements contained in Genesis 5^{32}, " And Noah was 500 years old : and Noah begat Shem, Ham and Japhet," do not give us any clue to the exact age of Noah at the birth of Shem. Shem is mentioned first, because he is the member of the family with whom the writer is mainly concerned.

The Old Testament is a narrative of the story of Redemption. Redemption is through the Messiah, Who is to come through a particular line of descent. He is progressively defined as the "seed of the woman" (Gen. 3^{15}), the "seed of Abraham" (Gen. 22^{18}), "the seed of Isaac" (Gen. 26^4) "the seed of Jacob" (Gen. 28^{14}), "the Shiloh of the Tribe of Judah" (Gen. 49^{10}) and "the seed of the House of David" (2 Sam. 7^{12-16}).

References to other families and other races are summary, and incidental. The grand theme of the whole of the Old Testament Scriptures is the coming of the Redeemer, and the things concerning the race from which He springs. References to other races are introduced only in so far as they bear upon the main theme of the Old Testament Scriptures as a whole.

This explains why Shem is mentioned first amongst the sons of Noah. He was not the eldest son, for in Genesis 10^{21} (a text misrendered in the R.V. but correctly translated in the A.V.), Japheth is distinctly described as his elder brother. In the same way, and for the same reason, Abram is mentioned before his elder brothers, Nahor and Haran, in Genesis 11^{26}, " And Terah lived seventy years, and begat Abram, Nahor and Haran." Similarly Issac is placed before Ishmael in 1 Chron. 1^{28}, " The sons of Abraham, Isaac and Ishmael," though Isaac was not the older, but the younger of the two.

| We arrive at the age of Noah at the birth of Shem by means of an induction from the facts contained in Genesis 7^6 and Genesis 11^{10}. From Genesis 7^6 we learn that Noah was 600 years old at the epoch of the Flood. From Genesis 11^{10} we learn that Shem was 100 years old, two years after the Flood. Therefore Shem was 98 years old at the Flood, that is Shem was 98 years old when Noah was 600. Therefore Shem was born when Noah was 502. This enables us to connect the Chronology of the ante-diluvian Patriarchs with the Chronology of the post-diluvian Patriarchs, and we may proceed in either of two ways. We may use the intermediate date of the Flood, or we may use the age of Noah at the birth of Shem, at which we have arrived

by means of a mathematical deduction from the statements of the Hebrew narrative.

THE NOAH-SHEM CONNECTION.

First Method.

AN. HOM.

1056. Noah born (see Chapter 4).

502. Add age of Noah at birth of Shem (Gen. 7 [6] with 11 [10]).

1558. Shem born.

100. Add age of Shem at birth of Arphaxad (Gen. 7 [6] with 11 [10]).

1658. Arphaxad born.

Second Method.

AN. HOM.

1056. Noah born (see Chapter 4).

600. Add age of Noah at the Flood (Gen. 7 [6]).

1656. Date of the Flood.

2. Add years after the Flood when Arphaxad was born (Gen 11 [10]).

1658. Arphaxad born.

The date of the Flood is treated as an epoch in the same way as the birth of one of the Patriarchs. It began on the 17th day of the 2nd month of the 600th year of Noah's age. Noah remained in the Ark for one whole year of exactly 365 days. But the expression "two years after the flood" in Gen. 11 [10] is not to be interpreted as meaning two years after the flood was over. The flood is treated as an epoch or point of time from which the Chronology is continued in the same manner as from the birth of one of the Patriarchs.

The Chronology of the Flood year throws an interesting light upon the primitive Hebrew calendar. The commencement of the Flood is dated the 17th day of the 2nd month of the 600th year of Noah's life (Gen. 7 [11]). The Ark rested on the 17th day of the 7th month (Gen. 8 [4]). The interval of five months between these two dates is described as an interval of 150 days, each of these five months consisting of 30 days. The Hebrews always reckoned 30 days to the month, except when they saw the New Moon on the 30th, which then became the 1st day of the new month. Moses may have followed this usage here. But Kennedy interprets him as reckoning 30 days to each of the first 11 months, and 24 days, or where necessary 25 days to the 12th month. Kennedy's account of the Flood year is as follows. The waters decreased continually till the 1st day of the 10th month, an interval embracing the remaining 14 days of the 7th month, and the two following months, or 74 days. The waters were dried up on the 1st day of the 1st month of the 601st year, after a further interval of 95 days, comprising a tenth month of 30 days, an eleventh month of 30 days, and a twelfth month of 24 days, making altogether 84 days to complete the twelve months of the lunar year, and a further 11 days to the eleventh day of the 1st month of the new lunar year to complete the 365 days of the solar year, the 600th year of Noah's life.

At this time Noah "removed the covering of the ark and looked, and behold the face of the ground was dry." Nevertheless he remained in the ark until the 27th day of the 2nd month of the new lunar year, a further interval of 46 days, comprising the remaining 19 days of the 1st month, and the 27 days of the second month of the new lunar year, when at the command of God he went forth out of the ark in which he had remained exactly 365 days.

From these particulars Kennedy concludes that in the primitive Hebrew calendar time is measured by the solar year of 365 days, but computed in terms of the lunar year of twelve months, viz. eleven months of 30 days, and a twelfth month of 24 days, when the lunar year or the 12 revolutions of the moon occupy 354 days, and 25 days when the lunar year or the 12 revolutions of the moon occupy 355 days. The facts as viewed by Kennedy may be graphically represented as follows :—

DIAGRAM OF THE FLOOD YEAR

ACCORDING TO

JOHN KENNEDY'S *New Method of Scripture Chronology.*

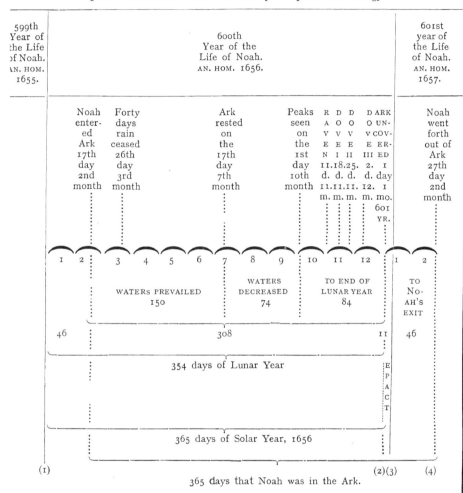

| 599th Year of the Life of Noah. AN. HOM. 1655. | 600th Year of the Life of Noah. AN. HOM. 1656. | 601st year of the Life of Noah. AN. HOM. 1657. |

Noah entered Ark 17th day 2nd month

Forty days rain ceased 26th day 3rd month

Ark rested on the 17th day 7th month

Peaks seen on the 1st day 10th month

R A V E N 11.18.25. d. 11.11.11. m. m. m.

D O V E I d. m.

D O V E II d. m.

D ARK O UN- V COV- E ER- III ED 2. 1 12. 1 m. mo. 601 YR.

Noah went forth out of Ark 27th day 2nd month

1 2 3 4 5 6 7 8 9 10 11 12 | 1 2

WATERS PREVAILED 150

WATERS DECREASED 74

TO END OF LUNAR YEAR 84

TO NO- AH'S EXIT

46   308   11   46

354 days of Lunar Year

E P A C T

365 days of Solar Year, 1656

(1)   (2)(3)   (4)

365 days that Noah was in the Ark.

(1) Beginning of the Solar Year AN. HOM. 1656, which this year coincides
with the Lunar Year.

(2) End of the Lunar Year of 354 days.

(3) End of the Solar Year of 365 days.

(4) End of the 365 days that Noah was in the Ark.

71

The Biblical year is the luni-solar year. Time is measured by the revolutions of the sun. The feasts are regulated by the revolutions of the moon, and the relations between the solar year are adjusted, not by astronomical calculation, but by observation of the state of the crops, and the appearances of the moon. The resulting system was perfect and self-adjusting. It required neither periodic correction nor intercalation.

According to Kennedy, Moses *measures* time by the *years* of the *sun*. He *computes* time by the *months* and *days* of the years of the moon, which are pinned down to the years of the sun. From the 17th day of the 2nd month of one lunar year to the 27th day of the 2nd month of the following lunar year is a period of $354 + 11 = 365$ days, viz. one complete lunar year and eleven additional days. These 365 days will invariably consist either of parts of two distinct lunar years, or else of one complete lunar year and part of another. When the last day of the lunar year is also the last day of the concurrent solar year we have what is called a year of commensuration. Such a year was the year AN. HOM. 1655, the 599th year of Noah's life, the year before the Flood.

When the 1st day of the lunar year is also the 1st day of the concurrent solar year, we have what is called a year of coincidence. Such a year was the year AN. HOM. 1656, the 600th year of Noah's life. The Flood year occupied 319 days of the solar year 1656, and 46 days of the solar year 1657, the year after the Flood. It also occupied 308 days of the lunar year concurrent with the solar year 1656, and 57 days of the lunar year concurrent with the solar year 1657. A year of commensuration is always followed by a year of coincidence.

The sun was appointed for the measurement of time or years. The moon for the regulation and determination of the periodic returns of the " seasons," i.e. the set feasts and solemn assemblies (Gen. 1[14], Psa. 104[19]).

The Mosaic Shanah (a word which like Mishna signifies repetition) invariably denotes a true, tropical solar year containing all the four seasons, and always returning to the same point in the ecliptic. These feasts were pinned down to the solar year, but they were computed and regulated by the months and days of the year of the moon. The first month was the month whose full moon either fell upon or followed next after the beginning of the solar year, Tekuphath hasshanah=the return of the year (Ex. 34[22], 1 Sam. 1[20] margin, 2 Chron. 24[23] margin, Psalm 19[6].)

From the Creation to the Exodus this "beginning of the year" was fixed at the autumnal Equinox in the month Tisri, but from the Exodus onward it was transferred by Divine command to the vernal Equinox, and to the month Abib, which was henceforth to be "the beginning of months, the first month of the year" (Ex. 12[2], 13[4]). So far Kennedy.

Sir Isaac Newton's account of the Hebrew calendar differs somewhat from Kennedy's. "All nations," he says in his *Chronology of Ancient Kingdoms Amended*, "before the just length of the solar year was known, reckoned months by the course of the moon, and years by the return of winter and summer, spring and autumn (Gen. 1[14], 8[22]; Censorinus, c. 19 and 20; Cicero in Verrem, Geminus, c. 6), and in making calendars for their festivals they reckoned 30 days to a lunar month, taking the nearest round numbers, whence came the division of the eclipitic into 360 degrees. So in the time of Noah's Flood when the moon could not be seen, Noah reckoned 30 days to a month, but if the moon appeared a day or two before the month, they began the next month with the first day of her appearing. That the Israelites used the luni-solar year is beyond question. Their months began with the new moons. Their first month was called Abib, from the earing of corn in that month. Their Passover was kept from the 14th day of the first month, the moon being then in the full. And if the corn was not then ripe enough for offering the first fruits, the festival was put off by adding an intercalary month to the end of the year, and the harvest was got in before Pentecost, and the other fruits gathered before the feast of the seventh month."

This intercalation is nowhere provided for in the Mosaic law, nor is it ever mentioned or referred to in the whole of the Old Testament. Nevertheless it undoubtedly follows as a necessary consequence of the system. For the revolution of the sun is completed in 365.242242 days, and that of the moon in 29.530588 days, so that 12 moons fill the space of only 354 or 355 of the 365 days in the year. The added month did not come into the calendar. We ourselves never speak of intercalating a 53rd week in our year.

Chapter VI. Comparative Chronology. Adam to Noah.

In calculating the Chronology of the ante-diluvian Patriarchs, the numbers used in Scripture are our only guide. The figures given above are those of the Massoretic Hebrew Text of the Old Testament.

Other numbers are given in the Septuagint Greek Text, and yet others again in the Samaritan Pentateuch, the sum of the numbers in the LXX. being 606 years longer, and the sum of the numbers in the Samaritan Version 349 years shorter, than those of the Hebrew Text. That the variations are due to contrivance or design, and not to accident, is plain from the systematic way in which the alterations have been made, the only question that arises is as to which of the three versions is the authentic original, and which the modified or concocted scheme.

The figures are here placed side by side in order that they may be easily compared and judgment passed upon their rival claims to originality.

THE ANTE-DILUVIAN PATRIARCHS.

Chronology of the Hebrew, Septuagint, and Samaritan Versions.

	Hebrew.			Septuagint.			Samaritan.		
	Age at birth of Son.	Resi-due.	Total.	Age at birth of Son.	Resi-due.	Total.	Age at birth of Son.	Resi-due.	Total.
Adam ..	130	+ 800	= 930	230	+ 700	= 930	130	+ 800	= 930
Seth ..	105	+ 807	= 912	205	+ 707	= 912	105	+ 807	= 912
Enos ..	90	+ 815	= 905	190	+ 715	= 905	90	+ 815	= 905
Cainan..	70	+ 840	= 910	170	+ 740	= 910	70	+ 840	= 910
Mahalaleel	65	+ 830	= 895	165	+ 730	= 895	65	+ 830	= 895
Jared ..	162	+ 800	= 962	162	+ 800	= 962	62	+ 785	= 847
Enoch ..	65	+ 300	= 365	165	+ 200	= 365	65	+ 300	= 365
Methuselah	187	+ 782	= 969	{167 + 802} {187 + 782}		= 969	67	+ 653	= 720
Lamech ..	182	+ 595	= 777	188	+ 565	= 753	53	+ 600	= 653
Noah (to the Flood) ..	600	+ 350	= 950	600			600		
Total ..	1656			2242 2262			1307		

The following variations are found in the Early Church Fathers, Theophilus and Africanus, and in the writings of the Jewish historian, Josephus.

THE ANTE-DILUVIAN PATRIARCHS.

Chronology of Theophilus, Africanus, and Josephus.

Age at Birth of Son.	Theophilus.	Africanus.	Josephus.
Adam	230	230	230
Seth	205	205	205
Enos	190	190	190
Cainan	170	170	170
Mahalaleel	165	165	165
Jared	162	162	162
Enoch	165	165	165
Methuselah	167	187	187
Lamech	188	188	182
Noah (to the Flood) ..	600	600	600
Total	2242	2262	2256

Theophilus agrees with the LXX. throughout, viz. with those copies which make the years of Methuselah at the birth of his son 167, and which are thus involved in the absurdity of making Methuselah survive the Flood by 14 years. He is followed by Eusebius, Augustine and Syncellus. But Africanus and Josephus and likewise the Paschal Chronicle, Demetrius and Epiphanius, follow those copies of the LXX. which adopt the unaltered Hebrew figure 187.

Theophilus and Africanus follow the LXX. in making the years of Lamech, at the birth of his son 188, whilst Josephus following the Hebrew Text gives the number as 182.

A careful study of these figures discloses the fact that originality belongs to the Hebrew Chronology to which the Septuagint adds 606 years, but from which the Samaritan deducts 349 years.

The main difference between the Hebrew and the LXX. consists in the addition of 100 years to the age of the six Patriarchs, Adam, Seth, Enos, Cainan, Mahalaleel and Enoch at the birth of their sons. This 100 years is carefully deducted from the residue so that the total remains the same in each case.

Jared and Methuselah, being already advanced in age at the birth of their sons, are left unaltered. The case of Lamech is exceptional, six years are added to his age before the birth of his son, and thirty years are deducted from the residue, so that the total number of the years of his life is 24 less than the number given in the Hebrew.

The alteration of the age of Lamech from 182 to 188 is accounted for as follows. Africanus starts like the LXX. with a total of 2262 years from Adam to the Flood. He looks to Peleg as the name in connection with which the millenary division of time is to occur, but he places the point of the division, or the epoch of the 3000th year from the date of the Creation, at the *death* of Peleg, not as Theophilus of Antioch does at the attainment of his 130th year. Like Theophilus, he omits the two years from the Flood to the birth of Arphaxad, a very common error which arises from the mistaken, but very general supposition, that Shem was Noah's eldest son, and was born when his father was 500, instead of when he was 502. The calculation then proceeds as follows :—

The Millenary scheme of Africanus.

Creation to the Flood	2262
Arphaxad to the birth of his son	135
Salah ,, ,, ,, ...	130
Eber ,, ,, ,, ...	134
Peleg ,, ,, ,, ...	130
Peleg, Residue	209
	3000

To make up this total, the first item must be 2262, that is Lamech's 182 must be altered to 188.

The majority of the Manuscripts of the LXX. give 167 as the age of Methuselah at the birth of his son, and this is confirmed by the Samaritan

Pentateuch, which has 67 (always a Century less than the LXX. until we get to Lamech).   But if Methuselah was 167 at the birth of Lamech, Lamech 188 at the birth of Noah, and Noah 600 at the Flood, Methuselah would be 955 at the date of the Flood, and since he lived to be 969, the LXX. is involved in the absurdity of making Methuselah survive the Flood by 14 years.   To remedy this the alteration of the age of Methuselah at the birth of his son from 187 to 167 was retracted, and the number 187 was restored.

The net effect of these alterations is to give the world an increased duration, and a more respectable antiquity.   The men who made the LXX. Version were Jews living in Egypt, about 250 to 180 years before Christ.   They were acquainted with the extravagant claims to antiquity put forward by the Egyptian priesthood.   They desired to modernise their view of the antiquity of the origin of the race, and to bring it into closer accord with the views that prevailed in the up-to-date Schools of learning at Alexandria, and this they did by adding some 606 years to the Hebrew Chronology of the Patriarchs who lived before the Flood.   The native Jews of Palestine cherished a deep and reverential regard for the very letter of Scripture, and would never dare to alter a single word.   Josephus describes their veneration for their Sacred Books as being so great that, " notwithstanding the lapse of so many ages, no one had ever dared to add to, or to take from them, or to alter anything in them."   He says that it was " innate in every Jew to regard them as the precepts of God, to abide by them, and if need be, cheerfully to die for them."

The translators of the Hebrew Scriptures into Greek, had no such compunctions.   They wished to make such a version as would commend the Hebrew Scriptures to the learned men of Alexandria, whose traditions laid claim to a remote antiquity by the side of which the Chronology of the Hebrew Scriptures seemed insignificant and contemptible.   Hence they contrived to add 606 years to the Chronology of the period before the Flood, and to make a similar, but larger addition of 880 years to the Chronology of the period from the Flood to Abraham.   The method and the motive of the alterations is perfectly clear.

The irregularity of the Hebrew numbers considering the notorious uncertainty of human life, is a reason for accepting the Hebrew Text as the genuine Original, whilst the more regular succession of the numbers in the LXX. makes it more likely that the LXX. was contrived as an improvement on the Hebrew, than that the irregular Hebrew numbers were designedly fabricated as an improvement on the more regular numbers of the LXX.

CHAPTER VII.   POST-DILUVIAN PATRIARCHS—FROM SHEM TO ABRAHAM.

(AN. HOM. 1558–2008).

THE Chronology of the Post-diluvian Patriarchs presents the same features as those already met with in dealing with the Ante-diluvian Patriarchs.

The 11th Chapter of Genesis supplies us with a list of Patriarchs in many respects similar to that which we have been studying in the 5th chapter.

The most notable differences are, (1) the reduction in the length of the lives of the Patriarchs placed at the head of the list, to about one half of that of the Patriarchs who lived before the Flood, and (2) its further reduction to about one half of the new standard of longevity, when we reach the name of Peleg, which stands very nearly in the middle of the list. Both lists of Patriarchs, the Ante-diluvian List, from Adam to Noah, and the Post-diluvian List, from Shem to Abraham, contain the same number of names, there being exactly ten names in each case. In this list the writer gives the age of the Patriarch at the birth of his son, and the residue of his years thereafter. The sum total of the years of the life of the Patriarch is not stated as it is in the case of the Ante-diluvian Patriarchs.

POST-DILUVIAN PATRIARCHS.

From the Flood to the Birth of Abram.

AN. HOM.

1656. The Flood—Shem aged 98 (Gen. 11[10]) (see Chapter 5).

   2. Add the years after the Flood when Arphaxad was born (Gen. 11[10])

1658. Arphaxad born. Shem aged 100.

  35. Add age of Arphaxad at birth of Salah (Gen. 11[12]).

1693. Salah born.

  30. Add age of Salah at birth of Eber (Gen. 11[14]).

1723. Eber born.

  34. Add age of Eber at birth of Peleg (Gen. 11[16]).

1757. Peleg born.

  30. Add age of Peleg at birth of Reu (Gen. 11[18]).

1787. Reu born.

  32. Add age of Reu at birth of Serug (Gen. 11[20]).

1819. Serug born.

  30. Add age of Serug at birth of Nahor (Abram's grandfather) (Gen. 11[22]).

1849. Nahor, Abram's grandfather, born.

  29. Add age of Nahor at birth of Terah (Gen. 11[24]).

1878. Terah born.

 130. Add age of Terah at birth of Abram (Gen. 11[26. 32], Gen .12[4], Acts 7[4]).

2008. Abram born.

The design of this genealogical list is to carry forward the Chronology from the date of the Flood to the birth of Abram.

CHAPTER VIII. THE TERAH-ABRAHAM CONNECTION.

Terah's age at the birth of Abraham = 130 years.

In Gen. 11 [26] we read, " And Terah lived 70 years, and begat Abram, Nahor, and Haran." We have already seen, in the parallel case of Noah and his three sons, that though Shem was mentioned first, he was not the eldest son of Noah, and was not born till two years after his father was 500 years old, as stated in Gen 5 [32].

We have now to show that in like manner, Abram, though mentioned first, was not the eldest son of Terah, and was not born till sixty years after his father was seventy years old, as stated in Gen. 11 [26].

We begin with the result obtained in our last chapter, that Terah was born AN. HOM. 1878. From Gen. 11 [32] we learn that Terah was 205 when he died. Therefore Terah died AN. HOM. 2083. From Acts 7 [4] we learn that when Terah died Abram left Haran.

The words of Stephen in Acts 7 make explicit what is implicit in Gen. 11 [27]–12 [5]. It is clear that there were two distinct calls given to Abram. In response to the first he left Ur of the Chaldees to go into the land of Canaan, but halted when he came to Haran, and dwelt there. In response to the second call he left Haran to go into the land of Canaan, " and into the land of Canaan they came."

The rendering of this passage in the A.V. is faulty in two respects, (1) the insertion of the word " had " in the phrase " Now the Lord *had* said unto Abram " in Gen. 12 [1] is inaccurate and misleading. There is nothing in the Hebrew Text to warrant it. It suggests to the reader that there was only one call instead of two. And (2) the division into chapters breaks the continuity of the narrative in which the connection between Gen. 11 [32] and Gen. 12 [1] is direct and immediate. It should read thus :—

" Terah died in Haran, and the Lord said unto Abram, Get thee out of thy country and from thy kindred, and from thy father's house, into a land that I will show thee . . . So Abram departed as the Lord had spoken unto him : and Abram was seventy and five years old when he departed out of Haran." Gen. 11 [32]–12 [4].

The consecutiveness of the narrative enables us to say that when Terah died at the age of 205, Abram left Haran at the age of 75, and came into the land of Canaan. But if Abram was 75 when Terah was 205, it follows that Abram was born when Terah was 130. We were, therefore, justified in adding, at the end of the list of the Post-diluvian Patriarchs the figures given in connection with the last name on the list, viz. that of Abram.

AN. HOM.
1878. Terah born (see Chapter 7).
 130. Add age of Terah at birth of Abram (Gen. 11 [26·32], Acts 7 [4],
        Gen. 12 [4]).
———
2008. Birth of Abram.

The lateness of Abram's birth in the life of his father explains how he could be only ten years older than his half-niece Sarah or Iscah (Gen. 11^{29}) and therefore of an age to marry her in spite of the fact that he belonged to a generation earlier than the generation to which she belonged. Sarah married her father Haran's much younger brother Abram. Similarly Milcah, Sarah's sister, married her father Haran's brother Nahor. Abram was probably Terah's son by a second wife. If so this would explain how Abram could say to Abimelech, She is the daughter (granddaughter) of my father Terah, but not the daughter (granddaughter) of my mother. Thus :—

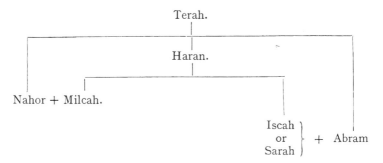

The credit of the discovery of the age of Terah at the birth of Abram is due to Archbishop Ussher. It is one of the principal improvements of his system, and a proof of the acuteness of his intelligence, and the keenness of his insight into the chronological bearing of the statements contained in the text of Holy Scripture.

CHAPTER IX. COMPARATIVE CHRONOLOGY—SHEM TO ABRAHAM.

THE Table of the Post-diluvian Patriarchs, with their ages at the birth of their sons, and the number of years in the residue of their lives as given in the Hebrew Text, has been manipulated in the LXX. and in the Samaritan Pentateuch, in the same way that the Table of the Ante-diluvian Patriarchs was manipulated by them.

The first of the following tables gives a comparative view of the Hebrew, LXX., and Samaritan figures for the age of each of the Ante-diluvian Patriarchs at the birth of his son, the residue of his years, and the total number of the years of his life. This third column is given in the Samaritan Pentateuch but is wanting in the case of the Hebrew and the LXX. It is here supplied in brackets for the sake of comparison.

The second table gives a comparative view of the figures adopted by the Early Christian Fathers, and by Josephus.

COMPARATIVE VIEW OF THE POST-DILUVIAN PATRIARCHS

According to the Hebrew, Septuagint, and Samaritan Texts.

	HEBREW.			SEPTUAGINT.			SAMARITAN.		
	Age at birth of Son.	Resi- due.	Total.	Age at birth of Son.	Resi- due.	Total.	Age at birth of Son.	Resi- due.	Total.
Shem (after the Flood) ..	[98] +2 +500 = (600)			[98] +2 +500 = (600)			[98] +2 +500 = 600		
Arphaxad ..	35 +403 = (438)			135 +400 = (535)			135 +303 = 438		
Cainan	— — —			130 + 330 = (460)			— — —		
Salah	30 +403 = (433)			130 + 330 = (460)			130 + 303 = 433		
Eber	34 +430 = (464)			134 +270 = (404)			134 +270 = 404		
Peleg	30 +209 = (239)			130 +209 = (339)			130 +109 = 239		
Reu	32 +207 = (239)			132 +207 = (339)			132 +107 = 239		
Serug	30 +200 = (230)			130 +200 = (330)			130 +100 = 230		
Nahor	29 +119 = (148)			$\left\{\begin{matrix}79\\179\end{matrix}\right\}$ +125= $\left\{\begin{matrix}204\\304\end{matrix}\right\}$			79 + 69 = 148		
Terah, to birth of Abram ..	130 +75 = (205)			70 +135 = (205)			70 + 75 = 145		
Total ..	352			942 (sic)			942		

Add 2nd Cainan ..	130
	1072
Add addition to Nahor	100
	1172

COMPARATIVE VIEW OF THE POST-DILUVIAN PATRIARCHS

According to the Early Christian Fathers, Theophilus, Africanus and Eusebius and the Jewish Historian, Josephus.

Age of Patriarch at birth of son.

	THEOPHILUS.	AFRICANUS.	EUSEBIUS.	JOSEPHUS.
Shem after the Flood ..	—	—	2	12
Arphaxad	135	135	135	135
Cainan	—		—	
Salah	130	130	130	130
Heber	134	134	134	134
Peleg	130	130	130	130
Reu	132	132	$\left\{\begin{matrix}132\\135\end{matrix}\right\}$	130
Serug	130	130	130	132
Nahor	75	79	79	120
Terah to birth of Abram	70	70	70	. 70
Total	936	940	942	993

We have now to consider the relative weight and value of the testimony of the following witnesses—The Hebrew, the LXX., the Samaritan, the Early Christian Fathers, and Josephus. All the authorites omit the second Cainan, except the LXX. Theophilus omits the two years after the Flood, and shortens Nahor's 79 years to 75. Africanus omits the two years after the Flood, but otherwise agrees with the LXX. Eusebius gives 135 for Reu, but as he makes the total 942, this must be an error for 132. Josephus is singular in making the interval between the Flood and the birth of Arphaxad 12 years instead of 2. He also adds an additional 41 years to the life of Nahor, making his years 120 instead of 79, thus adding altogether 51 years to the LXX. Chronology of the period. He also reverses the figures for Reu 130 instead of 132, and Serug 132 instead of 130.

We must not give to the testimony of the Early Christian Fathers an authority beyond its value. Their authority is not something additional to that of the LXX. It is the authority of the LXX. weakened by the fact that they manipulated the Text to make it fit in with their millenary chronological schemes. If we admit the testimony of Josephus, we have in favour of the longer Chronology before the Flood, two witnesses, the LXX. and Josephus ; after the Flood three witnesses, the LXX., Josephus and the Samaritan Text, the testimony of the Fathers being in each case included in that of the LXX. The alternative Chronologies for the period from Adam to the birth of Abram are two.

COMPARATIVE VIEW OF THE LONGER AND SHORTER PATRIARCHAL CHRONOLOGIES.

Alternatives.	Before the Flood.	After the Flood.	Total.
The HEBREW supported by the SAMARITAN before the Flood	1656	352	2008
The LXX. and JOSEPHUS supported by the SAMARITAN after the Flood	2256	993	3249

The interval from the creation of Adam to the birth of Abram was either 2008 or 3249. The Samaritan Text agrees with the Hebrew before the Flood, and with the LXX. and Josephus after the Flood.

The uncertainty does not arise from the want of testimony like that which occurs in the early Chronology of Greece, and many other countries where the times are uncertain because no evidence was preserved. It arises from a conflict between two different authorities, and we have to decide between

F

them. In the view of the present writer the evidence in favour of the orgin-
ality of the Hebrew Text and the derivative character of the LXX. under the
Hellenistic influences which prevailed at Alexandria (where the LXX. version
was made between B.C. 250 and 180) is overwhelming.

Clinton says the objection to the shorter Chronology of the Hebrew Text
founded upon the supposition of the deficient numbers of mankind vanishes
when the subject is better understood. "An army of Medes," he says,
"occupied Babylon about B.C. 2233, and this is the highest point to which
any authentic profane account will carry us." This, according to Clinton's
Chronology, was " 250 years after the Flood," by which time " the population
of the earth would amount to many millions." The translators of the Hebrew
Text into the Greek LXX. had a very obvious motive for enlarging the
Chronology. The history of the Chaldeans by Berosus, and the history of the
Egyptians by Manetho were published about this time, and they laid claim to
a remote antiquity for the beginning of their respective histories. It was
natural that the translators of the LXX. should augment the Chronology of the
period by the centenary additions, and by the insertion of the second Cainan,
in order to carry back the epoch of the Creation and the Flood to a respectable
antiquity, so that it might compare more favourably with that claimed for
Babylon and Egypt.

As there is no precedent in ante-diluvian times for placing the age of the
Patriarchs at the birth of their sons so low as from 30 to 35 years, it seems
probable that the Hebrew Text gives the true ages of the post-diluvian
Patriarchs, as in fact they were.

The LXX. and the Samaritan copyists, on the contrary, *adapt* the figures
and give the ages as 130 to 135, and thereby preserve the appearance of a
graduated instead of an abrupt fall in the ages of the post-diluvian
Patriarchs at the birth of their sons, and at the same time secure another
6½ Centuries for their Chronology, thus throwing the date of Adam another
650 years farther back than the date at which it is given in the Hebrew
Text.

Further traces of innovation and contrivance are disclosed in the sum
totals of the lives of the Patriarchs. These are no longer expressed, but they
are easily calculated, and a glance at the third columns of the three divisions
of the Table on page 80 will show that, whilst the Hebrew Record displays
considerable irregularity, the editors of the Septuagint and the Samaritan
Texts have graduated the figures in such a way that the life of each succeeding
Patriarch is nearly always somewhat shorter, or at all events not longer, than
that of his predecessor. Thus, according to the Hebrew Text, the life of Eber
is longer than that of Salah, and the life of Terah is considerably longer than
that of Nahor, whilst at Peleg we reach another abrupt shortening of the
period of human life from about 400 to 200, similar to the abrupt shortening
from about 800 before the Flood to 400 in the Partiarchs born immediately
after the Flood.

According to the Hebrew scheme Arphaxad and Salah both lived 403
years after the birth of their sons. If the plan adopted by the editors or
the copyists of the LXX. in the ante-diluvian scheme had been applied

here the residues of the lives of Arphaxad and Salah would have been reduced to 303, and the Chronology would not have been affected thereby.

But the editors of the LXX. appear to have had two motives, viz. two distinct kinds of critics, or potential raisers of plausible objections to the Hebrew Record, to conciliate. They must not only extend the Chronology of the period by adding another 6½ Centuries to the figures as given in the Hebrew Text, but they must also exhibit a graduated scale of reduction in the term of human life, minimizing the abruptness of the fall in the ages of the Patriarchs Arphaxad and Peleg, and lengthening the life of Nahor, who died, according to the Hebrew Text, at the comparatively early age of 148. Hence they make the residue of Arphaxad's years 400, whilst those of Salah are reduced to 330. According to the Hebrew Text, Eber's residue is 430 and his total 464, whilst Peleg, who comes next on the list, lived to be only 209. In order to break the abruptness of the fall from 464 to 209 in the standard of human longevity, Eber's 430 years' residue is changed into 270. The residues of Peleg, Reu and Serug, according to the Hebrew Text, are 209, 207 and 200 years respectively. But the reduction of human life in the case of Eber has been so great and so sudden that no further deduction can be made, so these residues are allowed to stand unaltered. Nahor does not live long enough to meet the requirements of the scheme ; he therefore receives an addition of 56 years to bring his age up to within a year of that of Terah, and of these 50 are apportioned to his age at the birth of his son, and the remaining 6 are added to the residue of his years. The reason why Nahor receives only 50 additional years to his age at the birth of his son, instead of the usual 100 years given to each of his predecessors, is, because the addition of the full Century would interfere with the fabricator's idea of the gradual decline in the standard of human life. For other reasons the figures were afterwards altered to 179, an addition of 150 years, in order to make the Chronology square with the presupposition of the Chiliasts, or millenary Chronologers. The net effect of all these alterations is that the list as given in the LXX. exhibits a carefully graded declension in the standard of human life instead of one that is like what we find in nature, irregular, abrupt and startling.

It is impossible to give any rational account of the derivation of the Hebrew figures from the LXX. on the supposition that those given in the LXX. are the original. The compilers of the Hebrew Text might conceivably have deducted the 6½ Centuries if they wished to shorten the Chronology, but no motive can be assigned for their wishing to do this, and even if they had reduced the Chronology of the period in this way no possible motive can be assigned for their interfering with the residues of the post-diluvian Patriarchs, which did not affect the chronological question at all. The sudden abridgment of human life by one half in the case of Arphaxad, as compared with the length of the lives of the Patriarchs who lived before the Flood, and the further sudden drop by another half in the days of Peleg, are not only without motive, but even if they could be shown to be the work of a capricious inventor, or a conscious forger, the results obtained are wholly gratuitous. In the case of the Hebrew numbers we have an irregular list, manifesting a total absence

of any indication of manipulation of contrivance.   In the case of the LXX. we
have unmistakable evidences of a two-fold motive (1) the lengthening of the
Chronology and (2) the graduation of the decline in the duration of human
life, in order to make the scheme plausible and palatable to the " Wisdom
of the Greeks."

In like manner the contriver of the Samaritan scheme manipulates the
figures of the Hebrew Text in accordance with his own personal preferences.
In the Table of the post-diluvian Patriarchs he adopts the longer Chronology adding the 6½ centuries to the Hebrew in the same way as the LXX.
has done, but he still more carefully graduates the decline in the standard
of human life, each succeeding Patriarch, including Eber and Terah, being
made to die in almost every case at an earlier age than his father.

The argument advanced for the longer Chronology of the LXX, and the
Samaritan versions, on the ground that the age of puberty at any period of
human history must bear a fixed proportion to the ordinary length of life
in that period, is a gratuitous assumption, wholly unsupported by testimony
and confuted by the facts recorded in the Old Testament, for in the period
to which Jacob, Levi and Kohath belonged, the age of puberty was the same
as it is amongst ourselves to-day, viz. about 14 or 15, but the average duration
of life was nearly double that of the standard three score years and ten of
the present day, for Jacob lived to be 147, Levi to be 137 and Kohath to
be 133.

The introduction of the second Cainan between Arphaxad and Salah,
in the LXX., adds another 130 years to the longer Chronology of that Version.
It is undoubtedly a spurious addition to the Hebrew Text.   The motive
was no doubt partly the desire to lengthen the Chronology, but the manner
in which this is done needs explanation.   Possibly the desire to form a second
list of 10 Patriarchs from the Flood to Abraham, corresponding with the list
of 10 patriarchs from Adam to Noah, may account for the insertion of the
extra name.   In that case it would seem to have escaped the notice of
the inventor of the extra name that the list of Patriarchs from the Flood to
Noah, as given in the Hebrew Text of Genesis 11 [10-26], already contains ten
names and can only be reckoned as nine when the name of Shem is omitted
from the list.

The origin and the motive of the insertion of the name of Cainan and his
130 years between Arphaxad and Salah, is amply explained from the
enumeration of the years of the period from Adam to Peleg given in the writings
of the Christain Chronologer Theophilus (Bishop of Antioch A.D. 176-186).

In his days the leading writers of the Christian Church were dominated
with the idea of six millenary ages of the world, which they regarded as
equally divided into two periods of 3,000 years each at the 130th year of Peleg's
life, when he begat his son Reu, Peleg's name signifying " division."   The following is the enumeration of the 3,000 years of this Period given by Theophilus.
He first adds 100 years to the life of Adam at the birth of Seth.   This makes
the period from Adam to the Flood 2,362 years, instead of 2,262 according
to the LXX.   He then adds, the years of Arphaxad 135, Salah 130, Eber 134
and Peleg 130 at the birth of their sons, which brings the total up to 2,891.

This calculation, it will be observed, like that of Africanus, misses out altogether the 2 years from the Flood to the birth of Arphaxad. For the reduction of the years of Methuselah from 187 to 167 a double motive may be assigned. It was done partly to approximate the age of Methuselah at the birth of his son to the ages of the patriarchs immediately preceding him, and partly to cover up, and so to prevent the detection of, the fraud in connection with the spurious addition of the 2nd Cainan, whose name is taken from the list of the Ante-diluvian Patriarchs in Genesis 5[9].

The rest of the story cannot be better told than as it is in the posthumous tract of John Gregorie, M.A., chaplain of Christ Church, Oxford, on " The Disproof of the Second Cainan," in which the matter is put thus :—

" By the period of Theophilus the interval from Adam to Phalec was 2,891 years : to this 110 years were to be added. First, then, to make it look unlike a cheat, they cut off 20 years from Methuselah's sum, and whereas Theophilus had reckoned him at 187, they set him down 176, as in some copies it still standeth. Then it was from Adam to Phalec 2,871 years. This done, they insert a new Cainan, assigning him 130 years, which added to the former sum precisely maketh up 3,000 years from Adam to the 130th year of Phalec."

It was only subsequently that the discovery was made that this reduction of the age of Methuselah, at the birth of Lamech, from 187 to 167, the 20 years being added to the residue of his 969 years, involved the absurdity of making him survive the Flood by a period of 14 years, whereupon the number was altered back to 167. Consequently the copies of the LXX. vary between the two numbers, some giving 187 and some 167.

The occurrence of these various readings in the LXX., as contrasted with the absence of various readings in the Hebrew Text, is an additional argument in favour of the originality of the Hebrew, and the derivative character of the Septuagint.

Many other arguments may be adduced to prove the spurious character of the addition of the second Cainan.

(1) It is omitted from the Hebrew Massoretic Text, and also from the Samaritan, as well as from all the ancient versions and Targums of Gen. 11[12].

(2) It is omitted from the Hebrew Text of the two passages 1 Chronicles 1[18.24], and also from many copies of the LXX. version of that passage, though 21 copies collated by Dr. Parsons have it, in verse 18, and 6 copies have it in verse 24.

(3) Josephus omits Cainan in his list of the Post-diluvian Patriarchs and so does Philo by implication, for he reckons ten generations before the Flood from Adam to Noah, and ten generations after the Flood from Shem to Abraham, which leaves no room for Cainan in the second group.

(4) Berosus (B.C. 284) and Eupolemus (B.C. 174) represent Abraham as living in the 10th generation after the Flood, whereas if the name of Cainan had been included Abraham would have been living in the 11th generation after the Flood.

(5) Origen marks the name of Cainan with an obelisk in his copy of the LXX., to mark his rejection of it as not genuine.

(6) Eusebius excludes him by reckoning only 942 years from the Flood to Abraham, and in this he is followed by Epiphanius and Jerome.

(7) The name is evidently a late invention of the Chiliasts, who reckoned up their Chronology by periods of a thousand years, and where the facts were stubborn they invented others, and thus retained their theory.

It is immaterial as to the date at which the name of Cainan was inserted in the LXX. version of Gen. 11 ^{12}, 1 Chron. 1 $^{18.24}$. Demetrius, a writer who flourished in the time of Ptolemy Philopator (B.C. 222–204) is quoted by Polyhistor as having reckoned 1070 years from the Flood to the birth of Abraham, and the two years from the Flood to the birth of Arphaxad, he invariably includes in the years before the Flood. The LXX. makes the period from the Flood to the birth of Abraham 942 years without, or 1072 years with Cainan. It is plain therefore from the 1070 + 2 years of Demetrius that the name of Cainan was included in the copy of the LXX. which he used. This, however, only proves the high antiquity of the error.

The fact that the name of the second Cainan occurs in the genealogy of Mary, the mother of our Lord, in Luke 3 ^{36}, is easily explained. The Bible, as it was held in the hands of the common people, in the time of our Lord, was the LXX. The LXX. was to them what our Authorized Version is to us. Scholars like Paul, and students of the Word like our Lord and His Apostles, had access to the Hebrew Text also, but Luke, the only writer of any book contained in the New Testament who was not a Jew (Col. 4 $^{10-14}$) and the one writer whose Gospel was specifically addressed to a Greek reader (Luke 1 ^{3}), would naturally use and quote from the Greek version in common use, and if the copy of the LXX. which he used contained the spurious addition of the name of the second Cainan, the error would of course be reproduced in his Gospel, just in the same way as any error of translation in the A.V. would be reproduced by any layman occupying a modern · pulpit, and acquainted only with the Scriptures in the Authorized Version.

It is just possible, of course, that Luke never wrote the word Cainan in Luke 3 ^{36}, for it is omitted in the Codex Bezae, the great Cambridge Uncial of the 6th Century, but the weight of traditional authority is in favour of his having taken the word from his copy of the LXX., for it occurs in all the great Uncials, ℵABΓΔΛΠ, etc., except the Codex Bezae D, though it is spelt Cainam instead of Cainan in some of them.

We have still to account for the alternative addition of 100 years to the life of Nahor at the birth of his son. Here again we trace the influence of the dominating idea of measuring the distance between the great epochs of the Scripture narrative by millenniums. If the Chiliast, who was not satisfied with the alteration of Nahor's age from the 29 of the Hebrew Text to the 79 of the original copies of the LXX., may be supposed to have been acquainted with the fact that Terah's age at the birth of Abram was not 70 but 130, this late alteration from 79 to 179 is satisfactorily explained by R. G. Faussett in his *Symmetry of Time*. Mr. Faussett supposes the addition of the further 100 years to the life of Adam at the birth of Seth, making it 330 instead of 230, to have been unacceptable. The period from Adam to the

Flood is restored, and stands at 2,262 as in the scheme of Africanus. We then proceed as follows :—

Millenary Scheme accounting for Nabor's Age—179.

Adam to the Flood	2,262
Shem after the Flood	2
Arphaxad	135
Cainan interpolated	130
Salah	130
Eber	134
Peleg	130
Reu	132
Serug	130
Nahor 79 + 100	179
Terah	130
To the call of Abraham	75
To the Exodus	430
	3,999

This, with the addition of the year of the Flood, which some have reckoned as an additional year independent of the years before and after, would make up the 4,000 years complete, and thus account for the addition of the further 100 years to the age of Nahor at the birth of Terah.

These millenary adaptations of the Chronology of the Scriptures have done much to bring the subject of Chronology into disrepute. The only way in which the credit of the Science can be restored is to adhere strictly to the actual statements of the original text, and to deal with these statements in accordance with the laws of the Science of History, which places the criterion of credibility and the test of truth in the testimony of witnesses at once honest, capable and contemporary. The identification of the dates of the dedication of Solomon's Temple and the birth of Christ with the years AN. HOM. 3000 and 4000 respectively must be jealously scrutinized, and the facts must not be warped in order to bring about the exhibition of this result.

Threefold attack on Biblical Chronology.

Three other branches of study have a direct bearing upon the Chronology of this period, and must be briefly, though but very inadequately, referred to here.

In the departments of Geology and evolutionary Biology, it has been maintained that the origin of man must be placed away back in the dim and distant past, some hundreds of thousands of years before the date assigned to it on any interpretation of the earliest historic records that have been preserved to us.

In the departments of Archæology and Anthropology, it has been maintained that the antiquity of man must be dated at a much earlier period than the 6000 years attributed to it in the Chronology of Ussher, as given by Bishop Lloyd in the margin of our Authorized Version, a scheme of Chronology which does not err by more than 38 years from that which lies embedded in the Hebrew Text, and also at a much earlier period than the 7500 years or thereabout required by the longer Chronology of the LXX.

In the department of Biblical Criticism doubt has been thrown upon the historic character of the testimony of the early chapters of Genesis, which have been regarded as a late compilation of myth and legend, the product of early human fancy, and of the working of the primitive mythopoetic faculty of man upon a rudimentary knowledge of the outer world.

I.   EVOLUTION AND THE ORIGIN OF MAN.

(1) *Evolutionary Biology.*

With regard to the evolutionary theory of the origin of man, it must be remarked, that however widely this theory has won the acceptance of acknowledged authorities in the world of learning and scholarship in the present day, it still remains an unproved hypothesis.   The theory is largely grounded upon (1) observed and admitted structural analogies between the skeleton of the anthropoid ape and that of man, (2) upon observed and admitted correspondences between homologous parts, such as the fin of a fish, the wing of a bird, the foreleg of a quadruped and the arm of a man, and (3) upon observed and admitted analogous stages of development in the prenatal condition of the offspring of man, corresponding with stages of development, illustrated in the classification or grouping of the various members of the animal world, as they rise in the scale of life, as determined by the principles of comparative anatomy.   The correspondence between the ontogenic or embryonic series, the taxonomic or natural history series, and the phylogenic or geologic or evolutionary series, is admitted.   But the fallacy of the evolutionary theory lies in the inference drawn from the fact.   The truth is that these homologous parts prove only a common Creator, not a common ancestor ; a common Author, not a common derivation.   Two works of art exactly resembling each other may be accounted for as products of one and the same artistic genius, without supposing the one to be derived or copied from the other. Two coins exactly alike prove a common matrix, not derivation the one from the other.   In like manner the resemblances that obtain between man and the lower animals, clearly prove the unity of their common Creatorship, whilst the transcendent differences between them prove with equal conclusiveness that the one is not evolved or derived from the other.

The theory of evolution requires us to believe that man was originally an absolute savage, and that something like at least 100,000 years must have elapsed from the first beginnings of human life to the development of the civilized condition of man in the present day.

There is no proof of this supposed priority of savagery to any form of civilization.   Sir Charles Lyall admits, in his " Antiquity of Man," that " we have no distinct geological evidence that the appearance of what are called the inferior races of mankind has always preceded in chronological order that of the higher races," and a similar confession was made by Mr. Pengelly, at the meeting of the British Association held at Bristol in August, 1875.   Sir

J. W. Dawson, President of the British Association in 1888, declares that the origin of man is to be fixed geologically within a moderate number of millenniums, say seven or eight.   He regards palæolithic man, to whom Professor J. A. Thompson, in his *Bible of Nature*, assigns an antiquity of 150,000 to 300,000 years, as the ante-diluvian of Scripture, and he finds indications of a general if not a universal Deluge, within the aforesaid human period of 7,000 or 8,000 years.

Belief in the enormously remote antiquity of man rests upon the assumption of slow and gradual emergence from a prior condition of brutishness and savagery, and proceeds by way of *a priori* reasoning on these supposed "origins," the arguments employed being in many instances of the most inconclusive and questionable kind.

Lord Salisbury, in his Presidential Address to the British Association in 1894, quoted Lord Kelvin as having "limited the period of organic life upon the earth to 100 million years," and Professor Tait as having "in a still more penurious spirit cut that hundred down to ten."   "On the other side of the account," he sarcastically remarks, "stand the claims of the geologists and biologists.   They have revelled in the prodigality of the cyphers which they put at the end of the earth's hypothetical age.   Long cribbed and cabined within the narrow bounds of popular Chronology, they have exulted wantonly in their new freedom."   Where the differences are so enormous they are clearly the result of the exercise of scientific imagination, and are not due to the scientific observation of facts.

(2) *Geology.*

The computations of the older geologists, based on the rate of deposits and the occurrence in them of human remains, flint implements, and other evidences of man's handiwork, are notoriously unreliable.   Professor Boyd Dawkins enters a caveat against such computations, and declares that in his view they have all ended in failure.   Mr. Pengelly, in his address to the British Association in 1888, allowed 5,000 years for the deposit of one inch of stalagmite in Kent's Cavern or 300,000 years for 5 feet.   But Professor Boyd Dawkins, in *Cave Hunting*, declares that it might have been formed at the rate of $\frac{1}{4}$ of an inch per annum, thus reducing the 300,000 years of Mr. Pengelly to 250 years.

The whole principle and method of these geological computations is vicious. Of course, if there is to be Science, there must be uniformity, but we do not arrive at science by assuming uniformity where it does not exist.   We have no warrant for the assumption that the earth was produced at a uniform rate of infinite slowness, by those forces, and those only, which are in operation at the present time.

Cave-bears, Hyenas, and mammoths were formerly referred by geologists to the Tertiary period, i.e. the period preceding the present Quaternary period, and from the fact that human skeletons were found alongside of mammoth skeletons in a cave at Aurignac, on the northern slopes of the Pyrenees, it was inferred that man belonged to the Tertiary period, and was therefore of very great antiquity. But it has now been proved, from the pile-buildings, that the first inhabitants of Europe, who belonged to the stone age, came from Asia not earlier than 2000 B.C., and therefore *after* the period at which the Deluge is placed in the Hebrew Chronolgy of the Old Testament. Hence the true inference is, not that man belongs to the earlier (Tertiary) period, but that mammoths belong to the later (Quaternary) or present period.

A glance at the following diagram will make clear the failure of the demand for an antiquity in the human race to be measured only in terms of geologic ages.

GEOLOGICAL TABLE OF ROCKS AND FOSSILS.

Graphic Representation of Fossil Remains.							
Fossils.	No Fossils.	Seaweed and Trilobites.	Ferns and Bone-clad Fish.	Pines and Reptiles.	Timber and Mammalia.	Timber and Man.
Series.	Stratified Schistose.	Llandovery Llandilo. Tremadoc.	Red Sandstone. Coal and Limestone. Old Red Sandstone.	Chalk, etc. Oolite. Portland. Bath, Lias, etc.	Pleiocene. Miocene. Oligocene. Eocene.	Recent, Prehistoric, Pleistocene or Glacial.
Systems.	Hauronian. Laurentian.	Silurian. Ordovician. Cambrian.	Permian or Dyassic. Carboniferous. Devonian.	Cretaceous. Jurassic. Triassic.	Tertiary.	Post-Tertiary.
Periods.	Eozoic.	Protozoic.	Deuterozoic.	Mesozoic.	Cainozoic.	Anthropozoic.
Rocks.	Archæan.	Primary.		Secondary.	Tertiary.	Quaternary.

The movement of evolution has been cyclic. Five cycles, Dynasties (Le Conte), Reigns (Agassiz), or Ages (Dana), have been traced by geologists in the fossil remains embedded in the crust of the earth. (1) Molluscs, (2) Fishes, (3) Reptiles, (4) Mammals, and (5) Man. The Archæan rocks of the earliest Eozoic period of the earth's existence contain no fossils at all. The Primary rocks of the Protozoic period contain no vertebrates. The earth was filled with molluscs of greater size, number and variety than at any other period in its history. In the Primary rocks of the Deuterozoic period, fishes were introduced and became dominant. They increased rapidly in size, number and variety, and usurped the empire of the sea, whilst the mollusca dwindled in size, and sought safety elsewhere. Amphibians appear in this period, but true reptiles only in the Secondary rocks of the succeeding Mesozoic period. Mammals begin to appear in this period, but not till we reach the Tertiary rocks of the Cainozoic period do they appear in such size, numbers and strength, as to overpower the great reptiles and secure the empire of the earth. We now reach the Quaternary rocks of the latest of the geologic ages, called the Anthropozoic period, because here for the first time fossil remains of man begin to appear. The Anthropozoic period is also called the Pleistocene or "most recent," the Glacial, and sometimes the Prehistoric period. Geology thus witnesses to the recent creation of man, of whom there is no trace till we reach this latest strata. "The low antiquity of our species," says Sir Charles Lyall, in his *Principles of Geology*, "is not controverted by any experienced geologist. If there be a difference of opinion respecting the occurrence in certain deposits of the remains of man and his works, it is always in reference to strata, confessedly of the most modern order."

On the question how long this period has lasted, or when it first begun, no answer can be given. So far as the facts are concerned, it is an open question, a question on which the natural science of Geology is incompetent to pronounce judgment. If the theory of evolution be assumed, if the "continuous progressive change, according to certain fixed laws, by means of resident forces," which it postulates, be taken for granted, if the countless ages which the theory demands for the evolution of the present condition of the world be conceded, then a fairly plausible theory of the past history of the world has been constructed.

But it must not be forgotten that it is only a construction put upon the facts, and not an explanation derived from the facts; that the theory is incapable of verification and that the rival theory of catastrophic "jumps," "saltations," "leaps," and "lifts" in nature, as opposed to the gradual continuous and infinitesimally slow process of evolution, gives a better explanation of the facts, and commends itself to the judgment of leading geological authorities, of equal repute with those who postulate for man an antiquity incomparably greater than that for which historic evidence can be produced.

The method of obtaining hundreds of thousands of years for the antiquity of the human race, by computing the time required for the deposition of certain alluvial deposits, in which human remains have been found, yields no reliable scientific results. Nothing is more uncertain than these geological computations. The rates of alluvial depositions are so variable, that they mock all calculations. Thus, a vessel containing many antiquities was discovered some years ago in a peat bog in Sundewitt, on the eastern coast of Schleswig. According to geological calculations it was *many thousands* of years old, but on being searched it was found to contain coins struck between A.D. 300 and 400. Cuvier's argument that the traditions and the historical consciousness of the race do not reach further back than 3,000 years before Christ, and that this would not have been possible, if the race were 100,000 years old, has never been refuted.

2.   ARCHÆOLOGY AND THE ANTIQUITY OF MAN.

Turning from the vague uncertainties of scientific hypothesis respecting the origin of man, to the historic records respecting his antiquity, we at once reach firmer ground.

The study of Egyptian and Chaldean history has materially affected our Chronology of the early history of civilization in these countries. An antiquity is now claimed for the commencement of the annals of these nations inconsistent with the date assigned to the Deluge (AN. HOM. 1656 = B.C. 2348 (Ussher). The Era of Menes, the first King of Egypt, is placed by some as high as B.C. 2717, whilst the Era of the Chaldean dynasty of Berosus, the earliest which has any claim to be regarded as historical, is placed somewhere about the year B.C. 2234. The validity of these claims depends upon the value we assign to the numbers of Manetho for Egyptian Chronology, to those of Berosus for Babylonian Chronology, and the astronomical calculations by which they are supposed to be confirmed.

The antiquity of civilization in Babylon and Egypt is ably treated by Canon Rawlinson, in his little volume on the *Origin of Nations*. Egypt and Babylon have Monuments to show which antedate all others on the surface of the earth. The conclusion at which Canon Rawlinson arrives with regard to Egypt is that the beginning of civilization there, can be traced back no further than 2250 or 2450 B.C.

The date of the Flood, according to the Hebrew Text of the Old Testament as stated by Ussher, is 2348 B.C. We ought, however, to add 38 years to Ussher's date and make it B.C. 2386, as the present writer hopes to be able to prove. Petavius' date is B.C. 2327, Clinton's B.C. 2482. These all follow the short Chronology of the Hebrew Text. In either case we are well within the limit of compatibility with Bible Chronology if we adopt Canon Rawlinson's lower date. The margin would be still greater if, with Canon Rawlinson, we adopted the Chronology of the LXX., according to which the date of the Flood is B.C. 3246. Hales' date is 3155, Jackson's 3170, Poole's 3159. These all follow the longer Chronology of the LXX. But this we have seen reason to reject.

(1) *Egypt.*

All the authorities are agreed that however far we go back in the history of Egypt, there is no indication of any early period of savagery or barbarism there. Menes, the first King, builds a great reservoir and a temple at Memphis. His son builds a palace there, and writes a book on Anatomy.

The Great Pyramid of Gheezeh, if not the oldest as well as the greatest and most wonderful structure on the earth's surface, falls very early in Egyptian history, and the hieroglyphics in it prove that even then writing had been long in use.

The epoch of the foundation of the Great Pyramid of Gheezeh is given by Piazzi Smith, Astronomer Royal for Scotland, in his Book, *Our Inheritance in the Great Pyramid*, as 2170 B.C. He regards the peculiarly constructed entrance passage as having been built for astronomical and chronological purposes.

The Great Pyramid is the greatest of all the Seven Wonders of the World, the most perfect as well as the most gigantic specimen of masonry the world has ever seen. It is the earliest stone building known to have been erected in any country. Its finished parts contain not a vestige of heathenism or idolatry. It was not built like the other pyramids as a tomb. Its author was not an Egyptian but a descendant of Shem, in the line of Abraham, but preceding him so early as to be somewhat nearer to Noah than to Abraham. It embodies exact mathematical knowledge of the grander cosmic phenomena of both earth and heavens. It is astronomically oriented on all its sides. Its passages are in the plane of the Meridian. It marks the period of the precession of the Equinoxes as a period of 25,827 years dating from the year 2,170 B.C., a period given by the famous astronomers Tycho Brahe and La Place as 25,816 years. It gives a practical solution of the theoretically insoluble problem of squaring the circle, for its vertical height is to twice the breadth of its base as the diameter to the circumference of a circle, a ratio expressed in mathematics by π or 3·14,159 etc. That is to say, its height is the radius of a theoretical circle, the length of whose curved circumference is equal to the sum of the lengths of the four straight lines of its base. It is a standard of linear measure, and each of its sides measures 365·242 sacred cubits of 25·025 British inches, thus measuring another incommensurable quantity, viz., the exact number of days in a year. It monumentalizes the size of the earth and its distance from the sun. In fact the marvels of mathematical and astronomical knowledge embodied in this unquestionably early structure go far to destroy the theory of the original savagery of primitive man.

The dates attributed to the Kings of Egypt in E. A. Wallis Budge's *Guide to the Egyptian Collections in the British Museum* go back as far as B.C. 4400, a date anterior to the period assigned in the Hebrew Text to the creation of the first man. But as a matter of fact there is a great diversity of opinion among Egyptologists as to the date of Menes, the first King of the first of the 31 dynasties, as the following list of authorities (from the *Encyclopædia Britannica*, 11th edition) will show:—

Date of King Menes and Beginning of Civilization in Egypt according to the views of leading Egyptologists.

Flinders Petrie (in 1906)	5510
Mariette, Director of the Cairo Museum	5004
Lenormant, a pupil of Mariette	5004
Flinders Petrie (in 1894)	4777
Dr. Brugsch, Director of the Berlin Museum	4400
E. A. Wallis Budge, British Museum	4400
Dr. Lepsius, Author of Chronology of the Egyptians ..	3892
Baron Bunsen (earlier view)	3623
Breasted (American, 1906)	3400
K. Sethe (German, 1905)	3360
Ed. Meyer (German, 1887)	3180
Baron Bunsen (later view)	3059
R. Stuart Poole (British Museum)	2717
Sir Gardner Wilkinson (our greatest English Egyptologist)	2691

All these are the views of men acquainted with the Monuments and competent to translate the Inscriptions. They differ from one another by as much as 2,000 years. This extraordinary variation is a proof of the fact that no sure basis has yet been discovered upon which to reach an assured scientific conclusion. The whole subject is involved in great obscurity and uncertainty.

The fact is the Egyptians themselves never had any Chronology at all. They had no Era. They were destitute of the chronological idea. It was not their habit to enter into computations of times. " The evidence of the Monuments in respect of the Chronology," says Mr. R. Stuart Poole, " is neither full or explicit." Baron Bunsen says, "Chronology cannot be elicted from them." The attempt to construct a Chronology of Egypt would have been abandoned altogether if it had not been for Manetho, an Egyptian priest of Sebennytus (c. B.C. 280-250) who composed a history of Egypt in Greek in the reign of Ptolemy Philadelphus.

Scarcely anything at all is known of him, except his history, the fame of which was much increased by the fact that he wrote it in the Greek language. The work itself is lost, but fragments of it are preserved in Josephus, Eusebius, Syncellus and other writers. The scheme of Manetho as given by Eusebius in his *Chronica*, is as follows :—

Egyptian Chronology according to Manetho.

Reign of Gods	13,900	years
Reign of Heroes	1,255	,,
Reign of Kings	1,817	,,
Reign of 30 Memphite Kings	1,790	,,
Reign of 10 Thinite Kings	350	,,
Reign of Manes and Heroes	5,813	,,
	24,925	
Thirty dynasties of Kings about	5,000	,,
(viz. 4,922, 4,954 or 5,329 years, according to various readings)	29,925	

The mythological character of the scheme is apparent. Nevertheless it has been adopted as the basis of numerous speculative chronological systems, or rather schools of Chronology, by Scaliger, Ussher, Bunsen, Poole, and other writers. The Long Chronology followed by Scaliger assumes that the 30 dynasties were all consecutive, and elevates the date of Manes to 5702 B.C. The Short Chronology followed by Ussher assumes that several of the dynasties were contemporary, and endeavours to square the figures of Manetho with the Hebrew Chronology, which dates the creation of Adam B.C. 4004 according to Ussher or B.C. 4042 according to the conclusion of the present writer.

The two principal authorities for the Chronology of Egypt are the Turin Papyrus, a list of Kings compiled in the 19th dynasty, which is in a terrible state of dilapidation, and the list of Kings and dynasties compiled by Manetho. Manetho is the only authortiy which offers a complete Chronology, and his evidence is very untrustworthy, being known only from late excerpts. For the 19th dynasty Manetho's figures are wrong wherever we can check them.

The Monuments themselves do not begin their records before the 19th dynasty or about B.C. 1590 (Budge, 1350 B.C.).

The source of the prevailing uncertainty is to be found in the fact that some of Manetho's dynasties are contemporary and not successive. This is admitted by every Egyptologist of note except Mariette and Flinders Petrie. Even Lenormant deserts his master here, and makes the 9th, 10th and 11th dynasties contemporary; also the 13th and 14th. Dr. Brugsch makes the 8th, 9th, 10th and 11th dynasties contemporary. Also the 13th and 14th, and several others. Baron Bunsen, Sir G. Wilkinson, and Mr. R. Stuart Poole carry out the principle of contemporaneousness further still.

There is also another source of uncertainty in the numbers of Manetho, arising from the fact that he is variously quoted by Eusebius and Africanus. Thus Eusebius gives 100 years, and Africanus 409 years, for the 9th dynasty. Eusebius makes the three Shepherd dynasties 103, 250 and 190 years. Africanus gives them as 284, 518 and 151, a difference of 410 years. There is no possibility of reconciling these differences, and no possibility of arriving at any assured scientific Chronology of Egypt from the materials in our possession.

Under these circumstances, Egyptologists choose the longer or the shorter period according to their own fancy. In reality Egyptian Chronology cannot be said to begin until the accession of the 18th dynasty. Even then it is far from exact, the best critics varying in their dates for this event as much as 200 years.

Canon Rawlinson places it about the year 1500 B.C. There was an older Egyptian Empire which may have come to an end about 1750 B.C., and to it the pyramids belonged. But its duration can only be guessed. Canon Rawlinson thinks it may have lasted 500 years or so. This would bring us to 2250 B.C. as the date of the establishment of civilization in the form of a settled government in Egypt, or about a hundred years after the date of the Flood (B.C. 2348, Ussher, or B.C. 2386 according to the present writer's interpretation of the Chronology of the Hebrew Text of the Old Testament).

The presuppositions which are necessary to give validity to the Chronology of the Egyptologists are admirably stated by Mr. E. A. Wallis Budge, in his *Guide to the Egyptian Collection in the British Museum,* and the impossibility of arriving at any assured scientific conclusion on the subject in the present state of our knowledge is frankly admitted.

To make a complete scheme of Egyptian Chronology he says " we need a complete list of the Kings of Egypt, and to know the order in which each succeeded and the number of years which he reigned. Now such a list does not exist, for the lists we have only contain selections of kings' names, and of many a King neither the order of his succession nor the length of his reign is known."

The authorities for the names of the Kings are tabulated as follows :—

Sources from which Egyptian Chronology is derived.

1. The Royal Papyrus of Turin.
2. The Tablet of Abydos.
3. The Tablet of Sakkârah.
4· The Egyptian Monuments of all periods, and
5. The King List of Manetho.

The Turin Papyrus was compiled about B.C.1500. It contained, when complete, the names of over 300 Kings, and gave the lengths of their reigns. The Tablet of Abydos was made for Seti I (of the 19th dynasty, B.C. 1350 according to Budge) and contained 76 names. The Tablet of Sakkârah contained 50 names.

The list of Manetho was compiled for King Ptolemy II, Philadelphus (B.C. 283–247), but the work itself is lost, and we only know it in the form in which it has come down to us in

(1) The Chronicle of Julius Africanus (A.D. 3rd century);
(2) The Chronicle of Eusebius (A.D. 265–340) ; and
(3) The Chronography of George the Monk (Georgius Syncellus of the 8th century A.D.).

The results preserved in Eusebius differ from those given by Africanus for almost every one of the 31 dynasties.

A great many credible facts may be gathered from these sources, but no scientific result can be arrived at by averaging the conflicting numbers of these discordant authorities.

Manetho is the only authority who provides materials for any kind of estimate of the duration of the period from Mena or Menes, who by general consent is allowed to have been the first dynastic King of Egypt. The deduction of 4,000 or 5,000 drawn by E. A. Wallis Budge stands midway between the extremes of Flinders Petrie (5,510) and Sir G. Wilkinson (2,691) but the laws of historical evidence do not on that account allow us to regard it as anything else than a guess. The conditions required to enable us to reach an assured scientific conclusion are these.

1. The trustworthiness of the List of Manetho. But this list cannot be trusted, for one version of it presents us with a list of 561 Kings who reign 5,524 years, whilst another gives the list as consisting of 361 Kings, who reign only 4,480 or 4,780 years.

2. The list must be shown to be successive. But every leading Egyptologist

except Mariette and Flinders Petrie admits that at least one if not six or eight of the dynasties were contemporary.

An attempt has been made to arrive at a Chronology of Egypt by means of astronomical observation and calculation. The calendar year of the Egyptians, the Vague or Wandering Egyptian year, contained 365 days exactly. The Sothic year, so called because it began on the day when the Dogstar Sothis or Sirius rose with the sun, was the same as the Julian year, and contained $365\frac{1}{4}$ days, or very nearly the same as the true tropical Solar year, on which the seasons depended. Consequently the 1st of Thoth or New Year's Day of each succeeding Vague Egyptian calendar year of 365 days fell $\frac{1}{4}$ day behind the New Year's Day of the Sothic or quasi-Solar year of $365\frac{1}{4}$ days, and in the course of 4×365 or 1,460 years it fell a whole year behind, having worked its way back through all the seasons of the year. By reckoning 1,461 Vague Egyptian Calendar years of 365 days to the Sothic period of 1,460 Sothic Julian or quasi-Solar years we can translate the dates of the heliacal risings of Sothis mentioned in terms of the Vague or Calendar year, into the corresponding terms of the ordinary Julian years. We learn from Censorinus, who wrote his *De die Natali* A.D. 238, that one Sothic period came to an end in A.D. 139. Hence three such Sothic periods must have begun in 4241 B.C. 2781, B.C. and 1321 B.C. respectively. The data obtained in this way will be reliable in proportion to the trustworthiness of Censorinus and the accuracy of the various astronomical observations and calculations involved. The evidence can only be dealt with by astronomical experts. It has not up to the present time led to any positive chronological result.

It is abundantly clear that whatever dates may be assigned to the Kings and Monuments of Egypt in the British Museum Guide, their authority is so much more a matter of subjective assurance than it is of objective certainty, that the idea of bringing them forward to controvert the definite chronological statements of the Hebrew Text of the Old Testament is simply preposterous.

(2) *Babylon.*

The antiquity of Civilization in Babylon can be traced back to the establishment of the Kingdom of Nimrod, the son of Cush, the son of Ham. the son of Noah, some two generations after the Flood (B.C. 2348, Ussher). Out of the land of Shinar, in which Babel or Babylon was situated, went forth Asshur (Gen. 10 [10, 11]) the son of Shem, driven out, the narrative suggests, by the slave-hunting Nimrod, the grandson of Ham. Asshur went forth out of Babylon and builded Nineveh and the other great cities of Assyria to the north of Babylon. There was, therefore, according to the Hebrew Record, a Semitic period of civilization in Babylon anterior to the Kingdom of Nimrod.

According to both profane and sacred history the earliest seats of civilization were Egypt and Babylon. In both these centres writing was practised and attention was paid to history, so that when the Greeks, through whom our knowledge of them is derived, became acquainted with them, they possessed historical records of an antiquity, greater than that which could

G

be claimed for any documents to be found elsewhere, except the writings of the Hebrew Old Testament. These records have been transmitted to us in the writings of Manetho the Sebennyte and Berosus the Chaldean. Attention was first drawn to the writings of Berosus and Manetho by Scaliger, the founder of modern Chronology, and their claims were acknowledged by historical critics like Niebuhr.

Berosus was an educated priest of Babylon, who lived about B.C. 260. He wrote in the Greek language three books of Babylonian-Chaldean history, in which he professes to derive his information from the oldest temple archives of Babylon. The work itself has been lost, but fragments of it have been preserved by Josephus, Eusebius, Syncellus and others. The scheme of Berosus, as given by Eusebius, in his *Chronicon*, is as follows :—

Babylonian Chronology according to Berosus.

10 Kings from Alorus, the first man, to Xisuthrus (Noah)	432,000	years
86 Kings from Xisuthrus to the Median Conquest	33,080	,,
8 Median Kings	224	,,
11 Kings	48	,,
49 Chaldean Kings	458	,,
9 Arabian Kings	245	,,
45 Kings down to Pul	526	,,
	466,581	,

The number 48 for the eleven Kings is very doubtful. According to the native tradition that Babylon was founded 1,903 years before its capture by Alexander the Great it should be 258. With this correction the figures of Berosus disclose a chronological scheme constructed in such a way as to fill the Great Babylonian Year or Cycle of 36,000 years, which is made up of the product of the Sossus (60 years) and the Nerus (600 years). Berosus' scheme is divided into two parts. The 432,000 years of the ante-diluvian dynasties to Xisuthrus or Noah is made up of 12 such cycles, 36,000 ×12= 432,000.

It has been suggested by Gutschmidt that the 36,000 cycle of the historical dynasties was probably made up as follows :—

Babylonian Chronology according to the conjecture of Gutschmidt.

Dynasty of 86 Chaldean Kings	34,080	years
,, ,, 8 Median Kings	224	,,
,, ,, 11 Chaldean Kings	258	,,
,, ,, 49 Chaldean Kings	458	,,
,, ,, 9 Arabian Kings	245	,,
,, ,, 45 Assyrian Kings	526	,,
,, ,, 8 Assyrian Kings	122	,,
,, ,, 6 Chaldean Kings	67	
	36,000	

The numbers are unaccompanied by any history, and are at once seen to be purely artificial. They may tell us something of the writer's subjective thought, but they have no relation to the truth of objective fact.

The antiquity of Assyria is a matter of dispute between the advocates of what is known as the Long Chronology of Ctesias and the Short Chronology of Herodotus.

Herodotus, the oldest Greek historian, usually styled the Father of History, was born at Halicarnassus, in Caria, Asia Minor, B.C. 484. According to Suidas he died about B.C. 408. He travelled widely in Egypt, Palestine, Phœnicia, and even penetrated as far as Babylon and Susa. He also visited all the countries situated on the shores of the Black Sea. In the course of his history he gives an account of the countries he visited, and whenever he gives the results of his own observations and enquiries he exhibits a wonderful accuracy and impartiality. When he is not an eyewitness he usually gives the authority on which he relies for his facts.

Ctesias of Cnidus, in Caria, Asia Minor, was a Greek physician and a historian contemporary with Herodotus. In early life he was physician to Artaxerxes Mnemon, whom he accompanied in B.C. 401 on his expedition against his brother Cyrus the younger. He wrote a history of Assyria and Persia in 23 books called *Persica*. As Court Physician to Artaxerxes Mnemon he resided for 17 years at the Court of Persia at Susa, where he had many opportunities of consulting the Persian royal archives, on which his history is professedly founded, whereas Herodotus only paid a flying visit to Babylon and was dependent for the most part upon the information given to him by others, though he too must have had access to some of the most important documents in the archives of the Persian Empire. Ctesias wrote his *Persica* in order to show that Herodotus was a "lying chronicler." Manetho also is said to have written a book against Herodotus. Ctesias introduces his work by a formal attack upon the veracity of his great predecessor. His history was designed to supercede that of Herodotus, and he proceeded to contradict him on every point on which he could do so.

He gives the date of the first establishment of a great Assyrian Empire at Nineveh as 1,000 years earlier than Herodotus. Its duration he reckons at 1,306 years as against the 520 years of Herodotus. He fixes the date of the Median Conquest of Assyria at B.C. 876. Herodotus makes it B.C. 600. He gives the duration of the Median Kingdom as 300 years. Herodotus gives it as 150 years.

The Long Chronology of Ctesias, which places the rise of the Assyrian Empire at about B.C. 2200, was followed by writers of ancient history like Cephalion, Castor, Nicholas of Damascus, Trogus Pompeius, Velleius Paterculus, Josephus, Clement of Alexandria, Eusebius, Augustine, Moses of Chorene, Syncellus, Dean Prideaux, Freret, Rollin and Clinton. Other historians have regarded his figures as extravagant, and have reduced them by as much as a thousand years.

Among the ancients the scheme of Ctesias was rejected by Aristotle, Plutarch, and Arrian. It was, however, widely accepted until the revival of learning, when Scaliger turned the scale against him. Scaliger is followed by

Volney, Heeren, Niebuhr, Brandis and Rawlinson.   Canon Rawlinson says, " It is surprising that the ancient Christian Chronologers did not at once see how incompatible the scheme of Ctesias is with Scripture.   To a man they adopt it and then strive to reconcile what is irreconcilable.   A comparison with the Old Testament Scriptures and with the native history of Berosus first raised a general suspicion of bad faith in Ctesias.   Freret is the only modern scholar of real learning who still maintains the paramount authority of Ctesias.   The *coup de grace* has been given to Ctesias by the recent Cuneiform discoveries, which convict him of having striven to rise into notice by a system of 'immoral lying,' whereunto the history of literature scarcely presents a parallel.   The Great Assyrian Empire, lasting 1,306 years, is a pure fiction ; his list of monarchs from Ninus to Sardanapalus is a forgery made up of names, the mere product of his own fancy.   He forges names and numbers at pleasure."

The *Persica* of Ctesias brings the history of the Persian Empire down to the year B.C. 398.   The work itself is lost, but we possess abridgments of it by Photius, an epitome of the second book by Diodorus Siculus, and numerous fragments quoted by Plutarch, Athenæus and 30 other authors, from Xenophon, B.C. 401, to Eustathius, A.D. 1160, whose names are given in the excellent collection of the *Fragments of the Persica of Ctesias*, by John Gilmore (Macmillan, 1888).

On the comparative merits of Herodotus and Ctesias, there has been much controversy, both in ancient and in modern times.   Herodotus was the abler and perhaps the more honest and trustworthy historian.   Ctesias appears to have had opportunities of access to sources that were denied to Herodotus, but we cannot be sure that he made an honest use, and gave a true and faithful account of them.

The classical accounts fix the Era of the Foundation of Babylon at B.C. 2230.   The artificial scheme of Berosus implies a belief that real human history had its commencement at Babylon somewhere between 2458 and 2286 B.C. The numbers of the Septuagint indicate for the date of Nimrod's Kingdom some such date as B.C. 2567.   The Hebrew Text places it at two generations after the Flood, or, according to Ussher, about B.C. 2218.   The fanciful character of the Scheme of Berosus, the doubtful nature of the figures given by Ctesias, and the artifiically and purposely exaggerated figures of the LXX. leave us no choice but that of the Hebrew Text, which points to a date some 100 years or more after the Flood.   The Monuments do not enable us to carry back the history of Babylon farther than to about B.C. 2025.   This allows 300 years for the Semitic Period and 150 for the previous Turanian period, and assumes an average of 25 years for the reigns of the 12 Semitic Kings of the former period and the 6 Turanian Kings of the latter.

Mr. E. A. Wallis Budge, in the Introduction to his *Guide to the Babylonian and Assyrian Antiquities*, says the earliest Babylonian Empire was that of Sargon of Agade, whose date, according to the cylinder of Nabonidus, would be about B.C. 3800 ; but recent excavation and research have shown that the scribes of Nabonidus exaggerated the interval between the period of Sargon and their own time, and that no means have yet been found for fixing a date for these early rulers in place of the traditional one.   Assuming the necessity of a lengthy period for the evolution of the complex social system, and the highly developed culture of the period of the Sumerian rulers who preceded Sargon of Agade, Mr. Budge estimates that the Sumerian Inscriptions point to a date as remote as B.C. 4000.

But, as with all arguments based on the evolutionary hypothesis, the conclusion is drawn from the unproved assumption of the infinitely slow and gradual rate of the progress made in those early days. From this assumed date of about B.C. 4000 Mr. Budge tells us that little or nothing is known of the country till we reach the period from 2500 to 2000 B.C., between which dates the history of the Monuments begins.

The date assigned to Sargon of Akkad, B.C. 3800, is obtained from the American Excavations of Nippur, where Mr. J. H. Haynes excavated the ruins of the Temple of El-Lil, removing layer after layer of debris, and cutting sections in the ruin down to the virgin soil. Here some large bricks were found stamped with the name of Sargon of Akkad. As the debris above them is 34 feet thick, it is calculated that the debris underneath the pavement, 30 feet thick, must represent a period of 3,000 years (Professor Jastrow, in *Encyclopædia Britannica*, 11th ed., article Babylonia and Assyria).

Chronological computations made on this principle, and which assume a uniform rate for the deposition of debris, are interesting and valuable, but like the similarly obtained geological computations, based on the rate of alluvial deposits, they are highly speculative, and cannot claim the character of exact scientific statements such as the use of the figures implies. When Professor Jastrow comes to deal with the actual chronology of the dynasties of the Kings of Babylon, whose names are obtained from the excavated ruins of the country, he at once reduces his figures to B.C. 2500.

The earliest dates assigned by other leading Assyriologists to the beginning of civilization in Babylon are as follows :—

Beginning of Civilization in Babylon according to leading Assyriologists.

Oppert	..	..	..	..	..	..	.. B.C. 2506
Sayce	..	..	..	..	..	..	.. ,, 2478
Winckler	..	..	..	..	..	..	.. ,, 2425
Delitzsch	..	..	..	..	..	..	.. ,, c. 2420
Maspero	..	..	..	..	..	..	.. ,, 2416
Marquart	..	..	..	..	..	..	.. ,, 2335
Hommel	..	..	..	..	..	..	.. ,, 2223
Niebuhr	..	..	..	..	..	..	., 2193
Hommel (alternatively)		..	..	..	..	,, 2050

There is, therefore, nothing in the Literary or the Monumental history of the early civilization of Babylon, which was older than Assyria, to require us to revise the date assigned to this event in the Hebrew Text, since all the earlier dates assigned to it are obtained by methods of computation which involve questionable assumptions, and can only yield highly speculative results.

Assyria and Babylon, Egypt and Phœnicia, all alike lay claim to a high antiquity. But whilst the literature of these mighty empires has perished, the Hebrew Scriptures remain.

(3) *Phœnicia.*

Of the events which took place before the Flood there are but few and faint memorials among heathen nations.   One of the most authentic may be found in the remains of the Phœnician History of Sanchoniathon, who is considered to be the most ancient writer of the heathen world.   His history is said to have been composed in the Phœnician language and collected from the archives of Phœnician cities.   It was translated into Greek by Philo of Byblos, a Syro-Phœnician Greek, who wrote in the 2nd century A.D.   For the preservation of the fragments of the work which remain we are indebted to Eusebius. Philo of Byblos professed to be translating an old Phœnician History, composed by a native priest called Sanchoniathon, in which he claims precedence for Phœnicia as the earliest nation to attain to a knowledge of science, art and civilization generally.

Some suppose that Philo of Byblos was himself the real author of the work. The fragments of it which remain consist of a mythical cosmogony, in which an account is given of the invention of the arts of hunting, fishing, building, architecture, navigation, metallurgy, embroidery and music, in which the ancient Phœnicians excelled.   But the great glory of the Phœnicians, and the most decisive mark of their early civilization, is their invention of the art of *alphabetic writing.*   Egypt and Babylon had anticipated them in the invention of a method of representing articulate sounds to the eye by means of pictures and figures, but the Phœnicians were the first to consummate the union of the written and the spoken word.

Nevertheless, the claim of Phœnicia to a civilization more ancient than that of Egypt or Babylon cannot be sustained.   The Monuments of Egypt furnish no evidence of Phœnician art or commerce earlier than the 18th dynasty, though the early Monuments of Egypt give the geography of Syria in great detail.   " If it be safe," says Kenrick, " to pronounce in any case on priority of knowledge and civilization, it is in awarding Egypt precedence over Phœnicia. . . . The commencement of the period of Phœnician commercial activity cannot be historically fixed.   It may ascend to the years 1600 or 1700 B.C. ; it may be several centuries earlier."   Canon Rawlinson prefers the later date, and concludes that whilst the Phœnicians may have emigrated from the shores of the Persian Gulf to those of the Mediterranean as far back as B.C. 1800, or even earlier, the rise of Phœnician civilization and the building of the old Phœnician capital Sidon, must be placed somewhere about the year B.C. 1600.

(4) *China.*

The case for the antiquity of China presents considerable difficulty. Dr. Edkins of Pekin, who writes an appendix on the *Antiquity of the Chinese* in Canon Rawlinson's *Origin of Nations,* concludes that " there is nothing in the Chinese classics which demands a longer period for the presence of the Chinese in their own country than 2,800 years."   In reaching the conclusion that early Chinese history requires " a longer Chronology than that which

Archbishop Ussher adopted," he is governed not by the evidence of historic testimony, but by hypothetical and speculative considerations, such as the time required to allow for the natural development of language, and of the differences which are found to exist between the different races residing in the various climates of our globe.

Du Halde states that the exact history of China begins with the reign of Yaou, B.C. 2357. Other Chinese historians commence their narrative of the history of China with the time of Fuhe, B.C. 2852. The reason for this extension of the history to a period 500 years earlier was the desire to embrace in the history the great legendary personage Fuhe. Confucius commences his history proper with the reign of Yaou, B.C. 2357, but he speaks of a succession of Wise Men who appeared between B.C. 2852 and 2357, and taught the arts of writing, hunting, fishing, agriculture, commerce, building, etc. These, however, partake of the character of legendary heroes. Dr. James Legge, who translated Confucius' *Book of History*, arrives at an unfavourable conclusion as to its historical character. He regarded it as half legend, and as containing the names of a number of Emperors which were invented by subsequent writers. The credible, self-consistent history of ancient China is believed by many to date from no earlier than B.C. 781, when the history written by Confucius commences. Mr. Mayers, in his *Chinese Reader's Manual*, treats the history of the period from B.C. 2852 to 781 as half mythical. He divides it thus :—

Chinese History.

B.C. 2852–1154. The legendary period.
,, 1154 – 781. The semi-historical period.
,,   781 –   . The period of trustworthy history.

There is, therefore, nothing in the high antiquity of China to conflict with the conclusion arrived at by Du Halde, whose admirable work on China stands unrivalled for the copiousness and correctness of the information it contains, that "two hundred years after the Deluge the sons of Noah arrived in North-West China."

(5) *Sir Isaac Newton's " Chronology of Ancient Kingdoms Amended."*

Before dismissing this subject, a reference must be made to that most fascinating work of Sir Isaac Newton, *The Chronology of Ancient Kingdoms Amended.* The book was published in 1728, the year after he died. We learn from the account which he gave of it, some five months before his death, to his friend Dr. Pearce, Bishop of Rochester, that Chronology was a pet subject of his. " He had spent 30 years," Dr. Pearce tells us, " at intervals, in reading over all the authors, or parts of authors, which could furnish any materials for forming a just account of the subject, that he had in his reading made collections from these authors, and had at the end of 30 years, composed from them his *Chronology of Ancient Kingdoms*, and that he had written it over sixteen times, making few alterations therein, but what were for the sake of shortening it, leaving out, in every later copy, some of the authorities and references on which he had grounded his opinion." A few days before his death, Bishop Pearce visited and dined with him at Kensington. " I found him," says Dr. Pearce, " writing over his *Chronology of Ancient Kingdoms* without the help of spectacles, at the greatest distance in the room from the window, and with a parcel of books on the table casting a shade on the table. " Sir," said I, " you seem to be writing in a place where you cannot well see." His answer was, " Little light serves me." He then told me that he was preparing his Chronology for the press, and that he had written the greatest part of it for that purpose."

In this work Sir Isaac Newton brings to bear upon a most intricate and difficult subject the wide and long continued reading, the unrivalled astronomical knowledge and the acute and penetrating insight of an intellectual giant.

His main conclusions, so far as they bear upon the antiquity of man, may be briefly summarized as follows :—

" Greek Antiquities are full of poetic fictions. They wrote nothing in prose before the Conquest of Asia by Cyrus. A little after the death of Alexander the Great (B.C. 323) the earliest Greek historians began to set down generations, reigns, and successions, and by putting reigns and successions as equipollent to generations, and 3 generations to 100 or 120 years, they have made the antiquities of Greece 300 or 400 years older than the truth. Eratosthenes wrote about 100 years after the death of Alexander the Great. He was followed by Apollodorus, and these two have been followed ever since by Chronologers. Plutarch quotes Aristotle as arguing from the Olympic disc which had the name of Lycurgus on it, making him contemporary with Iphitus and his companion in ordering the Olympic Festivals on the first Olympiad, B.C. 776. But Eratosthenes and Apollodorus, and others, computing their Chronology by the succession of the Kings of Sparta, make him 100 years older. Plutarch relates the unquestionably historic interview of Solon with Crœsus, but the Chronologers, by their method of computing, make it out that he was dead many years before the date of his visit to Crœsus."

" The Chronology of the Latins is still more uncertain. The records of the Latins were burnt by the Gauls B.C. 390, i.e. 64 years before the death of Alexander the Great, and Quintus Fabius Pictor, the oldest historian of the Latins, lived 100 years after that King."

" The Assyrian Empire began with Pul and Tiglath Pileser, and lasted 170 years ; accordingly Herodotus made Semiramis only 5 generations, or 166 years older than Nitocris, the mother of the last King of Babylon. But Ctesias made Semiramis 1,500 years older than Nitocris, and feigned a long series of Kings in Assyria whose names are not Assyrian, and have no affinity with the Assyrian names in Scripture."

" The priests of Egypt so magnified their antiquities as to tell Herodotus that from Menes to Moeris, whose date is B.C. 755, was 11,000 years, and they filled up the interval with feigned Kings who had done nothing, thus making the date of Menes and the commencement of civilization in Egypt B.C. 11,755."

" Eratosthenes and Apollodorus compute the time between the return of the Heraclides and the Battle of Thermopylæ by the number of the Kings of Sparta, viz. 17, and reckoning 36¼ years to each King they make the period 622 years."

Newton suggests that 18 or 20 years would be a more accurate estimate, and reduces the period to 340 years, a reduction of 278 years. He makes the taking of Troy 80 years earlier than the return of the Heraclides. The Argonautic Expedition he places a generation before the taking of Troy, viz. 33 years instead of 42, and the Wars of Sesostris in Thrace another generation, or 28 years instead of 75, before the Argonautic Expedition. Thus :—

Leading Events of Early Greek History.

	Received Chronology. B.C.	Sir Isaac Newton. B.C.
Wars of Sesostris	1300	965
Argonautic Expedition	1225	937
Taking of Troy	1183	904
Return of the Heraclides	1103	825
Battle of Thermopylæ	480	480
From Wars of Sesostris to Battle of Thermopylæ	820	485
	485	
A difference of	335 years	

Thus, according to Newton, the Chronologers, by their computation, have exaggerated the antiquity of Greek history, and antedated its earlier events by 300 or 400 years.

" The Europeans had no chronology at all before the times of the Persian Empire, and whatsoever Chronology thay now have of ancienter times hath been framed by reasoning and conjecture. First Pherecydes, the Athenian, wrote of the antiquities and ancient genealogies of the Athenians in the reign of Darius Hystaspes (B.C. 521–485). He was one of the first European writers of this kind, and one of the best. He was followed by Dionysius of Halicarnassus, Epimenides the historian, Hellanicus and Hipparchus. Then Euphorus, the disciple of Isocrates, formed a Chronology of Greece from the return of the Heraclides to the 20th year of Philip of Macedon. These all computed the years by the number of generations, or successive priestesses of Juno, or Archons of Athens, or Kings of Sparta. The Olympian Era was not used at all, and not even mentioned, nor any other Era till after the Arundelian Marbles were composed, 60 years after the death of Alexander the Great (in the fourth year of Olympiad 128) B.C. 264."

" Not till the following Olympiad, when Timæus Siculus wrote his history of Greece, was Chronology reduced to a reckoning of years. His Chronology was computed in the same way as that of his predecessors, but was expressed in terms of four years called Olympiads. Eratosthenes wrote 100 years after the death of Alexander the Great (B.C. 220). He was followed by Apollodorus, and these two have been followed by Chronologers ever since."

We see clearly that the basis and foundation on which the structure of

Greek Chronology was erected was largely subjective and fanciful, and we readily agree with the conclusion of Newton that, so far as the records of the history of the race are concerned, "Mankind cannot be much older than is represented in Scripture."

3. *Biblical Criticism and the Historical Character of the Biblical Records.*

We turn now to the department of Biblical Criticism, and to the doubts which have been raised as to the historical character of the events recorded in the early chapters of Genesis. These chapters have been assimilated to the myths and legends which are found in the story of their origins preserved by other nations, and accounted for as the product of the mythopoetic faculty of primitive man. They have also been shorn of their credentials, and regarded as a late compilation by writers who were not contemporary with the events they record, and therefore not qualified to give a true account of the events which they relate. These conclusions are now widely held by modern Biblical scholars. They are not only widely accepted, but they are also being vigorously propagated by those who occupy influential positions in the Colleges and Universities of England and her Colonies, as well as in all other centres of learning in Europe and America.

Nevertheless they are, in the view of the present writer, not only destitute of any reasonable foundation, and incapable of historic proof, but wholly unwarranted by the objective facts which have been urged against the authenticity of the early chapters of Genesis.

The method of the Higher Criticism as practised by its leading exponents, and the presuppositions involved in it as explained by them, are such as to exclude the possibility of arriving at a true estimate of the real value and authority of the Old Testament Scriptures. The Old Testament is nothing if it is not a revelation and a record of a Divine movement in human history, involving, in a very direct and special way, the universal sovereignty and the immediate activity of God, with a view to the redemption of man. Nevertheless the fundamental postulate of one of the leading advocates of the method is that no such activity can be admitted in any one single instance.

" So soon," says Kuenen, " as we derive a separate part of Israel's religious life directly from God, and allow the supernatural or immediate revelation to intervene in even a single point, so long our view of the whole continues to be incorrect. It is the supposition of a natural development alone which accounts for all the phenomena." This applies not merely to the early chapters of Genesis, but even to the very words of our Lord Himself and His interpretation of Old Testament passages ; for, in his work on *Prophets and Prophecy*, Kuenen says, " We must either cast aside as worthless our dearly bought *scientific method*, or must for ever cease to acknowledge the authority of the New Testament in the domain of the exegesis of the Old." This means, of course, that the said scientific method is of such a nature that it cannot possibly be applied without coming into conflict with the interpretation placed upon the Old Testament by our Lord and His Apostles, an interpretation so sure that if their testimony cannot be accepted on this point, it is quite certain that no other testimony can be accepted on any point whatsoever.

This fundamental postulate of Kuenen's, the impossibility of admitting the truth of any narrative which contains an element of the miraculous, rules out of existence the very thing which constitutes the distinctive characteristic of the Old Testament, and makes it different from every other literature in the world : its story of the creative, selective, directive, redemptive activity of God, both mediate and immediate, in the history of the human race. To postulate the absence from the literature of the Old Testament of an element which constitutes its distinctive characteristic, is to shut the door in the face of truth, and to make a scientific study of the literature impossible.

There are, however, other critics who admit the possibility and the actuality of the miraculous, and yet regard the early chapters of Genesis as unhistorical.

The more carefully these chapters are studied and compared with the mythical and legendary accounts of the origins of the race in other literatures, the more striking will be the contrast between them. One cannot read these chapters aright without being struck with the unique grandeur and sublimity of their language, and filled with wonder and amazement at the marvel and the glory of their message and content.

No one can place them side by side with the mythical accounts of other religions without being struck by the incomparable distinction which lifts them out of the class and category of all other writings, and proclaims them of another origin, and of another kind. And the one palpable difference between these chapters and all other forms of religious literature is the fact of their objective, historical character. The religions of Greece and Rome, of Egypt and Persia, of India and the East, did not even *postulate* a historical basis. The mythical period of the Greeks, though similar in form, was distinct in kind from the historic, the objective reality of the scenes and events described as belonging to each period was not even conceived of as belonging to the same order, or as being of the same kind. It is quite otherwise with the religion of the Old Testament. There the doctrine is bound up with the facts, and is so absolutely dependent upon them that without them it is null and void. If there is no first Adam there is no second Adam. The facts are the necessary substratum of the truths or doctrines of the Old Testament, as the truths or doctrines are the necessary substratum of the duties that arise out of them. The Chronology of the Old Testament is in strongest contrast with that of all other nations. From the Creation of Adam to the death of Joseph the Chronology is defined with the utmost possible precision, and only toward the end of the narrative of the Old Testament do doubts and difficulties and uncertainties arise. With all other Chronologies the case is exactly the reverse. They have no beginning. They emerge from the unknown, and their earliest dates are the haziest and the most uncertain, instead of being the clearest and the most sure. If the trustworthiness of testimony and the canons of credibility are accepted, the early chapters of Genesis will answer every legitimate test that can be applied to the determination of their genuine historical character.

The Mosaic authorship of the Pentateuch has long since been abandoned by many modern students of Biblical literature, and replaced by a theory of composite authorship and late compilation. The present writer believes that all the facts which have been pointed to in support of the new theory are susceptible of another interpretation consistent with the testimony of Scripture to the Mosaic authorship of these books.

It is nowhere directly stated, either in the Old Testament or the New, that Moses wrote the Book of *Genesis*, but it is everywhere affirmed that he is the author of the Book of the Law, of which the Book of Genesis is an integral part. In support of this we have the testimony of the Pentateuch itself. It is attributed to him five times in Exodus, once in Leviticus, twice in Numbers, and three times in Deuteronomy, where he is said to have spoken 94% of the words which the book contains. We have also the testimony of the rest of the Old Testament. It is attributed to him by Joshua, by the writers of 1 and 2 Kings, 2 Chronicles, Ezra, Nehemiah, Daniel and Malachi. We have again the testimony of the New Testament writers in John, in the Acts, in 2 Corinthians and in Hebrews. Twice it is attributed to Moses by our Lord Himself. We have the continuous, unbroken testimony of the entire Jewish nation and the Christian Church for 3,500 years, an array of positive evidence which ought by all the canons of Historical Criticism to make the Mosaic authorship of the Pentateuch an indubitable historical fact.

This conclusion is corroborated by the futility of the arguments that have been advanced against it. For instance, it is said (1) that Moses was not a writer but a man of action. But since *all* that we *know* of Moses is derived from the Old Testament, which says he *was* a writer, the argument not only fails, but discloses the frame of mind of the objector, which is that of a man who seeks to impose his views upon the facts instead of deriving his views from them.

Again, it is said, (2) since the pre-exilic writers do not quote the Priestly Code, it was not in existence till after the date of the return from the exile. But the fact is that they do quote it over and over again, e.g. in Amos 5^{21}, as frequently as they have any occasion to do so. "Genesis is referred to 149 times ; Exodus, 312 ; Leviticus, 285 ; Numbers, 168 ; while Deuteronomy is referred to 617 times." (Companion Bible, Appendix 92).

Again, it is urged, (3) that the state of religious culture was such that it could not have been produced in that early and barbarous age. But this is to beg the very question that has to be proved. The age of Moses was a highly civilized age, an age of schools, books and libraries, of an advanced stage of engineering, art and culture. Moreover the objection rests upon the highly speculative and unverified assumption that the more primitive the period the more it approximates to the condition of barbarism and savagery.

Finally, it is said that the Pentateuch is not by any one author, but is the composite work of many authors represented by the symbols J., E., JE., D., H., P., R^1., R^2., R^3., etc. whose hand can be traced in the various layers or strata, still visible in the closely knit, but still composite work, as it stands to-day. This theory has passed through six stages known as (1) the Document,

(2) the Fragment, (3) the Supplement, (4) the Crystallization, (5) the Modified Document, and (6) the Development Theory, each succeeding stage antiquating and disproving the truth of its predecessor.

Considerable use is made of the fact that in different passages different names of the Divine Being are used, as e.g. in Gen. 1–2 ^{4} the name Elohim or God ; in Gen. 2 ^{4}–3 ^{24} the name Jehovah Elohim, or Lord God, and in Gen. 4 the name Jehovah or Lord, these three passages being on these and other grounds attributed to three distinct authors.

But the facts as observed and stated are susceptible of another interpretation. The name Elohim (God) is always used when the reference is to the Deity in relation to the universe and man, as their Creator, and the word Jehovah (Lord) is similarly always used when the relation is that of Moral Governor and Responsible Agent, or that of rule and obedience to Moral Law or Divine Command ; just as we use the word Emperor instead of King for the Sovereign of England in relation to the Dependency of India. Similarly the name Elyon, translated Most High, is never used of the Divine Being except in relation to his sway over all the peoples of the earth. The names of the Divine Being are always used with a distinction of meaning, and application, and do not in any case suggest differences of authorship. The law of Recurrence, the Law of Synthetic Structure, the Law of Double Reference and the Law of the use of the Divine and other names, account for the facts adduced, far better than the hypothesis of composite authorship. The facts are admitted, but they do not support the theory.

A glance at the following diagram will show the relation in which the several theories of composite authorship that have been advanced, stand to each other.

MOSAIC v. COMPOSITE AUTHORSHIP OF THE PENTATEUCH.

The Six Hypotheses of the Advocates of Composite Authorship.

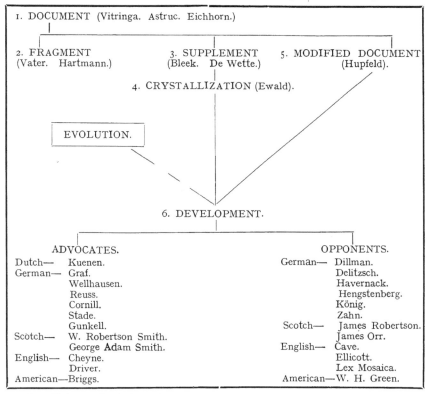

It will be noticed that the present theory not only gathers up in a comprehensive way the main features of three of the other theories, but derives its present plausibility and maintains its hold on the minds of the present generation of Biblical scholars, by incorporating the Doctrine of Evolution. The unverified assumptions and the highly speculative and hypothetical character of this doctrine render any statement into which it enters liable to subtle errors, which escape the notice and elude the attention of the unwary.

The positive evidence or testimony of the writers of the Old Testament in favour of the Mosaic authorship of the Pentateuch, may be briefly summarised as follows :—

I. *The Formation of the Book of the Law of Moses.*

   1. There was a definite book called the Book of the Law. (Josh. 1 [8]).
   2. It was commenced by Moses in obedience to the command of God (Ex. 17 [14]).

3. It contained the 10 Commandments, and the Book of the Covenant in Horeb in Ex. 20–23 (Ex. 24 $^{4-7}$).
4. It contained the renewed Tables of the Law and God's Covenant with Moses in Ex. 34 (Ex. 34 ^{27}).
5. It contained an account of the journeys of Israel during the 40 years in the wilderness (Numb. 33 ^{2}).
6. It contained the whole of Deuteronomy except the last chapter (Deut. 1 ^{5} where to "declare" means to "set forth in writing").
7. It contained the Song of Moses in Deut. 32, which Moses taught to the Children of Israel (Deut 31 $^{22. 30}$).
8. The limits of the Book were strictly defined (Deut. 4 ^{2}).

This Book of the Law formed the basis of the whole of the Old Testament. It was expounded and applied to the life of the nation by the Prophets, and to the life of the individual by the writers of the remaining books of the Old Testament.

II. *The Custody of the Book of the Law of Moses.*
1. Moses wrote it and placed it in the custody of the Priests, who placed it by the side of the Ark (Deut. 31 ^{9}, 31 $^{24-26}$).
2. The King had to make a copy of it for himself (Deut. 17 ^{18}).
3. The Priests had to read it in the hearing of all Israel once every seven years (Deut 31 $^{10-11}$).
4. It came into the custody of Joshua (Josh. 1 ^{8}).
5. Joshua wrote a copy of it upon the stones of an altar in Mount Ebal (Josh. 8 $^{31-35}$).
6. Just before his death Joshua directed all Israel to do all that was written in it (Josh. 23 $^{2-6}$).

III. *Subsequent additions to the Books of the Law of Moses.*
1. It was constantly added to by inspired men of later date, who received what they wrote, as Moses received what he wrote, direct from the Lord (Josh. 24 ^{26}, 1 Sam. 10 ^{25}).
2. Joshua himself wrote something in it in continuation of the history it contained, probably Deut. 34 and Joshua 1 to 24 ^{28} (Josh. 24 ^{26}).
3. Samuel continued the writing in the Book, and retained custody of it. He probably wrote Josh. 24 $^{29-33}$, the story of Joshua's death, the whole of Judges, the Book of Ruth, and 1 Samuel 1-24 (1 Sam. 10 ^{25}, where the "manner of the kingdom" means the constitutional limits of the newly established monarchy, and "*a book*" should be "*the book.*")

IV. *The Transmission of the Book of the Law of Moses.*
1. David had a copy of it, and gave one to Solomon (1 K. 2 $^{1-3}$).
2. Jehoshaphat had a copy of it and sent men throughout the length and breadth of his Kingdom to teach it to the people (2 Chron. 17 $^{7-9}$).

3. A copy of the Book was given to Joash at his coronation (2 Chron. 23 [11]).
4. Amaziah had a copy, and acted upon instructions contained in it (2 Chron. 25 [4], cp. Deut. 24 [16]).
5. In the reign of Josiah whilst the Temple was being repaired, Hilkiah the Priest discovered a copy of the long lost Book of the Law (2 Chron. 34 [14]).
6. Josiah had a copy, and observed the Passover in accordance with the directions contained in it (2 Chron. 35 [6]).
7. Ezra had a copy, which he described by various names, (Ez. 3 [2], 6 [18], 7 [6], 7 [10], 7 [14]).
8. Nehemiah had a copy, which he described in different ways (Neh. 8 [14], 10 [29], 13 [1]).
9. Daniel had a copy of it (Dan. 9 [11]).
10. Malachi had a copy of it (Mal. 4 [4]).

Throughout the whole period of the Old Testament from Moses to Malachi, the Book of the Law, which consisted of the five Books of the Pentateuch, and always included Genesis, was regarded as the genuine work of Moses, divinely authoritative and historically true. It continued to be so regarded by our Lord and his Apostles, by the whole Jewish nation, and by the entire Christian Church, until the beginning of last century, and it is so regarded to-day by those who accept the Canons of Credibility and believe the testimony of the witnesses who have certified its truth.

But testimony is never of such a character as to compel belief, it never amounts to demonstration, and it is always liable to be rejected when it comes into conflict with rationalistic, subjective presuppositions, which do not allow the mind to attach due weight and authority to the objective truth and value of the testimony of competent witnesses.

The book of Genesis, in these early chapters, deals with events that took place so early in the history of the human race that if we do not accept this testimony we are absolutely without any trustworthy and reliable history of the period which they cover. But allowance being made for the distance at which we stand from the period to which these chapters relate, and the tendency of time to destroy all manner of evidence, whether documentary or otherwise, which we might justly require in the case of more recent events, the wonder and the marvel is that so unique an account of the first 2,000 years of the history of the race remains with us to this day, fulfilling all the Canons of Credibility, and commending itself to our intelligent acceptance, as a truly historical record of a great but vanished past. That Moses incorporated earlier written records in the book of Genesis is proved by the express testimony of Gen. 5 [1].

We have now compared the Chronology of the period from Adam to Abraham as given in the book of Genesis, with all the evidence that can be alleged against its truth from the standpoint of Evolutionary Biology, Geology, Archæology, and Biblical Criticism, and after duly weighing, and carefully sifting, all the arguments adduced, we find that the attack has failed on every hand.

Returning to the study of the genuineness of the Record, on the positive side, we find it is amply attested by an incomparable array of incorruptible witnesses, and we proceed to the investigation of the next period of the Chronology, with the assurance that the foundations of the same, having been " well and truly laid," will bear the weight of any superstructure that may be placed upon it.

CHAPTER X. THE HEBREW PATRIARCHS—ABRAHAM, ISAAC, JACOB AND JOSEPH.

(AN. HOM. 2008–2369).

THE theme of the Old Testament is the purpose of God in Redemption. The early chapters of Genesis, which deal with the creation of the world and the fall of man, are introductory and preliminary. The first eleven chapters cover a period of time which is almost exactly equal to that covered by the remainder of the whole Bible, including the last book in the New Testament. It is a marvel of condensation. Its brevity precludes the application of the argument from silence. It is impossible to say that because things are not mentioned here, the author was not aware of them, or that they did not exist. The plan of the writer is selective. His history of these 2,000 years is little more than a genealogical chart, and *that*, for the most part, he traces only in one line of descent, through Seth and through Noah to Abraham, the father of the chosen race. There are indeed not a few precious fragments of historic truth respecting the origins of other nations, but they are not followed up. From the very beginning the centre of interest is the Messiah, who is first promised as the Seed of the woman in the protevangelium, Gen. 3 [15], and it is along the line of the ancestry of the Messiah that the early Chronology and the related history is given.

The Chronology of the remaining portion of Genesis is given on the same principles as that of the first eleven chapters. It follows the line of Abraham, through Isaac and Jacob and Joseph. As it is with the ante-diluvian and the post-diluvian Patriarchs, so it is with the Hebrew Patriarchs. The method adopted for measuring the time is that of giving the age of the father at the birth of his son, until we reach the name of Joseph. The age of Jacob at the birth of Joseph is nowhere directly stated, but it can be ascertained by an arithmetical calculation, or a historical induction.

We begin with the result reached in chapter 5. Abraham was born when Terah was 130, in the year AN. HOM. 2008. When Terah died, at the age of 205, Abraham left Haran, in obedience to the call of God, at the age of 75, in the year AN. HOM. 2083 (Gen. 11 [32], 12 [1], Acts 7 [4]).

The following Table shows the Chronology of the Hebrew Patriarchs from the birth of Abraham to the death of Joseph, as given in Genesis, chapters 11–50.

THE HEBREW PATRIARCHS—ABRAHAM, ISAAC, JACOB AND JOSEPH.

From the Birth of Abraham to the Death of Joseph.

AN. HOM.

2008. Abram born (see Chapter 8).

   75. Add age of Abram when he received the call from God (Gen. 11[32], 12[1], Acts 7[4]).

2083. Call of Abram, in obedience to which he left Haran and came into Canaan, immediately after the death of his father Terah.

   10. Add 10 years to Abram's marriage with Hagar (Gen. 16[3]).

2093. Abram, aged 85, married Hagar.

    1. Add 1 year to birth of Ishmael, Abram 86 (Gen. 16[16]).

2094. Ishmael born. Abram 86.

   14. Add 14 years to birth of Isaac (Gen. 21[5]).

2108. Isaac born. Abraham 100.

      Add 5 years to the great feast when Isaac was weaned, and became Abraham's SEED and HEIR. Ishmael cast out (Gen. 21[8-10]). This took place 400 years before the Exodus (Gen. 15[13], Acts 7[6]). The Exodus was 430 years after the call (Gen 12[1]), promise (Gen. 12[3], Gal. 3[17]) and covenant (Gen. 15[13]) of God with Abraham at the commencement of his sojourn, when he was 75 (Gen. 12[4]). Therefore the date of the Exodus was 2083+430=AN. HOM. 2513 (Ex. 12[40.41]). Therefore the 400 years sojourn of the SEED of Abraham commenced 2513-400 = AN. HOM. 2113, when Isaac was

    5.   5 years old.

2113. Isaac weaned at the age of 5, when he became Abraham's SEED and HEIR, Ishmael being cast out.

   32. Add 32 years to the death of Sarah.

      Sarah was 90 at the birth of Isaac (Gen. 17[17], 21[5]).

      Sarah died at the age of 127 (Gen. 23[1]), the only woman whose age is given in Scripture.

      Therefore Isaac was 127 – 90=37 when Sarah died.

2145. Sarah died aged 127.

    3. Add 3 years to the marriage of Isaac at the age of 40 (Gen. 25[20]).

2148. Isaac married at the age of 40.

   20. Add 20 years to the birth of Esau and Jacob (Gen 25[26]).

2168. Esau and Jacob born. Isaac aged 60.

   15. Add 15 years to the death of Abraham at the age of 175 (Gen. 25[7]).

2183. Abraham died aged 175 (2008+175=2183).

   25. Add 25 years to the marriage of Esau at the age of 40 (Gen. 26[34])
       (2168+40=2208).

2208. Esau married at the age of 40.

2208. Esau married at the age of 40.
　　　Add 37 years to the day when Jacob left home.
　　　Jacob left home at the age of 77 (2168+77=2245).
　　　　　Joseph stood before Pharaoh, aged 30 (Gen. 41 [46]).
　　　　　At the end of 7 years' plenty Joseph was 37 (Gen. 41 [29.30]).
　　　　　At the end of 2 years' famine, when Jacob came down into Egypt,
　　　　　　Joseph was 39 (Gen. 45 [6]).
　　　　　At the end of 2 years' famine, when Jacob came down into
　　　　　　Egypt, Jacob was 130 (Gen. 47 [9]).
　　　　　Therefore Jacob was 130 when Joseph was 39.
　　　　　　　,,　　　　,,　　　,,　91　,,　　　,,　　　,,　born.
　　　　　Jacob had served Laban 14 years when Joseph was born (Gen.30 [25]).
　　　　　Therefore Jacob was 91 – 14=77 when he left home for Padan
　 37.　　　Aram.
2245. Jacob left home for Padan Aram aged 77.
　　 7. Add 7 years to Jacob's marriage. Jacob married both Leah and
　　　　　Rachel at the same time. He served 7 years for Leah before his
　　　　　marriage and 7 years more for Rachel after it (Gen. 29 [21-28.30],
　　　　　30 [1.22.25.26.]31 [38-41]).
2252. Jacob at the age of 84 married *both* Leah and Rachel.
　　 7. Add 7 years to the birth of Joseph (Gen. 30 [25.26], 31 [38-41]).
2259. Joseph born. Jacob 91 (Gen. 30 [25], 31 [38-41]).
　　 6. Add 6 years to the time when Jacob returned to Canaan aged 97
　　　　　(Gen. 31 [41]).
2265. Joseph aged 6. Jacob returns to Canaan aged 97.
　　24. Add 24 years to the time when Joseph stood before Pharaoh, aged 30.
　　　　　(Gen. 41 [46]).
2289. Joseph stood before Pharaoh at the beginning of the 7 years of plenty,
　　　　　aged 30 (Gen. 41 [46]).
　　 7. Add 7 years of plenty. Joseph aged 37 (Gen. 41 [47]).
2296. At the end of 7 years of plenty Joseph aged 37 (Gen. 41 [47]).
　　 2. Add 2 years of famine when Jacob went down into Egypt (Gen. 45 [6]).
2298. At the end of 2 years of famine Jacob went down into Egypt, aged 130.
　　　　　Joseph aged 39 (Gen. 45 [6], 47 [9]).
　　17. Add 17 years to the death of Jacob (Gen. 47 [28]).
2315. Jacob died aged 147 (2168+147=2315). Joseph 56 (Gen. 47 [28]).
　　54. Add 54 years to the death of Joseph (Gen. 50 [26]).
2369. Joseph died aged 110 (2259+110=2369) (Gen. 50 [26].)

Each step in the progress of the Chronology is clearly explained in the
above table, and the " proof " is given in the " testimony " of the text of
Scripture cited. These proof texts are the historical data with which the
science of Chronology is built up. The result arrived at is characterized
by the accuracy and certainty of an exact science. It cannot be one year
more. It cannot be one year less. This is so mathematically exact and
so absolutely certain, that since Ussher proved that Terah was 130 when

Abram was born, no Chronologer, who accepts the text of the Old Testament, has ever made the period covered by the Book of Genesis from the Creation of Adam to the death of Joseph anything else but 2,369 years. The only exception is R. G. Faussett, who supposes that Abraham left Haran, not as Scripture says, *when his father Terah died*, but after an interval of 2 years.

The motive for this alteration is to provide the author with materials to illustrate his theory of the symmetry of time, so that e.g. each of the 21 7-year periods of Jacob's life may coincide with a year AN. HOM. divisible by the number 7. Thus e.g. he would be born in the year AN. HOM. $2170 = 7 \times 310$, instead of in the year AN. HOM. 2168. The temptation is great, but it is the very thing against which Chronologers must guard. No preconceived scheme, whether millennial, septenary, or of any other kind, must be allowed to warp the facts or to bend the figures into any particular symmetrical shape. The sole criterion of chronological truth is evidence, testimony, fact. Another motive for carrying the Chronology forward by 2 years is that Isaac may be 3 years old, instead of 5 years old, when he is weaned, 3 being the usual age at which children are weaned in the East, when the birth of one child is not soon followed by the birth of another (see 2 Macc. 7 [27], "My son, have pity on thy mother that gave thee suck 3 years," and cp. 1 Sam. 1 [21-23]. Josephus, Antiq. II. 9.6). The alteration does not affect the Chronology ultimately, for Faussett deducts the added two years from the interval between the death of Joseph and the birth of Moses, meanwhile every event from the birth of Abraham (AN. HOM. 2010 instead of 2008) to the death of Joseph (AN.HOM. 2371 instead of 2369) is placed 2 years too late.

We have now reached the epoch of the two promises (1) to Abraham's seed and (2) to Abraham himself, in connection with which, periods of 400 and 430 years are mentioned. It will be worth while for us to set out these two periods in detail.

The 430 years of Exodus 12 [40. 41] and Gal. 3 [17].

Exodus 12 [40. 41]. "Now the sojourning of the children of Israel (who dwelt in Egypt) was 430 years. And it came to pass at the end of the 430 years, even the selfsame day it came to pass, that all the hosts of the Lord went out from the land of Egypt."

Gal. 3 [17]. "The Covenant that was confirmed before of God in Christ, the law, which was 430 years after, could not disannul."

This sojourning includes the whole period from the call of Abram (Gen. 12 [1]) and the promise (Gen. 12 [3]) and the confirmation of the promise by a covenant (Gen. 15 [13-18]) to the going up out of Egypt, within 2 months of which the Law was given on Sinai.

From the call, promise and covenant of Gen. 12 [1-3],
Gen. 15 [13-18,] Gal. 3 [17]   ..   .. $= 2083$

To the going up out of Egypt, and the giving of the
Law on Sinai, Ex. 12 [40. 41], 19 [1. 2], Gal. 3 [17] ..   .. $= 2513$

years 430

The 400 years of Gen. 15^{13} and Acts 7^6.

Gen. 15^{13}. "And he said unto Abram, Know of a surety that
thy seed shall be a stranger in a land that is not theirs,
(and shall serve them;
and they shall afflict them);
four hundred years."

Acts 7^6. Stephen's speech—"And God spake on this wise, That
his seed should sojourn in a strange land
(and they should bring them into bondage;
and entreat them evil);
four hundred years."

Abraham's seed here means Abraham's posterity, viz. Isaac from the time
that he was weaned, and became Abraham's heir (Gal. 3^{29}-4^5) and
Isaac's descendants.

1. They were strangers and sojourners in Canaan (a land not theirs).
   From the weaning of Isaac and the casting out of
   Ishmael (Gen. 21^{10}) .. .. = 2113
   To the going down into Egypt (Gen. 47^9) .. .. = 2298
   ──────
   815

2. They were in favour in Egypt (a land not theirs)
   From the going down into Egypt
   (Gen. 47^9) .. .. = 2298
   To the death of Joseph (Gen. 50^{26}) = 2369 = 71

3. They were brought into bondage and
   affliction in Egypt,
   From the death of Joseph Gen. 50^{26}) = 2369
   To the Exodus (Ex. 12$^{40.\ 41}$) = 2513 = 144   215
   ────── ──────
   years   400

The structure of Gen. 15^{13} and Acts 7^6 shows that the first line corresponds
with the fourth line, the second and third lines being a parenthesis, so that
the term "400 years" refers to the whole period of the sojourning in Canaan
as well as in Egypt, and not to the sojourning in Egypt alone.

──────────

The 430 years of Ex. 12^{40} is 30 years longer than the 400 years of Gen. 15^{13},
because it includes the sojourning of Abraham himself as well as that of his
SEED. By a figure of speech the term "children of Israel" is made to
include Abraham himself. So Milton speaks of "Eve the fairest of all her
daughters."

DETAILS OF THE TWO PERIODS OF 400 & 430 YEARS.

PERIODS.	The 400 years.	The 430 years.
From the call, promise and covenant of Abram to the marriage of Hagar		10
From the marriage of Hagar to the birth of Ishmael		1
From the birth of Ishmael to the birth of Isaac		14
From the birth of Isaac to his being weaned and becoming the SEED at the casting out of Ishmael (Gen. 21 $^{8-10}$)		5
From the weaning of Isaac, when he became the SEED to the going down into Egypt	185	185
		215
From the going down into Egypt to the Exodus—(to make up the 400 years of Gen. 15 ^{13} and the 430 years of Ex. 12. $^{40-41}$)	215	215
	400	430

The method of fixing the date of the weaning of Isaac is strictly logical and mathematically exact. We begin with the call, promise, covenant or sojourning of Abraham, which took place immediately after the death of Terah, AN. HOM. 2083. There is the direct and positive testimony of the Hebrew Text for the fact that the period from that point to the Exodus was a period of 430 years; therefore the date of the Exodus must be 2083 + 430 = AN. HOM. 2513. We have again the direct and positive testimony of the Hebrew Text for the fact that the SEED of Abraham should be strangers and sojourners for a period of 400 years. That period ended with the Exodus, AN. HOM. 2513. Therefore it began 2513 – 400 = 2113, and since Isaac was born AN. HOM. 2108, he was then 5 years old. But Isaac became the sole HEIR (with which we may connect the word SEED) of Abraham on the day that he was weaned. On that day Abraham made him a great feast, to celebrate the event. Ishmael was Abraham's heir no longer. Isaac had taken his place. He mocked, and was cast out.

Some difficulty has been felt in reconciling the various statements of the number of the children of Israel who went down into Egypt, viz. the 66, the 70 and the 75 of Gen. 46 $^{26, 27}$ and Acts 7 ^{14}, and also in understanding how Jacob's great grandson Hamul, and Ard the youngest son of Benjamin, could have been born at the time when Jacob went down into Egypt, as Jacob was then only 130 years old. The following Tables will make these matters quite clear. They do not give a definite historical induction showing the exact date of the birth of Jacob's sons and grandsons. They are not therefore included in the Chronological Tables (Vol. II) which contain only those dates which are definitely fixed and demonstrably true. They are a demonstration of the *possibility* of ranging the events recorded within the limits of the 130

years of Jacob's life, without postulating any departure from the ordinary
course of nature respecting the age of puberty and the laws of human
generation.

THE CHILDREN OF ISRAEL WHICH CAME INTO EGYPT.
GEN. 46$^{5-27}$, ACTS 7^{14}.

	THE 66	THE 70	THE 75
THE SONS OF LEAH—Gen. 46$^{8-15}$.			
1. Reuben	I	I	I
2. Hanoch	I	I	I
3. Phallu	I	I	I
4. Hezron	I	I	I
5. Carmi	I	I	I
6. Simeon	I	I	I
7. Jemuel	I	I	I
8. Jamin	I	I	I
9. Ohad	I	I	I
10. Jachin	I	I	I
11. Zohar	I	I	I
12. Shaul	I	I	I
13. Levi	⌐	I	I
14. Gershon	I	I	I
15. Kohath	I	I	I
16. Merari	I	I	I
17. Judah	I	I	I
18. Er—not included in either—died in Canaan	–	–	–
19. Onan—not included in either—died in Canaan	–	–	–
20. Shelah	I	I	I
21. Pharez (sons of Judah)	I	I	I
22. Zarah by Tamar	I	I	I
23. Hezron (sons of)	I	I	I
24. Hamul Pharez	I	I	I
25. Issachar	I	I	I
26. Tola	I	I	I
27. Phuvah..	I	I	I
28. Job	I	I	I
29. Shimron	I	I	I
30. Zebulon	I	I	I
31. Sered	I	I	I
32. Elon	I	I	I
33. Jahleel	I	I	I
Carried forward	31	31	31

	THE 66	THE 70	THE 75
Brought forward	31	31	31
DINAH—Gen. 46[15]	I	I	I

THE SONS OF ZILPAH, Gen. 46 [16-18].

	THE 66	THE 70	THE 75
1. Gad	I	I	I
2. Ziphion	I	I	I
3. Haggi	I	I	I
4. Shuni	I	I	I
5. Ezbon	I	I	I
6. Eri	I	I	I
7. Arodi	I	I	I
8. Areli	I	I	I
9. Asher	I	I	I
10. Jimnah	I	I	I
11. Ishuah	I	I	I
12. Isui	I	I	I
13. Beriah	I	I	I
14. Serah (their sister)	I	I	I
15. Heber { sons of }	I	I	I
16. Malchiel { Beriah }	I	I	I

THE SONS OF RACHEL—Gen. 46[19-22].

	THE 66	THE 70	THE 75
1. Joseph—not included in the 66. Already in Egypt	–	ı	I
2. Manasseh—not included in the 66. ,, ,,	–	⊥	I
3. Ephraim—not included in the 66. ,, ,,			I
4. Benjamin	⊥	⊥	I
5. Belah	⊥	⊥	I
6. Becher	⊥	I	I
7. Ashbel	I	I	⊥
8. Gera	I	⊥	I
9. Naaman	⊥	⊥	I
10. Ehi	⊥	⊥	I
11. Rosh	⊥	⊥	I
12. Muppim	⊥	⊥	I
13. Huppim	I	I	I
14. Ard	I	I	I
Carried forward	59	62	62

	THE 66	THE 70	THE 75
Brought forward	59	62	62

THE SONS OF BILHAH—Gen. 46 [23-25].

	66	70	75
1. Dan	I	I	I
2. Hushim	I	I	I
3. Naphtali	I	I	I
4. Jahzeel	I	I	I
5. Guni	I	I	I
6. Jezer	I	I	I
7. Shillem	I	I	I

"ALL THE SOULS THAT CAME WITH JACOB INTO EGYPT, WHICH CAME OUT OF HIS LOINS, BESIDES JACOB'S SONS' WIVES" (Gen. 46 [26]) = ..   66

JACOB HIMSELF (Gen. 46 [8])   I

"ALL THE SOULS OF THE HOUSE OF JACOB WHICH CAME INTO EGYPT" (Gen. 46 [27]) =   70

After " Ephraim," in Gen. 46 [20] the LXX. (Septuagint), the Greek translation of the Old Testament used by Stephen, adds two sons of Manasseh and three sons of Ephraim, viz.

The sons of Manasseh
1. Machir   I
2. Gilead, (son of Machir)..   I
The sons of Ephraim.
1. Shuthelah   I
2. Talhath   I
3. Edem (or Bered or Becher), son of Shuthelah   I

"JACOB AND ALL HIS KINDRED" (Acts 7 [14])   75

PASSAGES OF SCRIPTURE RELATING TO THE CHILDREN OF ISRAEL WHICH CAME INTO EGYPT.

THE 66 SOULS.

Gen. 46 [26]—" All the souls THAT CAME WITH JACOB INTO EGYPT, WHICH CAME OUT OF HIS LOINS, besides Jacob's sons' wives, all the souls were threescore and six."

This excludes Jacob, Leah, Rachel, Zilpah, Bilhah, Joseph, Manasseh, Ephraim and the wives of Jacob's 12 sons.

THE 70 SOULS.

Gen. 46²⁷.—"All the souls of the house of Jacob which came into Egypt were threescore and ten."

Deut. 10²²—"Thy fathers went down into Egypt with threescore and ten persons."

This includes Jacob, Joseph, Manasseh and Ephraim, in addition to the 66—but excludes the wives of Jacob and his 12 sons.

THE 75 SOULS.

Acts 7¹⁴. Jacob and all his kindred, threescore and fifteen souls.

Gen. 46²⁰. The LXX. adds "And there were born unto Manasseh and Ephraim, whom his concubine the Aramitess bare him, Machir; and Machir begat Gilead. And the sons of Ephraim the brother of Manasseh were Shuthelah, Tahath; and the sons of Shuthelah, Edem (or Bered or Becher)."

This addition is probably taken from Numb. 26²⁸⁻³⁷ and 1 Chron. 7²⁰.

Numb. 26²⁹. "Of the sons of Manasseh; of Machir the family of the Machirites: and Machir begat Gilead."

Numb. 26³⁵. "These are the sons of Ephraim after their families; of Shuthelah the family of the Shuthalhites, of Becher the family of the Bachrites, of Tahan the family of the Tahanites."

1 Chron. 7¹⁴. The sons of Manasseh; whom his concubine Ashriel the Aramitess bare: she bare Machir the father of Gilead.

1 Chron. 7²⁰. "And the sons of Ephraim; Shuthelah, and Bered his son, and Tahath his son."

The Septuagint Version of the Old Testament was the version used by Stephen and sometimes by Paul.

Note also the adoption of Joseph's two sons Manasseh and Ephraim, by Jacob,—

Gen. 48⁵. "And now thy two sons, Ephraim and Manasseh, which were born unto thee in the land of Egypt before I came unto thee in Egypt, are mine; as Reuben and Simeon they shall be mine."

———

Jacob went down into Egypt (see above, Chapter 10) at the age of 130, being not necessarily more than 129 when his youngest great grandson Hamul, the son of Pharez, the son of Judah was born, and not necessarily more than 130 when his youngest grandson Ard the son of Benjamin was born. Dinah would have been at Shechem at the early age of 13, and Benjamin would have had a son at the early age of 16—unless some of Benjamin's sons were twins, in which case Dinah may have been older, and Benjamin may have married later. Benjamin may have had more than one wife, in which case the difficulty disappears.

THE AGE OF JACOB AND HIS DESCENDANTS, WHEN JACOB CAME INTO EGYPT.

Jacob left home (see above, Chapter 10) at the age of			..	..		..	77
Jacob married Leah and Rachel at same time, at the age of			..			..	84
Reuben born of Leah when Jacob was, say			..	..		..	85
Simeon ,, ,, ,,			..	..	..	••	.. 86
Levi ,, ,, ,,			..	..	..	..	.. 87
Judah ,, ,, ,,			..	••	..	..	.. 88
Pharez born when Judah was, say 20, and Jacob, say					..	..	108
Hezron born, Pharez say 20, Judah say 40, Jacob say						..	128
Hamul born, Pharez say 21, Judah say 41, Jacob say ..						..	129
Dan born of Bilhah, Rachel's maid when Jacob was, say ..				..		..	89
Napthali ,, ,, ,,			..		..	..	90
Gad born of Zilpah, Leah's maid when Jacob was, say ..				..		..	89
Asher ,, ,, ,,			..		..	..	90
Issachar born of Leah when Jacob was, say ..			..	..		..	90
Zebulun ,, ,,			..	..	..	..	91
Dinah ,, ,,			..	..	..	..	92
Joseph born of Rachel (see above, Chapter 10) when Jacob was..						..	91
Dinah at Shechem at age of, say, 13 when Jacob was, say ..				..		..	105
Benjamin born of Rachel when Jacob was, say ..			..		..	..	105

Belah born when Benjamin was, say 16 and Jacob say					..	..	121
Becher	,,	,,	,,	17	,,	..	.. 122
Ashbel	,,	,,	,,	18	,,	..	.. 123
Gera	,,	,,	,,	19		..	.. 124
Naaman	,,	,,	,,	20	..	..	.. 125
Ehi	,,	,,	,,	21	,,	..	.. 126
Rosh	,,	,,	,,	22	,,	..	.. 127
Muppim	,,	,,	,,	23	,,	..	.. 128
Huppim	,,	,,	,,	24	,,	..	•• 129
Ard	,,	,,	,,	25		..	.. 130

Some doubt has been cast upon the number of the children of Israel who went up out of Egypt as expressed (1) in Exodus 12[37], " 600,000 men beside children," (2) in Numb. 2[32] " 603,550," beside the Levites at the beginning of the 2nd year after they came out of Egypt, and (3) in Numb. 26[51], " 601,730 " at the close of the 40 years in the wilderness.

But these doubts are quite groundless. From the going down into Egypt, AN.HOM. 2298, to the Exodus, AN.HOM. 2513, is 215 years. Mr. Malthus has shown that with an abundant supply of food, a given population may continue to double its numbers in about 15 years, and in favoured cases, in even less time. At this rate of increase the 70 souls who went down into Egypt would have multiplied in 225 years to 2,293,760, which is perhaps about the number of the entire population including Levites, women and children ; the 600,000 mentioned in Ex. 12[37], Numb. 2[32] and 26[51], would be the adult males.

CHAPTER XI. THE JOSEPH-MOSES CONNECTION.

From the Death of Joseph to the Birth of Moses = 64 *years.*

(AN. HOM. 2369-2433)

THE Book of Genesis closes with the death of Joseph at the age of 110.   There the Patriarchal Chronology comes to an end, and it ends in a *cul de sac.*   We can go no further in this line, for the age of Joseph at the birth of Ephraim and Manasseh is not stated.   We must therefore turn back and start afresh.

Between the end of Genesis and the beginning of Exodus there is a great chronological gulf or chasm.   In Genesis we close with *Israel in favour* in Egypt under one dynasty.   In Exodus we open with the rise of a new King, of another dynasty, who " knew not Joseph," and with *Israel in affliction* in Egypt.   The Book of Exodus opens with a recapitulation of the names and the number of the children of Israel who came into Egypt, and of the bitter affliction which overtook them under the rule of the new Pharaoh— the Pharaoh of the Oppression.   But the exact point at which the chronological continuity of the narrative commences is the birth of Moses.   The problem is, then, how to bridge the gulf, and how to determine the exact number of the years between the death of Joseph and the birth of Moses.

The answer is given in the long number of the sojourning and the affliction of Abraham and his seed, which dates from the call of Abraham at the age of 75, viz. AN. HOM. 2083, and which ends at the Exodus.   This period is definitely stated to be a period of exactly 430 years.   Now we know that from the call of Abram to the death of Joseph (AN. HOM. 2083-2369) was a period of 286 years, and we know that from the birth of Moses to the Exodus was a period of 80 years (Ex. 2[11-15.23], Ex. 7[7], Acts 7[23-30]).   If we add these numbers (286 + 80 = 366) and subtract the sum of them from the number of years in the entire period (430 – 366 = 64), the remaining 64 years will be the exact length of the period between the death of Joseph and the birth of Moses ; between the close of the narrative of Genesis and the beginning of that of Exodus. There is here no appeal to Josephus, no speculative hypothesis, no assumption or conjecture.   The result is obtained by a historical induction from the facts and figures given in the Text itself, and is mathematically exact.

There are many similar cases of gaps or chasms, like this, in the Chronology of the detailed events given in the narrative of the Text of the Old Testament, but they are always made good by statements which bridge over the gulf by giving the entire length of a longer period which includes, and thereby specifies, the length of the gap or chasm left in the Chronology of the events as related in detail.

These chasms begin with very simple problems, easily solved, like that of the age of Noah at the birth of Shem, and that of the age of Terah at the birth of Abram.   They then become slightly more complex, as in the case before us, the problem of the length of the period between the death of Joseph and the birth of Moses.   After this they become much more complex and involved, as in the case of the Joshua-Judges connection and the Eli-Saul connection, whilst finally, in the determination of the length of the reigns of the Persian monarchs who occupied the throne between the first year of Cyrus and the second year of Darius Hystaspes, and in the length of the period between the first year of Cyrus and the Crucifixion, we reach the most difficult problems of all in Sacred Chronology.

Nevertheless, the solution is always given, either in the Record of the prophetic narrator, or else in the words of the prophet, and given with such precision that the Chronology can be fixed with as great a degree of certainty as the Chronology of any period in secular history.

The demonstration of the length of the period between the death of Joseph and the birth of Moses may be set out in tabular form as follows :—

THE JOSEPH-MOSES CONNECTION.

From the Death of Joseph to the Birth of Moses=64 years.

2369. Death of Joseph at age of 110 (see previous Chapter).
    Add 64 years to the birth of Moses, for,—
    Ex. 12$^{40, 41}$, Call of Abram to Exodus   ..   = 430 years
        See Chapter 10 on the 400 and the 430 years.
    From Call of Abram to death of Joseph (AN.HOM.
        2083–2369   ..   ..   = 286 ,.
        See Table of Hebrew Patriarchs, Chapter 10.
    ∴ Death of Joseph to Exodus   ..   ..   ..   = 144 ,.
    Ex. 2^{23}, Acts 7$^{29, 30}$, Flight of Moses to Exodus,
        when Moses was 80   ..   ..   ..   = 40 ,.
    ∴ Death of Joseph to flight of Moses, ...   = 104 ,.
    Ex. 2$^{11-15}$, Acts 7$^{23-29}$, Birth of Moses to Flight of
        Moses, ...   = 40 ,,
  64. ∴ Death of Joseph to Birth of Moses ..   ..   = 64 ,,
2433. Moses born.

CHAPTER XII. COMPARATIVE CHRONOLOGY—ABRAHAM TO MOSES.

Israel in Egypt.

THE statements of the Hebrew Text respecting this period have not been controverted by ancient testimony or modern discovery. The only doubt that has arisen is in connection with the silence of the Monuments of Egypt respecting so great an episode as the residence of the Israelites in Egypt, the career of Joseph and Moses, and so remarkable an event as the Exodus.

As Professor Sayce says : " There is no direct mention of the Israelites in Egypt on the Monuments or in the papyri, neither is there any representation of their servitude," but they belonged to the servant class of brickmakers and hewers of wood and drawers of water, and would not be likely to be portrayed on temples or walls or tombs. There is also no mention of the plagues, but the nations of antiquity never chronicled their misfortunes, their disasters, or their defeats, only their triumphs and their victories.

The Pharaoh of Joseph, the Pharaoh of the Oppression, and the Pharaoh of the Exodus have not been certainly identified, but it is very generally supposed that the Pharaoh of the Oppression was the great Rameses II, who reigned 67 years, and filled Egypt with statues of himself, and that the Pharaoh of the Exodus was his son and successor Merenptah, both of the 19th dynasty. No dates can be given, for the materials for fixing the same are wanting. Two schools of Egyptologists place the date of Rameses II at B.C. 1350 (Budge) and B.C. 1292 (Kent) respectively.

Dr. C. F. Kent thinks the Pharaoh of the Oppression may have been Amenophis IV of the 18th dynasty, whom Budge dates B.C. 1400, and Kent B.C. 1375. The Pharaoh of the Oppression has also been identified with one of the Hyksos or Shepherd Kings who were formerly dated B.C. 1750, but whose expulsion is dated by Kent about B.C. 1580.

Professor Sayce thinks the children of Israel came into Egypt in the time of the Hyksos or Shepherd Kings, and that on their expulsion there arose a new King, a Pharaoh of a new dynasty who knew not Joseph.

" The Oppression culminated," says Professor Sayce, " in the long reign of Rameses II, for whom the Israelites built the cities of Ramses and Pithom (Ex. 1 [11]). Ramses or Raamses was the name given to Zoan or Tanis, the old capital of the Hyksos, after its reconstruction by Ramses, and the city of Pithom was discovered only two years ago in the mounds of Tel-el-Maskhuta near Tel-el-Kebir. Inscriptions found on the spot show that it was built by Ramses II as a storehouse for corn or treasure. It contains store chambers strongly constructed, and divided by partition walls as much as 8 or 10 feet thick."

The bricks are sun-baked, some mixed with straw and others not. They may be seen to-day in the Museum at Cairo, where the visitor is also shown the mummies of Seti I, Ramses I, Ramses II (the supposed Pharaoh of the Oppression) and Merenptah (the supposed Pharaoh of the Exodus). The bricks were discovered by M. Ernest Naville, who regards the strawless bricks as the work of the Israelites to whom Pharaoh said, " I will not give you straw " (Ex. 5 [10]). If Ramses II was the Pharaoh of the Oppression, the Pharaoh of the Exodus must have been his son Merenptah whose reign was of short duration and full of disaster.

It must not be supposed that the Pharaoh of the Exodus was himself drowned in the Red Sea. The narrative in Exodus 14, and Moses' Song in Exodus 15, both expressly guard the reader against that supposition. The waters returned and covered the chariots and the horsemen, and all the host of Pharaoh that came into the sea after them ; there remained not so much as one of them, Ex.14 [28]—" all the host of Pharaoh that came into the sea " is a different expression from " Pharaoh and all his host." Again, in Ex. 15 [19], we read " the horse of Pharaoh went in with his chariots and with his horsemen," but not " Pharaoh and his horse."

The Merenptah Stele.

The one contemporary allusion to Israel in the Egyptian Monuments is the recently discovered triumphal Stele of this same Merenptah, son of Ramses II, also in the Cairo Museum. In this he speaks of his conquest of Canaan in the following words :—

> Plundered is Canaan with every evil.
> Ascalon is carried into Captivity.
> Gezer is taken.
> Yenoam is annihilated.
> *Israel is desolated*, her seed is not.
> Palestine has become a widow for Egypt.
> All lands are united, they are pacified.
> Everyone who is turbulent has been bound by King Merenptah.

The dates of the Egyptian Kings are uncertain, and naturally give rise to different schools of Chronologists, but there is no reason why uncertainty should be introduced into the Biblical Chronology where everything is clear, unambiguous and precise.

Misleading Hypotheses of the Higher Critics.

Nevertheless, many eminent and distinguished men, from François Lenormant of the Imperial Institute of France to Prof. C. F. Kent, Ph.D., Professor of Biblical Literature in Yale University, will persist in regarding the period of the residence of Israel in Egypt as a period of 430 years. Lenormant says, in his *Manual of the Ancient History of the East,* " The Hebrews remained 430 years in the fertile land of Goshen." Prof. Kent is still more confusing. He says truly enough that in Genesis 15[16] it is stated that the Hebrews were to return to Palestine in the fourth generation, which they did, as shown by the two passages which he quotes, Ex. 6[16-20] and Numb. 26[57-59].

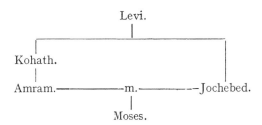

Prof. Kent's difficulty arises from inattention to the structure of Gen. 15[13]. " Know of a surety that

> A. thy seed shall be a stranger in a land that is not theirs,
>> B. and shall serve them ;
>> B. and they shall afflict them ;
> A. four hundred years."

The structure of this verse is admirably explained in the *Companion Bible,* sub. Gen. 15[13]. The Text is what is known as an Introversion, in which sentences A and A correspond to each other and relate to the same event, whilst sentences B and B likewise correspond to each other, and relate to another event. A and A relate to the whole period of the *sojourning* and the *servitude* in Canaan and in Egypt (400 years). B and B are parenthetic, and relate to the *servitude* in Egypt, and that alone (215 years.)

Gen. 15[14-16] gives further details relating to the period of the servitude in Egypt, referred to in Clauses B and B.

v. 14. " And also that nation, whom they shall serve, will I judge ; and afterward shall they come out with great substance."

v. 15. " And thou shalt go to thy fathers in peace ; thou shalt be buried in a good old age."

v. 16. " But in the fourth generation they shall come hither again ; for the iniquity of the Amorites is not yet full."

Clearly the point of departure for the reckoning of these generations, is the generation that went down into Egypt, viz. either that of Levi, in which case the four generations will be Levi, Kohath, Amram and Moses ; or that of Jacob, in which case the four generations will be Jacob, Levi, Jochebed and Moses. The children of Israel returned from Egypt in the generation of Moses, which was the fourth generation from that of Levi, the generation in which they went down into Egypt.

Prof. Kent then adds the misleading and groundless supposition, which he states as if it were a fact : " This implies a period of between 100 and 150 years." Now we know exactly how long this period was. From the going down into Egypt in the year AN. HOM. 2298 to the Exodus in AN. HOM. 2513 was exactly 215 years, no more and no less.

Then follows another quotation, which Prof. Kent introduces in such a way as to suggest that it contradicts the statement that Israel would return from Egypt in the fourth generation : " On the other hand, a late editor in Gen. 15[13] predicts that the period of foreign sojourn was to be exactly 400 years." So it did, but the period of " foreign sojourn " was not the residence of Israel in Egypt, which was 215 years, and not the sojourn of Abraham and his seed, which began AN. HOM. 2083, when Abram left his home and kindred in Haran, and lasted till the Exodus, AN. HOM. 2513, a period of 430 years, but was, as the Text most distinctly states, the sojourn of *Abraham's seed*, not therefore including the 30 additional years of Abraham's own sojourning, but only the years from AN. HOM. 2113 (when Isaac was weaned and became the heir of Abraham, Ishmael being disinherited) to AN. HOM. 2513, the period of 400 years named in the Text.

A further contradiction is suggested in the following sentence, in which Prof. Kent says, " Another compiler in Exodus 12[40] affirms that the time the Israelites dwelt in Egypt was 430 years." The Hebrew of Ex. 12[40] is accurately rendered in the Authorised Version, which reads, " Now the sojourning of the Children of Israel *who* dwelt in Egypt was 430 years." It is inaccurately rendered in the Revised Version, " Now the sojourning of the

children of Israel *which they sojourned in Egypt* was 430 years," the confusion
in the minds of the Revisers arising through the want of a proper understanding
of the Chronology of the period, which is very exact and always consistent
with itself.

Prof. Kent proceeds, "With this passage definitely in mind, the author
of Gal. 3[17] assigns 430 to the period from Abraham to Sinai." And correctly
so, for he understands the Chronology. The "promise" of Gal. 3[17] was given
immediately after Abram received and responded to the call of God to
leave his home and kindred and begin his sojourn, AN. HOM. 2083. The Law
was given in Sinai 2 months after the Exodus, AN. HOM. 2513, so that "the
period from Abraham to Sinai" is a period of exactly 430 years.

Prof. Kent implies that these "contradictions" are due to the fact that
the passages quoted are derived from different sources, which he describes
as the Northern Israelite history (E), the priestly writer (P), the late
priestly writer (P[2]), a late editor (R[1]), another compiler (R[2]). There is no
basis in fact for this discrimination between the supposed different sources.

The concluding sentence of Prof. Kent's paragraph is a striking evidence of
the blindness of an able scholar, and his inability to see the truth even when he
is writing it down with his own pen. He says, "Josephus and the translators
of the Samaritan and Greek Versions give the duration of the sojourn as
215 years, which is evidently a compromise between the shorter and the longer
periods suggested by the earlier writings." It is nothing of the kind. It
is the exact rendering into figures of the statements of the Hebrew Text,
which gives 215 years for the sojourn in Egypt, and which cannot possibly
be made to give anything else but 215 for it. The shorter period of 100 to
150 years is a baseless conjecture of Prof. Kent, which has no relation to any
Scripture fact or statement whatsoever. The longer period is a different
period altogether, beginning at another epoch, and referring to another event.

The Hebrew Text of Ex. 12[40] reads: "The sojourning of the children
of Israel who sojourned in Egypt was 430 years." The LXX. and the
Samaritan insert after Egypt the words "and in the land of Canaan," and
consequently read, "the sojourning of the children of Israel who sojourned
in Egypt and in the land of Canaan was 430 years." The added words agree
perfectly with the Hebrew, which is further elucidated, but in no way modified
by them. They correctly interpret the meaning of the Hebrew Text, and the
fact that the interpretation put upon it is correct is shown by its adoption
by Stephen (Acts 7[6]) and by the Apostle Paul (Gal. 3[17]). But the meaning
of the Hebrew is sufficiently clear without the explanatory addition when
the Text is properly translated.

The Chronology of the Old Testament is exact and accurate in every detail,
and will answer to any truly scientific test to which it is put, but to
misinterpret the Text, to infer therefrom what is not therein implied, or to
construe it in such a way as to make it mean what it was never intended to
mean, can only lead to misunderstanding and confusion.

A glance at the following diagram will make the matter clear.

DIAGRAM OF THE 215, THE 400 AND THE 430 YEARS

OF SOJOURN IN CANAAN, AND THE SOJOURN AND AFFLICTION IN EGYPT.

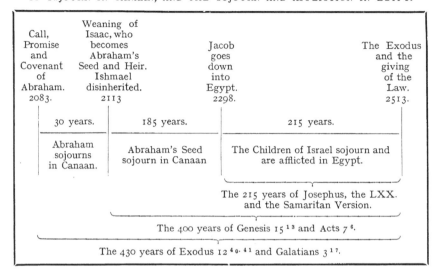

The Khammurabi Stele.

One other important discovery of recent years belongs to this period, one that has entirely vindicated the authenticity and re-established the authority of a unique passage in the Old Testament, formerly rejected by the critics as a late addition dating from about B.C. 300—the Khammurabi Stele and the 14th chapter of Genesis. The copy of the great Code of Laws drawn up by Khammurabi, King of Babylon (c. B.C. 2200 according to Budge), was discovered at Susa, in the winter of 1901-2. It contains a classified collection of laws, 282 in number, by which the Babylonians were to regulate their affairs. It was set up in Esagila, the temple of Marduk, in Babylon, was carried away by an Elamite King to Susa, and has now been brought to England and placed in the British Museum.

The 14th chapter of Genesis contains an account of an expedition of Chedorlaomer, King of Elam, and his allies, one of whom was Amraphel, King of Shinar, or Southern Babylonia, against the Kings of Sodom and Gomorrah, and their allies, four Kings against five. The account was condemned as unhistorical by the critics, partly because it was said to be incredible that a Babylonian campaign should be waged against a distant country like Palestine at that early age, and partly because the chapter represents a King of Elam as a leader of the invading army.

We now find from the Monuments that before the days of Abraham the Babylonian Kings led their armies as far west as Palestine, and even to Cyprus and Mount Sinai. Further, it is now known that in the time of

Abraham, Babylon was subject to the Aryan Kingdom of Elam and was divided into two states, the Southern one being called Sumer or Shinar, and the Northern one Akkad. The name Chedorlaomer is an Elamite name, meaning servant of the Elamite God Lagamur. Bricks in the British Museum tell us that Chedorlaomer had conquered Babylon, and that Eri-Aku, son of Kudur-Mabug, servant of the Elamite God Mabug, ruled at Larsa. But Eri-Aku of Larsa is Arioch of Ellassar, and Khammurabi of Sumer is Amraphel of Shinar or South Babylonia, whose Code of Laws has just been recovered.

PERIOD II. THE THEOCRACY—*Exodus to 1 Sam. 7.*

(AN. HOM. 2433–2513).

THE Chronology of this period is very simple; it consists of the first two periods, of 40 years each, of Moses' life. The Table is as follows:—

AN. HOM.

Birth of Moses to the Exodus.

2433. Moses born (see Chapter 11).

  40. Add 40 years to flight of Moses (Ex. 2$^{11\text{-}15}$, Acts 7$^{23\text{-}29}$).

2473. Flight of Moses.

  40. Add 40 years to the Exodus when Moses was 80 years old. (Ex. 2^{23}, 7^{7}, Acts 7$^{29\text{-}30}$).

2513. The Exodus.

       Hence Exodus 1^{6}–12$^{40.\ 41}$, from the death of Joseph, AN. HOM. 2369 to the Exodus, AN. HOM. 2513, covers a period of 144 years.

It is definitely stated that Moses was 80 years old when he and Aaron spoke to Pharaoh, and as the narrative is continuous, with no note of time to indicate anything to the contrary, we may conclude that the ten plagues all took place immediately afterwards, and that the Exodus was accomplished that same year. This is confirmed by the fact that 1½ months before the completion of the 40 years in the wilderness Moses died at the age of 120 years.

It is not definitely stated in the Text of the Old Testament that Moses was exactly 40 years old at the date of his flight, but we are told in Ex. 2^{11} that it took place " when Moses was grown," a phrase which meant " when Moses was 40 years of age," just as with us the phrase " coming of age " means arriving at the age of 21. This is the interpretation put upon the words by Stephen in Acts 7^{23}, and on this point he is a credible authority.

But even if we were doubtful as to whether Moses fled to Midian exactly at the age of 40, and led the people out of Egypt at the age of 80, the date of the Exodus would be unaffected by the doubt, and only two intermediate steps in the chronological ladder would be moved up or down, with compensation elsewhere to bring the Exodus down to the year AN. HOM. 2513 as stated in the above Table.

Chapter XIV. The Forty Years in the Wilderness.

(AN. HOM. 2513–2553)

In Chapter 13 we reached the conclusion that the narrative of Ex. 1^{6}–$12^{40.\,41}$ covers a period of 144 years, from the death of Joseph to the Exodus. We have now to show that the remaining portion of the Pentateuch, including the 15 days to the morrow after the Passover, viz. Nisan 15, AN. HOM. 2553 (Josh. $5^{10.\,11}$), of which details are given in Josh. 1^{1}–5^{10}, covers a period of exactly 40 years. The events of this period of 40 years are detailed in the following Tables :—

I. Bible Dates in Exodus $12^{40.\,41}$–40^{38}.

Israel in the Wilderness.

From the Exodus to the erection of the Tabernacle, Ex. $12^{40.\,41}$–40^{38}.

(1) From the Exodus to the wilderness of Sin.

From 15th day, 1st mo. 1st yr., Ex. $12^{2\text{-}6,\ 29\text{-}41}$, Num. 33^{3} .. .. $\left.\begin{array}{l}\\ \\ \\ \end{array}\right\}$ = 1

To 15th day, 2nd mo. 1st yr., Ex. 16^{1}.. .. ..

(2) From the wilderness of Sin to the Giving of the Law on Sinai.

From 15th day, 2nd mo. 1st yr., Ex. 16^{1} .. .. $\left.\begin{array}{l}\\ \\ \end{array}\right\}$ = –

To 15th day, 3rd mo. 1st yr., Ex. $19^{1.\,2}$ .. ..

(3) From the giving of the Law on Sinai to the erection of the Tabernacle.

From 15th day, 3rd mo. 1st yr., Ex. $19^{1.\,2}$ .. .. $\left.\begin{array}{l}\\ \\ \end{array}\right\}$ = $9\frac{1}{2}$

To 1st day, 1st mo. 2nd yr., Ex. 40^{17}.. .. ..

∴. Exodus $12^{40.\,41}$–40 covers a period of .. .. $\overline{11\frac{1}{2}}$

And the whole Book of Exodus covers a period of 144 yrs. $11\frac{1}{2}$ mos.

II. Bible Dates in the Book of Leviticus.

Israel in the Wilderness.

From the erection of the Tabernacle to the first census at Sinai.

From 1st day, 1st mo. 2nd yr., Ex. 40^{17} $\left.\begin{array}{l}\\ \end{array}\right\}$ .. .. 1 month.

To 1st day, 2nd mo. 2nd yr., Numb. 1^{1}

∴. The Book of Leviticus covers a period of 1 month.

III.   Bible Dates in the Book of Numbers.

Israel in the Wilderness.

From the first census at Sinai to the address of Moses in the plains of Moab.

(1) From the first census at Sinai to the sending out of
the spies at Paran.
From 1st day, 2nd mo. 2nd yr., Numb. 1^1 ..
To 20th day, 2nd. mo. 2nd yr., Numb. $10^{11.12}$, $\Big\} = 20$ days.
13^{17-30} ..   ..

(2) From the sending out of the spies at Paran
to the death of Miriam.
From 20th day, 2nd mo. 2nd yr., Numb.
$10^{11.12}$, 13^{17-20} ..   ..   .. $\Big\} = 37$ yrs. 11 mo. 0 days.
To — day, 1st mo. 40th. yr., Numb. 20^1.

(3) From the death of Miriam to the death of Aaron.
From — day, 1st mo. 40th yr., Numb. 20^1
To 1st day, 5th mo. 40th yr., Numb. 20^{28}, $\Big\} = $ 3 mo. 10 days.
$33^{38.39}$ ..   ..

(4) From the death of Aaron to the address of Moses
in the plains of Moab.
From 1st day, 5th mo. 40th yr., Numb.
20^{28}, $33^{38.39}$ ..   ..   .. $\Big\} = $ 6 mo. 0 days.
To 1st day, 11th mo. 40th yr., Deut. 1^3

∴ The Book of Numbers covers a period of .. 38 yrs. 9 months.

IV.   Bible Dates in the Book of Deuteronomy.

(Including the 15 days of Joshua 1^1–5^{10} to complete the 40 years in the
wilderness.)

Israel in the Wilderness.

From the address of Moses in the plains of Moab to the entry into Canaan.

(1) From the address of Moses in the plains of Moab to the death of Moses.
From 1st day, 11th mo. 40th yr. Deut. 1^3 ..   ..
To (say) 1st day, 12th mo. 40th yr. to make up the $\Big\} $ 1 month.
40 yrs. of Numb. 14^{33}, 32^{13}, Josh. 5^6. ..   ..

(2) The 30 days of mourning for Moses.
From 1st day, 12th mo. 40th yr., Numb. 14^{33}, 32^{13},
Josh. 5^6 ..   .. $\Big\} $ 1 month.
To 1st day, 1st mo. 41st yr., Deut. 34^8..   ..   ..

(3) From the end of the 30 days mourning to the entry into Canaan.
From 1st day, 1st mo. 41st yr., Deut. 34^8.
To 14th day, 1st mo. 41st yr., Josh. 1^{11} (3 days),
2^{16} (3 days), 3^1 (1 day), 3^2 (3 days), 4^{19} (10th day), $\Big\} \frac{1}{2}$ month.
5^6 (40 years), 5^{10} (14th day)   ..   ..   ..

∴ The Book of Deuteronomy, including Josh. 1^1–5^{10},
covers a period of   ..   .. $2\frac{1}{2}$ months.

These results enable us to continue the Chronology from the Exodus to the entry into Canaan, as follows :—

The Forty Years in the Wilderness.

AN. HOM.		YRS. MTHS.
2513. The Exodus (see previous Chapter)		
40. Add 40 years, viz. Events of Exodus 12 $^{40, 41}$–40 ..		11½
Events of Leviticus		1
Events of Numbers		38 . 9
Events of Deuteronomy including Josh. 1 ^{1}–5 ^{10}..		2½
2553		40 . 0

CHAPTER XV. THE SEVEN YEARS' WAR.
From the Entry into Canaan to the Division of the Land.
(AN. HOM. 2553–2560)

IN our last Chapter we arrived at the end of the 40 years in the wilderness, the crossing of the Jordan, and the encampment at Gilgal on the 14th day of the 1st month of the year AN. HOM. 2553. " The people came up out of Jordan on the 10th day of the 1st month and encamped in Gilgal " (Josh. 4 ^{19}). At that time the children of Israel who had been born in the wilderness were circumcised (Josh. 5 ^{2}). For the children of Israel walked 40 years in the wilderness (Josh 5 ^{6}) and they encamped in Gilgal and kept the Passover on the 14th day of the month, even in the plains of Jericho. "And they did eat of the old corn of the land on the morrow after the Passover, unleavened cakes and parched corn the selfsame day. And the manna ceased on the morrow after they had eaten of the old corn of the land ; neither had the children of Israel manna any more, but they did eat of the fruit of the land of Canaan that year " (Josh. 5 $^{10-12}$).

The Book of Joshua carries forward the Chronology from the entry into Canaan to the end of the Seven Years' War (at the conclusion of which Joshua divided up the land of Canaan amongst the twelve tribes), but no further.

We are told in Josh. 24 ^{29} that Joshua died at the age of 110 years, but it is not stated how long this was after the division of the Land, and we have no information as to the date of Joshua's birth, so that the date of his death is unknown.

The age of Caleb, however, is given, or rather it may be inferred or obtained by a historical induction, and by this means we arrive at the date of the conclusion of the war of the conquest of Canaan and the division of the Land amongst the twelve tribes, which thereupon immediately ensued.

The date of the Exodus, as we have seen in Chapter 13, is AN. HOM. 2513 (Ex. 12 $^{40, 41}$). The spies were sent out in the 2nd year after the Exodus— " And it came to pass on the 20th day of the 2nd month in the 2nd year, that the cloud was taken up from the Tabernacle of the Testimony. And the children of Israel took their journeys out of the wilderness of Sinai ; and the cloud rested in the wilderness of Paran," Numb. 10 $^{11, 12}$. " So they departed from the mount a three days' journey " (Numb. 10 ^{33}). They murmured, and God sent them quails, of which they ate for a whole month

(Numb. 11 ^{20}). Then Miriam and Aaron spoke against Moses, and Miriam was shut out of the camp for seven days. " And the people journeyed not until Miriam was brought in again " (Numb. 12 ^{15}). And afterward the people removed from Hazeroth and pitched in the wilderness of Paran (Numb. 12 ^{16}). From the wilderness of Paran (Numb. 13 ^{3}) Moses sent out the 12 spies, Numb. 13 ^{17}, " at the time of the first ripe grapes " (Numb. 13 ^{20}), " and they returned from searching the land after 40 days, and they went and came to Moses and Aaron and to all the congregation of the children of Israel into the wilderness of Paran, to Kadesh " (Numb. 13 $^{25\cdot\,26}$) Amongst the number of these 12 spies was Oshea the son of Nun, of the tribe of Ephraim (Numb. 13 ^{8}), whom Moses named Jehoshua (Numb. 13 ^{16}). With Caleb the son of Jephunneh (Numb. 13 $^{6\cdot\,30}$, 14 $^{6-10}$), he brought back a faithful report and endeavoured to still the murmuring of the people when they heard the evil report of the other ten spies (Numb. 13 ^{30}, 14 $^{6\cdot\,10}$).

At this time, viz. in the summer or early autumn of the year AN. HOM. 2515, Caleb was 40 years old. " Forty years old was I when Moses the servant of the Lord sent me from Kadesh-barnea to espy out the land " (Josh. 14 ^{7}). Therefore Caleb was born in the year AN. HOM. 2475. But at the division of the Land (Josh. 13 ^{1}, 14 ^{5}, and 15 ^{1}–19 ^{51}), on the conclusion of the war of conquest (Josh 14 ^{15}) Caleb said, " And now behold the Lord hath kept me alive, as he said, these 45 years, even since the Lord spake this word unto Moses while the children of Israel wandered in the wilderness; and now, lo, I am this day fourscore and five years old " (Josh. 14 ^{10}).

Hence it follows that the division of the Land took place at the end of the war of conquest, when Caleb was 85 years of age, viz. AN. HOM. 2475 + 85 = AN. HOM 2560, and that the war of the conquest of the Land was a Seven Years' War, for from the entry into Canaan in AN. HOM. 2553 (see the previous chapter) to the conclusion of the war. upon which the Land was divided up amongst the 12 Tribes, in the year AN. HOM. 2560, is a period of seven years.

These results may be exhibited in tabular form as follows :—

THE SEVEN YEARS' WAR.

From the Entry into Canaan to the Division of the Land.

(AN. HOM. 2553–2560).

AN. HOM.

2553. The entry into Canaan (see Chapter 14)

Add 7 years to division of the Land, for :—

Exodus (Ex. 12 $^{40\cdot\,41}$) see previous Chapter = 2513

Spies sent out in 2nd year after the Exodus
(Numb. 10 $^{11\cdot\,12}$, 13 $^{17-20}$) .. .. = 2515

At that date Caleb was 40 (Josh. 14 ^{7})

∴ Caleb was born 2515 – 40 .. .. = 2475

But at the division of the Land Caleb
was 85 (Josh. 14 ^{10}).

∴ Division of the Land took place in
2475 + 85 .. .. = 2560

∴ From entry of Canaan to division of

7. Land = 2560 – 2553 = 7 years

2560. Division of the Land at end of Seven Years' War.

CHAPTER XVI. THE JOSHUA-JUDGES CONNECTION.

From the Division of the Land to the Oppression of Cushan = 13 years.
(AN. HOM. 2560–2573).

THE determination of the length of this period has been a great puzzle to the Chronologers. To all of them except the author of the *Companion Bible* it has proved an insoluble problem. Ussher makes it 31 years. He reckons one year for the period from the division of the Land to the death of Joshua, and the election of the Elders (Judges 2[7]), " because from the birth of the promised seed Isaac (AN. HOM. 2108) to this time (AN. HOM. 2561) are reckoned 452 years, and from the rejection of Ishmael (AN. HOM. 2113) to this time (AN. HOM. 2561) 447 years, but between both we may count 450 years."

This is most unsatisfactory, for it not only puts an end to the method of stating the exact year in which an event occurs, the only system which deserves the name of Chronology at all, but it rests upon a forced construction of the passage in Acts 13[17-20], which cannot mean 450 years from the birth or the weaning of Isaac to the entry into Canaan, but must mean 450 years from the completion of the conquest of Canaan, " when he had destroyed seven nations," to the end of the Judgeship of Samuel. The length of the period from the division of the Land to the death of Joshua is nowhere directly stated or implied in Scripture. It cannot, therefore, be directly ascertained.

Ussher reckons an interval of 30 years, or one generation for the anarchy or misrule which succeeded from the death of Joshua to the beginning of the oppression of Cushan. This is not Chronology, if Chronology be a science at all, but the substitution of a good guess, or a subjective impression, for an objective fact, which latter is what we require in all true science.

Clinton fares little better. He says : " After the death of Moses, a chasm occurs in the Scripture Chronology. We are not informed what was the duration of the government of Joshua and the Elders, and of the interregnum or anarchy which followed. The notices of Scripture show that this period was not very long. The division of the Land was 45 years after the 2nd year from the Exode. The time of the anarchy included all the days of the Elders who overlived Joshua (Josh. 24[31]) and lasted till all that generation were gathered to their fathers, and there arose another generation which knew not the Lord (Judges 2[10]). *Caleb and Joshua might be about the same age,* about 40 at the Exode, which would bring the death of Joshua to the 30th year after the death of Moses. He was already old and stricken in years, six years after the death of Moses (Josh. 13[1]). Although the anarchy lasted till the Elders who overlived Joshua were dead, yet Othniel, who was a military leader in the sixth year after the death of Moses (Josh. 15[16. 17], Jud. 1[12. 13]), survived the anarchy 48 years (Jud. 3[8-11]). And Phineas was priest during the anarchy (Jud. 20[28]), who was at least 20 years of age in the last year of Moses, when the priesthood was promised to his posterity. His father Eleazar died soon after the death of Joshua (Josh. 24[33]). The interval then between the death of Moses and the first servitude may be pretty accurately filled, although *the years will be assigned upon conjecture and not upon testimony.*"

This is only another way of abandoning the science of Chronology and substituting for real dates a table of unverifiable conjectures.

Another method equally inadmissible is that of falling back upon the testimony of Josephus, a late compiler of the 1st Century A.D., who had no authentic information of the Chronology of this period beyond that which we ourselves have in the Text of the Old Testament, except those traditional Rabbinical conjectures which he preserves, and which are as inadmissible as the conjectures of the modern guesswork Chronologer.

Josephus makes the period from the death of Moses to the division of the land 5 years; from thence to the death of Joshua 20 years; from thence to the oppression of Cushan 18 years, or a total of 43 years from the death of Moses to the oppression of Cushan. This gives, if we deduct the 7 years from the death of Moses to the division of the Land, a period of 36 years for the Joshua-Judges chasm, from the division of the Land to the oppression of Cushan.

The results given by other Chronologers may be tabulated as follows. They are not obtained from the data afforded by the Text of the Old Testament, but have been arrived at by their own favourite method of subjective hypothesis and conjecture. They are therefore of no authority whatever. The variations between them are very numerous, and very large, another proof of the invalidity of the method by which they have been obtained.

THE JOSHUA-JUDGES CHASM.

From the Division of the Land to the Oppression of Cushan, according to the subjective opinions or guesses of Chronologers Ancient and Modern.

	YEARS.
Willis J. Beecher	11
Petavius	18
Du Fresnoy	19
Clinton	20
Sulpicius Severus	20
Paschal Chronicle	20
Clement of Alexandria	20
Theophilus	20
Eusebius	20 or 23 or 48 or 50
Hales	29
Blair	31
Ussher	31
Henry Browne	36
Des Vignoles	36
Josephus	36
Syncellus	38
A.V. Margin—Bp. Lloyd (B.C. 1444–1402)	42
Africanus	48
Pezron	61
Serrarius	71

All the data for determining the number of the years between the division of the Land and the oppression of Cushan are contained in the text of the Old Testament itself. The number of these years is 13. The honour of the discovery of this fact is due to the author of the *Companion Bible*, a work from which the present writer has obtained many illuminating suggestions. The *Companion Bible* is one of the most scholarly attempts to elucidate the meaning of the Scriptures which has appeared in recent years. It contains some errors, which will probably be removed from the second edition. It is dominated by the millenary idea, and the figures are sometimes bent to make the creation of Adam fall exactly 4,000 years before the actual date of the birth of Christ. The conjectural results suggested in part by *Lumen*, the author of the *Prince of the House of Judah*, and adopted by the author of the *Companion Bible* for the period of Ezra, Nehemiah and Esther, are probably erroneous, but his bold attempt to free the Chronology of the Bible from the tyranny of the Ptolemaic system is one of the many illustrations of the originality of the author's genius, and the keenness of his insight into the meaning of Scripture.

The number of years in the so-called Joshua-Judges chasm from the division of the Land to the oppression of Cushan is 13. This is involved in the length of the long period from the conquest and occupation of Heshbon by Joshua in the year before the entry into Canaan (Deut. 2) to its reconquest by Ammon 300 years later (Jud. 11 [26]). Now we know the length of every constituent portion of this period of 300 years, except the period from the division of the Land to the oppression of Cushan, and they amount altogether to 287 years. Therefore we conclude by an inevitable historical induction that that period must have contained exactly the remaining 13 years.

Before proceeding to the demonstration of this fact, the reader should glance at the bird's-eye view of the content of the Book of Judges given on page 48 in Vol II. in the form of a Table of the 12 Judges and the one usurper King, whose history is recorded in the Book of Judges, with the respective years of servitude, rest, usurpation and Judgeship, and other particulars respecting the twelve Judges.

From this Table it will be seen that the Judgeship of Shamgar was included in the 20 years of the 3rd servitude under Jabin. This is proved by the words of Judges 5 [6, 7]: " In the days of Shamgar the son of Anath, in the days of Jael, the highways were unoccupied, and the travellers walked through byways. The inhabitants of the villages ceased, they ceased in Israel, until that I Deborah arose, that I arose a mother in Israel."

This places the days of Shamgar, which are the days of Jael, in the 20 years of Jabin's servitude, which lasted " until that I Deborah arose," and were brought to a conclusion by the deliverance of Deborah and Barak.

It will also be seen that the 20 years of the Judgeship of Samson are included in the 40 years of the 6th servitude, under the Philistines. This is proved by the words of Judges 15 [20]: " And he judged Israel in the days of the Philistines twenty years." These facts are attested by the same authority as the rest of the facts related as happening during this period, viz. by the writer of the

Book of Judges. This writer was probably Samuel, who, no doubt, obtained all the facts from authentic contemporary records. According to oral tradition, dating perhaps from the very time, but first written down in the 1st Century A.D., in the Talmudic Tract *Baba Bathra*, Samuel wrote the Books of Judges, Ruth, and 1 Samuel 1–24. All the remaining periods of servitude, rest, usurpation and Judgeship in the Book of Judges are strictly consecutive and continuous. They are brought to a conclusion in Judges 16 ^{31}.

1 Samuel 1 resumes the narrative, which has been interrupted by three undated illustrative appendices, and is strictly continuous with the story of Samson and the Philistine servitude of Judges 13–16.

The 40 years of Eli's Judgeship begins where the 40 years of the Philistine servitude ends.

The story of Israel begins with the birth of Abram in Genesis 11. From that point on to the end of 2 Kings it is one continuous story throughout, interrupted by occasional illustrations like the two appendices in Judges 17–21, the Book of Ruth, and the five appendices in 2 Samuel 21–24.

We now return to the demonstration of the fact that the so-called Joshua-Judges chasm, or the period from the division of the Land to the oppression of Cushan, was a period of 13 years.

This is one of the most difficult problems of Old Testament Chronology. It can only be solved by giving the closest attention (1) to the structure of the Book of Judges as a whole ; (2) to the special characteristics of the general statements prefixed to the first four servitudes in Judges 2 $^{11-23}$,. and to the last two servitudes in Judges 10 $^{6-9}$. These are summary or prefatory statements of the nature of a preliminary survey of the whole periods of the four and the two servitudes respectively, with which the writer immediately afterwards proceeds to deal in detail ; and (3) to the structûre of the verse Judges 10 ^{8}. This verse, as it stands in the Hebrew, is an introversion, giving first an event and its time, and then another time and its event. The words " that year " refer to the 1st year of the Judgeship of Jair, in which the children of Ammon " broke and crushed " the children of Israel, and thereby recovered possession of Heshbon, and some part of the land of Israel, which they held during the 22 years of Jair ; whilst the words " eighteen years " refer to the time when, immediately after the death of Jair, they subdued and oppressed " *all* the children of Israel " on both sides of the river Jordan.

The 22 years of Jair will therefore be included in the Chronology as an entire period, complete in itself, and distinct from the 18 years of the 5th servitude under the children of Ammon, by which it is immediately succeeded. But neither of these two periods will be included in the 300 years of Jephthah (Judges 11 ^{26}), because in " that year," the 1st year of Jair, the children of Ammon " broke and crushed " the children of Israel, threw off their yoke, and recovered possession of Heshbon, and other towns, on the east side of Jordan, so that Jephthah could not say that " Israel dwelt in Heshbon and her towns, and in Aroer and her towns, and in all the cities that be along by the coast of Arnon " (Judges 11 ^{26}) at any time during the 22 years of the Judgeship of Jair. Still less could he say that Israel dwelt in these cities at any time during the 18 years of the Ammonite oppression when all Israel, on both sides of the Jordan, was completely subjugated and reduced to a state of servitude by the children of Ammon.

1. *The Structure of the Book of Judges as a whole.*

With regard to the first of these three important considerations, the structure of the Book of Judges as a whole, this will be to some extent apparent from the bird's eye view of the *content* of the Book of Judges given on page 48, in Vol. II, from which it will be seen that the book is a narrative of six apostasies, six servitudes, six cries to God, and six deliverances. The story gathers round the personalities of six deliverers and six other Judges, one Prophetess (Deborah) and one usurper King (Abimelech). The years of servitude, rest after deliverance, usurpation and Judgeship, are in each case unambiguously stated, as also the facts that the deliverance of Shamgar from the Philistines took place during the oppression of Jabin (Jud. 3^{31}, $5^{6.7}$) and that the Judgeship of Samson was exercised during 20 out of the 40 years of the Philistine oppression (Jud. 15^{20}, 16^{31}). The proof of the fact that the Judgeship of Eli is consecutive, and follows on immediately at the close of the 40 years of the sixth servitude under the Philistines, lies in the structure of the Books of Judges, Ruth and 1 Samuel taken together. It is one continuous story throughout. The story is interrupted by three appendices, which are given as detailed or concrete illustrations of the period of the Judges, an outline or skeleton of the history of which has been given in the previous chapters. We have first an illustration of the idolatry of the time, the story of Micah and the Danites (Jud. 17–18). Next an illustration of the immorality of the time, the story of the Levite and the men of Gibeah (Judges 19–21), and, by way of contrast, an idyllic picture of rustic piety and purity in the midst of infidelity and immorality. Then, in 1 Sam 1^{1}, the narrative is resumed. Take out the pictures, and the reading will be seen to be consecutive and continuous. There is, however, a change in the tone of the narrative as we pass from Judges 1–16 into 1 Sam. 1. Judges 1–16 gives the history of the times of the Judges properly so called. 1 Sam. 1–7 gives the history of the transition period from the Theocracy to the Monarchy. The difference is sufficient to account for the insertion of the three appendices, for in 1 Sam. 1 we turn down a page and commence a new chapter in Israel's history. But it must not be forgotten that the whole of the series of historical books from Genesis to 2 Kings is one consecutive, continuous narrative throughout.

In order to make the matter clear we append here a bird's-eye view of the *structure* of the Books of Judges, Ruth and 1 Samuel. This will show the consecutive, continuous character of the whole narrative, and also the transition character of 1 Sam. 1–7. It will also give us a key to the interpretation of the difficult phrase " that year " in Judges 10^{8}. It may be exhibited thus :—

BIRD'S-EYE VIEW OF THE STRUCTURE OF THE BOOK OF JUDGES.

Theocracy.

PART I.—FOUR SERVITUDES.

Jud. 1 ^{1}–2 ^{10}. Introduction.

Jud. 2 $^{11\text{-}23}$. Preliminary survey or summary statement prefixed to the
first four servitudes.

APOSTASY.—The children of Israel did evil in the sight of
the Lord.

SERVITUDE.—And he delivered them into the hands of their
enemies.

CRY TO GOD.—They groaned by reason of them that *broke
and crushed* them.

DELIVERANCE.—The Lord raised up Judges and delivered
them out of the hand of those that spoiled them.

Jud. 3 ^{7}.   The children of Israel did evil.

1st Servitude—Cushan, 8 years. Deliverance—Othniel.
Rest 40 years.

Jud. 3 ^{12}.   The children of Isarel did evil.

2nd Servitude—Eglon, 18 years. Deliverance—Ehud.
Rest 80 years.

(Jud. 3 ^{31}).   Parenthesis.—And after him Shamgar, he also delivered Israel,
viz. during Jabin's oppression (see Jud. 5 $^{6,\ 7}$). This
is not a continuation of the narrative, but an anticipatory summary statement of an event which took place
during the period dealt with in the next paragraph.

Jud. 4 ^{1}.   The children of Israel did evil *when Ehud was dead*. This connects the 80 years of rest by Ehud with the 20 years
of the oppression by Jabin, without leaving any room
for Shamgar's deliverance between these two periods.

3rd Servitude—Jabin, 20 years. Deliverance—Barak.
Rest 40 years.

Jud. 6 ^{1}.   The children of Israel did evil.

4th Servitude—Midian, 7 years. Deliverance—Gideon.
Rest 40 years.

Jud. 8 ^{33}–9 ^{57}. The Story of Abimelech.

Jud. 8 ^{33}. When Gideon was dead Abimelech 3 years.

Jud. 10 $^{1\text{-}5}$. Summary statement of two Judgeships.

Jud. 10 ^{1}. After Abimelech arose Tola.
Judged 23 years. Died and was buried.

Jud. 10 ^{3}. After him arose Jair.
Judged 22 years. Died and was buried.

This last statement is anticipatory. The historian completes his account
of Jair before commencing a new subject, though chronologically he has

only reached the first year of Jair. Cp. 2 Chron. 29$^{1.\ 2}$, a summary statement of the whole of the reign of Hezekiah, followed in verse 3 by a detailed account of it, beginning with the events of the first year.

PART II.—TWO SERVITUDES.

Jud. 10$^{6-16}$. Preliminary survey or summary statement prefixed to the last two servitudes.

> APOSTASY.—The children of Israel did evil in the sight of the Lord.
>
> SERVITUDE.—He sold them into the hands of the Philistines and the children of Ammon.
>> A. And they *broke and crushed* the children of Israel
>>> A. That year (=the 1st year of Jair).
>>> B. Eighteen years (=after the last year of Jair).
>> B. All the children of Israel on both sides of the Jordan.
>
> CRY TO GOD.—The children of Israel cried unto the Lord, saying we have sinned.
>
> REFUSAL TO DELIVER.—Go, cry to the gods which ye have chosen ; let them deliver you.
>
> REPEATED CRY TO GOD.—We have sinned. Deliver us this day only.
>
> RESPONSE.—His soul was grieved for the misery of Israel.

Jud. 10^{17}–12^6. Details of the Ammonite oppression and deliverance by Jephthah.

Jud. 12$^{7-15}$. Summary statement of four Judgeships.

Jud. 12^7.	Jephthah judged Israel 6 yrs., died and was buried				
Jud. 12^8.	Ibzan	,	,, 7	,, ,,	,,
Jud. 12^{11}.	Elon	,,	,, 10	,, ,,	,,
Jud. 12^{13}.	Abdon	,,	,, 8	,, ,,	,,

Jud. 13^1–16^{31}. Details of the Philistine oppression and Judgeship of Samson.

(Jud. 15^{20}). Parenthesis. — Samson judged Israel in the days of the Philistines 20 years.

APPENDICES.

Jud. 17–18. Appendix 1.—Micah and the Danites—Idolatry.

Jud. 19–21. Appendix 2.—The Levite and the men of Gibeah—immorality.

Ruth. Appendix 3.—The story of Ruth—piety and purity in the midst of infidelity and immorality.

Transition to Monarchy.

1 Sam. 1–7. Judgeships of Eli and Samuel.

Monarchy.

1 Sam. 8–2 K. Saul, David and Solomon, and the Kings of Israel and Judah.

2. *The Special Character of the Summary Statements, Jud.* 2$^{11-23}$ *and* 10$^{6-9}$.

From this analysis of the structure of the Book of Judges it will be seen that it is divided into two parts, each commencing with a summary statement of the fourfold cycle of events—apostasy, servitude, cry to God, deliverance —which are thereafter described in detail.

The difficult verse, Judges 10^8, occurs not in the continuous, consecutive narrative, but in the preliminary survey or summary statement of the last two servitudes, which are first mentioned together, and afterwards narrated in detail, the Ammonite oppression first, and then the Philistine. Though mentioned together in this summary way, they are two distinct servitudes, not one only, and they are consecutive, not contemporary.

3. *The Structure of the Verse Judges* 10^8.

Jair was a Gileadite. He had 30 sons that rode on 30 ass colts, a sign of princely rank and governmental authority ; and they had 30 cities called Havoth-Jair, or the villages of Jair, in the land of Gilead. It is not said that Jair *delivered* Israel, but only that he judged Israel 22 years, but in Judges 2^{18} we read that " when the Lord raised them up Judges then the Lord was with the Judge, and delivered them out of the hand of their enemies all the days of the Judge," so that, although it is not said that the Lord " raised up " Jair, but only that he " arose," it is most probable that the writer means us to understand that the Ammonites " broke and crushed " the children of Israel in the first year of Jair in such a way that they were able to recover Heshbon and the territory to the south allotted to Reuben, but not Gilead and the territory to the north allotted to Gad, and not any of the rest of the of the Land of Israel, until the death of Jair, when they crossed the Jordan and completely subjected all Israel on both sides of the river and oppressed them for 18 years until deliverance came by Jephthah.

The exact translation of the Hebrew of Judges 10^{8,9} is as follows :—

v. 8. A. And they broke and crushed the children of Israel
      A. In that year (=the first year of Jair).
      B. Eighteen years (=after the last year of Jair).
   B. All the Children of Israel who were beyond Jordan in the Land of the Amorites which is in Gilead.

v. 9. " And the Children of Ammon crossed over the Jordan to fight even against Judah and against Benjamin, and against the house of Ephraim, and Israel had great distress."

The construction of verse 8 is very difficult. The second sentence commencing with the words " eighteen years " begins very abruptly, and is elliptical, its verb having to be supplied from the first sentence. The meaning of this second sentence is expanded in the following verse. No other interpretation of the words makes the meaning more clear than that adopted above.

This interpretation, which makes the 22 years of Jair and the Ammonite oppression two complete and consecutive periods without any overlapping of the one by the other, is corroborated by the reckoning of St. Paul, who in Acts 13 [19, 20], gives a total of about 450 years for the period from the division of the Land by lot to the end of the Judgeship of Samuel. The figure is the exact sum of the number of years attributed to the servitudes, the years of rest, the usurpation and the Judgeships given in Judges and 1 Samuel 1–7, from the oppression of Cushan to the end of the Judgeship of Samuel, reckoning the 20 years of 1 Sam. 7 [2] as the length of the Judgeship of Samuel. But as the number of years for the so-called Joshua-Judges chasm, from the division of the Land to the oppression of Cushan, is not specified in the Old Testament, and must have occupied some years, St. Paul allows an indefinite addition to the 450 years by prefixing to it the word " about."

This interpretation is further corroborated by the fact that the 13 years which it gives to the so-called Joshua-Judges chasm, from the division of the Land to the 1st servitude under Cushan, makes up the years of the Theocracy from the Exodus to the 4th year of Solomon (omitting the six servitudes and the usurpation of Abimelech) to exactly 480 years, as stated in 1 Kings 6 [1].

This interpretation of Jud. 10 [8] is further supported by the fact that the only possible alternative interpretation of the words " that year," which makes them refer to the *last* year of Jair, would leave not a single year for the interval between the division of the Land and the oppression of Cushan. We may, therefore, regard the interpretation which makes " that year " in Jud. 10 [8] the *first* year of Jair as correct.

The determination of the length of the so-called Joshua-Judges Chasm, or the interval between the division of the Land and the oppression of Cushan, will then be arrived at in the manner indicated in the following Table.

K

THE SO-CALLED JOSHUA-JUDGES CHASM.

From the Division of the Land (Jud. 2⁶) to the beginning of the 1st Servitude under Cushan (Jud. 3⁸).

PERIODS.	years.	years.	years.
From the Conquest of Heshbon to its re-conquest by Ammon, probably in the 1st year of Jair (Jud. 10 $^{3\text{-}8}$, 11 ^{26}) ..			300
DEDUCT.			
From Conquest of Heshbon to Entry (Ex. 12 $^{40\cdot 41}$, 40 ^{17}, Deut. 2 $^{14\text{-}37}$, Josh. 4 ^{19}, 5 ^{6})		1	
From Entry to Division of Land, 2253–2260		7	
[Here follows the so-called Joshua-Judges Chasm]			
From 1st Servitude, under Cushan, to 1st Year of Jair, viz. :—			
1st Servitude, under Cushan (Jud. 3⁸)	8		
Rest by Othniel (Jud. 3 ^{11})	40		
2nd Servitude, under Eglon (Jud. 3 ^{14})	18		
Rest by Ehud (Jud. 3 ^{30})	80		
Judgeship of Shamgar (Jud. 3 ^{31}) included in 3rd Servitude under Jabin (Jud. 5 $^{6\text{-}7}$)			
3rd Servitude, under Jabin (Jud. 4 ^{3})	20		
Rest by Barak (Jud. 5 ^{31})	40		
4th Servitude, under Midian (Jud. 6 ^{1})	7		
Rest by Gideon (Jud. 8 ^{28})	40		
Usurpation of Abimelech (Jud. 9 ^{22})	3		
Judgeship of Tola (Jud. 10 ^{2})	23	279	287
∴ The so-called Joshua-Judges Chasm, from the Division of the Land to the 1st Servitude under Cushan .. .. } =			13

We may now add to our Chronology the following additional link :—

AN. HOM.

2560. Division of the Land (see Chapter 15).

   13. Add 13 years, to the 1st Servitude under Cushan (Jud. 3⁸) as determined by the above Table.

2573. Beginning of 1st Servitude under Cushan.

CHAPTER XVII. THE JUDGES INCLUDING SAMUEL = 450 YEARS.

(AN. HOM. 2573–3023)

THE following Table exhibits the Chronology of the period of the Judges, from the 1st servitude under Cushan to the election of Saul. The years of servitude, rest, usurpation, and Judgeship, are set out in four different columns, and it will be seen that the four totals amount to exactly 450 years. St. Paul, in his address at Antioch in Pisidia, says : " He divided their land to them by lot. And after that he gave unto them Judges about the space of 450 years until (ἕως = up to and including) Samuel the Prophet." Acts 13 $^{19\cdot 20}$. Here again the minutest accuracy is observed.

It will be seen that the number of the years from the oppression of Cushan to the end of Samuel's Judgeship is not " about," but exactly 450 years.

St. Paul is, however, quite right in using the word "about," and he was compelled to use it in order to be accurate, because the period of which he is speaking is the period from the division of the Land to the end of the Judgeship of Samuel. It includes, therefore, the so-called Joshua-Judges chasm of 13 years, and as this is not specified in the Text of the Old Testament, and not included in the 450 years that are specified, St. Paul is obliged to allow for this space, and he does so quite naturally and quite accurately by describing this period as a period of " *about* 450 years."

ISRAEL UNDER THE JUDGES.

From the 1st Servitude, under Cushan to the Election of Saul.

PERIODS.	Servi-tude.	Rest.	Usur-pation.	Judge-ship.
1st Servitude, under Cushan	8	—	—	—
Rest by Othniel ..	—	40	—	—
2nd Servitude, under Eglon	18	—	—	—
Rest by Ehud ..	—	80	—	—
(Judgeship of Shamgar included in 3rd Servitude, under Jabin, Jud. 3^{31}, $5^{6, 7}$)	—	—	—	—
3rd Servitude, under Jabin	20	—	—	—
Rest by Barak ..	—	40	—	—
4th Servitude, under Midian	7	—	—	—
Rest by Gideon	—	40	—	—
Usurpation of Abimelech	—	—	3	—
Judgeship of Tola	—	—	—	23
Judgeship of Jair	—	—	—	22
5th Servitude, under Ammon	18	—	—	—
Judgeship of Jehptah	—	—	—	6
Judgeship of Ibzan	—	—	—	7
Judgeship of Elon	—	—	—	10
Judgeship of Abdon	—	—	—	8
6th Servitude, under the Philistines..	40	—	—	—
(Judgeship of Samson included in 6th Servitude, under the Philistines, Jud. 15^{20})	—	—	—	—
Judgeship of Eli	—	—	—	40
Judgeship of Samuel	—	—	—	20
(N.B.—1 Sam. 7^{13-17} is a Review, not a continuation of the history)				
Totals	111	200	3	136

THE WHOLE PERIOD OF THE JUDGES.

Years of Servitude	111
Years of Rest	200
Years of Usurpation	3
Years of Judgeship	136
	450

We are now in a position to continue the Chronology from the 1st servitude, under Cushan, to the election of Saul, and this is done in the following Table :—

CHRONOLOGY OF THE PERIOD OF THE JUDGES.

From the 1st Servitude, under Cushan to the Election of Saul.

AN. HOM.

2573. 1st Servitude, under Cushan (see Chapter 16).

   8. Add 8 years' Servitude under Cushan (Jud. 3 ^{8}).

2581. Rest by Othniel.

  40. Add 40 years' Rest by Othniel (Jud. 3 ^{11}).

2631. 2nd Servitude, under Eglon.

  18. Add 18 years' Servitude under Eglon (Jud. 3 ^{14}).

2639. Rest by Ehud.

      Judgeship of Shamgar (Jud. 3 ^{31}) included in 20 years of 3rd
        Servitude, under Jabin (Jud. 5 $^{6, 7}$).

  80. Add 80 years' Rest by Ehud (Jud. 3 ^{30}).

2719. 3rd Servitude, under Jabin.

  20. Add 20 years' Servitude under Jabin (Jud. 4 ^{3}).

2739. Rest by Barak.

  40. Add 40 years' Rest by Barak (Jud. 5 ^{31}).

2779. 4th Servitude, under Midian.

   7. Add 7 years' Servitude under Midian (Jud. 6 ^{1}).

2786. Rest by Gideon.

  40. Add 40 years' Rest by Gideon (Jud. 8 ^{28}).

2826. Usurpation by Abimelech.

   3. Add 3 years' Usurpation of Abimelech (Jud. 9 ^{22}).

2829. Judgeship of Tola.

  23. Add 23 years' Judgeship of Tola (Jud. 10 ^{2}).

2852. Judgeship of Jair.

  22. Add 22 years' Judgeship of Jair (Jud. 10 ^{3}).

2874. 5th Servitude, under Ammon.

  18. Add 18 years' Servitude under Ammon (Jud. 10 ^{8}).

2892. Judgeship of Jephthah.

   6. Add 6 years' Judgeship of Jephthah (Jud. 12 ^{7}).

2898. Judgeship of Ibzan.

   7. Add 7 years' Judgeship of Ibzan (Jud. 12 ^{9}).

2905. Judgeship of Elon.

  10. Add 10 years' Judgeship of Elon (Jud. 12 ^{11}).

2915. Judgeship of Abdon.

   8. Add 8 years' Judgeship of Abdon (Jud. 12 ^{14}).

2923. 6th. Servitude, under the Philistines.

      Judgeship of Samson 20 years (Jud. 16 ^{31}) included in 40 years
        of 6th Servitude, under Philistines (Jud. 15 ^{20}).

2923. 6th Servitude, under the Philistines.
  40. Add 40 years' Servitude under Philistines (Jud. 13 [1]).
2963. Judgeship of Eli.
  40. Add 40 years' Judgeship of Eli (1 Sam. 4 [18]).
3003. Judgeship of Samuel.
  20. Add 20 years' Judgeship of Samuel, 1 Sam. 7 [2]. (N.B.—1 Sam. 7 [13-17]
      is a review, not a continuation of the history).
3023. Election of Saul.

CHAPTER XVIII. THE ELI-SAMUEL CONNECTION.

From the Death of Eli to the beginning of the Reign of Saul = 20 years.

(AN. HOM. 3003–3023)

THE so-called Joshua-Judges chasm fills the interval between the last dated event of the Seven Years' War of conquest, viz. the division of the Land by Joshua and the first dated event of the 450-year Period of the Judges, viz. the oppression of Cushan. It is determined with great difficulty, by means of [the fact implied in Jephthah's message to the children of Ammon (Jud. 11 [14-28]).

The argument of Jephthah is this. The children of Ammon were dispossessed by the Amorites, not by the children of Israel. The children of Israel obtained their title to the land by the conquest of Sihon, the Amorite King of Heshbon, which took place in the year before the entry into Canaan, when they took possession of " all the coasts of the Amorites from Arnon even unto Jabbok."

The right of conquest had been supported and maintained by the fact of the uninterrupted possession of the land in spite of the attack of Balak, King of Moab, to wrest it from them, which had failed. The Lord God of Israel had dispossessed the Amorites and given the land to Israel and their claim had been made good by their uninterrupted possession of it for a period of 300 years from the conquest of Heshbon in the year before the entry into Canaan to " that year," the year in which the children of Ammon " broke and crushed " the children of Israel and recovered the territory which Israel had taken from the Amorites, but which the children of Ammon now claimed as originally belonging to them.

With great difficulty, but with a considerable degree of historic certainty we have fixed upon an interpretation of the words " that year " in Jud. 10 [8], which identifies it with the first year of Jair, the year which immediately succeeded, but which was not included in the 300 years of Jephthah.

We now approach the discussion of another chronological problem of almost equal difficulty and complexity, and one which has given rise to an equal number of divergent interpretations or rather, " guesses at truth," there being no *direct statement* as to the exact length of the period from the death of Eli to the end of Samuel's Judgeship at the election of Saul.

The determination of the number of years in this period *which coincides exactly with the administration of Samuel* is, however, quite simple and quite decisive. The administration of Samuel occupies the interval of those twenty years mentioned in I Sam. 7[2].

These years include the fraction of the year during which the Ark was for 7 months in the land of the Philistines, and the whole period of its stay at Kirjath-jearim down to the battle of Mizpeh, at which the Philistines were defeated and the cities which they had taken from Israel were restored to Israel from Gath even to Ekron.

Whereupon the people began that clamour for a King which led to the election of Saul.

This interpretation is necessitated by a proper understanding of the structure of I Samuel 7. The analysis of the chapter by Professor Henry Preserved Smith into two sections derived from two sources or documents, is in the highest degree subjective and fanciful, and rests upon no assured basis of objective fact. He assumes the existence of an " Eli document " which begins with I Sam. 4 or 5, and extends to the end of I Sam. 7[2], the phrase " for it was 20 years " being eliminated by Stenning as a subsequent interpolation or addition by a late redactor. The rest of the chapter Prof. H. P. Smith regards as derived from a " Samuel document," the symbol for which is the abbreviation Sm., whilst Stenning makes I Sam. 7[2]-8[22] the work of a second Elohistic narrator, who is designated by the symbol E[2].

An analysis of the structure of the chapter shows that the first verse belongs to the narrative contained in Chapter 6. There is no reason to doubt the uncontradicted tradition preserved in the Talmudic Tract *Baba Bathra,* that the author of the first 24 chapters of this book was Samuel himself, and there is no real ground for the assumption of interpolations and later additions by subsequent editors of the Book and redactors of its text. At verse 2 a new epoch is reached and a new subject is introduced, and this should have been marked by the division of the chapter, or the placing of a paragraph mark (¶) at this point.

The author proceeds to tell the story of the first great religious revival brought about by the 20 years of Samuel's quiet, unobtrusive, but pervasive religious teaching, at the close of which the people returned to God, and under the leadership of Samuel obtained a great victory over their enemies at Mizpeh, and thus recovered their independence (I Sam. 7[2-12]).

This brings the narrative of the Judgeship of Samuel to a close, and the next consecutive event is the rejection of the Theocracy and the demand for the appointment of a king in I Sam. 8.

But before finally dismissing the closing period of the Theocracy, the author sums up in a few brief and pregnant sentences the whole story of the Judgeship of Samuel, down to the appointment of King Saul, and intimates that not only down to that point but beyond it, even all the days of his life, Samuel continued to act as Judge. The summary of the Judgeship of Samuel is contained in I Sam. 7[13-17]. Like the summary of the reign of Saul, in I Sam. 14[47-52], it is retrospective and prospective, not continuous. It tells us that the hand of the Lord had been against the Philistines all the days of Samuel, and that this antagonism had now culminated in the great victory at Mizpeh, as a result of which the cities which the Philistines had taken from Israel were restored to Israel, and a period of peace ensued, during which the Philistines came no more into the land of Israel.

This summary statement also tells us something of the method of Samuel's administration. He was accustomed to go on circuit from Bethel to Gilgal, and from Gilgal to Mizpeh, after which he returned to his home at Ramah, where he established a centre of religious worship, and where he exercised his function as Israel's Judge all the days of his life, for he continued his work as Judge even after the appointment of King Saul.

Since 1 Sam. 7^{13-17} is a retrospective and prospective summary of the administration of Samuel, the continuity of the narrative will be exhibited by connecting 1 Sam. 8^4, the gathering of the Elders to Samuel to demand a King, with 1 Sam. 7^{12}, the setting up of the stone Ebenezer in memory of the great victory at Mizpeh, and the period of 20 years named in 1 Sam. 7^2 must be interpreted as covering the whole period of Samuel's administration previous to the victory of Mizpeh and the election of Saul, by which it was immediately followed.

This result is obtained from a close attention to the structure of the chapter. It is obtained from a careful consideration of the statements made in the Text itself, and it may be accepted as a true exposition of the author's intention and meaning.

But it does not stand alone. It is corroborated, and indeed necessitated, by the figures given by St. Paul in Acts 13^{19-20}, in which he states that the period from the division of the Land up to and including ($\tilde{\epsilon}\omega\varsigma$) Samuel was a period of about 450 years. The word "about" is introduced to cover the period between the division of the Land and the oppression of Cushan.

The 450 years is made up of the 19 figures specified in the Book of Judges (including 1 Sam. 1–7,) as the number of years contained in each of the six servitudes, the four periods of rest, the one usurpation of Abimelech and the remaining eight Judgeships, of which the last is the Judgeship of Samuel, and which must have been a period of 20 years, as otherwise the years of the period as defined by St. Paul would not have amounted to the total of 450 years.

There can be no doubt that, whether the Apostle Paul was right or wrong, in the figures which he gives, he obtained them by the process of simple addition. He took each figure as it is given in the text of the Old Testament narrative of the period under review, and the result was as follows. Nobody can make it either one year more or one year less :—

Details of the 450 years of St. Paul in Acts 13^{20}.

		YEARS.
Cushan	.. ..	8
Othniel	.. ..	40
Eglon	.. ..	18
Ehud..	.. ..\ ..	80
Jabin	.. ..	20
Barak	.. ..	40
Midian	.. ..	7
Gideon	.. ..	40
Abimelech	.. ..	3
Tola ..	.. ..	23
Jair ..	.. ..	22
Ammon	.. ..	18
Jephthah	.. ..	6
Ibzan..	.. ..	7
Elon ..	.. ..	10
Abdon	.. ..	8
Philistines	.. ..	40
Eli ..	.. ..	40
Samuel	.. ..	20

Total 450 years.

This result is further corroborated by its agreement with the total of 480 years given in 1 Kings 6^{1}, which is made up of all the figures given for the various periods of the history from the Exodus to the commencement of the building of the Temple in the 4th year of Solomon, always omitting the years of the six servitudes, and the one usurpation, as not to be included in the reckoning of the years of Isra-El, governed by God, and also the years of Shamgar's Judgeship, as falling within the period of the oppression of Jabin, and those of Samson as falling within the period of the oppression of the Philistines.

The Table on p. 49, in Vol. II, Chronological Tables, gives a complete view of the entire period of the Judges, apportioning the number of years assigned to each period in the Text of the Old Testament, and showing its agreement with the number of years in the longer periods of the 300 and the 480 years specified in the Old Testament, and the 450 years specified in the New Testament.

CHAPTER XIX. COMPARATIVE CHRONOLOGY—MOSES TO SAMUEL.

THE so-called Samuel or Eli-Saul chasm, which fills the interval between the last year of Eli and the 1st of Saul, has been as great a puzzle to the Chronologers as the so-called Joshua-Judges chasm.   They all persist in the error of supposing that the period is not definitely implied in the statements of the Old Testament, and they either fall back upon Josephus or some other unauthoritative source, or else proceed to fill the gap by setting down the figure which appeals most strongly to their own imagination.   The result is the production of an immense variety of discordant figures obtained by guesswork, all alike destitute of any semblance of authority or value. The following Table may be compared with the list of guesses hazarded by Chronologers, ancient and modern, as to the length of the period of the so-called Joshua-Judges chasm, given in Chap. 16.

Eli-Saul Connection.

From the Death of Eli to the beginning of the Reign of Saul.
According to the subjective opinions of Chronologers, ancient and modern,
or as Clinton phrases it, as " variously supplied by conjecture."

	YEARS.
Jewish Chronicle (included in reign of Saul)	0
Eusebius	0
Petavius	0
Clement of Alexandria	0 or 9
Theophilus	12 or 23
Josephus (Eli and Saul=52)	12 or 23
De Tournemine in Du Fresnoy	20
Syncellus	20 or 40
Ussher (Eli omitted as contemporary with Philistine Servitude)	21
Hales (Eli and Samuel=72)	32
Clinton (32 years are not too much to assume)	32
Africanus	38 or 50 or 108
Willis J. Beecher (Waiting 20, Samuel 19)	39
Companion Bible	40
Jackson	41
A.V. Margin=Bishop Lloyd (B.C. 1141–1095)	46
Paschal Chronicle	60

This method of writing history, which records only those facts and dates which lie on the surface, leaving the gaps between them to be " supplied by conjecture," is not one that will commend itself to the modern student of Biblical Chronology.

History and geography are descriptive Sciences. They are not, like physics, chemistry and biology, *general* Sciences in which hypotheses are allowable, because they can always be tested and verified or disproved by observation and experiment. The Sciences of history and geography depend entirely on direct observation and testimony, and where that is wanting they lose the character of Sciences altogether, unless the problems encountered can be solved by historical induction from well attested facts from which the information required can be deduced by way of inference. It is in this manner alone that the problems of Biblical Chronology can be solved, and the Joshua-Judges, the Samuel and other apparent chasms in the continuity of the Chronology bridged over.

It is for this purpose that the long periods of Scripture are given ; to them recourse must be had in every case in which there is a break in the continuity of the dates given in the narrative of the history. The result will show that every gap or chasm in the Old Testament history can be bridged over, and that the materials given in the Text of the Old Testament are sufficient to construct a continuous Chronology of dated events from the creation of Adam to the " cutting off " of the Messiah, without recourse to any outside source of information, or to the adoption of problematical results " supplied by conjecture."

The 480 years of 1 Kings 6[1].

The long period of 480 years mentioned in 1 Kings 6[1] has occasioned a considerable amount of perplexity. Some Chronologers, like Ussher, have adopted it into their chronological system and thereby vitiated their entire scheme from that point onward to the extent of 114 years. Others, like Jackson, Hales and Clinton, regard it as " a forgery foisted into the Text," and reject it altogether. Others, again, have not only accepted the number 480 as authentic, and bent the Chronology of the Old Testament to make it accord with this figure, but they have even ventured upon the task of correcting St. Paul, and emended the Text of the New Testament in Acts 13[17-20] in order to bring it into accord with the 480 years of 1 Kings 6[1].

This " amended," or rather this corrupted Text, is the basis of the translation of Acts 13[17-20] in the Revised Version, a rendering which absolutely precludes the possibility of putting any intelligible construction on the words of Acts 13[19-20].

The Authorised Version translates the true Text of ςTi. D[2], E, H, L, P, and many others, item D*d., syr., ar., æth., " when He had destroyed seven nations in the land of Canaan, He divided their land to them by lot. And after that He gave unto them Judges about the space of 450 years until Samuel the prophet."

The Revised Version translates the " emended " Text of Gb[1]א A, B, C, and 7 cursives, which yields this nonsense, " when He had destroyed seven nations in the land of Canaan, He gave them their land for an inheritance for about 450 years ; and after these things He gave them Judges until Samuel the prophet."

The great blot of the R.V. throughout the New Testament, is the overrating of the authority of Westcott and Hort's pet MSS. א and B., two MSS. regarded as amongst the earliest and best authorities by one school of Textual critics led by Westcott and Hort, but really two faulty copies carelessly made by Eusebius for the Emperor Constantine, containing numerous errors, and by no means worthy to be adopted as a standard Text, as is clearly proved by an opposing school of Textual critics led by Burgon and Scrivener.

How could St. Paul have been guilty of perpetrating a sentence which limits the inheritance of the Land by the people of Israel to the time of Eli, and then placing the period of the 14 Judges between Eli and Samuel! Fortunately, the Authorised Version adheres to the better MS. authorities, and gives not only an intelligible but also a true rendering of Paul's great speech at Antioch in Pisidia.

We will first prove (I) that the true extent of the period from the Exodus to the 4th year of Solomon is 594 years : (1) from the Text of the Old Testament, and (2) from the address of St. Paul at Antioch recorded in the New Testament (Acts 13[17-20]).   We will then explain (II) the nature of the mistake of Ussher, who is followed in this matter by Bishop Lloyd, in the dates given in the margin of the A.V., and finally we will explain (III) the real significance of the phrase " the 480th year," as used by the author of the Text, 1 Kings 6[1], and the exact meaning which he intended to convey thereby.

1. *From the Exodus to the 4th year of Solomon* = 594 *years.*

I. And first the true extent of the period which lies between the two epochs, the Exodus and the 4th year of Solomon, in which the building of the Temple was commenced, is 594 years.   Our first step is (1) to prove the accuracy of this figure (594 years) from the Text of the Old Testament.   The Table of the 25 dated events of the 480 years of 1 Kings 6[1], given on p. 49, in Vol. II, contains full details of the entire period, together with the chapter and verse references which prove the truth of the number assigned to each dated event, except the 13 years of the Joshua-Judges connection and the 20 years, of the Eli-Saul connection, detailed proof of the length of which is given in chapters 16 and 18.   The Table is as follows :—

Chronology of the Period from the Exodus to the 4th year of Solomon.

(1) *According to the Old Testament.*

1. The Wilderness Period	40	years.
2. The Seven Years' War	7	,,
3. The Joshua-Judges Connection	13	,,
4. 1st Servitude (Cushan)	8	,,
5. Rest by Othniel	40	,,
6. 2nd Servitude (Eglon)	18	,,
7. Rest by Ehud	80	,,
Judgeship of Shamgar included in 3rd Servitude (Jabin)	—	
8. 3rd Servitude (Jabin)	20	,,
9. Rest by Barak	40	,,
10. 4th Servitude (Midian)	7	,,
11. Rest by Gideon	40	,,
12. Usurpation of Abimelech	3	,,
13. Judgeship of Tola	23	,,
14. Judgeship of Jair	22	,,
15. 5th Servitude (Ammon)	18	,,
16. Judgeship of Jephthah	6	,,
17. Judgeship of Ibzan	7	,,
18. Judgeship of Elon	10	,,
19. Judgeship of Abdon	8	,,
20. 6th Servitude (Philistines)	40	,,
Judgeship of Samson included in 6th Servitude (Philistines)	—	
21. Judgeship of Eli	40	,,
22. Eli-Saul Connection = Judgeship of Samuel	20	,,
23. Reign of Saul	40	,,
24. Reign of David	40	,,
25. Reign of Solomon to 4th year	4	,,
Total	594	,,

Our next step is to prove the accuracy of this figure (594 years), from the address of St. Paul at Antioch, in Pisidia, recorded in Acts 13 [17-22] so far as it covers the same ground.

Chronology of the Period from the Exodus to the 4th year of Solomon.

(2) *According to St. Paul in Acts* 13 [17-22].

PERIODS.	Years stated by St. Paul.	Years omitted by St. Paul.
1. The Wilderness Period	40	—
2. The Seven Years' War	—	7
3. Division of the Land to 1st Servitude (Cushan)	—	13
4. After that He gave unto them Judges, until (= $\check{\epsilon}\omega\varsigma$ i.e., up to and including) Samuel the Prophet..	450	—
5. Saul	40	—
6. David	—	40
7. Solomon, to his 4th year	—	4
Period covered by St. Paul's statement	530	64
Period omitted from St. Paul's statement	64	
Total ..	594	

The ground covered by St. Paul's figures alone exceeds the 480 years of 1 Kings 6 [1], to which has to be added the whole of the 40 years of the reign of David and three smaller periods, which brings the total for the entire period up to 594 years, in exact accordance with the text of the Old Testament.

2. *Ussher's mistaken Interpretation of* 1 *Kings* 6 [1].

II. We now proceed to explain the nature of the mistake of Ussher, whose dates were first printed, with some slight modifications, in the margin of the A.V. in Bishop Lloyd's Bible, published A.D. 1701. The dates in the margin of the A.V. are in the main exceedingly accurate and reliable. Those in the margin of the Book of Genesis are correct to the last detail. Ussher's dates are seriously astray only (1) in respect of this period, which Ussher assumes to be a period of 480 instead of 594 years, an error of 114 years which vitiates to that extent all previous dates expressed in terms B.C., and all subsequent dates expressed in terms A.M. or AN. HOM.; (2) in respect of the period of Ezra, Nehemiah and Esther, perhaps the most difficult and perplexing chronological period in the whole of the Old Testament; and (3) in the marginal note to 2 Kings 15 [1], in accordance with which Ussher abridges the Chronology by a period of 11 years, by dating the accession of Uzziah (Azariah) from the 16th year of Jeroboam II instead of from his 27th year, thereby omitting an interregnum of 11 years after the reign of Amaziah of Judah, and reducing the interregnum after Jeroboam II of Israel from 22 years to 11 years.

Ussher's method of reckoning the Chronology of the Judges abridges the period from the division of the Land to the accession of Saul by exactly 114

years.   This is done intentionally and purposely, the object being to cut off 114 of the 594 years between the Exodus and the 4th year of Solomon in order to c rowd all the events between these points into the 480 years of 1 Kings 6 [1].
Ussher's error in this period may be tabulated as follows :—

Chronology of the Period from the Exodus to the 4th year of Solomon.

Table of Ussher's Mistakes.

	YEARS.		TOO MUCH.	TOO LITTLE.
Joshua-Judges Connection	.. 31 instead of 13	= 18		—
Rest by Othniel	.. 62	,, 40	= 22	—
Rest by Ehud	.. 20	,, 80	= —	60
Rest by Barak	.. 33	,, 40	= —	7
Rest by Gideon	.. 9	,, 40	= —	31
Abimelech	.. 4	,, 3	= 1	—
Jair	.. 4	,, 22	= —	18
Eli contemporary with the Philistine Servitude	0	,, 40	= —	40
Eli-Saul Connection (Samuel Judgeship) ..	21	,, 20	= 1	—
			42	156
Deduct errors in excess				42
Net abridgement of the Chronology				114

Ussher's dates are quite correct down to the division of the Land, AN. HOM. 2560 = B.C. 1444 (Josh. 14 [1], A.V. margin).   He then omits these 114 years in order to square his Chronology with the 480 years of 1 Kings 6 [1].   In order to secure this result he assumes that the figures for some of the periods of rest are figures that include the years of the previous servitude, and that the Judgeship of Eli is contemporary with the Philistine oppression.   Consequently his date for the accession of Saul is AN. HOM. 2909 = B.C. 1095 (1 Sam. 11 [14], A.V. margin) instead of the true date which is AN. HOM. 3023, or just 114 years later than Ussher's date.

3. *The real Significance of the Phrase "the 480th year," in* 1 *Kings* 6 [1].

III. We now turn to the examination of the real significance of the phrase " the 480th year " as used by the author in 1 Kings 6 [8], with a view to ascertaining the exact meaning which he intended to convey to his readers by the use of it.
The Text is undoubtedly genuine, though many attempts have been made to alter, or to get rid of it.   Thus the LXX. has " the 440th year."   Jackson regards the number 480 as spurious.   Clinton rejects it.   Hales boldly declares it to be " a forgery foisted into the Hebrew Text."
The indefatigable Petavius, on the contrary, not only adhered to the Hebrew verity, reprobating every departure from or emendation of the Massoretic Text, but actually pronounced an anathema against those " who dared to assert that the number 480 years was corrupt."

A glance at the Table of the 480 years of 1 Kings 6 [1] (see Vol. II, Chronological Tables, p. 49) will at once disclose the fact that the number 480 is arrived at by omitting from the 594 years of the entire period, the 111 years of the six servitudes and the 3 years of the usurpation of Abimelech.

The writer is not computing the Chronology of the world.   He is computing the Chronology of Isra-El, i.e. of the chosen people as *Governed-by-God*, in other words, he is computing the years of the Theocracy that lie between these two crucial epochs, the Exodus at which it began and the commencement of the building of the Temple; at the dedication of which, just 10 years later, the full cycle of seventy-sevens of these Theocratic years was completed.   The dedication of the Temple is manifestly an event of first-rate importance in the history of the religion of Israel, and in the relation of Israel to the government of Jehovah.

Hebrew names compounded of the passive participle and the Divine name El, are intended to immortalize that special form of the activity of God which the action of the verb denotes.   At Peni-El, " faced by God," Jacob the " heeler," who had outwitted Esau and outbargained Laban, and prevailed with men, became Isra-El, " *Governed-by-God*."   Similarly Samu-El, " heard by God," denotes a child of prayer (1 Sam. 1 [20]) and a man of prayer (1 Sam. 7 [9], 8 [6], 12 [19-23], 15 [11]; Ps. 99 [6]; Jer. 15 [1]).   Dani-El, " judged by God," a man whose judgment is not his own but God's.

Why, then, are these 114 years of servitude and usurpation omitted? Because the author is computing the years of the Theocracy, of the government of God, of Isra-El, and during those years Israel was not Isra-El, not governed by God, but under the heel of the oppressor and the usurper.   Hence they are not included in the Theocratic years of the reckoning of God, though they are reckoned in the computation of the years of the age of the World.

The method appears strange and almost impossible to the modern mind, with its highly developed historical sense, its worship of truth, its keen scent for fact, and its pantheistic indifference to distinctions of good and evil.   Nevertheless, there are days in the history of individuals and years in the history of the nations which we would fain blot out of the calendar of time.   Job desired for the day of his birth that it might perish, that it might " not be joined to the days of the year, nor come into the number of the months." We cannot deal thus with the objective facts and events of time, but we can with the chronicle and the record of them.

The monarchs of Assyria, and other nations of antiquity, left copious records of their conquests and their victories, but they did not chronicle their disasters and their defeats.   The nations of the East were accustomed to treat their history in this way.   They kept account of the years of prosperity, but they omitted from their Chronology altogether the years of national humiliation and disgrace.   We do not write our histories in this way, but

" East is East and West is West,
And never the twain shall meet."

It is a first principle of statistical Science that no list of figures compiled for one purpose should be used for another purpose.   The purpose of the compiler determines the classification and hence the number of the units.   All kinds of statistics are lawful if we use them lawfully.

If I am asked the duration of the Kingdom of England from the accession of William the Conqueror to that of Queen Victoria, I reply 1837 – 1066 = 771 years.   But if the purpose of the enquiry is to institute a comparison between a monarchy and a republic then I must deduct the 11 years marked " Abasi-leutus," or " Commonwealth," between the reigns of Charles I and Charles II, and possibly other periods of Regency, and the 771 years of the duration of the Kingdom will be reduced to 760 or something less.

Now the writer of I Kings 6[1] is computing the years of the Theocracy, the years of God's rule, the years of Isra-El, when she was herself, when she was *isra-El*, when she was *Governed-by-God*, and the sum total of these years is correctly given.

During the years of the servitudes the people of Israel were not ruled-by-God, for " He delivered them into the hands of Spoilers that spoiled them, and sold them into the hands of their enemies round about."   He sold them into the hand of Cushan-rishathaim.   They served Eglon—not Jehovah.   He sold them into the hand of Jabin.   He delivered them into the hand of Midian. Abimelech reigned over Israel—not God.   He sold them into the hands of the Philistines and into the hands of the children of Ammon.   These are the keynotes of the history of the periods of oppression and usurpation.

It is abundantly clear that these are no Theocratic years at all, and cannot be included in the reckoning of the years of God when He ruled over Israel and Israel served Him.   Nothing can be clearer than the fact that these are the years which the writer of I Kings 6[1] omits, except the fact that he omits them intentionally and purposely, and does not for a moment pretend to be making an ordinary chronological statement.   He does not even say that the space between the two epochs was a period of 480 years.   He records a fact which took place in the 480th year, by which he means the 480th theocratic year after the children of Israel were come up out of the land of Egypt.

Contemporary Events in Egypt.

There are no synchronisms between the history of Israel during the period from the birth of Moses to the end of the administration of Samuel (AN. HOM. 2433 –3023), and the history of Egypt, Assyria and Babylon, or Greece, either in the literary records which have been preserved to us, or in the Monumental Inscriptions that have been discovered in recent times.

With regard to Egypt, the identification of the Pharaoh of the oppression has not yet been established.   We have to choose between two rival schools. Those who adopt the *Long Chronology* identify the Pharaoh of the Exodus with Achencheres, Amosis or Amenophis, one of the Pharaohs of the 18th dynasty, and date the Exodus somewhere near the year B.C. 1500.   Those who adopt the *Short Chronology* identify the Pharaoh of the Exodus with Merenptah (also called Amenophis in the story of Manetho), the son of Rameses the Great, one of the Pharaohs of the 19th dynasty, and date the Exodus.. somewhere near B.C. 1300.

According to those who adopt the *Short Chronology*, the Pharaoh who " made the children of Israel to serve with rigour " (Ex. 1^{13}) and " made their lives bitter with hard bondage " (Ex. 1^{14}), the Pharaoh for whom " they built treasure cities Pithom and Raamses " (Ex. 1^{11}), and who died sometime after Moses was 40 years old (Ex. 2^{23} with Acts $7^{23.30}$), was Rameses II, whose long reign of 67 years, and whose extensive and enormous Monumental remains ought to form a distinct chronological landmark.

The *Short Chronology* rests upon the identification of the Pharaoh of the Exodus with Merenptah, whose reign is dated B.C. 1328–1309. But the only authority for this identification is the account of the Exodus given by Manetho and preserved in Josephus, who, however, regards it as of little or no authority.

The story is that the King, whose name is given as Menophis or Amenophis, but who must be identified with Merenptah the Son of Rameses II, resolved to propitiate the gods by purging the land of Egypt of all lepers and unclean persons. These, to the number of 80,000, were banished to the city of Avaris (Pelusium). Here they chose for their leader an apostate priest of Heliopolis, whose name, Osarseph, was changed to Moses. He gave them new laws, bidding the people to sacrifice the sacred animals. He fortified the city, and called in the aid of the shepherds who had been expelled from Avaris and had settled in Jerusalem. These now advanced to Avaris with an army of 200,000 men. " The King of Egypt marched against them with an army of 300,000, but returned to Memphis through fear of an ancient prophecy. He then fled to Ethiopa, whence he returned after an absence of 13 years, drove the rebels out of Egypt, and pursued them to the frontier of Syria." (Philip Smith's *Ancient History*).

The story evidently confuses reminiscences of the Hyksos or Shepherd Kings of the 18th dynasty (c. 1500) with the Exodus of the Israelites. It is a manifest invention of the priests of Egypt, a perverted Egyptian version of the great national disaster by which the chariots and the horsemen and all the hosts of Pharaoh were overtaken when " the Lord overthrew the Egyptians in the midst of the Sea." The mention of lepers recalls the sign of Moses' leprous hand. The people's choice of Moses as their leader, their acceptance of new laws at his hands, the mention of Jerusalem and the description of Moses as an apostate priest, one therefore who was " learned in all the wisdom of the Egyptians," may be regarded as so many dim reflections of the underlying truth which the legend perverts and yet preserves. The name of the King of Egypt—Amenophis, though he is here identified with Merenptah of the 19th dynasty, is more probably that of the real Amenophis of the 18th dynasty.

The *Long Chronology* rests upon the identification of the Pharaoh of the Exodus with one of the Egyptian Kings of the 18th dynasty, whom Africanus calls Amosis, whose date is somewhere about B.C. 1525, and whom he describes as the first King of the 18th dynasty.

But both the Greek and the Armenian copies of Eusebius place the Exodus under the 9th King of the 18th dynasty, whose name was Achencheres, and who was either the son or the grandson of Amenophis III.

The history of the Empire of the Pharaohs for this period is full of

obscurities.   It was a time of continual revolution and civil discord.   Revolts
occurred in most of the provinces, and disorder reigned for nearly half a century
after the death of Amenophis III.

The following dates have been assigned to the Exodus by various members
of these two rival schools.

THE LONG CHRONOLOGY $\left\{\begin{array}{l}\textit{Pharaoh} = \textit{one of the Kings of the 18th dynasty.}\\ \textit{Exodus} = c.\ 1500\ \text{B.C.}\end{array}\right.$

	B.C.
The Hebrew Text (according to Ussher)	1491
Ussher	1491
A.V. Margin (Bishop Lloyd)	1491
Bengel	1497
Bede	1499
Willis J. Beecher	1501
Eusebius (Achencheres, 9th King, 18th Dynasty)	1512
Africanus (Amosis, 1st King, 18th Dynasty)	1525
Petavius	1531

THE SHORT CHRONOLOGY $\left\{\begin{array}{l}\textit{Pharaoh} = \textit{Merenptah, son of Rameses II, one of}\\ \qquad\qquad \textit{the Kings of the 19th dynasty.}\\ \textit{Exodus} = c.\ 1300\ \text{B.C.}\end{array}\right.$

	B.C.
Jewish Rabbinical Tradition A.M. 2447	1314
Owen C. Whitehouse (Angus' Bible Handbook)	1320
Baron Bunsen	1328
Lepsius	1328

The theory of Lepsius has now been abandoned by recent scholars, and
a new theory framed by Mahler, Edouard Meyer and others, has taken its
place.   Hence we have a third school of Chronologers and a still shorter
Chronology, amongst the advocates of which the following names deserve
mention :—

	1st year of Merenptah.
A. H. Sayce	1280
E. A. W. Budge (British Museum Guide)	1263
Breasted	1225
Flinders Petrie	1207

All Egyptian dates for this period are, however, purely conjectural.   The
date of the Exodus is fixed quite definitely in the Hebrew Text, and as there
is nothing certainly known in the records of Egypt to conflict with the Hebrew
date there is no reason why it should not be accepted.   The Exodus occurred on
the 14th of Nisan, in the year AN. HOM. 2513, a year which would be expressed
by Ussher as B.C. 1492, but in terms of the scheme of the present writer as
B.C. 1530 (Bible dates), and in terms of the ordinary received Chronology as
B.C. 1612 (Ptolemaic dates).

There are no synchronisms during this period, AN. HOM. 2433–3023 in Babylonian history.   The contemporary monarchs were the Kings of the Kassite dynasty (B.C. 1780–1203), the dynasty of Isin (B.C. 1203–1030), the Dynasty of Elam (B.C. 1030–1025) and the second dynasty of Babylon (B.C. 1025–730) (Prof. Jastrow's dates).

There are no synchronisms during this period with the events of Assyrian history.   Babylon was conquered by Tilgath-in-Aristi I (son of Shalmaneser I), King of Assyria about B.C. 1270.   The kings of the daughter colony, Assyria, continued to rule the mother city, Babylon, from this time onward for about 600 years, till the destruction of Nineveh by Nabopolassar, King of Babylon, and Cyaxares the Mede, in or before the year B.C. 606.

There are no synchronisms during this period with the history of Greece. The date usually assigned to the taking of Troy is B.C. 1184.   Sir Isaac Newton places it in the year B.C. 904.

PERIOD III. THE MONARCHY—1 *Sam.* 8 *to* 2 *Kings.*

CHAPTER XX. SAUL, DAVID AND SOLOMON.

I. Saul.

VERY little is known of Saul in the way of Chronology. The Old Testament gives neither the year of his coronation, the length of his reign, nor the year of his death.

There is only one date given for his reign, and that is to Commentators and Revisers, both ancient and modern, a puzzle and a mystery. In 1 Sam. 13[1] we read, "Saul reigned one year ; and when he had reigned two years over Israel" he established a standing army. The meaning of this verse unquestionably is that Saul had now, at this point in the narrative, reigned one year, viz. from his first anointing by Samuel at Ramah, to his second anointing by him at Gilgal after the defeat of Nahash.

The historian proceeds to tell us that he reigned over Israel two years, that is he reigned two years over the whole of Israel now that he was publicly recognised and accepted by all the people at Gilgal, for before, at the public recognition at Mizpeh, there were some who dissented from the appointment and despised him (1 Sam. 10[17-27]).

The implication is that at the end of this two years the Lord cast him off, and anointed David in place of him. The remaining 37 years of his reign is not recognised as legitimate ruling, but is regarded rather as a tyranny, and a persecution. During the two years of his recognised rule over Israel he defeated Moab, Ammon, Edom, the Kings of Zobah, the Philistines and the Amalekites, and thus delivered Israel out of the hands of those that spoiled them (1 Sam. 14[47-48]). Then he invaded and conquered Amalek, but here he disobeyed the word of the Lord in sparing Agag, and the Lord cast him off, three years after his first anointing at Mizpeh, and two years after the commencement of his reign over all Israel at his second anointing at Gilgal.

The translation of the verse in the Revised Version is utterly unwarranted, and the marginal note is distinctly misleading. The R.V. rendering is "Saul was (thirty) years old when he began to reign, and he reigned two years over Israel." The marginal note reads as follows : "The Hebrew Text has 'Saul was a year old. The whole verse is omitted in the unrevised LXX. but in a later recension the number 30 is inserted.'"

Now the truth is the Hebrew Text does not say "Saul was a year old." To say that it does is to charge it with perpetrating a folly of which it is incapable. And the charge is a false one. What the Hebrew Text says is not " Saul was a year old," but *"Saul was a year old in his reigning"* or " *in his Kingdom,"* literally " a son of one year in his reigning," accurately " Saul had been reigning one year." The description of the LXX. which omits the verse altogether as " the unrevised LXX." when it is nothing else but the original LXX. itself, and of the LXX. of Origen's Hexapla, in which Origen himself has *interpolated* the word " thirty " as a " later recension," implying the superiority of Origen's interpolated text to the original LXX., is an inexcusable and a gratuitous misrepresentation of the facts of the case. The translators of the LXX. *omitted* the verse altogether simply because they did not understand it. Origen *perverted* it because he did not understand it. The Revisers prefer the perverted text of Origen to the imperfect text of the original LXX., which omits the text altogether, and both to the true Text as it stands in the Hebrew Verity. If modern interpreters, instead of reading modern ideas into the Text of these ancient writers, would place themselves at the point of view of the writers, we should be spared some of these superfluous " emendations." In truth the Text, as it stands in the Hebrew, is both correct and complete. These first three years are carefully distinguished and marked off from the remaining 37 years of Saul's reign because they are regarded as being years of a different character. The first three years are years of the legitimate rule of Saul, the Lord's anointed. The last 37 years are years of the unrecognised and illegitimate tyranny of Saul, the usurper of David's throne, and the rejected of the Lord.

Josephus says : " Now Saul, when he had reigned 18 years while Samuel was alive, and after his death two (and twenty), ended his life in this manner." There may have been some authentic record to which Josephus had access, and from which he obtained the information here given, and this is all the more probable, because the length of Saul's reign was also known to St. Paul, who gives it in his address at Antioch in Pisidia, as a " space of 40 years " (Acts 13 [21]).

II. David.

Full details are given of the Chronology of David's reign. He was thirty years old when he began to reign, and he reigned 40 years. In Hebron he reigned over Judah seven years and six months ; and in Jerusalem he reigned thirty and three years over all Israel and Judah (2 Sam. 2 [11], 5 [4. 5], 1 Chron. 29 [27]).

Willis J. Beecher, therefore, adds 41 years to the Chronology for the reign of David, assuming that the odd six months would be counted to David as an additional year. But there is no ground for this supposition. The statement in 2 Sam. 2 [11] from which that of 2 Sam. 5 [5] is derived is quite peculiar. The Hebrew specifies 7 years and 6 months as " the number of days that David reigned in Hebron."

The usual chronological statements of the years of the Kings reckon quite accurately in whole years, without introducing fractions of a year. For these whole years are always *calendar* years from New Year's Day (Nisan 1st) to New Year's Day. They are not measured from the day of the King's accession to the day of his death. They are designed like the years of the Patriarchs in Genesis, and the reigns of the Kings in Ptolemy's Canon, and in the Assyrian Eponym Canon, to mark the succession of the years in a given chronological Era.

It is not so with a chronological statement which contains fractions of a year like this of David's 7½ years in Hebron. Here we have a statement measuring the exact duration of David's reign in Hebron, as measured from the day of his accession to the day of his removal to Jerusalem. When the statement is reproduced in terms of calendar years in 1 Chron. 29 ^{27}, the number assigned to David's reign is not 41 but 40 years.

This is confirmed by the 480 years of 1 Kings 6 ^{1}, for if we give David 41 years, that figure would have to be altered to 481. We could not make David's reign 41 years in that list and still retain the number 480 by reducing the Joshua—Judges chasm to 12 instead of 13, for if we did that we should reduce Jephthah's 309 to 299. These numbers are so locked and inter-locked, so checked and doubly checked, that it is next to impossible to " correct " any one of them without throwing the whole system into confusion.

 . Other dated events are mentioned as taking place in the reign of David.

(1) In 2 Sam. 15 ^{7} we read, " And it came to pass after 40 years, that Absalom said unto the King, I pray thee, let me go and pay my vow, which I have vowed unto the Lord, in Hebron." It is the story of the commencement of Absalom's rebellion. If we knew the point of departure from which the 40 years are reckoned we should be able to fix the date of the event, but we do not.

Hales suggests an " emendation " of the Text, and would read 4 years with the Syriac, Arabic, several MSS. of the Vulgate, Josephus and Theodorus, instead of 40, " the present reading being utterly inexplicable."

The proposal is wholly gratuitous. The 40 years is not reckoned from the time of the events detailed in the preceding verses, 1 Sam. 15 $^{1-6}$, but from some previous event, whether, as Dr. John Lightfoot, Ussher and the *Companion Bible* suggest, from the anointing of David, or from some other event, is uncertain.

As the last four chapters of the Book (2 Sam. 21-24) contain five appendices on (1) the Gibeonites (2 Sam. 21), (2) David's Song (2 Sam. 22), (3) David's last words (2 Sam. 23 $^{1-7}$), (4) David's mighty men (2 Sam. 23 $^{8-39}$), and (5) David's census (2 Sam. 24), incidents which are not arranged in chronological order, and which do not form part of the consecutive history of David ; and as almost the very next incident of the consecutive history (1 Kings 1) is the story of David's last days and death, there is no reason why the 40 years may not be reckoned *from the 1st year of the reign of David.* In that case, 1 Sam. 15 ^{7}, " It came to pass after 40 years," means it came to pass in the 40th and last calendar year of David's reign, the 41st as it would be called by us if we reckoned from the day of his accession instead of from the following New Year's Day, as the writers of the Old Testament reckon. As however one cannot be *quite sure* that this is the epoch from which the 40th year is reckoned, the event is not inserted in the Chronological Tables.

(2) The other dated event belonging to David's reign is the appointment of Officers of State, which took place in the fortieth year of his reign (1 Chron. 26 ^{31}).

III. Solomon.

" The time that Solomon reigned in Jerusalem over all Israel was 40 years " (1 Kings 11 ^{42}, 2 Chron. 9 ^{30}).

The dated events of his reign are the following :—" In the fourth year of Solomon's reign, in the month Zif, which is the second month, he began to build the house of the LORD " (1 Kings 6 $^{1.37}$), " in the 2nd day of the 2nd month of the 4th year of his reign" (2 Chron. 3 ^{2}). In the 11th year in the month Bul, which is the 8th month, the House was finished throughout, so he was 7 years (more exactly 7 years and six months) in building it (1 Kings 6 ^{38}).

In the 11th year he commenced to build his own house, and with this he was occupied for 13 years until the 20th year of his reign (1 Kings 7 ^{1}, 9 ^{10}, 2 Chron. 8 ^{1}).

Accuracy of the Round Numbers used in the Old Testament.

The remarkable fact that each of the first three Kings of Israel, Saul, David and Solomon, are said to have reigned 40 years, has been used to cast a doubt upon the accuracy of the record, these figures being used, it is said, as round numbers, and signifying nothing more than a rough approximation to the lifetime of one generation.

The same argument has been applied to other periods of 20, 40 and 80 years in respect of the 40 years in the wilderness, and the periods of rest in the Book of Judges. The argument could not be applied to the Kings of Israel and Judah from Rehoboam and Jeroboam onward without modification, as there, only one out of the 19 Kings of Judah, and only one out of the 19 Kings of Israel, is credited with either 20 or 40 years.

Nevertheless, it has been urged that multiples of five occur with great frequency in the ages of the Kings of Judah, and the years of their reign, and that the natural inference is that the figures given are round numbers or approximations (D. R. Fotheringham, *Chronology of the Old Testament*). But the total number of the ages and reigns of the Kings of Judah is 36. Of these we should expect, on the theory of averages, that at least 7 would end in a 5 or a 0. As a matter of fact, seven end in a 5 and two in a 0, from which the true conclusion is that the figures given are not approximations, but exact statements of matters of fact.

The same can be said with regard to the periods of 20, 40 and 80 years. The entire list is as follows :—

Periods of 20, 40 *and* 80 *years mentioned in Scripture.*

The Wilderness Period	..	..	..	..	.. 40	years
Othniel	..	..	..	..	.. 40	,,
Ehud ..	..	..	..	..	.. 80	,,
Jabin ..	..	..	..	..	.. 20	,,
Barak ..	..	..	..	..	.. 40	,,
Gideon	..	..	..	..	.. 40	,,
The Philistines	..	..	..	..	.. 40	,,
Eli ..	..	..	..	..	.. 40	,,
Samuel	..	..	..	..	.. 20	,,
Saul ..	..	..	..	..	.. 40	,,
David ..	..	..	..	..	.. 40	,,
Solomon	..	..	..	..	.. 40	,,

The wilderness period is not an approximation, for it is calculated to the day, and full particulars are given of 17 distinct events with the year, the month, and the day of the month on which they happened, especially at the beginning and at the end of the period.

It is not true of David's reign, for this is divided into two parts of $7\frac{1}{2}$ and 33 years respectively. We have no warrant for concluding that the remaining periods of 20, 40 and 80 years may not be made up in the same way either to the day, as in the case of the wilderness period, or within six months, the fraction of a year being allowed for in the Chronology as in the case of the reign of David.

The number of the Kings of England from William the Conqueror to Queen Victoria is 35. On the theory of averages we should expect the number of years in the reigns of 7 of these to end in a 5 or a 0. As a matter of fact, 12 or nearly double that number end in one or other of these figures, yet no one supposes that the length of the reigns of the Kings of England is an approximation.

The Book of Judges is a very condensed account of a long period of time. Its space is apportioned at the rate of 5 pages to the Century. A writer on English Architecture would not be guilty of chronological inaccuracy if he dealt in a similarly brief space with the various styles of Gothic Architecture, tabulating them as follows : 11th Century, Norman ; 12th Century, Transition ; 13th Century, Early English ; 14th Century, Decorated ; and 15th Century, Perpendicular. As a matter of fact, each of these styles dates from at least a decade or so before the opening year of the Century to which it mainly belongs. But the Chronology of the entire period is not affected thereby. And it must not be supposed that the round numbers used in Scripture are introduced in such a way as to make the Chronology, as a whole, inaccurate or inexact. The reckoning by forties is just as accurate as the reckoning by Centuries. If these numbers are approximations they are self-compensating and self-correcting, and conduct us to a point quite definite and quite exact, for their totals agree with the long numbers measuring long periods by which smaller component numbers are checked. All the above periods of 40 years are checked either by St. Paul's 450 years, in Acts 13 [20], or by the 480 years of 1 Kings 6 [1], and some of them by both of these long numbers.

We are therefore justified in rejecting the theory of round numbers or approximations, and taking the numerical statements of Scripture at their face value. We continue our Chronology from the election of Saul to the accession of Rehoboam and Jeroboam as follows :—

AN. HOM.

3023. Saul (see Chapter 17).

40. Add 40 years for the reign of Saul (Acts 13 [21]).

3063. David.

40. Add 40 years for the reign of David (2 Sam. 5 [4, 5], 1 Chron. 29 [27]).

3103. Solomon.

40. Add 40 years for the reign of Solomon (1 Kings 11 [42], 2 Chron. 9 [30]).

3143. Rehoboam and Jeroboam.

CHAPTER XXI. ISRAEL AND JUDAH TO THE FALL OF SAMARIA.

The Gordian Knot of Bible Chronology.

(AN. HOM. 3143–3413).

[*In reading this Chapter continual reference must be made to the Chronological Tables, which are printed separately in Vol. II so that they may lie upon the table at the required opening, ready for use.*]

WE now reach the crux of the Chronology of the Old Testament, the period of the Kings of Judah and Israel, " the Gordian knot of Sacred Chronology," as Hales terms it. As was to be expected, we here meet with an unusually large number of attempts to cut the Gordian knot by means of so-called emendations, corrections and rejections of the Text by lame Chronologers, who, one and all, conclude that if they cannot make the figures agree, it is not their own interpretation of the figures, but the Text which is at fault.

And yet there is not a single difficulty that has been raised which is not capable of a simple and easy solution without doing violence to the Text ; there is not a single difficulty that has not been satisfactorily cleared up in standard works by able Chronologers from the *Chronicle of the Old Testament* by Dr. John Lightfoot, in the 17th Century, to Willis J. Beecher's *Dated Events of the Old Testament*, and the scholarly work of the author of the *Companion Bible*, in our own day.

" In casting up the times of the collateral Kingdoms," says Dr. Lightfoot, " your only way is to lay them in two columns, one justly paralleling the other, and run them both by years, as the Text directs you. But here is nicety indeed, not to see how strangely they are reckoned, sometimes inclusive, sometimes otherwise—for this you will easily find ; but to find a reason why they be so reckoned. Rehoboam's years are counted complete ; Abijam's are current. Whereas it is said that Jeroboam reigned 22 years—and his son Nadab 2 years ; you will find by this reckoning that Nadab's 2 years fall within the sum of his father's 22. This may seem strange, but the solution is sweet and easy from 2 Chron. 13^{20}. The Lord smote Jeroboam with some ill disease, that he could not administer or rule the kingdom, so that he was forced to substitute Nadab in his lifetime. And in one and the same year, both father and son die."

" Divers such passages as these you will find in this story of the Kings. Ahaziah 2 years older than his father (2 Chron. 22^2), Baasha fighting 9 years after he is dead (2 Chron. 16^1), Jotham reigning 4 years after he is buried (2 Kings 15^{30}), Joram crowned King in the 17th year of Jehoshaphat (2 Kings 1^{17} with 1 Kings 22^{51}), and in the 22nd year of Jehoshaphat (2 Kings 8^{16}), and after Jehoshaphat's death (2 Chron. 21^1)."

" For resolution of such ambiguities, when you have found them, the Text will do it, if it be well searched. This way, attained to, will guide you in marking those things that seem to be contradictions in the Text, or slips of the Holy Ghost, in which always is admirable wisdom."

" Admirable it is to see how the Holy Spirit of God in discords hath showed the sweet music. But few mark this, because few take a right course in reading of Scripture. Hence, when men are brought to see flat contradictions, as unreconciled there be many in it, they are at amaze and ready to deny their Bible. A little pains right spent, will soon amend this wavering and settle men upon the Rock, whereon to be built is to be sure."

The key to the solution of all these difficulties is given by Willis J. Beecher, in an article on " The Kings of Israel and Judah," in the American *Presbyterian Review* for April, 1880.

" In recording dates," he says, " these narratives follow a simple and consistent system. The following rules are obeyed with entire uniformity, in all the dates of the period under consideration :—

" Rule 1. All the years mentioned are current years of a consecutive system. The first year of a King is not a year's time beginning with the month and day of his accession, but a year's time beginning (1) the preceding, *or* (2) the following New Year's Day—the New Moon before the Passover, Nisan 1st.

" Rule 2. When a reign closes and another begins during a year, that year is counted to the previous reign (Judaite mode).

" Rule 3. Regularly in the case of the earlier Kings of Israel, and occasionally in other cases, the broken year is counted to the following reign as well as to the previous reign (Israelite mode).

" Rule 4. When we use the ordinal numbers (1st, 2nd, 3rd, etc.) which date the beginning or the end of a reign to check the cardinal numbers (1, 2, 3, etc.), which denote its duration, we must count both sets as designating complete calendar years. That is, we must count the date given in the ordinal as being either the opening or the close of the year designated by the ordinal. Otherwise the units represented by the two sets of numbers are of different sorts, and cannot be numerically compared."

The Hebrew Text of the history of this period is self-consistent and self-contained. All the data required for the resolution of any difficulties that may arise are to be found in the Text itself.

There is no need to fall back upon Josephus. Still less is there any need to introduce any of the harmonizing expedients of the LXX. or any of the " emendations," " restorations " and " corrections " of the Text by modern critics, who present us with a view of the history as *they* think it *ought* to be, not with a view of the history as it is.

Similarly the use of " Sothic Cycles," the calculation of eclipses and other astronomical methods and expedients for settling Bible Dates, are all alike inadmissible. They are liable to errors of observation on the part of the original observer, to errors of calculation on the part of the modern astronomer, and consequently to errors in the identification of the observed and recorded eclipse with the eclipse reached by astronomical calculation.

They are used mainly in support of assumptions and pre-suppositions already arrived at by the method of hypothesis and conjecture. They may be true or they may not, but in any case they cannot be erected into a standard by which to correct the data given in the Hebrew Text.

Modern Egyptologists make much of astronomical data. Each advocate regards his own scheme as thereby invested with the certainty of a mathematical calculation. But there are many such schemes, and they differ from each other by more than a century. As Willis J. Beecher says, " Each chain has links of the solid steel of astronomical computation, but they are tied together with the rotten twine of conjecture."

A few years ago the scheme of Lepsius was generally accepted by those modern Egyptologists by whom the Biblical data were discarded. A Sothic Cycle known as that of Menôphres, terminated A.D. 139, and as the cycle contains 1,461 years it began B.C. 1322. By this calculation they date the Exodus in the year B.C. 1320. The inference depends for its validity upon the truth of the following hypotheses, every one of which partakes of the character of an unverified conjecture :—

1. The trustworthiness of the *testimony* of Censorinus, the chronological scheme constructor, who lived A.D. 238, and who states in his work *De die Natali* that a Sothic period came to an end A.D. 139. The testimony may be authentic and reliable, but as it is not contemporary, but given just a century after the event, it is at all events liable to error.

2. The accuracy of the *calculation* of Censorinus, and the truth of the underlying assumption that the period of 1,460 Sothic years of $365\frac{1}{4}$ days does actually correspond with the period covered by 1,461 of the vague or calendar years of 365 days, and that these vague years were used in the historical records of Egypt throughout the entire period of 1,460 Sothic or 1,461 vague calendar years.

3. The accuracy of the *calculation* of modern astronomers as to the heliacal rising of Sirius, the rising of the dogstar with the sun in the year B.C. 1322.

4. The accuracy of the *identification* of this cycle (B.C. 1322 to A.D. 139) with the Sothic cycle of Menōphres.

5. The accuracy of the *identification* of this Menōphres with Merenptah the son of Rameses the Great.

6. The accuracy of the *identification* of Merenptah with the Amenophis IV, to whose reign Manetho, as reported by Josephus, assigns the Exodus.

7. The trustworthiness of the *testimony* of Manetho, as preserved in Josephus, in referring the Exodus to the reign of this Amenophis IV, and the accuracy of the identification of Manetho's story of the expulsion of the lepers with the Biblical story of the deliverance of Israel out of Egypt, by Moses, at the Exodus.

Lepsius held that the year B.C. 1322 was connected with the reign of Merenptah, the immediate successor of Rameses the Great. It was based on astronomical calculations of the Sothic cycle, and was generally accepted by modern scholars a few years ago.

But to-day the theory of Lepsius is abandoned for another theory also based on astronomical calculations of the Sothic cycle, and elaborated by Mahler, Edouard Meyer, Prof. Breasted, and others. Its advocates claim that their methods are exact, but their results are various and incompatible. The year in which Merenptah succeeded Rameses II is given by Flinders Petrie as B.C. 1207, by Sayce as B.C. 1280, and by Breasted as B.C. 1255.

But the most striking feature in the whole process and method of these scientific calculations is the fact that the synchronism of Amenophis III of Egypt with Burna-buriash of Babylon and Asshur-uballet of Assyria, who are said to have flourished about B.C. 1430, which was formerly used in confirmation of the Lepsian dates, is now used in confirmation of these other dates, which differ from that of Lepsius by 42, 97, and 115 years respectively, " each method abundantly convincing to those already convinced before ! "

These quasi-infallible dates arrived at by modern investigators are erected into a standard by which to amend and to correct the dates of the Hebrew Text of the Old Testament. But this is correcting standard coin of the realm by means of counterfeit fabrications.

The authentic documents of the Hebrew Old Testament are both accurate and self-consistent, complete and self-sufficient. The facts and the events, the dates and the periods there given, are as accurate and as reliable as those other statements upon which we base our confidence in the goodness of God, and rest in hope of eternal Salvation.

We read in Hales' *Analysis of Sacred Chronology*, the following proud and startling paragraph.

" We are now competent to detect some errors that have crept into the correspondences of reigns ; and which have hitherto puzzled and perplexed Chronologers, and prevented them from critically harmonizing the two series ; not being able to distinguish the genuine from the spurious numbers.

"1. 1 *Kings*, 22 ⁴¹. Jehoshaphat began to reign over Judah in the *fourth* year of Ahab. It should be the *second*.

2. 1 *Kings* 22 ⁵¹. Ahaziah the son of Ahab began to reign over Israel in the *seventeenth of* Jehoshaphat. It should be the *twentieth*.

3. 2 *Kings* 1 ¹⁷. Jehoram the son (?) of Ahaziah began to reign over Israel in the *second* year of *Jehoram* son of Jehoshaphat. It should be in the *twenty-second* year of *Jehoshaphat*, as also where it is again incorrectly stated in the *eighteenth* (2 Kings 3 ¹).

4. 2 *Kings* 8 ¹⁶. Jehoram son of Jehoshaphat began to reign over Judah, in the fifth year of the reign of Joram the (grand) son of Ahab. It should be,

(1) the fifth year from the death of Ahab, or

(2) the third year of Joram's reign.

'Jehoshaphat being then King of Judah' is an anachronism and an interpolation in the Massoretic Text.

5. 2 *Kings* 13 ¹⁰. Jehoash began to reign over Israel in the thirty-seventh year of Joash King of Judah. It should be in the *thirty-ninth* year; as in the Aldine Edition of the Greek Septuagint.

6. 2 *Kings* 15 ³⁰. Hoshea slew Pekah King of Israel in the *twentieth* year of Jotham. But Jotham only reigned sixteen years (2 Kings 15 ³³). It should be in the *third* year of Ahaz, as collected from 2 Kings 16 ¹."

Clinton follows in the same groove, though not quite in the same vein. Chronologers generally follow each other like a flock of sheep, each one reproducing and propagating the errors of his predecessor. He says :—

"1. 2 *Chron.* 16 ¹⁻³. Baasha came up against Judah in the 36th year of the reign of Asa. As in the 36th year of Asa, Baasha was dead, we must either (1) correct the numbers to the 26th, or (2) we must understand them to mean the 36th year of the Kingdom of Judah.

2. 2 *Chron.* 22 ². Forty-two years for the age of Ahaziah are wrong, on account of 2 Kings 8 ²⁶, where it is given " 22 years," and on account of the age of his father who died at forty.

3. 1 *Kings* 22 ⁵¹. The 17th year of Jehoshaphat is inconsistent with the other coincidences given. (So he alters it to the 19th, as Hales does.)

4. 2 *Kings* 3 ¹. The 18th of Jehoshaphat was the 1st of Joram. This is evidently impossible ; for between the accession of Jehoshaphat and the accession of Joram son of Ahab are 18 years complete of Ahab and two years of Ahaziah.

5. 2 *Kings* 1 ¹⁷. Joram son of Ahab is said to have succeeded his brother in the 2nd of Jehoram King of Judah, but as the 1st of Jehoram King of Judah was the 5th of Joram King of Israel, and the 8th of the King of Judah was the 11th or 12th of the King of Israel, this date, the ' 2nd of Jehoram,' is evidently wrong.

"6. 2 *Kings* 8 [16]. The phrase, ' Jehoshaphat being then King of Judah,' we may perhaps explain thus : Jehoram began to reign while his father was yet living (as in the accession of Solomon), and Jehoshaphat died at the commencement of the 25th year, which is therefore the 1st Jehoram.

7. 2 *Kings* 13 [10]. The 37th year of Joash is inconsistent with the other dates. The LXX. has the 39th year, which might be the true reading.

8. 2 *Kings* 15 [1]. We may concur with Jackson, De Vignoles and Greswell in rejecting the 27th year of Jeroboam as corrupt."

All these difficulties are due to (1) misinterpretation of the words of the Text, or (2) unwarrantable inferences drawn by the Chronologer, not from the words of the Text, but from assumptions made by the Chronologer in construing it.

Thus 2 *Chron.* 16 [1-3]. Baasha came up against Judah in the 36th year of the reign of Asa. The text says the 36th year of the מלכות = malchuth = *Kingdom* of Asa, which Kingdom dates from the 1st year of Rehoboam, and which is here contrasted with the Kingdom of Baasha, which dates from the 1st year of Jeroboam. To make it mean the 36th year from the accession of Asa is an error of interpretation.

Again, 2 *Kings* 13 [9. 10]. Jehoash of Israel began to reign in the 37th year of Joash, King of Judah. It is said that this should be the 39th. Here it is *assumed* that Jehoash of Israel did not begin to reign until after his father Jehoahaz was dead, and as his father did not die till two years later in the 39th of Joash of Judah, the inference *drawn from the Chronologer's assumption* is that Jehoash of Israel did not begin to reign till the 39th year of Joash of Judah. But the Text says he began to reign in the 37th year of Joash of Judah, and the true inference *drawn from the Text* is that Jehoash was Co-Rex with his father, during the last two or three years of his father's reign.

In like manner it can be shown that every other supposed inconsistency is not in the Text, but in the mind of the critic ; that the Text is susceptible of another interpretation, and that the construction put upon it by the critic is a false one. This is done in the ensuing Chronological Table of the Kings of Judah and Israel, where each difficulty is explained in accordance with the statements of the Text.

The Table is divided into three periods :—

1. From the 1st of Rehoboam to the death of Ahaziah of Judah, which synchronises with the period from the 1st of Jeroboam to the death of Jehoram of Israel, both these monarchs having been slain at the same time by Jehu.

2. From the 1st of Athaliah to the 6th of Hezekiah, which synchronises with the 1st of Jehu to the 9th of Hoshea, the Text giving the synchronism, " the sixth year of Hezekiah, that is the ninth year of Hoshea," as the date of the fall of Samaria (2 Kings 18 [10]).

3. From the fall of Samaria in the 6th of Hezekiah to the captivity. The captivity is dated from the 3rd year of Jehoiakim. The following year is characterised by the synchronism, " the fourth year of Jehoiakim that was the first year of Nebuchadrezzar " (Jer. 25 [1-11]). The captivity lasted for 70 years (Jer. 25 [12]).

In the first of these three periods, Rehoboam and Jeroboam start level, and their years are parallel or co-numerary as far as they both continue. Similarly, in the second of these three periods, Athaliah and Jehu start level, and their years are parallel or co-numerary as far as they both continue. In the third period, which forms the subject of our next chapter, we have the reckoning of the one Kingdom of Judah only.

The reigns of the Kings of the first two periods are so locked and interlocked, that it is impossible for any error to have crept into the Chronology between the year of the disruption and the year of the fall of Samaria.

The accuracy of the Chronology of the Kingdom of Judah from the fall of Samaria to the captivity is likewise guaranteed, being checked by the long numbers which measure the intervals between two distant events, e.g. the period from the 13th year of Josiah, when the ministry of Jeremiah began, to the 4th year of Jehoiakim, is stated to have been a period of 23 years (Jer. 25 [1-3]).

The synchronism contained in Jer. 25 [1] is the most important date in the Bible. It connects all the previous dates of Sacred Chronology down to the 4th year of Jehoiakim, with all the dates of Profane Chronology that can be connected with the 1st year of Nebuchadnezzar, for these two years are here identified, and to know any one date in a complete system of Chronology is to know every date connected with it.

We have inserted in Vol. II, pp. 50 and 51, two Tables giving a bird's-eye view of the Kings of Judah and Israel, the years of their reigns, and other particulars contained in the Hebrew Text.

Scripture Chronology deals only with integral years. It reckons a broken year sometimes as one whole year, which it gives to the outgoing King, and sometimes as two whole years, of which it gives one to the outgoing, and one to the incoming King, the year being thus reckoned twice over. It follows from this fact that the Chronology of the period cannot be ascertained by applying the process of simple addition to the figures denoting the length of the reigns of the various Kings. This is easily demonstrated.

In the first period the sum of the reigns of the 6 Kings of Judah from Rehoboam to Ahaziah of Judah is 95 years. The sum of the reigns of the 9 Kings of Israel from Jeroboam to Jehoram of Israel is 98 years. The true Chronology of the period is 90 years. The explanation of the figures 95 and 98 lies in the fact that in them some years have been reckoned twice over.

In the second period the sum of the reigns of the 6 Kings and 1 Queen of Judah from the 1st of Athaliah to the 6th of Hezekiah, together with the interregnum of 11 years, is 176 years. The sum of the reigns of the 10 Kings of Israel from the 1st year of Jehu to the 9th year of Hoshea, including the interregnums of 22 and 8 years respectively, is 175, reckoning a full year each to Zechariah and Shallum.   The true Chronology of the period is 174 years, and the explanation of the figures 176 and 175 years is the same as before.

In the third period the sum of the reigns of the 6 Kings of Judah from the 6th year of Hezekiah to the 3rd year of Jehoiakim is 114.   The true Chronology of the period is also 114 years.

We now proceed to consider the case of each reign in detail.   The figures cannot be treated mechanically.   They can only be interpreted and understood in the light of the accompanying narrative.

The fact that Ahab and his two successors, Ahaziah of Israel and Jehoram of Israel, all reigned in the same calendar year, is illustrated by the knowledge gained from the Assyrian Inscriptions that Ahab of Israel and Benhadad of Syria, were engaged in military operations against Shalmaneser II (III) of Assyria, in the 21st year of Ahab's reign, which led to the appointment of Ahaziah of Israel as Co-Rex during his father's absence at the war.   But Ahaziah was incapacitated by his fall through a lattice in his upper chamber (2 Kings 1[2]).   Hence the appointment of his brother Jehoram, either as Deputy or Pro-Rex, whilst Ahaziah was ill, or as Co-Rex with his father Ahab on Ahaziah's death.   In that 18th year of Jehoshaphat, Ahab was in his 22nd year and died. Ahaziah of Israel was in his 2nd year as Co-Rex with his father Ahab, and he died.   Thereupon Jehoram of Israel ascended the throne, and, in the usual Israelite mode of computation, the same year, the 18th of Jehospaphat, is also given to him as the incoming King, and reckoned as his first year.

The last year of Edward IV was the year 1483.   If his son Edward V had been associated with him in 1482 and had died, and been succeeded by Richard II in 1483 instead of 1485, we should have had a parallel case in English History.   Edward IV, Edward V and Richard II all on the throne in the same calendar year.

Similarly, the character of Jehoram of Judah, one of the most wicked Kings that ever sat upon the throne of Judah (2 Chron. 21), explains why he should have been made Pro-Rex with his father in the 17th of Jehoshaphat (the 18th year of Jehoshaphat = the 1st year of Jehoram of Israel being his second year—2 Kings 1[17], 3[1]), then deposed by his godly father Jehoshaphat and subsequently re-appointed, or possibly, prompted by his own wickedness to usurp (2 Chron. 21[4]) the throne of his father, in the 22nd year of Jehoshaphat, Jehoshaphat himself being then (in the 22nd of Jehoshaphat = the 5th of Jehoram of Israel) King of Judah (2 Kings 8[16]). |

Ussher is correct here.   Clinton is wrong.   Ussher does not "suppose" three beginnings of the reign of Jehoram of Judah.   He incorporates these three beginnings in his scheme as a *fact* definitely stated in the Hebrew narrative.

Clinton does not think the three beginnings probable, but circumstances alter cases, and our business is not to construe the Chronology as we think it ought to be, but as the Hebrew writer says it is.

If we adhere to the facts as given in the Hebrew Text, and never so much as attempt to " emend," to " correct," or to " restore " a single one of them, we shall find that we are here presented with a Chronology of the Kings of Israel and Judah which is at once both self-consistent, self-sufficient and correct in every detail.

1. *First Period—Rehoboam to Jehu.*

We begin with the reigns of Rehoboam and Jeroboam. We gather from the narrative that these both commenced in the same calendar year. The 40th year of Solomon is their accession year. The following year is their first year. The 17 years of Rehoboam run parallel with the first 17 years of Jeroboam.

Rehoboam was succeeded by Abijah, who began to reign in the 18th year of Jeroboam, and reigned 3 years (1 Kings 15 [1, 2]). As Abijah's first year is the 18th year of Jeroboam, either his accession year was the 17th of Jeroboam = the 17th of Rehoboam, or else Rehoboam reigned out his 17th year to its close, and Abijah began his reign at the very beginning of the New Year. In either case the three years of Abijah will be the years 18, 19 and 20 of Jeroboam.

The words " began to reign " used throughout this entire period and spoken of almost every King, alike in the A.V. and in the R.V., is not an accurate translation of the Original. The Hebrew is always " he reigned," not " he began to reign."

The intention of the writer is to give us, not the actual day of the King's accession, but the calendar year of the chronological Era in which he came to the throne. As a matter of fact, he may have acceded to the throne in the year which, by the Judaite mode, is reckoned as the last year of the outgoing King, and by the Israelite mode as both the last year of the outgoing King and the year 1 of the incoming King. By the Israelite mode of computation the same year is reckoned twice over.

Abijah's three years are the years 18, 19 and 20 of the reign of Jeroboam. From 1 Kings 15 [9, 10] we learn that Asa " reigned " in the 20th year of Jeroboam, and that his reign consisted of 41 calendar years. As the 20th year of Jeroboam is already given to Abijah, this 20th year of Jeroboam is Asa's accession year, and Asa's year 1 is Jeroboam's year 21. Of course Asa did reign in the 20th year of Jeroboam, but only during a fraction of it. The Chronology ignores the fraction, and on the Judaite mode of reckoning gives the whole year to Abijah.

Should we make the mistake of entering Asa's year 1 as parallel with Jeroboam's year 20, then Asa's year 2 will be Jeroboam's year 21, and Asa's year 3 will be Jeroboam's year 22, which is Nadab's year 1. But by 1 Kings 15 [25-33], Nadab reigned in the 2nd year of Asa, 2 years, and Baasha reigned in the 3rd year of Asa. We must therefore place Asa's year 1 parallel with Jeroboam's year 21, and Asa's accession year parallel with Jeroboam's year 20. What the narrative tells us is that during Abijah's year 3, he died and was succeeded by Asa, whose year 1 begins at the close of Abijah's year 3.

Asa 1 = Jeroboam 21. Therefore Asa 2 = Jeroboam 22. Jeroboam reigned 22 years and was succeeded by Nadab (1 Kings 14 [20]), who also reigned in Asa's year 2 (1 Kings 15 [25]). This year, Asa's year 2, is therefore reckoned twice over ; it is given to Jeroboam, the outgoing King, as his year 22, and also to Nadab as his year 1. This is the Israelite mode of reckoning.

Nadab reigned 2 years (1 Kings 15 [25]). His year 1 is Asa's year 2. Therefore his year 2 is Asa's year 3. But in Asa's year 3, Baasha slew Nadab and reigned in his stead (1 Kings 15 [28-33]). Therefore Asa's year 3 is both Nadab's

M

year 2 and Baasha's year 1. Again, the same year is reckoned twice over. It is given to Nadab, the outgoing King, as his last year, and to Baasha the incoming King, as his first year, according to the Israelite mode of reckoning.

Baasha reigned 24 years (1 Kings 15 [33]). His year 1 is Asa's year 3. Therefore his year 24 is Asa's year 26. But in Asa's year 26 Elah reigned (1 Kings 16 [8]). Hence Asa's year 26 is reckoned twice over, once as the last year of Baasha and again as the 1st year of Elah, according to the Israelite mode of reckoning.

Elah reigned 2 years (1 Kings 16 [8]). His year 1 is Asa's year 26. Therefore his year 2 is Asa's year 27. But in Asa's year 27 Zimri slew Elah and reigned 7 days (1 Kings 16 [10-15]).

Then the people made Omri King, but half the people followed Tibni, and they both reigned as rival Kings from Asa's year 27 till Tibni died (1 Kings 16 [16-22]). Again the year Asa 27 is reckoned twice over, to Elah the outgoing King, and to Omri and Tibni as their year 1, according to the Israelite mode of reckoning. On the death of Tibni, in Asa's year 31, Omri reigned over Israel alone (1 Kings 16 [22-23]). But Asa's year 27 was Omri and Tibni's year 1. Therefore Asa's year 31 was Omri and Tibni's year 5.

Omri reigned 6 years, that is one year more, in Tirzah. He then bought the hill of Samaria and built his new capital there (1 Kings 16 [23-24]). Omri reigned altogether 12 years (1 Kings 16 [23]). Since Asa's year 27 was Omri's year 1, Omri's year 12 was Asa's year 38. But Asa's year 38 is Ahab's year 1 (1 Kings 16 [29]). Hence Asa's year 38 is reckoned twice over to the outgoing King Omri as his 12th and last year, and to the incoming King Ahab as his first, according to the Israelite mode of reckoning.

The verse 1 Kings 16 [23], like many others, would be much clearer if instead of the mistranslation " began to reign," we read simply " reigned," as it is in the Hebrew Text. Omri *began* to reign over part of Israel in Asa's year 27. He *began* to reign over all Israel in Asa's year 31. He reigned altogether 12 years from Asa's year 27 to Asa's year 38.

Asa reigned 41 years (1 Kings 15 [10]). Asa's year 38 was Ahab's year 1. Therefore Asa's year 41 was Ahab's year 4. But in Ahab's year 4, Jehoshaphat reigned in Judah (1 Kings 22 [41]). Asa's year 41 is therefore Jehoshaphat's accession year, and Jehoshaphat's year 1 is the next year, Ahab's year 5. The whole of the broken year, Ahab's year 4, is given to the outgoing King Asa, and none of it to the incoming King Jehoshaphat, according to the Judaite mode of reckoning.

Should we make the error of reckoning Ahab's year 4 as Jehoshaphat's year 1, we shall be tripped up when we reach the years of Ahaziah and Jehoram of Israel, and the critics who fall into this trap will immediately begin to cry out for an " emendation " of the Text to make it square with their error.

So far all is clear. Each figure given is found to be correct. The Judaite method of reckoning is applied to the Kings of Judah, the Israelite method to the Kings of Israel.

But now we reach the most difficult and puzzling problem of the Ahaziahs and the Jehorams of Israel and Judah, the Gordian knot of the Chronology

of the Kings of Israel and Judah.   Many Chronologers have cut the knot.
But very few have untied it, amongst whom honourable mention must be
made of Ussher, Willis J. Beecher, and the Author of the *Companion Bible.*

The problem is not an easy one, and it can only be solved by giving careful
attention to the history of the period and the character of the Kings.

Three Kings of Israel and three Kings of Judah are concerned.   A mnemonic
will serve to fix them in their proper place and to distinguish one from another.
A. follows A., and J. follows J., and the two successors of Ahab and Jehoshaphat
are of the same names, but follow in reverse order.   Thus we have the following successions :—

> In Israel : (1) Ahab, (2) Ahaziah, (3) Jehoram.
> In Judah : (1) Jehoshaphat (2) Jehoram, (3) Ahaziah.

Ahab married Jezebel and became a thorough-paced Pagan.   Jehoshaphat
" walked in the ways of Asa his father doing that which was right in the eyes
of the Lord."   After a while Jehoshaphat joined affinity with Ahab.

There was first a *family* alliance (2 Chron. 18 [1]).   Jehoshaphat's son, Jehoram
of Judah, married Ahab's daughter Athaliah.   Then there was a *commercial*
alliance.   Jehoshaphat joined himself with Ahab's son, Ahaziah of Israel, to
make ships to go to Tarshish (2 Chron. 20 [36]).   Finally, there was a *military*
alliance.   Jehoshaphat joined his armed forces with those of Ahab, and went
up with him against Ramoth-gilead (1 Kings 22 [1-40]).

Jehoram of Judah was one of the worst men that ever sat on the throne of
David.   His wife Athaliah was the daughter of Jezebel, and whatever was
not bad in her husband when she married him was made bad by her.   He
killed off all his brethren (2 Chron. 21 [4]).   She killed off all the descendants
of her son Ahaziah (except Joash who was saved by Jehoshabeath).   Jehoram
of Judah walked in the ways of the Kings of Israel like as did the house of
Ahab.   He rose up against (וַיָּקָם עַל) the kingdom of his father (2 Chron. 21 [4]),
not " was risen up to " in the sense of being made a partner of the kingdom,
as suggested in the A.V. marginal note, but " he rose up against the
rule of his father and slew all his brethren with the sword, and divers also
of the princes of Israel."   This looks like laying violent hands upon the Kingdom.   Jehoram of Judah caused the inhabitants of Jerusalem to commit
fornication and compelled Judah thereto (2 Chron. 21 [11]).   Elijah rebuked him,
his enemies stripped him of all his substance, the Lord smote him with a
foul disease, and in the end " he departed without being desired."

When Ahab and Jehoshaphat went out to war they left the care of their
Kingdoms to their sons.   Hence we find Jehoram of Judah Pro-Rex with
Jehoshaphat, and Ahaziah of Israel Co-Rex with Ahab, both in the same
year.   Next year Ahab dies in battle at Ramoth-gilead.   Ahaziah of Israel
falls through the lattice and dies, and his brother Jehoram of Israel succeeds
to the Kingdom.   This explains how it is that there were three Kings of
Israel in one and the same calendar year.

Meanwhile Jehoshaphat returns to Jerusalem.   He resumes the control
of affairs, and the Pro-Rexship of Jehoram of Judah comes to an end, and with
it the reckoning of Jehoram of Judah's years in 2 Kings 1 [17], which makes

Jehoram of Israel's year 1 = Jehoshaphat's year 18, which again = Jehoram of Judah's year 2.

Then comes Jehoshaphat's death and the sole Kingship of Jehoram of Judah. He began his second count as Co-Rex in Jehoram of Israel's 5th year (2 Kings 8 [16, 17]) = Jehoshaphat's year 22. This, then, was Jehoram of Judah's year 1 as Co-Rex, *Jehoshaphat being then King of Judah*, if Hales and Clinton, who would delete these words as an interpolation, only knew it.

Jehoshaphat died in Jehoram of Judah's year 4 as Co-Rex, whereupon Jehoram of Judah begins to reign for the third time, now as sole King, but he continues the count of the years of his Co-Rexship and calls the next year his 5th year. He reckons himself King from the time of the first year of his Co-Rexship, and consequently he calls the year after the year of Jehoshaphat's death his year 5.

This explains the apparent incongruity of his beginning to reign three times over, 1st as Pro-Rex, when his father went to war, 2nd as Co-Rex, during his father's lifetime, when Jehoshaphat gave gifts and cities to all his sons, but gave to Jehoram of Judah the Kingdom because he was the firstborn (2 Chron. 21 [3]), and 3rd as sole King when his father died.

Ahaziah of Israel is said to have reigned 2 years, but both he and his father died in the same year, and both these years belong to each of them, whilst the second of them belongs also to Jehoram of Israel. All this is correctly stated in the Text (1 Kings 22 [51], 2 Kings 1 [17], 3 [1]), according to the Israelite mode of reckoning.

Since Jehoram of Israel's year 1 = Jehoram of Judah's year 2 (2 Kings 1 [17], 3 [1]) = Ahab's year 22 = Ahaziah of Israel's year 2 = Jehoshaphat's year 18, it follows that Jehoram of Judah's year 1 as Pro-Rex = Jehoshaphat's year 17.

Since Jehoram of Judah's year 1 = Jehoram of Israel's year 5 = Jehoshaphat's year 22 (2 Kings 8 [16, 17]), it follows that he must have been removed from the Pro-Rexship (the count of his years as Pro-Rex having ceased), and begun to reckon again as Co-Rex, making Jehoshaphat's year 22 the year 1 of his Co-Rexship, the years of which are continued throughout the rest of his life, so that when he becomes sole King on the death of Jehoshaphat his years are counted on just as if he were already King. In all this there is no departure from the ordinary Judaite mode of reckoning. The facts are all perfectly clear and are all clearly stated. They can only be understood by keeping the eye on the Chronological Table which exhibits them. (See Vol. II, p. 24.)

When Jehoram of Judah was smitten with the foul disease he was obliged to associate his son Ahaziah of Judah with himself as Co-Rex. Hence Ahaziah of Judah reigned in Jehoram of Israel's year 11, viz. as Co-Rex (2 Kings 9 [29]).

But since Jehoram of Israel's year 5 is Jehoram of Judah's year 1, it follows that Jehoram of Israel's year 11 is Jehoram of Judah's year 7. Hence Jehoram of Judah's year 7 is Ahaziah of Judah's year 1 as Co-Rex. The next year is Jehoram of Israel's year 12 = Jehoram of Judah's year 8 = the year in which Jehoram of Judah died (2 Kings 8 [17]), consequently in which Ahaziah of Judah became sole King (2 Kings 8 [25]) and reigned one year (2 Kings 8 [26]). This one year is Jehoram of Israel's year 12, and Ahaziah of Judah's year 1 as sole King.

But now for the first time in the records of the Kings of Judah we get one and the same year counted twice over, and given to the outgoing King, Jehoram of Judah, and also to the incoming King, Ahaziah of Judah. This just shows what thorough-paced heathens these two Kings of Judah had become, the one the husband, and the other the son, of Athaliah, the daughter of Jezebel. We cannot affect to be surprised that under the domination of paganizing Israelitish influences, the Judaite method of reckoning is displaced by the Israelite mode of reckoning.

Ahaziah of Judah is the King whose age, as given in 2 Chron. 22 [2,] shows him to have been " two years older than his father." Yet, as Dr. John Lightfoot says, there is always " admirable wisdom " in these " slips of the Holy Ghost." " Strange variations yet always Divine," " discords in which the Holy Ghost hath showed sweet music."

Compare the two passages :—

> 2 *Kings* 8 [26] : " Two and twenty years old was Ahaziah when he began to reign."
>
> 2 *Chron.* 22 [2] : " Forty and two years old was Ahaziah when he began to reign."

A plain contradiction, if ever there was one, either in the Bible or out of it, yet one put there *intentionally* and on purpose to convey a Divine Truth.

The two golden rules for the solution of Bible difficulties like this are, (1) look to the original Hebrew, and (2) read carefully the context. We translate—

> 2 *Chron.* 22 [2] : A son of 42 years was Ahaziah when he began to reign.

If, therefore, we look back 42 years, we shall come to his father. Now from AN. HOM. 3231, the first year of Ahaziah, deduct 42 years, and we reach the year AN. HOM. 3189. Referring to the Chronological Tables we find that the year AN. HOM. 3189 was the first year of Omri, the founder of a new dynasty—so that just as the sacred writer reckons the years of the Kingdom of Asa from the true origin of the Kingdom in the first year of Rehoboam (2 Chron. 16 [1,] see Chronological Tables AN. HOM. 3178 = 16th year of Asa), so here he reckons the years of Ahaziah from the accession of the dynasty of Omri.

Now look to the context. Complete the translation of the verse :—

> 2 *Chron.* 22 [2] : A son of 42 years was Ahaziah when he began to reign, and he reigned *one* year in Jerusalem, and his mother's name was Athaliah, the daughter of Omri. He also walked in the ways of the house of Ahab. He did evil, like the house of Ahab. He went down to see Joram the son of Ahab. And the destruction of Ahaziah was of God by coming to Joram. For he went out with Joram against Jehu, whom the Lord had anointed to cut off the house of Ahab. And when Jehu was executing judgment upon the house of Ahab, and found the princes of Judah and the sons of the brethren of Ahaziah, he slew them. And he sought Ahaziah, and they caught him (for he was hid in Samaria), and when they had slain him they buried him, for they said he is the son of Jehoshaphat who sought the Lord with all his heart.

But the Holy Ghost will not have him for a son of David's line at all.   He is the son of Athaliah, the daughter of Omri and Jezebel.   He is no seed of David.   He is an imp of the house of Ahab, a son of the house of Omri, and as such a " son of 42 years," for the dynasty of the house of Omri was exactly 42 years old.

That is not the " modern " way of writing history, but it is the way of the Old Testament writers, and the way of the New Testament writers too, and if we want to understand their writings we must put ourselves at their point of view, and not force our meaning into their words.

This interpretation is confirmed by St. Matthew, who will have it that Rehoboam begat Abijah, and Abijah begat Asa, and Asa begat Jehoshaphat, and Jehoshaphat begat Jehoram, but Jehoram did not beget Ahaziah—nor Joash—nor Amaziah—but only the fourth in the direct line of descent, " Jehoram begat Uzziah," his great-great-grandson. " Let the posterity of the wicked be cut off, and in the generation following let their name be blotted out.   Let the iniquity of his fathers be remembered with the Lord ; and let not the sin of his mother be blotted out.   Let them be before the LORD continually, that He may cut off the memory of them from the earth" (Psa. 109 $^{13\text{-}15}$). " For I the Lord thy God am a jealous God, visiting the iniquity of the fathers upon the children unto the third and fourth generation of them that hate Me " (Ex. 20 ^{5}). St. Matthew will have it that from David to the carrying away to Babylon are 14 generations, not 17, and that these three men are no true seed of the royal line of David.   Their ancestry must be traced to the house of Omri.

The modern critic wants facts, and will have it that the Bible must be interpreted like any other book.   But the Bible is not written from the same standpoint as any other book, and whilst it gives all the facts that the critics need, it also gives something more.   It gives the Divine interpretation and the real meaning of the facts.

2. Second Period—Jehu to the Fall of Samaria.

We have reached the end of another chapter in the history of the Kings of Israel and Judah.   Jehu slays both Ahaziah of Judah and Jehoram of Israel, and seizes the throne of Israel.

Athaliah destroys the seed royal, and usurps the throne of Judah.   Athaliah and Jehu start level as Rehoboam and Jeroboam did.   Jehu's year 1 is Athaliah's year 1, and with this year a new Era is introduced. " Jehu slew (the seventy sons and) all that remained of the house of Ahab in Jezreel, and all his great men, and his kinsfolks, and his priests, until he left him none remaining (2 Kings 10 ^{11}). He gathered together " all the prophets of Baal, all his servants, and all his priests," and slew them.   Thus Jehu destroyed Baal out of Israel (2 Kings 10 $^{19.\ 25.\ 28}$).

In the Kingdom of Judah, Jehoiada engineers a great political revolution, inspires a great religious revival, and sets Joash on the throne of Judah. Athaliah is slain in the 7th year of her usurpation.   The house of Baal is broken down, and Mattan, the priest of Baal, is slain (2 Kings 11 $^{4\text{-}21}$).

In these circumstances, it is natural to expect that the reigns of the succeeding Kings of both Kingdoms are computed by the Judaite mode of reckoning, and, as a matter of fact, this is just what we find.

The new Era begins with Jehu's year 1, which is also Athaliah's year 1. From this point onward, the Israelite mode of reckoning is discarded except in the one solitary instance of the 1st year of Jeroboam II, which is reckoned twice over, once to his predecessor and once to himself.

From 2 Kings 11 [1, 3, 4, 21] we learn that Athaliah reigned 6 years, and was slain in the 7th, and from 2 Kings 12 [1] that Joash of Judah reigned in Jehu's year 7. So that Jehu's year 7 = Athaliah's year 7 = Joash of Judah's year 1.

Jehu reigned 28 years (2 Kings 10 [36]) and Jehu's year 7 = Joash of Judah's year 1. Therefore, Jehu's year 28 = Joash of Judah's year 22.

Jehoahaz of Israel's year 1 = Joash of Judah's year 23 (2 Kings 13 [1]), and Jehoahaz of Israel reigned 17 years (2 Kings 13 [1]). Therefore, Jehoahaz of Israel's year 17 = Joash of Judah's year 39.

Jehoahaz of Israel was succeeded by Jehoash of Israel. As Jehoahaz of Israel's last year was Joash of Judah's year 39, Jehoash of Israel's first year was Joash of Judah's year 40 (2 Kings 13 [9]). Jehoash of Israel's year 1 (as sole King) = Joash of Judah's year 40. But Jehoash of Israel reigned (as Co-Rex) in Joash of Judah's year 37 (2 Kings 13 [10]). Therefore, Jehoash of Israel was Co-Rex with his father Jehoahaz of Israel during the last three years of his father's reign.

This is not a supposition or a hypothesis. It is a fact stated by implication in the Text itself, and being contained in the Text it is of equal authority with any other statement contained in the same Text.

These Co-Reigns occur frequently in the history of Israel and Judah, from the time when Solomon was made King in the reign of David onward. They are also equally frequent in the annals of other Eastern nations.

They do not become any less frequent by being referred to as " gratuitous," "fictitious" and "absurd." They are there in the Text itself. There is frequently a hint given in the Text as to the reason for them. In this case, the reason for the appointment of Jehoash of Israel as Co-Rex may have been the absence of Jehoahaz of Israel in his Syrian wars, when " the King of Syria made them (the people of Israel) like dust by threshing " (2 Kings 13 [7]).

Amaziah succeeded Joash of Judah in Jehoash of Israel's year 2 as sole King (2 Kings 12 [21], 14 [1]). He reigned 29 years (2 Kings 14 [2]).

Jehoash of Israel reigned 16 years as sole King (2 Kings 13 [10]). Since Jehoash of Israel's year 2 as sole King = Amaziah's year 1, Jehoash of Israel's year 16 = Amaziah's year 15. But Amaziah's year 15 = Jeroboam II's year 1 (2 Kings 14 [23]). Hence Amaziah's year 15 is a broken year, and is reckoned twice over, once as Jehoash of Israel's last year as sole King, and once as Jeroboam II's first year, according to the Israelite mode of reckoning, which reappears here for the last time.

Amaziah lived after the death of Jehoash of Israel 15 years. Then a conspiracy was hatched against him. He fled from Jerusalem, and was slain at Lachish in Jeroboam II's year 15 (2 Kings 14 [17-22]). The interregnum which followed lasted for some time. The word " then " in 2 Chron. 26 [1] is a mistranslation. It represents the Hebrew *Vav*, which contains no note of time, and should be translated simply " And."

Judah was divided into two parties. The conspirators gained their object. They slew King Amaziah and held their own for some years, but in the 27th year of Jeroboam II the scales were turned, and the other party, the people of Judah, got the upper hand and made Uzziah (Azariah) King instead of his father Amaziah (2 Kings 14^{21}, 15^1).

From the 15th year of Jeroboam II when Amaziah was slain (2 Kings 14$^{17-22}$), to the 27th year of Jeroboam II when Uzziah was made King instead of his father Amaziah (2 Kings 15^1), is a period of 11 years during which the throne of Judah was vacant.

Hence, Ussher is wrong in deleting these 11 years from the Chronology. He *assumes* that Jeroboam II was Co-Rex with his father Jehoash of Israel, for the long period of 11 years, being made Co-Rex in Jehoash of Israel's year 5. He *assumes* that the 27th year of Jeroboam II in 1 Kings 15^1 is the 27th year of this *assumed* Co-Regency which began in the 5th year of Jehoash of Israel, the 27th year of this assumed Co-Regency being the 16th year of Jeroboam II's reign as sole King. (See 2 Kings 15^1, marginal note). This is one of the few blemishes in Ussher's work.

He fell into the error because he had an axe to grind. He wanted to make our Lord's birth fall exactly 4,000 years after the creation of Adam. For this purpose he wanted to get rid of 7 years. He cuts out 11 years here and gets back 4 of them, one at a time, later on. But there is no room for doubt. The fact of the 11 years interregnum is as stable as any other fact which lies embedded in the Text, and cannot be ignored without throwing the whole scheme of the Chronology of the Text into hopeless confusion.

Josephus made the same error as anyone else may do, quite easily, who is satisfied with a superficial and a cursory, instead of an attentive reading, of the narrative. But the interregnum is there and it cannot be got rid of. The gap of 11 years between Amaziah and Uzziah must be charted down.

For 15 years Uzziah and Jeroboam II reigned together, Uzziah in Judah and Jeroboam II in Israel. Jeroboam II reigned 41 years (2 Kings 14^{23}, 15^8). Jeroboam II's year 27 was Uzziah's year 1. Therefore Jeroboam's year 41 was Uzziah's year 15. Then follows a gap of 22 years from the year after Jeroboam II's year 41, or Uzziah's year 16, to Uzziah's year 37, both inclusive, or from Uzziah's year 15 to Uzziah's year 38, both exclusive, an interregnum in the Kingdom of Israel of 22 years.

By deleting the 11 years interregnum in the Kingdom of Judah, Ussher reduces the interregnum of the Kingdom of Israel by 11 years, viz. from 22 to 11. (See A.V. marginal note, 2 Kings 14^{29} and 15^1.) These years must be restored.

Ussher's own notes are as follows : " Jeroboam seemeth to have been taken into the consortship of the Kingdom by his father Joash, going to war against the Syrians." " After Amaziah came Uzziah or Azariah, in the 27th year of Jeroboam, King of Israel, *reckoning from the time that he began to reign in consortship with his father*." Ussher makes Uzziah (Azariah) succeed Amaziah immediately after Amaziah has completed his 29th year, which he identifies with the 16th year of Jeroboam II's reign as sole King, and which he calls the 27th year of Jeroboam II's reign. He ought to have inserted an interval between Amaziah and Uzziah, and made Uzziah succeed Amaziah after an interregnum of 11 years, in the 27th year of Jeroboam II, as stated in 2 Kings 15[1].

No account is given of the events which occurred in Israel during this interregnum which lasted 22 years, but the history indicates very plainly the straitened character of the times, and suggests a reason for the interregnum, for we are told that the country was overrun by enemies, and the name of Israel was in danger of being "blotted out from under heaven" (2 Kings 14[26, 27]). Some mystery seems to hang over this period. During the first part of it Assyrian history is also a blank.

It is the time of the Prophet Jonah (2 Kings 14[25]) with his dread message : "Yet 40 days and Nineveh shall be destroyed." It is the time of the earthquake, two years before which Amos began to prophecy (Amos 1[1]), an earthquake that was remembered even to the days of Zechariah, nearly 300 years later, the terror of which Zechariah uses as an image of the terror of the Day of Judgment.

It was a time when the affliction of Israel was bitter, for "there was not any shut up nor left in Israel" (2 Kings 14[26]). The author of the *Companion Bible* suggests that the words "shut up" are to be interpreted as meaning "protected," like those shut up in a fortress, and that the word "left" is a mistranslation. He derives the word so translated from the Hebrew word עָזַב *âzab*, to fortify, not from the Hebrew word עָזַב *âzab*, to leave, to forsake. The meaning then is "there was no fortress and no fortification," or "no protection and no defence" against their foes. The bitterness of Israel's affliction at this time may possibly be connected with the Civil War by which the Kingdom of Israel was torn asunder from the reign of Jeroboam II to the close of its history.

At the close of this interregnum of 22 years, in the 38th year of Uzziah, Zachariah the son of Jeroboam II reigned over Israel for six months (2 Kings 15[8-10]), and was slain by Shallum.

In the following year, the 39th year of Uzziah, Shallum reigned one month and was slain by Menahem (2 Kings 15[13, 14]).

In the same year, the 39th year of Uzziah, Menahem slew Shallum and reigned over Israel. Here we notice the adoption of the Judaite mode of reckoning the reigns of the Kings of Israel. This year, the 39th of Uzziah, is the accession year of Menahem. For he reigned 10 years, and if this 39th year of Uzziah's was his first year, there would be a break of one year between his last year and the first year of his son Pekahiah.

Therefore Menahem's year 1=Uzziah's year 40, Menahem's year 10 = Uzziah's year 49. Pekahiah's year 1=Uzziah's year 50 (2 Kings 15[23]), Pekahiah's year 2=Uzziah's year 51 (2 Kings 15[23]).

Pekah's year 1=Uzziah's year 52 (2 Kings 15[27]). Jotham's year 1= Pekah's year 2 (2 Kings 15[32])=the year after Uzziah's year 52, which year 52 was Uzziah's last year (2 Kings 15[2]).

Jotham reigned 16 years (2 Kings 15[33]), and since Jotham's year 1=Pekah's year 2, Jotham's year 16, his last year=Pekah's year 17. But Pekah's year

17 was also Ahaz's accession year, for he reigned in the 17th year of Pekah (2 Kings 16[1]). Consequently Pekah's year 18=Ahaz's year 1, and Pekah's year 20 his last year on the throne=Ahaz's year 3.

We now reach one of the most interesting, and, at the same time, one of the most illuminating puzzles of the Chronology of this period. We read in 2 Kings 15[30], that Hoshea slew Pekah in the 20th year of Jotham, which is the year after the 20th of Pekah. Now Jotham only reigned 16 years altogether, and if Jotham's year 20 is the date intended, *we* should call this Ahaz's year 4. But in the Text it is called the 20th year of Jotham.

Why is this? The history supplies a reason in the character of the wicked King Ahaz. Two characters in the narrative of the Kings of Israel and Judah are marked with an index finger of horror and scorn, as pointing to the names of two persons singled out for fierce execration and perpetual reproach. In 2 Kings 9[37], we read " This is Jezebel," and in 2 Chron. 28[22], " This is that King Ahaz."

It was Ahaz who " made molten images for Baalim," who " burnt his children in the fire after the abominations of the heathen," who " made Judah naked and transgressed sore against the Lord." The cup was full. The writer could say no more. " *This is that King Ahaz.*" "And" (not " for " as in A.V. and R.V.), with a fine finishing touch of irony the writer adds this last mark of his contempt and scorn, " he sacrificed to the gods of Damascus which smote him, and he said, Because the gods of the Kings of Syria help them, therefore I will sacrifice to them, that they may help me. But they were the ruin of him, and of all Israel." That explains the Chronology. As Dr. John Lightfoot quaintly observes, " The Holy Ghost choozeth rather to reckon by holy Jotham in his grave, than by wicked Ahaz alive," and instead of the 4th year of Ahaz we get the 20th year of Jotham.

Pekah was slain by Hoshea in the 20th year of Jotham, i.e. in the 4th year of Ahaz, i.e. in the year after the 20th year of Pekah. So then he was dethroned in his 20th year, and slain the year after the 20th, and last year of his reign.

Then comes another gap, an interregnum or a period of anarchy lasting 8 years. For although Pekah's throne was empty in the 4th year of Ahaz, Hoshea did not himself begin to reign till the 12th of Ahaz (2 Kings 17[1]).

Ahaz's year 12 is Hoshea's year 1. For Hoshea reigned 9 years (2 Kings 17[1]), and Hoshea's year 9 = Hezekiah's year 6 (2 Kings 18[10]), and Hoshea's year 7 = Hezekiah's year 4 (2 Kings 18[9]). Therefore Hoshea's year 4 = Hezekiah's year 1. But Hoshea's year 4 is also Ahaz's year 15 because Hoshea's year 3 is Hezekiah's accession year (2 Kings 18[1]). Therefore Hoshea's year 3 = Ahaz's year 14, and consequently Hoshea's year 1 = Ahaz's year 12 (2 Kings 17[1]). Therefore the gap between Pekah's year 20, his last year on the throne, and Hoshea's year 1, is the gap between Ahaz's year 3 and his year 12, both exclusive, or the gap between Ahaz's year 4 and his year 11, both inclusive, and this is a period of 8 calendar years.

Hoshea's year 1 = Ahaz's year 12 (2 Kings 17[1]). Therefore Hoshea's year 3 = Ahaz's year 14. And Ahaz reigned 16 years (2 Kings 16[2]). But Hoshea's year 3 = Hezekiah's accession year (2 Kings 18[1]). Therefore Hezekiah was

Co-Rex with Ahaz during Ahaz's years 14, 15 and 16. Ahaz's year 14 = Hezekiah's accession year. Ahaz's year 15 = Hezekiah's year 1. Ahaz's year 16 = Hezekiah's year 2.

The year in which Hezekiah began to reign as Co-Rex with his father(Ahaz's year 14), is Hezekiah's accession year. As soon as he got firmly into the saddle he took matters into his own hands. He was 25 years of age, and in the first year of his reign, and the very first month of it (2 Chron. 29 [3]), and on the very first day of the month (2 Chron. 29 [17]), he made a clean sweep of the idolatrous practices of his father Ahaz.

He opened the doors of the house of the Lord which Ahaz had shut up (2 Chron. 28 [24]). He removed the high places, broke in pieces the stone statues of Baal, cut down the wooden images of Ashtoreth, and " brake in pieces the brasen serpent that Moses had made, and called it Nehushtan (a piece of brass) " (2 Kings 18 [4]). They cleansed the Sanctuary in 16 days (2 Chron. 29 [17]). It was now too late to keep the Passover at the proper time in the 1st month, so they observed the feast on the 14th day of the 2nd month.

The remnant of Israel that were escaped out of the hands of the Kings of Assyria were invited to attend this great Passover (2 Chron. 30 [6]), and they came from Ephraim and Manasseh and Issachar and Zebulum (2 Chron. 30 [18]), and there was no Passover like it since the time of Solomon (2 Chron. 30 [26]).

"And Hezekiah rejoiced, and all the people, that God had prepared the people: for the thing was done suddenly " (2 Chron. 29 [36]).

It was a sudden *coup d'état*. It had been prepared for by the inspiring ministry of Isaiah, and the secret influence of Hezekiah during his Co-Rexship with his father. When Ahaz died, the revulsion of the people was deep and widespread. This first year of Hezekiah, when he was 25 years of age, was not his accession year as Co-Rex (the 14th of Ahaz), and not his first year as Co-Rex (the 15th of Ahaz), but his first year as sole King, in the year after Ahaz's death. That explains how it was that the great religious revival broke out so suddenly on the 1st day of the 1st month of Hezekiah's reign as sole King. It had been prepared for. The people were ready for it. It met with an immediate response, and it spread like wildfire throughout the two Kingdoms.

A difficulty has been raised respecting the age of Ahaz at the birth of his son Hezekiah, who is said from a comparison of 2 Kings 16 [2] and 2 Kings 18 [2] to have been born when his father was only 8 years old. But Ahaz was 20 when he began to reign (2 Kings 16 [2]), and 36 when he died and Hezekiah was 25 when he began to reign as sole King the year after the 16th of Ahaz (2 Kings 18 [2]). Hence Hezekiah was 25 when Ahaz was 37, i.e. Ahaz was 12 when Hezekiah was born, not 9 as he would have been if he had been 25 in his accession year, the 14th of Ahaz. Hezekiah was 25, not in his accession year as Co-Rex, but in his first year as sole King.

CHAPTER XXII.   JUDAH FROM THE FALL OF SAMARIA TO THE CAPTIVITY.

(AN. HOM. 3406–3520)

SAMARIA fell in the 9th year of Hoshea, which was the 6th year of Hezekiah, the year AN. HOM. 3406. The account of the fall of Samaria in 2 Kings 18 [9, 10] is very condensed but perfectly accurate. We know from the records of Assyria that it was taken by Sargon. Scripture says, "Shalmaneser came up against Samaria and besieged it." So he did. "And at the end of three years," not " *he* took," but " *they* took it," implying that someone else was concerned in the actual taking of the city beside Shalmaneser, who began the siege.

This is not the place to discuss the authorship of the so-called Deutero- or Trito-Isaiah. But it may be pointed out that the critical year of the reign of Hezekiah was the 14th. It was the year of Sennacherib's invasion, when the angel of the Lord went forth and smote in the camp of the Assyrians 185,000, and when they arose early in the morning they were all dead corpses (2 Kings 18 [13]–19 [37], Is. 36.37). It was the year of Hezekiah's sickness, when the Lord brought the shadow 10 degrees backward by which it had gone down in the dial of Ahaz (2 Kings 20 [1, 6, 11], Is. 38). It was the year of the embassy of Merodach-baladan of Babylon (2 Kings 20 [12-21], Is. 39).

It was the year in which Isaiah said to Hezekiah, "Behold, the days come, that all that is in thine house, and that which thy fathers have laid up in store until this day, shall be carried to Babylon ; nothing shall be left, saith the Lord. And of thy sons that shall issue from thee, which thou shalt beget, shall they take away ; and they shall be eunuchs in the palace of the King of Babylon" (Isaiah 39 [1, 6, 7]). These three great events, the destruction of the host of Sennacherib of Assyria, the sickness of Hezekiah, and Isaiah's prophecy of the Babylonian captivity, all fell out in the same year and made it the great critical year of Hezekiah's life.

They are all recorded in Isaiah 36–39, a passage which forms the true second part of Isaiah, the connecting link between Isaiah 1–35, and Isaiah 40–66. These last 27 chapters should not be called the second, but the third part of Isaiah. The Prophet foresaw and foretold, not only the captivity, but also the return from Babylon. This is the subject elaborated in these last 27 chapters of Isaiah, and the present writer agrees with Professor R. G. Moulton and the Poet Tennyson in believing that, with the preceding 39 chapters, they form one indivisible literary and artistic whole, and are the work of one and the same man. They belong to the last fifteen years of the reign of Hezekiah, from this his 14th year, to his 29th and last.

Up to this point, the Chronology has been so locked and interlocked by checks and cross-checks, that it has been almost impossible for anyone to err in regard to it, provided that the statements in the Text are strictly adhered to in every case. From the accession of Manasseh to the reign of Josiah, we have no check on the numbers given, but from the 13th year of Josiah onward, they are checked by the long periods in the Prophets (Jer. 25 [1-3]), and by synchronisms with the years of the reign of Nebuchadnezzar (2 Kings 24 [8-12], 25 [2-8], Jer. 32 [1], etc).

But in the Kingdom of Judah, the Chronology always follows the Judaite mode of reckoning, and never counts a year twice over, or gives it to both the outgoing and the incoming King, with the one single exception of the case of Ahaziah the son of Athaliah, the daughter of Ahab and Jezebel, an exception which proves the rule, for Ahaziah is not reckoned as a true descendant of the line of David, but " an imp of the house of Omri," whose years are naturally computed by the Israelite mode of reckoning.   Apart from the special circumstances of this case, the reigns of the Kings of Judah are always reckoned as calendar years, the broken year being always reckoned to the outgoing, and never to the incoming King, the outgoing King's last year being always regarded as the incoming King's *accession* year, and the following calendar year as the *first* year of his reign.   We cannot be wrong in applying the Judaite mode of reckoning to the cases of Manasseh, Amon and Josiah, the only three cases in which the mode of reckoning cannot be checked.

Manasseh reigned 55 years (2 Kings 21 [1]).   Fifty-five calendar years must be allotted to him in full in our Chronology of his reign.   Amon reigned 2 years (2 Kings 21 [19]).   Two years must be allotted to him.   Josiah reigned 31 years (2 Kings 22 [1]).   Thirty-one years must be allotted to him.

Jehoahaz reigned 3 months, the whole of which was included in the Josiah's year 31.   If his reign had gone over into the New Year he would have been described as having reigned one year.   It is of the essence of the method of the Chronology that it deals only with whole years.   Fractions do not count ; they do not come into the Chronology at all.

Jehoiakim reigned 11 years.   His accession took place either during the 31st year of Josiah, which would then be called his accession year, or else immediately after, at the beginning of the New Year.   In either case Jehoiakim's year 1 is the calendar year that follows next after Josiah's year 31.

The correctness of these results is proved by the long period given in Jeremiah 25 [1-3].   The 4th year of Jehoiakim was one of the most critical years in the history of Judah.   It was the year in which Jeremiah prophesied that both Jerusalem and the cities of Judah, and all the world, from Egypt to Media, should serve the King of Babylon 70 years (Jer. 25 [11-26]).

It was the year which synchronised with the 1st year of Nebuchadnezzar King of Babylon (Jer. 25 [1]), the most important synchronism in the whole Bible, for it enables us to connect the Sacred Chronology, from the creation of Adam to the 4th year of Jehoiakim, with the recorded dates of profane history from that point, both forward and backward, as far as they have been faithfully preserved and accurately ascertained from the writings and Monuments of antiquity.

Finally, it was the year in which Jeremiah solemnly recounted the results of the work of the past 23 years of his ministry, thereby giving us this valuable synchronism.   "From the 13th year of Josiah, the son of Amon King of Judah, even unto this day (the 4th of Jehoiakim), these 23 years, the word of the Lord hath come unto me, and I have spoken unto you rising up early and speaking ; but ye have not hearkened " (Jer. 25 [3], R.V.).   What are " these 23 years ? "

They are as follows :—

The 23 years of Jeremiah 25 [3].

1 = Josiah's year							13
2	,,	,,					14
3	,,	,,					15
4	,,	,,					16
5	,,	,,					17
6	,,	,,					18
7	,,	,,					19
8	,,	,,					20
9	,,	,.					21
10	,,	,,					22
11	,,	,,					23
12	,,	,,					24
13	,,	,,					25
14	,,	,,					26
15	,,	,,					27
16	,,	,,					28
17	,,	,,					29
18	,,	,,					30

19= Josiah's year 31 = Jehoiachin's 3 mos. = Jehoiakim's accession year.

20= Jehoiakim's year							1
21	,,	,,					2
22	,,	,,					3
23	,,	,,					4

This enables us to bridge the gulf between the last year of Josiah and the 1st of Jehoiakim, and proves conclusively that the computation given above is correct.

CHAPTER XXIII. COMPARATIVE CHRONOLOGY—SAUL TO THE CAPTIVITY.

We have now traced the history of the Hebrew people during the period of the Monarchy, from the first year of Saul to " the 4th year of Jehoiakim . . . that was the first year of Nebuchadnezzar " (Jer. 25 [1]), as it is recorded by contemporary prophetic narrators in their own annals. The Chronology is so precise, and the history of the Kingdom of Israel is so closely locked and interlocked with that of the Kingdom of Judah, that it is next to impossible for any error to have crept into it. The connections are so perfect that to alter any one text by one single year, is to throw the Chronology of the whole into hopeless confusion. No method for the better preservation of a chronological Record for all succeeding generations could be devised or even imagined. We may rely absolutely on the authenticity and the correctness of every chronological statement in this Record, as it has been preserved to us, and as we have it in our hands to-day.

There are numerous other witnesses by whose testimony the chronological data for this period, as given in the Old Testament, can be tested, and it is not too much to say that wherever it has been thus brought into court, its accuracy and its authenticity have been amply and invariably vindicated. " In every case where we can test it by contemporaneous Monuments, the authenticity of which is doubted by no one," says Prof. A. H. Sayce, " we find it confirmed and explained even in the minutest details."

These other witnesses may be grouped under three heads—Egypt, Moab and Assyria.

1. *Egypt.*

In Egypt we have the celebrated *Shishak Inscription,* on the south wall of the temple of Amon at Karnak. This Temple is one of the noblest examples of the majesty and sublimity of Egyptian architecture. Karnak is situated on the right bank of the river Nile, a very short distance from the site of Thebes, now Luxor, the ancient capital of Egypt. Karnak is the " populous No," or better, as in the margin, the " No-Amon " of Nahum 3 [8].

Shashanq I, or Sheshonk I, as the name is now pronounced by the modern guide to the temple ruins, is the Shishak of the Old Testament. To him Jeroboam fled when Solomon sought to kill him (1 Kings 11 [40]). In the fifth year of King Rehoboam, Shishak came up against Jerusalem, plundered the Temple and took away all the treasures of the hing's House (1 Kings 14 [25, 26], 2 Chron. 12 [2-9]).

Shishak was the founder of a new dynasty, the 22nd or Bubastite dynasty, so called because it alone of all the 31 dynasties had its capital at Bubastis.

Near the close of his 21st year, Shishak commissioned Haremsaf, his Chief of Public Works, to execute a memorial of his conquests, and the result was the great bas-relief on the walls of the temple of Amon at Karnak. In this Inscription, Shishak mentions the names of 133 cities of the Kingdom of Judah, like Beth-horon, Gibeon, Mahanaim, Shunem, Megiddo, etc., as taken by him during this invasion.

He does not give the exact date of his warlike operations in Palestine, but we know from 1 Kings 14 [25] that it was in the 5th year of Rehoboam's reign (B.C. 982–966), viz. in the year B.C. 978. We can never be sure of any Egyptian dates at this early period, but several computations have been made from various approximate data.

The Egyptian Monuments generally give the year of the reign of the King in whose reign they are executed, but the King *may* have lived on a year or more after executing his last Monument. His years will therefore be expressed by the highest number found on any Monument plus an unknown remainder.

The later King Shabaka, the So of 2 Kings 17 [4], was on the throne when Sargon invaded Palestine in B.C. 720, and for an unknown period before that event. Professor Breasted, in his *Ancient Records*, gives the minimum length of the Kings from that date back to the 1st year of the 22nd dynasty, which was the 1st year of Shishak, as follows :—

Egyptian Kings from Shishak to Shabaka.

Accession of Shabaka or So	..	..	..	B.C.	720	years	+
1 King, 24th dynasty	..	..	..	..	6	,,	+
3 Kings, 23rd ,,	..	..	..	..	37	,,	+
6 Kings, 22nd ,,	..	..	..	..	230	,,	+
				B.C.	993	,,	+

A similar computation from the accession of Tirhaka, B.C. 701+, makes the number 998+. To this we must add the unknown number of years that So had reigned before his defeat by Sargon, and the unknown number of years that each of the other ten Kings reigned after the date of the latest Monument we moderns have happened to discover. We must then deduct the unknown number of years by which these reigns overlap each other. But if we suppose these additions and subtractions to cancel each other, we shall probably not be more than 5, 10, 15 or 20 years out.

Shishak's Inscription was executed in the 21st year of his reign. If his 1st year was B.C. 998 (or 993), and his invasion of Palestine the year before that of his Inscription, that would bring the date of his expedition against Rehoboam to the year B.C. 978 (or 973), i.e. *in the exact year (or within 5 years)* of the 5th year of Rehoboam, B.C. 978. This is quite as exact as we could expect.

Other estimates for the accession of Shishak are Brugsch 980, Marriette 980, Whitehouse 966, Lepsius 961, Flinders Petrie 952. The lowest of these is within 26 years of the 5th year of Rehoboam, and is quite a possible synchronism, but the date which *is* excluded by the synchronism is the Assyrian date c. B.C. 947, which, by omitting the blank of 51 years between Ramman Nirari III and Ashurdân III (B.C. 834–783), makes the 20th year of Shishak c. 927, or 51 years after the 5th of Rehoboam.

This is a decisive argument, from the uncertain but approximate dates of Egypt, against the omission of the 51 years from the Chronology of Assyria, but the Egyptian Monuments have no testimony to bear against the Biblical date of the 5th year of Rehoboam, for the invasion of Judah by Shishak.

We must not, however, lay too much stress upon any argument connected with Egyptian Chronology. The data are so uncertain that no reliance can be placed upon any conclusion derived from them. In order to show the highly speculative nature of the Chronology of Egypt adopted by modern Egyptologists, it will be necessary to examine the *method* by which their chronological results are obtained.

We cannot do better than take the chapter on " The Revision of Chronology," by Prof. W. M. Flinders Petrie, in his recently published *Researches in Sinai* (1906). Prof. Petrie stands almost alone amongst Egyptian Chronologists in the contention that none of Manetho's dynasties are contemporary. " Every instance of double reckoning, or, contemporary dynasties of Kings in Manetho," he says, " has broken down on examination. Not a single overlapping period can be proved against him." Hence Prof. Petrie's date for the 1st dynasty is B.C. 5510.

The principal sources of our knowledge of Egyptian Chronology are (1) the Turin Papyrus, a list of Kings compiled in the 19th dynasty ; (2) the list of Kings and dynasties preserved by Manetho, of the 3rd century B.C., a list known to us only in fragments at second or third hand, and much altered in the process of transmission ; and (3) the records of the Monuments.

The Turin Papyrus is illegible and incomplete. The list of Manetho is incomplete and self-contradictory. The Monuments do not give any chronological data earlier than the 19th dynasty, say about B.C. 1590.

Failing authentic sources of information, recourse is had to the method of *astronomical calculation.*

The Egyptians ignored leap year, and counted only 365 days to every year. Hence every month slipped back $\frac{1}{4}$ of a day every year, a whole day every four years, a whole year every $365 \times 4 = 1{,}460$ years. This period of 1,460 years was called the Sothic period. At the commencement of the period, the star Sirius, called by the Egyptians Sothis, first appeared in the glow of sunrise at early dawn just before the sun.

Censorinus (A.D. 238) says one Sothic period commenced A.D. 139. Consequently, other Sothic periods must have commenced B.C. 1322, 2782, 4242 and 5702, at regular intervals of 1,460 years.

A papyrus from Kahun, now at Berlin, states that there was a rising of Sirius on the 17th of the month Pharmuthi in the 7th year of Senusert III, of the 12th dynasty, which may have been the year B.C. 1874, or the year $1874 + 1460 = $ B.C. 3334, and consequently the close of the 12th dynasty was either in the year B.C. 1786, or in the year B.C. 3246.

The Berlin school of Egyptologists assume that the closing year of the 12th dynasty was the year B.C. 1786. Professor Petrie assumes that it was the year B.C. 3246. There is no Monumental evidence that can be brought forward by the advocates of either of the two schools to decide between them.

In order to arrive at any conclusion on the matter they have to fall back upon the already discarded Turin Papyrus and Manetho, which differ from each other by a period of 258 years, which are only known to us in illegible fragments, which offer self-contradictory testimony, which cannot be checked by the Monuments during the period of the first six dynasties, and one of which, Manetho, is said to be in error wherever he can be checked by them.

Apart from which Professor Petrie himself admits that even if all these difficulties were removed, astronomical calculations in regard to the precessional movement of the Pole may introduce a difference of two or three Centuries from the dates which he adopts.

Under these circumstances the proper course is to admit that we are not in possession of the materials necessary to enable us to arrive at a scientific conclusion on the matter, and every date ascribed to an Egyptian Monument in the British Museum, on grounds similar to those explained above, ought to be marked with a query.

2. *Moab.*

" I Mesha am son of Chemosh-[Gad ?], King of Moab, the Dibonite. My father reigned over Moab 30 years, and I reigned after my father. And I erected this high place to Chemosh at Kahara (a Stone of Sal)vation for he saved me from all despoilers (?) and let me see my desire upon all my enemies. Omri was King of Israel, and oppressed Moab many days, for Chemosh was angry with his land. His son succeeded him, and he also said, I will oppress Moab. In my days he said, Let us go and I will see my desire on him and on his house, and Israel said I shall destroy it for ever. Now Omri took the land Medeba and occupied it his days and half his son's days (or he and his son and his son's) son forty years. And Chemosh

N

had mercy on it in my days ; and I built Baal Meon, and made therein the reservoir and I built Kirjathaim.   And the men of Gad dwelled in the land (Ataro)th from of old, and the King of Israel restored (At)aroth, and I assaulted the city and captured it."

So runs the opening sentence of this ancient Monument, the discovery of which, by Rev. F. Klein, of the Church Missionary Society, in 1868, created intense interest throughout all Europe.

It is the oldest Semitic lapidary record yet discovered ; in the course of a couple of Centuries it will be 3,000 years old.   It takes us half way back to the Bible date for the beginning of the race.   It exhibits the most ancient specimen of alphabetical writing yet discovered.   It is older than two-thirds of the Old Testament itself.   Its principal interests are theological and linguistic, but it has also a historic, and even a chronological value, corroborating as it does the authenticity of the Biblical Record.

Dr. Ginsburg, in his excellent monograph on *The Moabite Stone*, gives a facsimile of the Stone itself, an introduction, a translation and a commentary. He has also added an interesting account of its discovery.

The Omri here described as the oppressor of Moab, is the King of Israel mentioned in I Kings 16[16-28].   His date is B.C. 936-925.   His son would be Ahab (B.C. 925-904) and his son's son Jehoram of Israel (B.C. 904-893). Mesha's father's reign of 30 years would be during the reigns of Baasha (B.C. 960-937) and Elah (B.C. 937-936), and part of Omri's reign.   The forty years of the oppression of Moab would be the remainder of Omri's reign and the reign of Ahab (B.C. 925-904), and part of Jehoram of Israel's reign (B.C. 904-893).   (See Vol. II, Chronological Tables, pp. 23.24).

Upon the accession of Ahaziah of Israel we read (2 Kings I[1], 3[4, 5]): "Then Moab rebelled against Israel after the death of Ahab. . .   And Mesha, King of Moab, was a sheepmaster, and rendered unto the King of Israel (Jehoram of Israel) 100,000 lambs and 100,000 rams, with the wool.   But it came to pass when Ahab was dead, that the King of Moab rebelled against the King of Israel."

Whereupon Jehoram of Israel, with Jehoshaphat of Judah, and the King of Edom, made war against Moab (2 Kings 3[6-25]).   "And when the King of Moab saw that the battle was too sore for him, he took with him 700 men that drew swords, to break through even unto the King of Edom : but they could not. Then he took his eldest son that should have reigned in his stead, and offered him for a burnt offering upon the wall.   And there was great indignation against Israel : and they departed from him and returned to their own land" (2 Kings 3[26.27]).

The last phrase is euphemistic.   It means that though Moab was at first defeated and hard pressed, in the end the allies were beaten back, and there was aroused against Israel a feeling of intense indignation, in the strength of which Mesha renewed the battle, the siege was raised and victory remained with Mesha.

It was in the days of Jehoram of Judah (B.C. 905-893), which run almost exactly parallel with those of Jehoram of Israel (B.C. 904-893), that Edom also revolted from Judah.   "In the days of Jehoram of Judah, Edom re-

volted from under the hand of Judah and made a King over themselves "
(2 Kings 8 20).

There was a weakening of power in both Israel and Judah. Mesha took
advantage of it and threw off the yoke, and then erected this triumphal pillar
to commemorate the result.

The Moabite Stone fits in exactly with the Old Testament narrative.
They mutually illustrate and confirm each other.

The great value of the Moabite Stone lies in the fact that it is a history
of events which were contemporary with the Inscription which records them.
And this ancient witness, a witness in the presence of which most of the coins,
manuscripts and Inscriptions of antiquity are comparatively young, has come
forth out of the dark recesses of past millenniums, to corroborate the
authenticity of the Hebrew Records contained in the Old Testament. It
brings us face to face with the very times of Omri and Ahab, Elijah and
Elisha, Jehoshaphat and Jehu.

3. Assyria.

However great the interest and value of the *Shishak Inscription* and the
Moabite Stone may be, on various accounts, they cannot for one moment
be compared for chronological purposes with the interest and value of the
Cuneiform Inscriptions recently discovered in Assyria, Babylon and Persia.

Throughout the Middle Ages, Nineveh remained unknown to Europe. The
natives of the district had, however, preserved the name and the tradition
of the site of Nineveh among the mounds of Nunia, opposite Mosul, on the
Tigris. It was pointed out to Benjamin Tudela, A.D. 1160, and its ruins
were described by Rauwolf (1573), Sherley (1599), Tavernier (1644), Thevénot
(1663), the Jesuit writer of the *Lettres Édificantes* (1675), Otter (1734), Niebuhr
(1766) and Ollivier (1794). But the discovery of the Cuneiform Inscriptions
of Assyria, Babylon and Persia, was the romance of the 19th Century. The
mounds of Nineveh were explored by Rich in 1820, and by Commander Jones
in 1852. In 1850 Botta excavated Khorsabad (Dur-Sarrukin or Sargonsburg),
the great northren suburb of Nineveh, containing the vast palace of Sargon II.
Sir H. Layard excavated Kouyunjik (Central Nineveh) with its palaces
of Sennacherib and Ashur-bani-pal, and Nimrûd (Calah) with its N.W. palace
of Ashur-nasir-pal, its S.W. palace of Esar-haddon, and its central palace of
Shalmaneser II (III). These excavations were continued by Mr. Rassam
and others, and are still proceeding.

In 1847 Sir Henry Rawlinson published the text of the Behistun Inscription
in three languages—(1) Persian, (2) contemporary Elamite or Susian, and
(3) Assyrian or Babylonian. The Behistun Inscription provided the key
for the decipherment of the Assyrian Inscriptions, as the Rosetta Stone
provided the key to the interpretation of the Egyptian Inscriptions.

Grotefend, Burnouf, Lassen, Dr. Hincks, and George Smith, took a leading
part in the interpretation of the Cuneiform characters inscribed on slabs,
bulls, cylinders, tablets, bricks, etc., now treasured up in the British Museum
and the Louvre, through which a new world of ancient history has been

opened up to the astonished gaze of modern Europe. These inestimably precious treasures of antiquity lay buried with a hoard of clay documents, till they were dug up by Layard and interpreted by Dr. Hincks, Sir H. Rawlinson, and other pioneers in the art of deciphering these ancient records.

These important lapidary documents, which have been used in constructing a Chronology of the ancient Empires of Assyria and Babylon during the period of the Hebrew Monarchy, may be classified as follows :—

Assyrian Cuneiform Inscriptions.

A. The Historical Inscriptions of the Kings.
    I. Shalmaneser II (III), B.C. 911–876. (Assyrian Dates = B.C. 860–825).
    II. Tiglath-Pileser III (IV)   745–727.
    III. Shalmaneser IV (V) .. 727–722.
    IV. Sargon II   .. .. 722–705.
    V. Sennacherib .. .. 705–681.
    VI. Esar-haddon .. .. 681–668.
    VII. Ashur-bani-pal.. .. 668–626.
B. The Assyrian Eponym Canon.
C. Fragmentary Lists of Assyrian Eponyms.
D. The Synchronous History of Assyria and Babylon.

The dates given in the present work are those adopted by Willis J. Beecher, in his *Dated Events of the Old Testament.* The Assyrian dates, which precede the great gap, B.C. 834–783, are all 51 years later. After we reach the reign of Shalmaneser III (IV), B.C. 783–773, they coincide. The Assyrian dates are adopted by E. A. Wallis Budge, in his *Guide to the Babylonian and Assyrian Antiquities in the British Museum,* and by many other Assyriologists, but, in the view of the present writer, they are 51 years too recent.

A. The Historical Inscriptions of the Kings.

I. Shalmaneser II, B.C. 911–876 (Assyrian dates = B.C. 860–825), is called Shalmaneser III by recent writers like C. H. W. Johns, in *Ancient Assyria,* published 1912, on account of the recent discovery of an earlier King of the same name.

Shalmaneser's long reign of 35 years was a protracted military campaign against Babylon, Mesopotamia, Armenia and the peoples of Asia Minor. The Hittites of Carchemish were compelled to pay tribute, and Hamath and Damascus were subdued.

Prof. Sayce says : " In B.C. 854 (Assyrian Dates) = B.C. 905, a league formed by Hamath, Arvad, Ammon, Ahab of Israel and other neighbouring Princes, under the leadership of Damascus, fought an indecisive battle against him at Karkar, and other battles followed in 849 (= B.C. 900) and 846 (= B.C. 897). In 842 (= B.C. 893) Hazael was compelled to take refuge within the walls of his capital. The territory of Damascus was devastated, and Jehu of Samaria (whose ambassadors are represented on the black obelisk now in the British Museum), sent tribute. . . . . Shalmaneser II (III) built a palace at Calah, and the annals of his reign are engraved on an obelisk of black marble which he erected there (*Encyclopædia Britannica, 11th Edition, Article—Shalmaneser II.*)

The position of the palace of Shalmaneser II (III) is indicated in the following diagram of ancient Nineveh, its suburbs and its palaces.

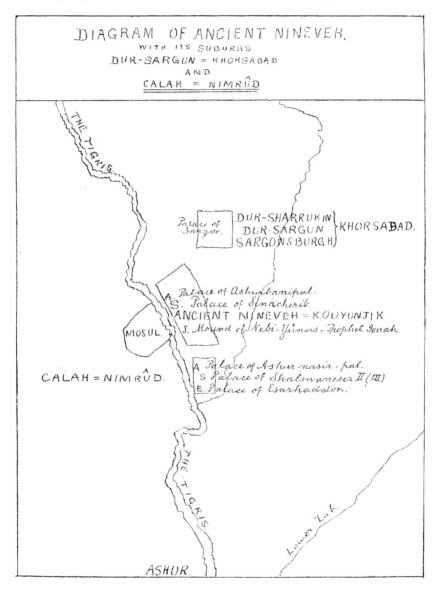

Shalmaneser II (III) has left us an account of his conquests during the first 31 years of his reign down to B.C. 880, the year in which the Black Obelisk was finished. Then his son Ashur-danin-apli rebelled against him, and the remaining four years of his reign was a time of civil war. Shalmaneser II (III) held Calah, but Nineveh, Asshur and most of the chief cities of Assyria went over to his rebel son Ashur-danin-apli. Shalmaneser died B.C. 876 after 31 years of undivided rule, and 4 years of divided rule. He was then succeeded by his other son and legal successor, Shamshi-Adad (= Shamshi-Ramman II), who had to fight two years more before he won his crown in B.C. 874.

Shalmaneser II (III) has left us the following Monumental Inscriptions :—

1. The Kurkh Monolith (Rawlinson's *Cuneiform Inscriptions*, vol. iii, p. 8). In this he says that in the 6th year of his reign he left Nineveh, crossed the Tigris and the Euphrates, and came to Syria where he captured

   12,000 chariots, 1,200 carriages and
   20,000 men of Ben-hadad of Syria,
   700 chariots, 700 carriages and
   10,000 men of Irhuleni of Hamath, and
   2,000 chariots and 10,000 men of Ahab of Sirhala (Israel),

   overthrowing all the 12 Kings whom Ben-hadad of Syria had brought him. This was in the sixth year of his reign, B.C. 905 (Assyrian dates B.C. 854).

2. The Bull Inscription (Rawlison's *Cuneiform Inscriptions*, vol. iii, p. 5, No. 6). In this he says :—

   " In my 18th year the sixteenth time the river Euphrates I crossed. Hazael of Syria . . . I overthrew. 18,000 men of his army with weapons I destroyed. 1,121 of his chariots, 470 of his carriages, with his camp, I took from him. To save his life he fled. After him I pursued, in Damascus his royal city I besieged him . . . In those days the tribute of Tyre and Zidon, of Jehu son of Omri, I received."

   This event is referred to in the following Inscription :—

3. The celebrated Black Obelisk of Shalmaneser II (III) in the British Museum (Layard, p. 98, l. 2). Here the Inscription runs :—

   " Tribute of Jehu son of Omri, silver, gold, bowls of gold, cups of gold, bottles of gold, vessels of gold, maces, royal utensils, rods of wood I received from him."

From these three Inscriptions it will be seen that Shalmaneser came into touch with Israel on two distinct occasions. In the sixth year of his reign (B.C. 905) he says he took 2,000 chariots and 10,000 men from Ahab, who was one of 12 Kings joined together in alliance against him, under the leadership of Ben-hadad of Syria. And in the 18th year of his reign (B.C. 893) he fought another campaign against Hazael of Syria, the successor of Ben-hadad, at which time he received tribute from Jehu.

This exactly fits in with the Biblical narrative. A reference to Vol. II, Chronological Tables, p. 24, AN. HOM. 3220–3232 will show that the 6th year of Shalmaneser II (III) (B.C. 905) is the 21st year of Ahab, and that the 18th year of Shalmaneser II (III) (B.C. 893) is the year of Jehu's accession.

Shalmaneser's 6th year could not have been later than the 21st year of Ahab, for in his 22nd, which was his last year, he was not in alliance with Ben-hadad of Syria, but at war with him. In 1 Kings 22 [1, 2] we read that after a series of wars between Ben-hadad of Syria and Ahab of Israel, " they continued 3 years without war between Syria and Israel, and it came to pass in the 3rd year " that Ahab and Jehoshaphat went up to Ramoth-gilead and fought a battle against the King of Syria, in which Ahab was killed.

The three years' truce between Syria and Israel was the truce of the 19th, 20th and 21st years of Ahab. During these three years Ben-hadad formed the league of the 12 Kings, and in the last of them, i.e. in the 6th year of Shalmaneser's reign, which was the 21st year of Ahab's reign, the year B.C. 905, Ben-hadad and Ahab fought against Shalmaneser and were defeated. In this year Ahaziah the son of Ahab was associated with his father as Co-Rex of Israel, during his father's absence at the war. In the following year, the 22nd year of Ahab, B.C. 904, Ahab was no longer in alliance with Ben-hadad, but was fighting against him at Ramoth-gilead, with his ally Jehoshaphat of Judah.

But if Shalmaneser's 6th year could not have been *later* than the 21st year of Ahab (the year B.C. 905), his 18th year could not have been *earlier* than the accession year of Jehu (the year B.C. 893), for in that year Jehu first came to the throne. The synchronism is therefore absolutely exact. It is also determinative. It fixes this and every other date at which the history of Assyria comes into contact with the history of Israel and Judah. It could not have been one year earlier, for then Jehu could not have paid tribute. It could not have been one year later, for then Ahab was not in alliance with, but was fighting against, Ben-hadad, and the year after that he died.

Schrader dates the battle of Karkar in the 6th year of Shalmaneser, B.C. 854 (Assyrian dates), i.e. B.C. 905. He contrasts this with Ussher's date for the reign of Ahab, B.C. 918–897, but this should be 925–904, when it is seen to be in perfect agreement.

Schrader dates the payment of tribute by Jehu in the 18th year of Shalmaneser, B.C. 842 (Assyrian dates), i.e. B.C. 893. He contrasts this with Ussher's date for the reign of Jehu, B.C. 884–856, but this should be 893–865, when, again, it is seen to be in perfect agreement. Here, as everywhere, the Chronology of the Assyrian Inscriptions, when rightly interpreted, is in exact agreement with that of the Old Testament (see Vol. II, Chronological Tables).

II. Tiglath-pileser III (B.C. 745–727) is called Tiglath-pileser IV by the most recent writers, as e.g. by C. H. W. Johns, in *Ancient Assyria*, published 1912. It will be noticed that from the year B.C. 783 onward the Assyrian dates and those of Willis J. Beecher coincide, the gap or blank of 51 years extending over the period B.C. 834 to 783, and affecting only those dates which lie before these years.

Tiglath-pileser III (IV) was a military upstart, a usurper. He probably owed his elevation to the throne of Assyria to a discontented army. We know nothing of his origin, but he never lays claim to royal descent. Later on, when he came to the throne of Babylon, he was known as Pulu or Poros. He has been identified by George Smith and Schrader with Pul. Pil-Eser is his Assyrian name, the termination *Eser* being merely a title occurring in many Assyrian names, like Shalmaneser, Esar-haddon, etc. Pul or Pulu is his Babylonian name. It is found also in Scripture (2 Kings 15^{19}, 1 Chron. 5$^{6, 26}$). Porus is the Greek form of the name found in Ptolemy's Canon. According to the cuneiform Inscriptions, Tiglath-pileser III (IV) or Pul, conquered Chinzer, King of Babylon, B.C. 731 and died B.C. 727. According to Ptolemy's Canon, Porus succeeded Chinzer, and began to reign in Babylon in 731 and died in 727. Tiglath-pileser III (IV), Pul, Pulu, and Porus have, therefore, been identified as one and the same person.

He built himself a palace at Calah, the modern Nimrûd, on the ruins of an old palace of Shalmaneser II (III). Many years later Esar-haddon, a King of another dynasty, used the marble slabs of Tiglath-pileser III (IV) for a palace of his own, turning their faces to the wall and cutting his own inscriptions on their backs.

Hence, the chronological annals of Tiglath-pileser III (IV) are lost, and the only Inscriptions of his that we have left are some mutilated fragments, the date of which it is impossible to determine. Mr. George Smith says, the dates given for the reign of Tiglath-pileser III (IV) are only approximate calculations, and future discoveries may alter them considerably.

It is very important to remember this, as the dates attributed to some of the expeditions of Tiglath-pileser III (IV) do not agree with the dates given in the Old Testament, unless we assume that they were expeditions undertaken by him when he was acting as the General of Ashur-dàn III (773–754) or Ashur-nirari (754–745) before he seized and mounted the throne himself, B.C. 745.

The Inscriptions of Tiglath-pileser III (IV) like those of most Assyrian Monarchs are of two kinds.

(1) Annalistic Inscriptions giving details of dated events arranged in chronological order and written down year by year according to the individual years of the King's reign.

(2) Summarising triumphal Inscriptions giving a general review of all that has happened during an extended period of time, in which the facts are grouped, not chronologically, but geographically, or in the order of their importance, or on some other principle.

Tiglath-pileser III (IV) mentions (1) Azariah of Judah (= Uzziah, 806–755) as a great military power to whom certain cities turned when they revolted from Assyria; (2) Menahem of Israel (768–758) as one who paid tribute to him; (3) Rezin of Damascus and Pekah of Israel (755–735, dethroned 736) as defeated and deposed by him; (4) Yauhazi or Joachaz (Ahaz, 739–723) as submitting to his dominion and paying tribute ; and (5) Hoshea (736–719, King of Israel 727–719) as set up by him, not as King but as governor, as Gedaliah was set up later on by Nebuzaradan for Nebuchadnezzar.   Thus, altogether no fewer than five Kings of Judah and Israel are mentioned by Tiglath-pileser III (IV) in those of his Inscriptions which have a bearing on the Chronology of the Old Testament.

These Inscriptions are as follows :—

1. Rawlinson's *Cuneiform Inscriptions*, vol. iii, p. 9, No. 2, date unknown ; George Smith says its probable date is B.C. 738.

This is an Inscription on a fragment of a marble slab used by Tiglath-pileser III (IV) in his central (S.E.) palace at Calah (Nimrûd).   It was subsequently transported by Esar-haddon and used by him in his S.W. palace at Calah (Nimrûd).   It contains this passage (Schrader i, 210 ; George Smith, *Assyrian Eponym Canon*, p.117). :—

"In the course of my campaign . . . . . tribute of the Kings . . . .
Azrijahu of Judah . . . . . Asurijahu of Judah (Azariah=Uzziah).

2. Rawlinson's *Cuneiform Inscriptions*, vol. iii, p. 9, No. 3, date unknown ; George Smith says its probable date is B.C. 738.

This is an Inscription on another fragment of a marble slab used by Tigath-pileser III (IV) in the same way.   It contains this passage (Schrader, i, 212 ; George Smith, *Assyrian Eponym Canon*, pp. 117–118).

"Of Azariah my hand mightily captured . . . Nineteen districts of the town Hamath, together with the towns in their circuit, which are situated on the sea of the setting sun, which in their faithlessness made revolt to Azrijahu (Azariah = Uzziah), I turned into the territory of Assyria.   My officers, my governors I placed over them."

It will be noted, (1) that this Inscription is undated ; (2) that it does not say that Azariah (Uzziah) paid tribute to Tiglath-pileser III (IV), but that Tiglath-pileser (received) tribute from certain Kings who had revolted from him and turned to Azariah (Uzziah), and that he pulled down and destroyed the cities of these Kings.   If the Inscription was written as George Smith suggests, B.C. 738, the revolt of the Kings was a prior event to the campaign of Tiglath-pileser III (IV), and might well have been as long prior as some time before B.C. 755, the last year of Uzziah's reign.

Schrader says : "The Azariah (Uzziah) here mentioned must be a contemporary of Tiglath-pileser III (IV).   The date of Uzziah's death according to the ordinary Chronology (of the Bible) is 758, while Tiglath-pileser, according to the Assyrian fivefold guaranteed Canon, did not ascend the throne till B.C. 745.   There gapes here a chronological discrepancy which refuses to be explained away.   If the Assyrian Chronology, certified as we have said fivefold, be the correct one, the Biblical cannot be correct."

There is here no discrepancy whatever.   The Inscription does not say when these 19 Cities revolted to Uzziah, but only when Tilglath-pileser destroyed them.   It does not say whether he destroyed them before he ascended the throne of Assyria, as General of Ashur-dân III (773–754), or as General of Ashur-nirari (754–745), or after he ascended the throne B.C. 745. On the one hand, there is no reason why these cities should not have revolted to Uzziah long before the campaign of Tiglath-pileser III (IV) ; and on the other, there is no reason why Tiglath-pileser III (IV) should not have made his military expedition long before he came to the throne of Assyria, B.C. 745, for he exacted tribute from Merodach-baladan of Babylon in B.C. 751, six years before he came to the throne. And to crown all, this Inscription, like every other Inscription of Tiglath-pileser III (IV) yet recovered, is *an undated, mutilated fragment,* the date having been *given to it,* and not *derived from it.* All which proves that this, like all other " contradictions " in the Old Testament, is derived from the "assumptions," and inspired by the animus of the critic. Prof. Owen C. Whitehouse thinks the Inscription probably refers to a King of the land of Yâdi and not to Azariah (Uzziah) of Judah at all.

3. Rawlinson, *Cuneiform Inscriptions,* vol. iii, p. 9, No. 3, date unknown ; George Smith says its probable date B.C. is 738 (cp. 2 Kings 15 [19]).

This is an Inscription on the same fragment of the marble slab as the Inscription last mentioned, containing the name of Azariah (Uzziah).

Azariah (Uzziah) is mentioned on lines 2 and 10. Menahem on line 29.

Here we read (Schrader i, 244 ; George Smith, *Assyrian Eponym Canon,* p. 120) :—

> " The tribute of Kustaspi of Kummuha, Resin of Syria, Menahem of Samaria and (here follow the names of 14 other Kings and one Queen) I received." Then follow the words, "In my 9th year." Judah is not included in the list. Uzziah was King there, and he had a standing army of 307,050 men (2 Chron. 26 [13]).

Schrader and other Assyriologists attribute these Inscriptions to Tiglath-pileser, and as the year preceding the 9th year of his reign was the year B.C. 737, and Menahem died 21 years before, B.C. 758, there is here an apparent discrepancy between the interpretation of these fragmentary Inscriptions by Assyriologists, and the Chronology of the Old Testament.

But it is by no means certain that the above Inscriptions do relate to the *reign* of Tiglath-pileser III (IV). Willis J. Beecher thinks they belong to the 8th year of Ashur-dân III (B.C. 773–754), the year B.C. 765, when Tiglath-pileser III (IV), some 20 years before he seized the throne, was acting as General of the army of Ashur-dân. The subject of the Inscription is an expedition to Hamath, 19 districts of which had revolted to Azariah (Uzziah), and in that very year, the 8th year of Ashur-dân III, the year B.C. 765, the Assyrian Eponym Canon mentions the fact that there was an expedition to Hadrach.

The identification of these Inscriptions as belonging to Tiglath-pileser may be granted, but it must be remembered that it is only a " conjecture," not a directly attested fact. George Smith speaks of " the deplorable state in which the annals of Tiglath-pileser III (IV) are found." He says, " It is very difficult to arrange them in their chronological order," " the dates assigned to them are only approximate calculations," and "future discoveries may alter them considerably."

The process by which Schrader dates the payment of tribute by Menahem to Tiglath-pileser in the year B.C. 738 is as follows :—

There is nothing in the Inscription itself to yield this date. It is only an inference from a study of the Assyrian Eponym Canon. From this Schrader says certain things may be "presumed," and certain other things must be "assumed," but "whether Menahem of Samaria was among the Princes who rendered homage in the 3rd year of Tiglath-pileser III, which he identifies with the year B.C. 738, *cannot be determined with certainty*. Meanwhile the above *conjecture* would be justified *if* G. Smith had really, on a basis of palæographic facts, connected the plate Layard 45 with the plate Rawlinson, vol. iii, p. 9, No. 1."

Since G. Smith himself says the dates in question are only "approximate calculations," and that "future discoveries may alter them considerably," and since Willis J. Beecher finds equal support in the Assyrian Eponym Canon for his conjecture that the payment of tribute by Menahem belongs to the 8th year of Ashur-dân, the year B.C. 765, when Tiglath-pileser was perhaps acting as his General, we may allow the matter to remain where it is. One conjecture disagrees with the Chronology of the Old Testament. Another conjecture agrees with it. Either conjecture meets all the facts contained in the Assyrian Inscriptions, and these Inscriptions contain no fact which contradicts the facts of the Old Testament.

4. Rawlinson's *Cuneiform Inscriptions*, vol. iii, p. 10, No. 2. Probable date B.C. 740 to 730.

This is a summarising or triumphal Inscription by Tiglath-pileser III (IV), on a fragment of one of the marble slabs from his palace at Nimrûd.

It reads as follows (Schrader i, 246 ; G. Smith, *Assyrian Eponym Canon*, p. 123).

> "The cities Gil(ead), Abel (Beth-maacha ?) . . . which is the boundary of the land of Beth-omri (Samaria) I turned in its entire extent into the territory of Assyria. I set my Officers and Viceroys over it (cp. 2 Kings 15 [29], 16 [9-16], 1 Chron. 5 [6. 26], Isaiah 7 [1—9 1]).
>
> .   .   .   .
>
> The land of Beth-omri (Samaria) . . . the goods of its people and their furniture I sent to Assyria. Pekaha (Pekah) their King . . . and Asui (Hoshea) I appointed over them . . . their tribute of them I received."

(Cp. 2 Kings 17 [1,] but this refers only to Hoshea's appointment as Governor under the King of Assyria like that of Gedaliah (2 Kings 25 [23]) under the King of Babylon, not to the first year of his reign as King, which was several years later).

The date attributed to this Inscription by the Assyriologists is B.C. 740 to 730, which agrees perfectly with the Biblical date of the deposition of Pekah, B.C. 736, and his being slain by Hoshea the following year, B.C. 735, or as it is called in 2 Kings 15 [30] the 2cth year of Jotham, though Jotham had been dead 4 years, and this was really the 4th year of the reign of Ahaz, " the Holy Ghost choosing rather to reckon by holy Jotham in his grave than by wicked Ahaz alive " (Dr. John Lightfoot).

Schrader translates inaccurately, " Pekah their King I slew." There is nothing in the Original to correspond with this rendering. The Assyrian text reads " Pa-ka-ha sarra-su-nu ... du ... ma." " Pekah their King ... ed." There is no " I " at all in it. And there is no " kill " or " slay " in it, only the termination of some verb unknown indicating a past tense *-ed*. All the rest is conjecture, read into the text by Schrader (may we not add), in order to manufacture a contradiction to the Text of the Old Testament, which tells us that Pekah was slain a year later by Hoshea ? It might just as well be conjectured to have been " Pekah their King escaped," or " Pekah their King I defeated," or " Pekah their King I dethroned," or " Pekah their King I imprisoned."

From 2 Kings 15 [25-27] we learn that Pekah slew Pekahiah and reigned from the 52nd year of Uzziah, B.C. 755, for 20 years (inclusive reckoning) to B.C. 736.

From the above Inscription of Tiglath-pileser III (IV) we learn that about that time he was removed and Hoshea appointed as governor in his place. And from 2 Kings 15 [30] we learn that in the following year, B.C. 735, he was slain by Hoshea.

5. Layard's *Inscription*, p. 66 ; Smith's *Assyrian Eponym Canon*, p. 124. Probable date, according to George Smith, B.C. 734–730.

This is a tiny fragment of an Inscription of Tiglath-Pileser, which tells us nothing more than we have already learned from the previous Inscription. It reads " Samaria alone I left. Pekah their King. . . ."

6. Rawlinson's *Cuneiform Inscriptions*, vol. ii, p. 67. Probable date, according to George Smith, B.C. 732. (Schrader i, 249 ; Smith, *Assyrian Eponym Canon*, p. 124).

This is a summarising triumphal Inscription of Tiglath-pileser III (IV), embracing the events which belonged to the period " from the beginning of my rule (sarrutu) to the 17th year of my reign (palu), i.e. from B.C. 745, or perhaps earlier, to B.C. 728. It records the fact that Tiglath-pileser III (IV) received tribute from a very large number of Kings, amongst which we find the name of Yauhazi of Judah (=Ahaz, B.C. 738–723), (cp. 2 Kings 16 [8], 2 Chron. 28, Is. 7 [1]–9 [1]).

This beginning of rule (sarruti) is in other cases expressly distinguished in the Inscriptions from the first year of the King's reign. The year in which a new monarch ascended the throne was reckoned, not to the new monarch, but to his predecessor. Any events which happened during that portion of the calendar year which followed the accession of the new monarch were described as happening in " the beginning of his rule "—the following year being reckoned the " first year " of his reign (Schrader, *Cuneiform Inscriptions and the Old Testament*, vol. ii, p. 94), cp. Jer. 26 [1], 27 [1], 28 [1], 49 [34].

III. Shalmaneser IV (V) (727–722).

No Monuments have been found bearing Inscriptions by this monarch. Some scholars think he may have left some, but that they were destroyed by his successor Sargon II, who was a usurper and the founder of a new dynasty. Other scholars have conjectured that Shalmaneser IV (V) and Sargon II are one and the same person.

IV. Sargon II (B.C. 722–705).

Sargon II, the successor of Shalmaneser IV (V), was a mighty warrior. It is generally supposed that he was a usurper, who may have been concerned in a revolution resulting in the overthrow of his predecessor. He gives no genealogy of himself, but he claims royal descent from 350 royal predecessors. If this claim be true his revolution may have been a counterstroke leading to a reversion of the crown to some collateral branch of the older dynasty of Ashur-dân III, which was overthrown some 23 years before by Tiglath-pileser III (IV) B.C. 745.

Sargon II was the first King of Assyria to come into actual conflict with Egypt, which he defeated at the famous battle of Raphia, near the frontier of Egypt, not immediately, but soon, after the capture of Samaria. Shabaka or Seveh, the " So, King of Egypt," of 2 Kings 17[4], paid tribute to Sargon II, and it is quite possible that Sargon II went up the Nile and partly destroyed the Ethiopian No-Amon or Thebes referred to in Nahum 3[8], in fulfilment of Isa. 20[1-6], as his great grandson, Ashur-bani-pal, destroyed it again, twice over, three generations later.

But in spite of the vast resources of the mighty empire of this powerful ruler, his magnificent achievements and his glorious conquests were all forgotten. *Sic transit gloria mundi.* There was no reference to him in classic literature. There was just the incidental mention of his name in Isaiah 20[1], the unsupported witness of one single verse of Scripture, and that was all that was known of him. Critics and scholars doubted whether there ever was such a " King of Assyria " who sent his Tartan against Ashdod and took it, just as to-day, there are scholars and critics of very considerable reputation who doubt whether there ever was such a person as Belshazzar, the King of the Chaldeans, or Darius the Mede, who took the Kingdom from him.

For 25 Centuries Isaiah was the sole witness to the existence of Sargon II. To-day, through the corroboration of the Monumental Inscriptions, he is known to have been Assyria's great master mind, the Emperor of the then known world.

Sargon II's reign of 17 years (722–705) was one long series of military expeditions. He conquered Samaria, Elam, Babylon, Hamath, Egypt, Armenia, Ashdod, Ethiopia, Babylon (a second time) and Cyprus, together with a host of smaller states, transporting the inhabitants of one conquered territory to another. The most noteworthy of his conquests were :—

B.C. 722. His accession year—His first capture of Samaria, upon which he imposed tribute, but which soon afterwards rebelled again. (Other documents place his accession two years later, in the year 720.)

B.C. 721. His first year—His conquest of Merodach-baladan of Babylon.

B.C. 720. His second year—His conquest of Shabaka = " So, King of
Egypt," at Raphia.
(Other documents make this his accession year, so that
his first year may be either 722, 721, 720 or 719, according
to the documental authority followed, and the method
of reckoning employed).

B.C. 711. His 11th year—Conquest of Azuri, King of Ashdod. This
is the event referred to in Isaiah 20. It is very fully
described by Sargon II, in his great summarising triumphal
Inscription at Khorsabad.

B.C. 710. His 12th year—Conquest of Merodach-baladan of Babylon,
whom he dethroned, reigning there himself for five years
as King of Babylon (710–705). Ptolemy's Canon gives
the name Arcean as King of Babylon for these five years,
B.C. 710–705.

Like all great warriors and world conquerors, Sargon was a great builder.
He built a palace for himself, and called the place after his own name,
Dur-Sharrukin or Dur-Sargon, now Khorsabad, or Northern Nineveh. All
the more important Monuments of Sargon II, were obtained from Khorsabad
by M. Botta, the French explorer, who sent them to the Louvre.

Sargon II also restored the palace of Ashur-nasir-pal (B.C. 936–911), built
some 200 years earlier at Calah, the modern Nimrûd. He repaired the walls
of Nineveh proper, the modern Kouyunjik, and made it the first city in the
Empire.

The Inscriptions of Sargon II are for the most part well preserved. They
include,

1. Sargon II's Annals, which give detailed accounts of the events of
each year of his reign.
2. The great summarising triumphal Inscription at Khorsabad.
3. The Bull Inscription at Khorsabad.
4. A triumphal Inscription on a Stele of Sargon II which he sent to
Cyprus, which was discovered on the site of ancient Citium, and
which is now preserved in the British Museum.
5. A clay cylinder Inscription.
6. Sundry Inscriptions on pavements, slabs, bricks, vases, etc.

Of these, seven have some bearing on the Chronology of the Old Testament.
They are as follows :—

1. Botta, 145, I. (Smith, *Assyrian Eponym Canon*, Extract 21, p. 125 ;
Schrader i, p. 263).

This is a short passage from Sargon II's great triumphal Inscription at
Khorsabad, dated by George Smith B.C. 722. It is in a very mutilated
condition but contains the following passages :—

".... Samaria .... I carried off 50 chariots, my royal portion ....
.... tribute the same as that of the Assyrians I fixed upon them."

2. *Fastes* of Oppert, lines 23 to 25 ; Smith's *Assyrian Eponym Canon*, Extract, 22, p. 125 ; Schrader i, p. 265.

This is a passage from Sargon II's Annals, dated by Smith B.C. 722 (?). It appears to refer to the same event as the foregoing Inscription, viz. the first capture of Samaria by Sargon in 722, i.e. in the 3rd year of Hezekiah, and three years before its final fall.   It reads as follows :—

> " Samaria I besieged, I captured, 27,290 people dwelling in the midst of it I carried captive, 50 chariots from among them I selected, and the rest of them I distributed.   My general over them I appointed, and the taxes of the former King I fixed on them " (cp. 2 Kings 17 [13]).

These two extracts appear to refer to events that took place prior to the siege of Samaria by Shalmaneser IV (V), referred to in 2 Kings 17 [5], and Sargon appears to be acting as the General of Shalmaneser IV (V).

3. *Annals of Sargon*, lines 36–57 ;   Smith, *Assyrian Eponym Canon*, Extract 23, p. 125.   Dated 720.

This is a mutilated Inscription, respecting the defeat of Sibahki (= So, King of Egypt, 2 Kings 17 [4]), at Raphia.   It reads as follows :—

> " In   my   second   year . . . . . . Damascus,   Samaria . . . .
> . . . .
> . . . . . . Sibahki . . . . . to his aid, with him to make battle and war, to my presence came.   In the name of Assur my lord their overthrow I struck, and Sibahki the ruler, who had slight courage, fled away alone and got off.
> " Hanun in hand I captured, and his family to my city Assur I sent.
> " Raphia I pulled down, destroyed, in the fire I burned, 20,033 people and their abundant goods I carried captive."

4. *Fastes* of Oppert, lines 25 and 26 ; Smith, *Assyrian Eponym Canon*, Extract 24, p. 126 ; Schrader ii, p. 87.   Botta, 145, 2, 1–3.

This is an extract from Sargon II's summarising triumphal Inscription at Khorsabad.   It also refers to the Battle of Raphia.   It is dated by Smith B.C. 720, and reads as follows :—

> " Hanun, King of Gaza, with Sibahe, General of Egypt, in Raphia, to make battle and war, to my presence came.   Their overthrow I struck. Sibahe the attack of my soldiers avoided, fled away, and his place could not be seen.   Hanun, King of Gaza, in hand I captured."

5. Rawlinson's *Cuneiform Inscriptions*, vol. i, p. 36, line 20 ; Smith, *Assyrian Eponym Canon*, Extract 29, p. 129 ; Schrader i, p. 269.

This is from Sargon II's clay cylinder Inscription.   It is dated by Smith B.C. 715, and reads as follows :—

> " Sargon (?) Conqueror of the Tamudu (an Arabian tribe), Ibadidi, Marsimani, and Hayapa, who the rest of them enslaved, and caused them to be placed in the land of Beth-omri (Samaria)."

6. Smith, *Assyrian Eponym Canon*, Extract 30, p. 129.

This is the great Ashdod Inscription (cp. Isa. 20) contained in Sargon II's Kouyunjik Cylinder and Khorsabad Inscription.

It is distinctly dated here " In the 9th year of my reign," i.e. B.C. 713 if he dates his accession from B.C. 722, or B.C. 711 if he dates his accession from B.C. 720. In his Annals he gives this expedition under the 11th year of his reign.

This shows that there were two ways of reckoning the accession of Sargon. His accession year was 722. His first year 721. He had another accession year 720, and his royal Eponym Year was 719.

Similarly Shalmaneser II (III) ascended the throne B.C. 860 (Assyrian dates) = B.C. 911. His first year was B.C. 859 (Assyrian dates) = B.C. 910 and his royal Eponym Year B.C. 858 (Assyrian dates) = B.C. 909.

From the time of Tiglath-pileser III (IV) (745–727) onward, says Schrader (ii, p. 168 note), the year of the King's accession is also reckoned as the first year of the new series of Eponyms. The Canons vary in their mode of reckoning the first year of the King. Sometimes it is his accession year, sometimes the year after his accession, sometimes the year after that.

George Smith says (*Assyrian Eponym Canon*, p. 21) the general practice was to count the regnal years from the first New Year's Day after the King's accession, and to call the period between the accession and the first New Year's Day, " the beginning of the reign." Nevertheless, there are cases in which the year of accession is considered as the first year, thus giving two reckonings. Thus :—

Shalmaneser II (III's) year of	Accession	=860.	His 1st year	860 or 859
Tiglath-pileser III (IV's)	,,	=745	,,	745 or 744
Sargon II's	,,	=722	,.	722 or 721
Sennacherib's ..	,,	=705	,,	705 or 704
Nebuchadnezzar's ..	,,	=605	,,	605 or 604

Sargon's Ashdod Inscription, as taken from the Kouyunjik Cylinder, is as follows :—

" In my 9th year, to the land beside the great sea, to Philistia and Ashdod I went.

" Azuri of Ashdod hardened his heart not to bring tribute, and sent to the Kings round him, enemies of Assyria, and did evil. Over the people round him I broke. . . . .

" Ahimite . . . . his brother I raised and appointed over his Kingdom before his face. Taxes and tribute to Assyria like those of the Kings round him I appointed over him.

" But the people. . . . . revolted against their King . . . . and drove him away . . . . and appointed Yavan, not heir to the throne, to the Kingdom over them. . . .

" I, Sargon, crossed, the Tigris and the Euphrates . . . . Yavan heard of my expedition . . . . and fled away . . . . to the border of Egypt, the shore of the river, the boundary of Meroe."

7. Botta, 149, 6 ; Schrader, ii, p. 89.

This is another account of the Ashdod Expedition from Sargon's Annals, dated the eleventh year of his reign instead of the ninth, as in the preceding Inscription.   It reads as follows :—

" Azuri, King of Ashdod, hardened his heart not to pay tribute, and sent
to the Princes of his neighbourhood, demands to revolt from Assyria.
Accordingly, I wreaked vengeance, and changed his government over
the inhabitants of his district.   Achimite, his own brother, I
appointed to be governor over them.   The Hittites, who thought to
revolt, despised his rule, raised Yaman, who had no claim, to the
throne, and who, like the former, refused recognition of authority
over them.   In the rage of my heart, my whole army I gathered
not, did not even collect my baggage ; with my chief warriors,
who did not retreat from the victorious track of my arms, I advanced
to Ashdod.   The above Yaman, as he of the approach of my
expedition heard from far, fled to a district of Egypt, which is
situated on the frontier of Milukka (Meroe or Ethiopia) ; not a
trace of him was seen.   Ashdod Gimt-Ashdudim, I besieged, I
captured ; his goods, his wife, his sons, his daughters, the treasures,
possessions, valuables of his palace, together with the inhabitants
of his land, I destined for capture.   Those towns I restored again.
The inhabitants of the countries which my hands had seized . . . .
in the East I settled there.   I treated them like unto the Assyrians.
They tendered obedience. . . . The King of Milukka (Meroe or
Ethiopia) cast Yaman into iron chains, and caused him to take his
distant way to Assyria, and appear before me."

This is the background that lies behind the words of Is. 20^{1-6}: "*In the year* that Tartan came unto Ashdod (when Sargon the King of Assyria sent him), and fought against Ashdod and took it : at the same time spake the Lord by Isaiah the son of Amoz, saying, Go and loose the sackcloth from off thy loins, and put off thy shoe from thy foot.   And he did so, walking naked and barefoot."

This was the sign upon Egypt and Ethiopia that so should the King of Assyria lead away the Egyptians prisoners, and the Ethiopians captives, naked and barefoot, to the shame of Egypt and Ethiopia.

The enterprise of Sargon against Ashdod was connected with an enterprise against the great Western Power on the Nile.   After the fall of Ashdod, Sargon either went to Thebes (the No-Amon of Nahum 3^8, A.V. margin) and partly destroyed it, as his great grandson Ashur-bani-pal did more completely, twice over, about half a century later, or else Egypt and Ethiopia surrendered to Sargon without fighting, for they betrayed and gave up Yaman the King of Ashdod, who had fled to them for refuge, and sued for peace.

If the dates of Sargon's reign are rightly computed by the interpreters of the Assyrian Inscriptions, the year that Sargon II took Ashdod was his 11th year—the year B.C. 711—the 14th year of Hezekiah, the year of the destruction of the 185,000 of the host of Sennacherib, the year of the sickness of Hezekiah,

o

and the year of the embassy of Merodach-baladan of Babylon (2 Kings 18–20, Is. 36–39).

There is no reason why Sargon II should not have made his son Sennacherib his Tartan or Commander-in-Chief, and associated him with himself on the throne of Assyria in B.C. 711, six years before Sargon II died, and Sennacherib became sole King of Assyria. The word Tartan occurs only in 2 Kings 18[17] and Is. 20[1]. It may be the title of Sennacherib as Crown Prince and Co-Regent with his father Sargon, and Commander-in-Chief of the army. The Ashdod expedition, the Lachish payment of tribute, the blasphemous letter episode, and the destruction of the host of Sennacherib all belong to one and the same year, the 14th year of Hezekiah, the year B.C. 711. We have no right to assume that Sennacherib undertook none of his military expeditions before he ascended the throne in B.C. 705. He may very well have been associated with his father in the throne and Commander-in-Chief of the army in the year 711, for we know that he was " Crown Prince and Viceroy in Assyria during the last few years of Sargon's reign " (C. H. W. John's *Ancient Assyria*), just as Nebuchadnezzar was Co-Regent with, and Commander-in-Chief of, the army of his father Nabopolassar, and just as Belshazzar was Co-Regent with, and Commander-in-Chief of, the army of his father Nabonidus.

V. Sennacherib (B.C. 705–681).

Sennacherib was the son of Sargon II (722–705), and the father of Esar-haddon (681–668). He was a typical Assyrian monarch. His whole life was taken up in warlike expeditions, conquering and crushing and subduing other nations, and taking tribute from them, and in the erection of great palaces and other buildings. He was nearly always at war with Babylon. He defeated Merodach-baladan, and appointed Belibus as his Viceroy there. Later on he conquered Merodach-baladan again, and appointed his own son, Ashur-nadin-shum, King of Babylon, and finally he was himself King of Babylon for 8 years, a period which is reckoned as an interregnum in Ptolemy's Canon.

He conquered Armenia, Media, Sidon, Tyre, Edom, Ashdod, Ashkelon, Libnah and Lachish. He defeated Egypt at Eltakeh between Ekron and Timnath, and took the seal of So, King of Egypt, which was discovered in his palace at Kouyunjik, a building extending over 8 acres of ground. He restored another palace at Neby Yunas (the prophet Jonah), also at Nineveh. He was the first Assyrian monarch to make Nineveh the seat of government.

His Inscriptions are on clay cylinders, marble slabs, and colossal bulls. We have bas-reliefs of his wars and building operations, terra cotta bowls, bricks, alabaster plate, and a crystal throne. There is also an Inscription of his on the Rock at Bavian, to the north of Nineveh, and another at Nahr-el-Kelb, on the coast of Syria, which he made by the side of an Inscription placed there by Rameses the Great 600 years before.

Those which refer to the Chronology of the Old Testament may be tabulated as follows :—

1. Rawlinson's *Cuneiform Inscriptions*, vol. i, 43, 15 ; *The Inscription of Constantinople* of Schrader i, 279 ; The Memorial Tablet, lines 13 to 15, of Smith's *Assyrian Eponym Canon*.

Here we read :—" From Elulæus King of Sidon I took his Kingdom, Ethobal I raised to his throne and imposed on him the tribute of my rule ; the extensive territory of the land Judah, Hezekiah its King, I compelled to obedience."

2. Rawlinson's *Cuneiform Inscriptions*, vol. i, 7, No. J ; Schrader i, 280 ; The Lachish Slab, No. 28, in the Assyrian Saloon of the British Museum.

This is a bas-relief of Sennacherib sitting on a throne amid the vines and fig-trees outside the city of Lachish, receiving tribute. It bears the Inscription : " Sennacherib, King of hosts, King of Assyria, seated himself upon an exalted throne and received the spoil of the city Lachish."

3. Rawlinson's *Cuneiform Inscriptions*, vol. i, 37–42. The Taylor six-sided clay Cylinder, Schrader i, 280.

This was executed in the Eponymy of Bel-emur-ani, B.C. 691, and contains an account of Sennacherib's *eight* military expeditions.

The Inscription on the Bellino Cylinder, executed B.C. 702, contains an account of *two* of these campaigns. The Inscription on the Colossal Bulls of Kouyunjik, executed B.C. 700, contains a parallel account of the *third* of these campaigns. The Inscription on the C. Cylinder (George Smith's *Assyrian Discoveries*, p. 296), executed B.C. 697, contains an account of *four* of these campaigns.

These parallel accounts add little to the matter contained in the celebrated Taylor Cylinder.

The most important of all the Inscriptions of Sennacherib is the account he gives of his third campaign.

Unfortunately, none of the events recorded by Sennacherib are dated. Earlier monarchs, like Shalmaneser II (III) and Tiglath-pileser III (IV) record the events which happened " in the first, second, third, etc., year of my reign." The later monarchs, Sennacherib, Esar-haddon, and Ashur-bani-pal, do not give dates. They record only the events which happened " in my first, second, third, etc., military campaign."

This third campaign of Sennacherib embraces :—

1. An expedition to the towns of Phœnicia and Philistia.
2. An expedition against Zedekiah of Ashkelon.
3. An expedition against the Ekronites, whose King, Padi, had been deposed and sent as a prisoner to Hezekiah because he was loyal to Assyria. Hezekiah gave him up, and Sennacherib restored him. While Sennacherib was engaged here he was attacked by the Egyptians and Ethiopians, whom he defeated at Eltakeh, between Ekron and Timnath.
4. An expedition against Hezekiah, on the date of which Schrader founds his whole case for the untrustworthiness of the Biblical Chronology, and the necessity of substituting for it the Chronology of the Monuments.

The account of Sennacherib's third campaign is a long one, but it must be given in full :—

" As for Hezekiah of Judah, who had not submitted to my yoke, 46 of his strong cities, together with innumerable fortresses and small towns dependent on them, by overthrowing the walls and open attack, by battle engines and battering-rams I besieged, I captured ; I brought out from the midst of them and counted as a spoil 200,150 persons, great and small, male and female, besides mules, asses, camels, oxen, and sheep without number. Hezekiah himself I shut up like a bird in a cage in Jerusalem, his royal city. I built a line of forts against him, and I kept back his heel from going forth out of the great gate of his city. I cut off his cities which I had spoiled from the midst of his land, and gave them to Metinti, King of Ashdod ; Padi, King of Ekron ; and Zil-baal, King of Gaza, and I made his country small. In addition to their former tribute and yearly gifts, I added other tribute and the homage due to my majesty, and I laid it upon them. The fear of the greatness of my majesty overwhelmed him, even Hezekiah, and he sent after me to Nineveh, my royal city, by way of gift and tribute, the Arabs and his body guard whom he had brought for the defence of Jerusalem, his royal city, and had furnished with pay, along with 30 talents of gold, 800 talents of pure silver, carbuncles, and other precious stones, a couch of ivory, thrones of ivory, an elephant's hide, an elephant's tusk, rare woods of all kinds, a vast treasure, as well as the eunuchs of his palace, and dancing men and dancing women, and he sent his ambassador to pay homage (or tribute) and to make submission."

It will be seen from this extract that Sennacherib claims a victory, but he did not take Jerusalem, though he sent an army against it. He is evidently trying to cover up a fact which looks like virtual defeat.

When this passage is compared with 2 Kings 18^{13}–19^{37}, 2 Chron. 32, Is. 36–37, 38^1, 39^1, chronological difficulties at once arise, for Sennacherib began to reign B.C. 705, and this was his third campaign. Therefore, says Schrader, " for this event the only possible date is B.C. 701. But Hezekiah died B.C. 700, and his fourteenth year in which these events took place, according to the Chronology of the Old Testament (2 Kings $18^{2. 13}$, 20^{1-6}) was the year B.C. 711.

" We see," says Schrader, " that one of the two systems must be abandoned. We cannot doubt against which of the two sentence must be passed. Our verdict must be pronounced against the Scriptural system. It must be abandoned in the presence of the corresponding statements of the Monuments and the Eponym Canon. In the Monuments we possess the additional advantage of gaining access to documents which have not, like Scriptural writings, notoriously been subjected in the course of Centuries to numerous alterations. We must acknowledge the artificial character of the Biblical Chronology."

Many attempts have been made to explain this discrepancy. Rawlinson suggests that there were two campaigns by Sennacherib. Kleinert suggests that the redactor put " Sennacherib " by mistake for " Sargon." Fausset thinks the case is hopeless and we must admit a copyist's error in putting the 14th instead of the 27th year of Hezekiah. Budge adopts Rawlinson's theory of an earlier campaign ending in victory as described by Sennacherib, and a later campaign, about two years after, ending in the destruction of the 185,000 men of Sennacherib's army by the angel of the Lord, who smote them " perhaps with a plague." George Smith thinks we should read 24th instead of 14th, and Samuel Kinns, in *Graven on the Rock*, says there is some error of transcription in 2 Kings 18 [13].

But there is really no need for any of these expedients. The whole difficulty arises from supposing that Sennacherib could not have undertaken a warlike operation of this kind during his father Sargon's lifetime—a pure assumption, wholly gratuitous, and capable of being satisfactorily disproved. Hezekiah's 14th year is the year B.C. 711. There is some doubt as to Sargon's first year, but his accession year was either B.C. 722 or 720. Hezekiah's 14th year was Sargon's 11th, and Sargon reigned 17 years. Six years, therefore, before he came to the throne, in B.C. 705, Sennacherib undertook this expedition, and received the submission of Hezekiah with the silver and the gold in the name of the King of Assyria.

George Smith says, "Sennacherib held some official rank during his father's reign, and it is quite possible that he commanded the expedition in B.C. 711 as his father's deputy. In the Tablet K 2169, Sennacherib is called "Rabsaki" (Rabshakeh) or General, and "great royal son," that is, heir to the throne; and he is said to possess his own scribe. The passage reads :—

"Tablet of Aia-suzubu-ilih the Scribe of the Rabshakeh, of Sennacherib, the great royal son of Sargon, King of Assyria."

The title, "great royal son," was assumed by Asshur-bani-pal when he was associated with his father on the throne.

Schrader says, "According to the Assyrian Eponym Canon, Sennacherib began his reign in the year B.C. 705. Therefore the campaign must have fallen subsequent to that year." Why must it? Why could not Sennacherib have conducted it before he came to the throne? Schrader says, "The Inscription does not inform us in the least in which year or years of Sennacherib's reign these eight campaigns occurred." But neither does it inform us that they occurred in the reign itself, i.e. between B.C. 705 and 681.

On the contrary, we know from an Inscription on a tablet enclosed in a clay envelope, and sent as a letter by Sennacherib to his father—No. 105 in Table-case D in the Nineveh Gallery of the British Museum—that Sennacherib sent to his father extracts from despatches which he had received concerning imperial affairs.

In the account of his fourth campaign, Sennacherib says : "Merodach-baladan, on whom I, in my first military expedition, inflicted a defeat, and whose force I had broken in pieces, dreaded the onset of my powerful weapons and the shock of my mighty battle." Why may not that first campaign have been undertaken by Sennacherib before he came to the throne? Did not Edward the Black Prince prove himself a famous warrior? Yet he never came to the throne of England at all.

Sargon conquered Merodach-baladan and dethroned him B.C. 710. Sennacherib's first campaign was against Merodach-baladan. Why may not he have been the Tartan or Commander-in-Chief in the war against Merodach-baladan, B.C. 710, five years before he came to the throne, and also in the war against Ashdod, in the 14th year of Hezekiah, B.C. 711, six years before he came to the throne?

Schrader says, "We have no means of directly fixing the date of

Sennacherib's third campaign "—the one against Hezekiah.   Yet this is the very one whose date he declares to be irreconcilable with the Biblical date, the 14th year of Hezekiah, B.C. 711 (2 Kings 18 13), and what makes it irreconcilable is not anything in the Monuments, but the *assumption* that Sennacherib could not have conducted a military expedition during Sargons' reign, as we know Sargon's Tartan did (Is. 20 1), and whether Sennacherib was that Tartan or not, we know that he was Crown Prince and Viceroy, or Co-Rex with his father Sargon, during the last five years of Sargon's reign.

Schrader is puzzled by the fact that Merodach-baladan was defeated and dethroned by Sargon in B.C. 710, and then again by Sennacherib in 704.   He asks, " Was this Merodach-baladan, by whom Sennacherib was confronted, identical with the Babylonian King of the same name, whom Sargon defeated and dethroned, or was he distinct from the above, perhaps his successor and son " ?

The solution of the difficulty is perfectly simple.   *Quod facit per alium facit per se*—what one does through another, one may be said to do oneself. What Sargon did through his son Sennacherib, he did himself.   It was one and the same Merodach-baladan, one and the same defeat, by one and the the same Sargon in his 12th year, which was Hezekiah's 15th year, B.C. 710, through one and the same Sennacherib, in his first campaign, in the *beginning* of his *rule*, five years before his accession, and six years before the first year of his *reign*.

This is borne out by Sennacherib's Inscriptions on the Taylor cylinder, the Bellino cylinder, and the Memorial Tablet, in each of which he says that he conquered Merodach-baladan " *ina ris sarruti* " (in the beginning of my *rule*), not " *ina ris pale-ja* " (in the beginning of my *reign*).

Prof. Sayce interprets the Biblical Record in another way.   He takes 2 Kings 18 13-16 as referring to the events of the 14th year of Hezekiah, B.C. 711, and 2 Kings 18 17–19, the destruction of Sennacherib's host, to a later date, viz. Sennacherib's 4th year, and Hezekiah's 24th, B.C. 701.   The interpretation is not perhaps positively excluded by the Text of the Old Testament, but in view of the words of 2 Kings 20 1. 6. 12 it seems more probable that the whole of 2 Kings 18 13–20 19 belongs to the 14th year of Hezekiah (B.C. 711). It is not necessary to decide what the explanation of the difficulty is.   It is enough to prove that no necessary contradiction between the Old Testament and the Monuments has been made out.

There is no reason why Sennacherib may not have been Co-Regent in the field with Sargon, as Nebuchadnezzar was with his father Nabopolassar, and Belshazzar with his father Nabonidus.   Sennacherib appointed his son Ashur-nadin-shum, King of Babylon, and Esar-haddon appointed his two sons, the one King of Assyria and the other King of Babylon.   The practice of appointing a Co-Regent during the King's life was very commonly adopted in all the countries of the East.

Schrader's whole case for the untrustworthiness of the Bible Chronology rests, as he himself tells us, upon this discrepancy between the Biblical date of Sennacherib's expedition, in the 14th year of Hezekiah, B.C. 711, and the Assyrian Monumental date for Sennacherib's accession, B.C. 705.   But both these statements are true.   There is no discrepancy between them.   Schrader's attack has failed, and the Bible Chronology stands.

VI. Esar-haddon (681–668).

Esar-haddon was the most potent of the Kings of Assyria.   He conquered Media, Phœnicia, Egypt and Ethiopia, and drove Tirhakah out of Egypt. He conquered the sons of Merodach-baladan, and made Babylon directly subject to the Assyrian Crown, residing by turns at Nineveh and Babylon instead of governing Babylon by Viceroys.

Esar-haddon was a great builder.   He built no new city, but he restored many old ones.   He rebuilt Babylon, which his father had destroyed, and which had lain waste for 10 years.   He began to build a great palace for himself at Calah, the modern Nimrûd, using for this purpose the slabs inscribed and used before by Tiglath-pileser III (IV), but it was never finished.   He rebuilt or restored temples at Nineveh, viz. at Nebi Yunus (Prophet Jonah), at Erech, Sippara and Borsippa.

He abdicated B.C. 668, after proclaiming his son Ashur-bani-pal King of Assyria and his son Shamash-shum-ukin King of Babylon.

The colossal Stele of Esar-haddon at Samaal represents him holding a cord attached to rings in the lips of two lesser figures, Tirhakah of Egypt and Baal of Tyre.

His Inscriptions include baked clay, six-sided cylinders, giving the annals of his reign and a summary of the same.   A black basalt Memorial Stone in archaic Babylonian characters, a bas-relief (cut in the rock at Nahr-el-Kelb near Berût, in Syria, close to the ancient highway from Egypt to Syria by the side of six other similar Assyrian and three Egyptian Inscriptions), cylinders, slabs, tablets, etc., giving his name, titles, genealogy and building operations. Four of his Inscriptions have a bearing on the subject of Old Testament Chronology, and the authenticity of the Bible Records so far as they refer to him.

1. A brick Inscription (I, Rawlinson 48, No. 3 ; Schrader, vol. ii, p. 20).   It reads as follows :—
" Esar-haddon, King of Assyria, son of Sennacherib King of Assyria." This agrees with 2 Kings 19[37].

2. The broken clay cylinder (III, Rawlinson 15, col. 1, 18 foll.) on the defeat of his two paricidal brothers who killed their father and fled to Armenia (Schrader ii, 17.)   It bears the following Inscription :—
" The terror of the great gods, my lords, overthrew them.   They saw and dreaded the meeting.   Istar the mistress of conflict and battle, who loved my priesthood, raised my hands, broke their bow, cleft through their battle array ; in their assembly resounded the cry ' This is our King.' "   This corroborates 2 Kings 19[37].

3. The great cylinder Inscription (I, Rawlinson 47, V, 11–13 ; Schrader ii, 39 ; Smith, Assyrian Eponym Canon, Extract 37, p. 139, date B.C. 680).
" I gathered 22 Princes of the land of Khatti (the Hittites) who dwell by the sea, and in the midst of it, all of them I summoned."

3A. A supplement to 3.   A broken clay cylinder (III, Rawlinson 16, c. V ; Schrader ii, 39–41 ; Smith, *Assyrian Eponym Canon*, Extract 37, p. 139.   Probable date B.C. 680), which gives the names of these 22 Princes.   They are as follows :—

1. Baal, King of Tyre.
2. Manasseh, King of Judah.
3. Khausgabri, King of Edom.
4. Mushuri, King of Moab.
5. Zilbel, King of Gaza.
6. Mitinti, King of Askelon.
7. Ikasamu, King of Ekron.
8. Milkiasap, King of Byblos.
9. Matanbaal, King of Arados (Arvad).
10. Abibal, King of Samsimuruna.
11. Puduil, King of Beth-Ammon.
12. Ahimelech, King of Ashdod.
Etc., etc.

There is a similar list given by his son Ashur-bani-pal in the next reign, in which all the names are the same except that Jakinlu takes the place of Matanbaal, and Amminadab that of Puduil.

These Inscriptions prove that Manasseh paid tribute to both Esar-haddon and Ashur-bani-pal in accordance with 2 Kings 21[13, 14], and 2 Chron. 33[11–19].

4. A baked cylinder (V, Rawlinson 45, col. 1, 24 ; Schrader ii, 61 ; Smith, *Assyrian Eponym Canon*, Extract 36, p, 137-8.   Probable date, B.C. 680), in which Esar-haddon says : " I gathered together all the Kings of the land of Khatti (Hittites) and of the sea coast.   Another town I caused to be built. Esarhaddonstown I called it.   The inhabitants of the mountains carried away by my bow, and those of the Eastern sea I settled in that spot.   My Officer the Viceroy I placed over them."

This corroborates Ezra 4[2], in which the adversaries of Judah, who opposed Zerubbabel and hindered the rebuilding of the Temple, say that it was Esar-haddon who brought them there.

If the captivity of Manasseh (B.C. 696–641), related in 2 Chron. 33[11], took place in the reign of Esar-haddon (B.C. 681–668), this would explain why he was deported by the King of Assyria to *Babylon*, and not to *Nineveh*, and as Esar-haddon was of a mild, forgiving nature, he would readily forgive and restore Manasseh, as he did the son of Merodach-baladan (2 Chron 33[12, 13]). In that case, there would be at least 28 years in which Manasseh could carry out his reformation.   If the captivity of Manasseh was due, as Schrader suggests, to his being suspected of complicity in the rebellion of Shamash-shum-ukin against Ashur-bani-pal, B.C. 648, he may have had to appear before Ashur-bani-pal at Babylon, to clear himself of suspicion and to furnish guarantees of faithfulness to Ashur-bani-pal ; upon which he would naturally be restored (2 Chron. 33[12, 13]).   In that case, there would be only seven years in which Manasseh could carry out his reformation, as he died B.C. 641.

The most probable conclusion is that of George Smith, which is as follows :

In the days of Ahaz, whose first year was the year B.C. 738, Isaiah prophesied and said, " Within 65 years shall Ephraim be broken from being a people " (Is. 7 [8]).

The adversaries who hindered the building of the Temple by Zerubbabel, were planted in Samaria by Esar-haddon, and some of these were Babylonians (Ez. 4 [2, 9]).

Manasseh King of Judah was carried away to Babylon by the King of Assyria (probably Esar-haddon), 2 Chron. 33 [11]

Esar-haddon gathered all the Kings of the land of the Khatti and of the sea coast (Palestine) and settled in that district the inhabitants of the Mountains and the Eastern Sea. He summoned to his presence the 22 Kings of the land of the Khatti, amongst whom he mentions Manasseh King of Judah (*Esar-haddon's Inscriptions*, Rawlinson i, 45, col. 1, lines 23 and 24 ; i, 47 ; v, 11–13 and iii, 16, c.V.)

Esar-haddon was King of Babylon B.C. 681–668. " Some of the dates of Esar-haddon," says George Smith, " are uncertain, but the time of the revolt and conquest of Palestine is fairly certain. In B.C. 673 or 672 Esar-haddon carried into captivity the remnant of Israel, and sent Manasseh, King of Judah, prisoner to Babylon. In the following year, B.C. 671, Manasseh was released."

Now from B.C. 738 to 673, the year in which Esar-haddon transplanted the inhabitants of Samaria into his Eastern provinces and re-peopled Samaria with Babylonians, etc., is exactly 65 years, and this occasion, rather than the first capture of Samaria by Sargon in B.C. 722, or its final fall in B.C. 719, was the one on which Ephraim was " broken from being a people." Thus, the Assyrian cuneiform Inscriptions throw a welcome light on a difficult verse in Isaiah, and show how his prophecy was fulfilled.

VII. Ashur-bani-pal (668–626).

The Inscriptions of Ashur-bani-pal give the history of his reign down to the year 640. Then the accounts cease. In accordance with the will of his father he became King of Assyria, and his brother Shamash-shum-ukin became King of Babylon.

In 661 he captured and plundered Thebes, the No-Amon of Nahum 3 [8], expelled the Ethiopians, and reinstated Psammeticus as King of Egypt under Assyrian protection and support.

In 648 his brother, Shamash-shum-ukin rebelled. He was besieged, and burnt himself in his palace, and Ashur-bani-pal ruled Babylon himself as King Kandalanu from B.C. 647 to his death in B.C. 626.

It is almost impossible to say when Nineveh and the Empire of Assyria fell. Ashur-bani-pal was the last great monarch. His accounts cease at B.C. 640.

Greek traditions say he lived in ease and indulgence, but we have no contemporary records. He was a cultured, leisurely man, interested in books and libraries. He left war to his warriors. He was a great builder. He created a great library, collecting and copying tens of thousands of clay tablets from every possible source, embodying the masterpieces of the age, together with works on astronomy, mathematics, grammar, dictionaries, deeds, letters, documents and lists of Eponyms. His library was situated first at Calah, and afterwards at Nineveh.

Ashur-bani-pal was probably succeeded by his two sons, Ashur-etil-ilani and Sin-shar-ish-kun (Saracos), who may have reigned the rest of the time, but there is no record, only traditions.

Assyria fell some time after 626.   The Greek tradition is that Psammeticus held Egypt, that Nabopolassar, the King of Assyria's Viceroy at Babylon, proclaimed himself King of Babylon, and with the help of Cyaxares the Mede took Nineveh B.C. 625, whereupon the Empire of Assyria was divided between Psammeticus who took Egypt, Nabopolassar who took Babylon, and Cyaxares who took Media.

C. H. W. Johns says it is difficult to harmonise the accounts that have reached us of these times, "and even the exact date of the fall of Nineveh is not certain.   It is usually set at B.C. 606."

We shall not, perhaps, be far out if we suppose that Ashur-bani-pal died in or about the year B.C. 626, that Nineveh was besieged by Nabopolassar of Babylon and Cyaxares the Mede, and fell in B.C. 625, that Ashur-bani-pal's two sons maintained a precarious existence as in some sense Kings of Assyria between B.C. 625 and 606, the elder, Ashur-etil-ilani, occupying the throne for the first six years (B.C. 625–619) and the younger Sin-shar-ish-kun (Saracos) for the remainder of the period (B.C. 619–606), at the end of which we may date the final fall and destruction of Nineveh B.C. 606.

But as George Smith says, in his *Assyrian Eponym Canon*, " No Assyrian date can be fixed with any certainty after the accession of Nabu-pal-uzer, or Nabopolassar, at Babylon, in B.C. 626, and this event appears to have been closely followed by the death of Ashur-bani-pal, King of Assyria."

The only Inscription of Ashur-bani-pal that bears upon the events recorded in the Old Testament is the Inscription on—

1. Cylinder C, Ashur-bani-pal (III, Rawlinson 27), its probable date, according to George Smith, being B.C. 668.

This is in a very mutilated condition, but more recently a duplicate of the Inscription made upon it has been discovered, numbered—

1a. Rassam 3, from which we obtain the full text (Schrader ii, 41 ; Smith, *Assyrian Eponym Canon*, Extract 41, p. 143), probable date B.C. 668 :—

" To Egypt and Ethiopia I directed the march. In the course of my expedition
1. Baal, King of Tyre.
2. Manasseh, King of Judah.
3. Kausgabri, King of Edom.
4. Musuri, King of Moab.
5. Zilbel, King of Gaza.
6. Mitinti, King of Ashkelon.
7. Ikasamsu, King of Ekron.
8. Milkiasap, King of Byblos.
9. Jakinlu, King of Arados.
10. Abibaal, King of Samsi-muruna.
11. Amminabad, King of Beth-Ammon
(and 11 others, making)
22 Kings of the side of the sea and the middle of the sea, all of them tributaries dependent on me, to my presence came and kissed my feet."

The payment of tribute by Manasseh is not mentioned in the Bible, but the Inscription of Ashur-bani-pal accords very well with what we might expect from 2 Kings 21 [13, 14] and 2 Chron. 33 [11-19].

In Ezra 4 [9, 10] we read of the great and noble Asnapper who brought over and set in the cities of Samaria, the Dinaites, the Apharsathchites, the Tarpelites, the Archevites, the Babylonians, the Susanchites, the Dehavites and the Elamites.

This Asnapper has not yet been definitely identified. He may have been (1) Esar-haddon (cp. Ezra 4 [2]), or (2) a General of Esar-haddon (though no General of that name has yet been met with in the Assyrian Inscriptions), or (3) most probably Ashur-bani-pal himself. In favour of this is the epithet "great and noble" or "great and mighty," and the fact that Ashur-bani-pal was the only Assyrian monarch who penetrated into the heart of Elam and gained possession of Susa (Schrader ii, p. 65).

This brings us to the close of the list of the historical Inscriptions of the Kings.

B. The Assyrian Eponym Canon.

One of the most important chronological documents ever discovered was that found by Sir Henry Rawlinson, among the inscribed terra cotta tablets which Mr. Layard and other explorers brought from Nineveh—the Assyrian Eponym Canon. This consists of a Canon or list of the annual Eponyms.

The Eponym was an Officer resembling, in some respects, our Lord Mayor. He held office for one year, and his name was appropriated to the function of denoting the year in which he held office, as one of a continuous series of years forming a chronological Era.

Sir H. Rawlinson distinguished 4 copies of the Canon, all imperfect, which he named Canons I, II, III and IV. Since then, other fragments have been found belonging to Canon I and some additional copies, also fragmentary, which have been named Canons V, VI and VII.

Canon I is the principal and standard copy. It begins with the Eponymy of Vul-nirari or Ramman-nirari, B.C. 911 (Assyrian dates) = B.C. 962, which corresponds with the 1st year of Asa, and ends in the year B.C. 659 (the 37th year of Manasseh).

Canon II extends from B.C. 893 (Assyrian dates) = B.C. 944 to B.C. 691.

Canon III from B.C. 810 (Assyrian dates) = B.C. 861 to B.C. 647.

Canon IV from B.C. 753 to 697, but originally it contained names now lost, bringing it down to about B.C. 637.

Canon V preserves names from B.C. 817 (Assyrian dates) = B.C. 868 to BC. 728.

Canon VI has a few names between B.C. 819 (Assyrian dates) = B.C. 870 and B.C. 804 (Assyrian dates) = B.C. 855, and also some further names between B.C. 708 and 700.

Canon VII has a few names between B.C. 829 and 822 (Assyrian dates) = B. C. 880 to 873, and some further names between B.C. 768 and 748, and between B.C. 732 and 723.

By piecing together the various parts of the VII Canons a list of the annual Eponyms of Assyria has been made out for the period from B.C. 911 (Assyrian dates)=B.C. 962 to B.C. 647.

There are several gaps of a few years in which a number of names have been lost, and it is believed by one school of Assyriologists that a whole block of 51 consecutive names, from B.C. 834 to 783, has been dropped out, so that the names from B.C. 783 and upwards (Assyrian dates) are really those of the Eponyms for B.C. 834 and upwards.

This view of the Canon is the one that agrees with the Chronology of the Old Testament. It is the view held in a modified form by Prof. Oppert, Rev. D. H. Haigh, Willis J. Beecher and other authorities, whilst Schrader, Sir H. Rawlinson and E. A. W. Budge (in the British Museum Guide) regard the Canon as we have it as complete, and adhere to the Assyrian dates, which throw all Old Testament and all Egyptian synchronisms above the year B.C. 783,-51 years out of joint.

George Smith cannot be claimed by either side. He says, " My own theory for the solution of the problem is founded on the principle of taking the Assyrian records to be correct as to Assyrian dates and the Hebrew Records as to Hebrew dates." And he regards the Ahab and Jehu mentioned on the Stele of Shalmaneser as two other persons, not to be identified with the Ahab and the Jehu of the Old Testament.

Of course, the Canon itself gives us no dates. On the side of the *Shorter Chronology* of the Assyrian dates there is simply the list of names which constitute the Canon, confirmed by certain long numbers which may be regarded as proving that the later Assyrian scribes, who compiled and copied and preserved these Eponym lists, held them to be continuous, but the authority of these scribes is that of late compilers, not that of contemporary witnesses, and it would be quite easy for a list of 51 names to be lost, or destroyed by accident (e.g. by fire), or purposely, by the founder of a new dynasty who wished to obliterate the records of his predecessors.

The records of Shalmaneser II (III) were probably destroyed by the usurper Sargon, and the records of the blank period of 51 years, B.C. 834–783, may have been similarly destroyed by Ashur-dân III when he came to the throne in B.C. 773. Syncellus says the records for this period were tampered with, and he assigns this as the reason why Ptolemy's Canon went back no further than B.C. 747. In a similar way, during the French Revolution, the country mansions were all fired in order that the title deeds contained in them might be destroyed.

A more exact parallel would be that of the Order of the Privy Council, giving the official authorization which led to the printing of the words, " Appointed to be read in Churches," by the King's printer, Robert Barker, in the original copies of the Version now universally known as the "Authorised Version." This Order was destroyed, together with other records of the Privy Council in a fire which occurred at Whitehall in January, 1618 (old style). This leaves a gap of several years in the records of the Privy Council, and it has led many to the erroneous conclusion that the Authorised Version never was officially authorised at all.

C. Fragmentary Lists of Assyrian Eponyms.

The list of Assyrian Eponyms, which has been drawn up by piecing together all the information given in the VII Canons, contains also the occasional record of the most striking event of any particular year.

Thus, we have " B.C. 722, Eponym of the Ninip-ilai, accession of Sargon, siege of Samaria." " B.C. 711, Eponym of Ninip-alik-pani, expedition to Ashdod." " B.C. 668, Eponym of Marlarmi, Esar-haddon died."

These addenda are derived from certain fragmentary lists of Eponyms which contain notes of the principal events of each year (Rawlinson's *Cuneiform Inscriptions*, vol. ii, plates 52, 69 ; Schrader, vol. ii, pp. 188-197).   These lists extend from (B.C. 817 Assyrian dates=)B.C. 868 to B.C. 728.

D. The Synchronous History of Assyria and Babylon.

There is no Babylonian Eponym Canon or list of annual officials in Babylon, but there are certain documents which may be called Babylonian chronicles, written in the Persian period, which give lists of dynasties and Kings, and the number of years they reigned.

There are also fragments of writings that give a synchronous history of the two countries.

The history of Assyria was interwoven with that of Babylon from the very earliest times, and these documents describe the relations and the exploits of the various contemporary Babylonian and Assyrian Kings, sometimes dating events by the year, the month and the day, but they exist only in a mutilated condition, and do not give us a continuous Chronology.

PERIOD IV. GENTILE DOMINION—2 *Kings* 24 *to Esther.*

CHAPTER XXIV. THE CAPTIVITY.

(AN. HOM. 3520–3589).

[*It is very desirable that in reading this chapter, the Chronological Tables in Vol. II should be kept open at page 30 for constant reference.*]

THE date of the captivity is the 3rd year of Jehoiakim, the year AN. HOM. 3520, B.C. 605, the 21st year of Nabopolassar, Nebuchadnezzar's father, as King of Babylon, in which year Nebuchadnezzar, being associated with his father on the throne, was also " King of Babylon," though the year he was Co-Rex with his father is not reckoned as his first year.

We learn from Daniel 1^{1-7} that " In the third year of the reign of Jehoiakim King of Judah, came Nebuchadnezzar King of Babylon unto Jerusalem, and besieged it. And the Lord gave Jehoiakim into his hand with part of the vessels of the house of God," and certain of the seed royal, amongst whom were Daniel, Shadrach, Meshach and Abed-nego. This was in accordance with the prophecy of Isa. 39^7, uttered in the 14th year of Hezekiah, B.C. 711, just 106 years before.

The following year, the fourth of Jehoiakim, was the first year of Nebuchadnezzar. The synchronism is given in Jer. 25^1. This is one of the most important dates in the Bible. It is the link which connects together the years of sacred and profane Chronology. By it all events of Bible history from the creation of Adam onward, are brought into chronological relation with the events of our own day, so far as the record of the years has been accurately preserved from the 1st year of Nebuchadnezzar onward.

The 4th year of Jehoiakim was also the 23rd year of Jeremiah's prophecies, which began in the 13th year of Josiah (Jer. 25^3). It was the year in which Jeremiah's memorable prophecy of the 70 years' captivity in Babylon was uttered. All the Kingdoms of the world were to serve the King of Babylon for 70 years (Jer. 25^{8-26}). Then Sheshach, or Babylon herself, was to be punished in a similar way. All nations were to serve the King of Babylon, and his son, and his son's son (Jer. $27^{6.7}$).

In the same year, Jeremiah was charged to commit to writing all the prophecies that he had uttered during the 23 years of his prophetic ministry (Jer. $36^{1.2}$). Baruch his scribe was told not to seek great things for himself, for the Lord was about to bring evil upon all flesh, nevertheless Baruch's life would be spared (Jer. 45^{1-5}).

It was the year in which Pharaoh-necho, who had gone as far East as Carchemish, on the river Euphrates, in order to obtain his share of the plunder arising from the fall of Nineveh and the Empire of Assyria, was smitten by Nebuchadnezzar (Jer. 46 [2]), so that he " came not again any more out of his land : for the King of Babylon had taken from the river of Egypt unto the river Euphrates, all that pertained to the King of Egypt " (2 Kings 24 [7]).

The following year, B.C. 603, was the 5th of Jehoiakim and the 2nd of Nebuchadnezzar. Daniel had been three years, in training (Dan. 1 [5]), viz. from the accession year of Nebuchadnezzar when he was Co-Rex with his father (B.C. 605) to the 2nd year of his reign as sole King (B.C. 603). . Nebuchadnezzar was on the eve of a great career, his mind was filled with thoughts of Empire, and he dreamed his dream of the great image of gold and silver and brass and iron which Daniel interpreted as a revelation of the purposes of God, respecting the four great World Empires of Babylon, Medo-Persia, Greece and Rome (Dan. 2 [1-45]).

Jehoiakim reigned altogether 11 years. He was made King by Pharaoh-necho (B.C. 608) and served him for three years, when his capital was besieged and himself bound in fetters (B.C. 605) by Nebuchadnezzar, who intended to carry him to Babylon (2 Chron. 36 [6]), but he was afterwards released and allowed to retain his throne as a vassal King under Nebuchadnezzar. He served Nebuchadnezzar three years, to his 5th year (2 Kings 24 [1]), then (B.C. 603) he turned and rebelled. Nebuchadnezzar was too busy in other parts of his Dominion to deal with him just then, but he allowed him to be harassed by bands of Chaldees, Syrians, Moabites and Ammonites (2 Kings 24 [2]).

In this 5th year of Jehoiakim a fast was proclaimed in Jerusalem (Jer. 36 [9]). Jehoiakim sat in the winter-house, with a fire burning on the hearth before him. Jehudi read to him from the Roll of the prophecies of Jeremiah, and Jehoiakim took the Roll and cut it with a penknife and cast it into the fire (Jer. 36 [21-23]).

Five years later Nebuchadnezzar came up against Jerusalem in the 7th year of his reign (B.C. 598), and took 3,023 Jews (Jer. 52 [28]).

What happened to Jehoiakim, or how he met his death, is only told in the form of prophecy. He died unlamented, in the 11th year of his reign, and was buried with the burial of an ass, drawn and cast forth beyond the gates of Jerusalem (Jer. 22 [18, 19]).

He was succeeded by his son Jehoiachin, who only reigned three months.

There is a double statement with respect to the age of Jehoiachin at the time when he began to reign. Both statements are equally true, but the two writers who make them reckon the years from a different starting point. In 2 Kings 24 [8] we read, " Jehoiachin was 18 years old when he began to reign," viz. in the 11th year of his father Jehoiakim. This same year was also the 8th year of Nebuchadnezzar, and it was this fact which was in the mind of the writer of 2 Chron. 36 [9], when he said, " Jehoiachin was " *a son of 8 years* " when he began to reign." The expression " son of " is used with a great deal of latitude, and is made to cover almost any genitive relation or reference to a point of origin or commencement. Here the words are used to express the number of years between the accession of Jehoiachin and the 1st year of the new Era of the reign of Nebuchadnezzar.

The author of the *Companion Bible* thinks Jehoiachin did actually begin to reign as Co-Rex with his father ten years before, in the 1st year of Jehoiakim, which is a possible alternative interpretation of the words, " Jehoiachin was a son of eight years when he began to reign."

If we refuse to place ourselves at the point of view of the writer in order that we may understand his meaning, and instead, insist on forcing *our own* thought into his words, we shall have to admit a careless copyist's error, the word " eight " having been written down by the transcriber instead of the word eight(een) by the omission of the word for 10 in the Hebrew, which is also a possible alternative theory of the origin of the Text, though not an interpretation of it.

But with a knowledge of the author's method of writing the Chronology and dating the events, gained from 2 Chron. 16[1] (the 36th year of the *Kingdom* of Asa), and 2 Chron. 22[2] (Ahaziah was " a son of 42 years " when he began to reign), we ought to be prepared for the new method of dating which he adopts here.

In this same year, the 8th of Nebuchadnezzar, in which Jehoiachin ascended the throne, Nebuchadnezzar came up against Jerusalem and beseiged it. Nebuchadnezzar took Jehoiachin, his mother, his servants, his officers, and all the mighty men of the land, and carried them away to Babylon, together with the treasures of the house of the Lord, and the treasures of the King's house, and 10,000 captives, including 7,000 mighty men of valour, 1,000 craftsmen and smiths ; all that were strong and apt for war, the King of Babylon brought captive to Babylon (2 Kings 24[8-16]).

Amongst the number of these captives were Ezekiel and Mordecai. In Ezek. 1[1,2], Ezekiel says he was among the captives by the river Chebar in the 5th year of Jehoiachin's captivity, B.C. 593, which was the 4th year of Zedekiah and the 12th year of Nebuchadnezzar. And in Ezek. 40[1], he speaks of the great vision which he had in the " 25th year of our captivity," thus including himself amongst the number of the captives carried away with Jehoiachin. All his prophecies are dated with reference to this event (Ezek. 1[2], 8[1], 20[1], 24[1], 26[1], 29[1,17], 30[20], 31[1], 32[1,17], 33[21], 40[1]).

In Esther 2[5,6] we read, " Now in Shushan the palace there was a certain Jew, whose name was Mordecai, the son of Jair, the son of Kish, a Benjamite, who had been carried away from Jerusalem with the captivity which had been carried away with Jeconiah (Jehoiachin), King of Judah, whom Nebuchadnezzar King of Babylon had carried away." From this it is perfectly clear that Mordecai is the man whom the writer means to indicate as having been carried away with Jeconiah in the 8th year of Nebuchadnezzar. His name appears as one of the leaders of those who returned with Zerubbabel (Ezra 2[2], Neh. 7[7]), but in consequence of the misdating of the Books of Ezra, Nehemiah and Esther, this verse has been misinterpreted, and made to mean that it was not Mordecai, but Kish, his grandfather, who was carried away with Jeconiah.

In 2 Chron. 36[10], we read that at the return of the year (A.V. margin), or " when the year was expired," King Nebuchadnezzar brought Jehoiachin to Babylon and made Zedekiah King over Judah and Jerusalem. This probably means that Zedekiah did not actually begin to reign till after the New Year's Day following the year in which Jehoiachin reigned. Hence we date the

last year of Jehoiakim and the three months of Jehoiachin in the 8th of Nebuchadnezzar, the year B.C. 597, and the 1st year of Zedekiah, in the 9th of
Nebuchadnezzar, the year B.C. 596.

In the year AN. HOM. 3532 = B.C. 593, i. e. 390 years after the disruption in
AN. HOM. 3143 = B.C. 982, in the 5th day of the 4th month of the 5th year of
Jehoiachin's captivity, Ezekiel began to prophesy.

This fact is referred to in the type or sign given to the Prophet in the 1st
year of his prophecy and recorded in Ezek. 4 [4-6].

> " Lie thou also upon thy left side and lay the iniquity of the house of Israel
> upon it : according to the number of the days that thou shalt lie
> upon it, thou shalt bear their iniquity.
> " For I have laid upon thee the years of their iniquity, according to
> the number of the days, 390 days : so shalt thou bear the iniquity
> of the house of Israel.
> " And when thou hast accomplished them, lie again on thy right side,
> and thou shalt bear the iniquity of the house of Judah 40 days :
> I have appointed thee each day for a year."

The 390 years of the iniquity of Israel are the years from the disruption
to the date of the prophecy. The 40 years of the iniquity of Judah are the
40 years of the prophecies of Jeremiah from their commencement in the 13th
year of Josiah, B.C. 626, to the 10th year of Zedekiah, B.C. 587, in which year
Zedekiah shut him up in prison (Jer. 32 [1-3]).

The date of Ezekiel's first prophecy is given as the 5th day of the 4th
month of the 30th year of some Era which is not expressly defined, but this
30th year is identified with the 5th year of Jehoiachin's captivity (Ezek. 1 [1.2]).
Reckoning back these 30 years, we find that the first year of this Era was the
year B.C. 622, the 17th year of Josiah, the year of the discovery of the Book
of the Law, and of the great religious revival which culminated in Josiah's
great Passover in his 18th year, B.C. 621. It may mark the year of the fall of
Nineveh and the end of the Empire of Assyria, which occurred at some time
after B.C. 626, but the exact date of which cannot be definitely ascertained.

In Jer. 28 [1-3] we read of another event which occurred in the 4th year of
Zedekiah (B.C. 593). In the 5th month of this year, Hananiah, the false
prophet, spoke to Jeremiah in the house of the Lord, and said, "Within two
full years will I bring again into this place all the vessels of the Lord's House
that Nebuchadnezzar took away."

In the following year, B.C. 592, in the 5th day of the 6th month of the 6th
year of Jehoiachin's captivity, Ezekiel had his vision of the chambers of
imagery (Ezek. 8 [1]).

In the year after this, B.C. 591, on the 10th day of the 5th month of the 7th
year of Jehoiachin's captivity, we read of the remarkable experience of the
cessation of prophecy, when the Elders come to enquire of Ezekiel, but there
is no answer from God (Ezek. 20 [1]).

In the year B.C. 589, we reach the remarkable prophecy of the boiling
cauldron, Ezek. 24 [1-29.] It is dated the 10th day of the 10th month of the
9th year of Jehoiachin's captivity, and as the years of Jehoiachin's captivity

are always one more than the years of Zedekiah's reign, the date of the prophecy is the 10th day of the 10th month of the 8th year of Zedekiah. This is the Epoch of the 70 years of Jehovah's indignation with Israel, another 70 years, quite distinct from the 70 years of Daniel's captivity.

The prophecy comes to Ezekiel precisely one year before the day on which Nebuchadnezzar laid siege to Jerusalem. Ezekiel is bidden to "write the name of the day, even of this same day, the King of Babylon set himself against Jerusalem this same day." It was a memorable day, the beginning of a prophetic period, and Ezekiel was told to note it down. It marked the commencement of the fury and the vengeance which Jehovah now began to execute upon Jerusalem.

The city was like a pot set on a fire and made to boil, a parable of the condition of the inhabitants of Jerusalem when the city was besieged by Nebuchadnezzar. The indignation lasted till the building of the Temple was recommenced in the 2nd year of Darius B.C. 589–520 (see Vol. II, Chronological Tables, pp. 30 and 34, and cp. Zech. 1 [7-12]).

Alternative dates have been proposed for the commencement of this period of 70 years, viz. the following year, B.C. 588, when the siege of Jerusalem began, or the year, B.C. 586, when the city was taken, but the true date is given in Ezek. 24 [1.] The name of the day which Ezekiel was charged to write was the 10th day of the 10th month of the 9th year of Jehoiachin's captivity, B.C. 589, on the anniversary of which day, exactly a year later, "the King of Babylon set himself against Jerusalem."

In B.C. 588 Nebuchadnezzar pitched against Jerusalem and besieged it (2 Kings 25 [1,] Jer. 39 [1,] 52 [4]), on the 10th day of the 10th month of the 9th year of Zedekiah. On the 12th day of the 10th month of the 10th year of Jehoiachin's captivity, also B.C. 588, Ezekiel prophesied that Egypt should be desolate for 40 years (Ezk. 29 [1. 11. 12]).

The following year, B.C. 587, was the 10th year of Zedekiah, the 11th year of Jehoiachin's captivity, the 18th year of Nebuchadnezzar, the 2nd year of the siege of Jerusalem, and the last of the 40 years of Jeremiah's prophecies before the fall of Jerusalem (Ezek. 4 [4-6]).

In this year, Jeremiah bought his uncle Hananeel's field (while Nebuchadnezzar was besieging Jerusalem, Zedekiah having shut him up in prison), as witness to his faith in the future of the Land, in spite of its present desperate state (Jer. 32 [1-12]).

In this year also, Nebuchadnezzar took 832 souls (Jer. 52 [29]).

In this year, Ezekiel prophesied against Tyre, on the 1st day of the 11th year of Jehoiachin's captivity, because she rejoiced over the calamity of Jerusalem, and said, "Aha, Jerusalem is broken" (Ezek. 26 [1]). On the 7th day of the 1st month of the 11th year of Jehoiachin's captivity, Jeremiah prophesied against Egypt, and said, I have broken Pharaoh and will scatter Egypt (Ezek. 30 [20]). On the 1st day of the 3rd month of the 11th year of Jehoiachin's captivity he prophesied again against Egypt, and declared that Egypt should fall like Assyria, the Cedar of Lebanon (Ezek. 31 [1-3]).

The following year, B.C. 586, is the year of the fall of Jerusalem. It was.

the 11th of Zedekiah, the 12th of Jehoiachin's captivity, and the 19th of Nebuchadnezzar's reign.

We learn from 2 Kings 25 [1-4], Jer. 39 [2] and 52 [4-7], that on the 9th day of the 4th month of the 11th year of Zedekiah, the famine prevailed, and the city was broken up, and from 2 Kings 25 [8] and Jer. 52 [12] that on the 7th day of the 5th month of the 11th year of Zedekiah, "which was the 19th year of Nebuchadnezzar," Nebuzar-adan burnt the Temple and broke down the walls.

From 2 Kings 25 [18-21] we learn that shortly after the 7th day of the 5th month of the 11th year of Zedekiah, the high priest, Seraiah, who was the father of Jehozadak (1 Chron. 6 [1-15]) and Ezra (Ez. 7 [1-5]) was brought before Nebuchadnezzar at Riblah, in the land of Hamath, and there slain. " So Judah was carried away out of their land" in the 5th month of the 11th year of Zedekiah (2 Kings 25 [21], Jer. 1 [3]). Six months later, in the 7th month of the 11th year of Zedekiah, Gedaliah, who had been appointed governor of Judah by Nebuchadnezzar, was slain by Ishmael (2 Kings 25 [25], Jer. 41 [1]).

We are now in a position to give the Chronology of the period from the first year of Rehoboam to the 11th year of Zedekiah, to which we append a similar Chronology of the Kings of Israel.

Kings of Judah.

AN. HOM.

3143. Rehoboam (see chapter 30).

17. Add 17 years, reign of Rehoboam (1 Kings 11 [43], 14 [21]).

3160. Abijam.

3. Add 3 yrs. reign of Abijam (1 K. 15 [1, 2]).

3163. Asa.

41. Add 41 yrs. reign of Asa (1 K. 15 [9, 10]).

3204. Jehoshaphat.

25. Add 25 yrs. reign of Jehoshaphat (1 K. 22 [41, 42]).

3229. Jehoram sole King.

Add 3 yrs. reign of Jehoram as sole King + 4 years Co-Rex with Jehoshaphat + 1 yr. reckoned to Ahaziah = 8 yrs., (cp. 1 K. 22 [50], 2 K. 1 [17], 3 [1], 8 [16, 17], and see Vol. II, Chronological Tables, p. 24,

3. AN. HOM. 3220–3232.)

3232. Ahaziah sole King.

Add 1 yr. reign of Ahaziah (cp. 2 K. 8 [25, 26], 9 [29] and see Vol. II,

1. Chronological Tables, p. 24, AN. HOM. 3231–3232).

3233. Athaliah.

6. Add 6 yrs. reign of Athaliah, (2 K. 11 [1, 3, 4, 16]).

3239. Joash.

40. Add 40 yrs. reign of Joash (2 K. 12 [1]).

3279. Amaziah.

29. Add 29 yrs. reign of Amaziah (2 K. 12 [21], 14 [1, 2], [17-22]).

3308. Interregnum.

Add 11 yrs. interregnum (see Vol. II, Chronological Tables, p. 26,

11. AN. HOM. 3308–3318).

3319. Uzziah.

AN. HOM.

3319. Uzziah.

52. Add 52 yrs. reign of Uzziah (= Azariah) (2 K. 14 ^{21}, 15 $^{1\cdot 2}$).

3371. Jotham.

16. Add 16 yrs. reign of Jotham (2 K. 15 $^{32\cdot 33}$).

3387. Ahaz.

16. Add 16 yrs. reign of Ahaz (2 K. 15 ^{38}, 16 $^{1\cdot 2}$).

3403. Hezekiah sole King.

    Add 27 yrs. reign of Hezekiah as sole King+2 yrs. as Co-Rex with
        Ahaz = 29 yrs. (2 K. 16 ^{20}, 18 $^{1\cdot 2}$.   See Vol. II, Chronological
27.   Tables, pp. 27, 28, AN. HOM. 3400–3429).

3430. Manasseh.

55. Add 55 yrs. reign of Manasseh (2 K. 20 ^{21}, 21 ^{1}).

3485. Amon.

2. Add 2 yrs. reign of Amon (2 K. 21 $^{18\cdot 19}$).

3487. Josiah.

30. Add first 30 yrs. reign of Josiah.

3517. Jehoahaz (3 months).

    Add 31st year of Josiah, (2 K. 21 $^{23\text{-}26}$, 22 ^{1}), which includes 3 months
1.   of Jehoahaz (2 K. 23 $^{30\cdot 31}$).

3518. Jehoiakim.

10. Add first 10 yrs. of reign of Jehoiakim.

3528. Jehoiachin (3 months).

    Add 11th yr. of Jehoiakim (2 K. 23 ^{36}), which includes 3 months of
1.   Jehoiachin (2 K. 24 $^{6\text{-}8}$).

3529. Zedekiah.

10. Add first 10 yrs. of Zedekiah.

3539. 11th and last year of Zedekiah (2 K. 24 $^{17\cdot 18}$), in which Jerusalem
    was taken by Nebuchadnezzar, and Zedekiah's captivity began
    (2 K. 25 $^{1\text{-}21}$).

Kings of Israel.

3143. Jeroboam (see Chapter 20).

21. Add 21 years+1 reckoned to Nadab = 22 (1 Kings 12 ^{20}, 14 ^{20}).

3164. Nadab.

1. Add 1 yr. +1 reckoned to Baasha = 2 (1 K. 15 ^{25}).

3165. Baasha.

23. Add 23 yrs.+1 reckoned to Elah = 24 (1 K. 15 $^{28\cdot 33}$).

3188. Elah.

1. Add 1 yr.+1 reckoned to Omri = 2 (1 K. 16 ^{8}).

3189. Omri, Tibni and Zimri (see Vol. II, Chronological Tables, p. 23,
    AN. HOM. 3189–3200).

11. Add 11 yrs.+1 reckoned to Ahab = 12 (1 K. 16 $^{22\cdot 23}$).

3200. Ahab.

AN. HOM.

3200. Ahab.
  20. Add 20 yrs. + 2 Co-Rex with Ahaziah = 22 (1 K. 16 ^{29}).

3220. Ahaziah.
      Add 1 yr. + 1 reckoned to Jehoram = 2 (1 K. 22 ^{51}). (See Vol. II,
  1. Chronological Tables, p. 24, AN. HOM. 3220–3221).

3221. Jehoram.
      Add 12 yrs. reign of Jehoram (2 K. 1 ^{17}, 3 ^{1}). (See Vol. II, Chronological
  12. Tables, p. 24, AN. HOM 3221–3232.)

3233. Jehu.
  28. Add 28 yrs. reign of Jehu (2 K. 9 $^{13. 24. 27. 33}$, 10 ^{36}).

3261. Jehoahaz.
  17. Add 17 yrs. reign of Jehoahaz (2 K. 10 ^{35}, 13 ^{1}).

3278. Jehoash sole King.
      Add 15 yrs. + 1 reckoned to Jeroboam II = 16 (2 K. 13 $^{9. 10}$). (See Vol. II,
  15. Chronological Tables, p. 25, AN. HOM. 3275–3293.)

3293. Jeroboam II.
  41. Add 41 yrs. reign of Jeroboam II (2 K. 14 $^{16. 23}$).

3334. Interregnum.
      Add 22 yrs. interregnum. (See Vol. II, Chronological Tables, p. 26,
  22. AN. HOM. 3334–3355.)

3356. Zechariah.
  1. Add 1 yr. for Zechariah (6 mos.), (2 K. 14 ^{29}, 15 ^{8}).

3357. Shallum.
      Add 1 yr. for Shallum (1 mo.), (2 K. 15 $^{10. 13}$, and accession of
  1. Menahem, 2 K. 15 $^{14. 17}$).

3358. Menahem.
  10. Add 10 yrs. reign of Menahem (2 K. 15 $^{14. 17}$).

3368. Pekahiah.
  2. Add 2 yrs. reign of Pekahiah (2 K. 15 $^{23. 24}$).

3370. Pekah.
  20. Add 20 yrs. reign of Pekah (2 K. 15 $^{25-27}$).

3390. Interregnum.
      Add 8 yrs. Interregnum. (See Vol. II, Chronological Tables, p. 27,
  8. AN. HOM. 3390–3397.)

3398. Hoshea.
  8. Add first 8 yrs. of Hoshea.

3406. 9th and last year of Hoshea (2 K. 17 ^{1}). Final fall of Samaria and
      deportation of its inhabitants by Sargon, B.C. 719, three years
      after its previous capture by Sargon, B.C. 722, when he took the
      city, but left the inhabitants and imposed tribute upon them
      (2 K. 17 $^{1-23}$).

News of the fall of Jerusalem travelled to the East. The city fell in the
5th month of the 11th year of Zedekiah. Five months later, on the 5th day

of the 10th month of the 12th year of Jehoiachin's captivity (the same year, B.C.
586), one that had escaped from Jerusalem came to Ezekiel and said, " The
city is smitten."

Harold Browne, in his excellent *Ordo Sæclorum : Chronology of the Holy
Scriptures*, p. 167, makes the years of Zedekiah's reign coincide with the years
of Jehoiachin's captivity. This he thinks he proves from 2 Kings 25[1] and
Ezek. 24[1], the 10th day of the 10th month of the 9th year of Zedekiah being
equated to the 10th day of the 10th month of the 9th year of Jehoiachin's
captivity. But he is mistaken. Ezek. 24[1] is prophetic. Ezekiel sees Nebuchadnezzar pitching against Jerusalem, not in contemporary vision at the very
moment at which he is doing so, but in prophetic vision, exactly one year ahead
to the very day.

In consequence of Browne's error he is tripped up when he comes to Ezek.
33[21], where *his* reckoning makes the man who escapes from Jerusalem reach
Ezekiel in Chaldea 1 year and 5 months after the city is smitten, instead of
5 months after the event. It was just a four or five months' journey (Ezra 7[9]),
and the news of such an event could not fail to reach Ezekiel and the Jews in
captivity within about four or five months of the event. But rather than
abandon his own error, he charges it upon the Hebrew Text. The Hebrew
reading of Ezek. 33[21] is "in the 12th year." Browne alters it to "*the
eleventh ! "*

In this same year, B.C. 586, on the 1st day of the 12th month of Jehoiachin's
captivity, Ezekiel dates his lamentation for Pharaoh, in which he declares that
the Lord will make Egypt desolate (Ezek. 32[1]), and also the further prophecy
on the 15th day (of the same month) of the 12th year of Jehoiachin's captivity,
his wail for Egypt (Ezek. 32[17]) with its terrible refrain : —

> All of them slain, fallen by the sword,
> Gone down uncircumcised into the pit,
> Into the nethermost parts of the earth,
> Into the midst of hell.

Four years later there was another expedition of some kind against Jerusalem, for in that year (B.C. 582), the 23rd year of Nebuchadnezzar, Nebuzar-adan
took 745 souls, making a total of 4,600, for three expeditions in the 7th, 18th
and 23rd years of Nebuchadnezzar, which, however, does not include those
carried away with Jehoiachin in the 8th year of Nebuchadnezzar (Jer. 52[28-30]).

Our next note of time is in the year B.C. 573, on the 10th day of the beginning
of the 25th year of Jehoiachin's captivity, which was the 14th year after the
city was smitten. Ezekiel had a wonderful vision of the new Land, the new
city, and the new Temple, the account of which forms the climax of his Book
(Ezek. 40–48, especially 40[1]).

Two years later, in B.C. 571, on the 1st day of the 1st month of the 27th
year of Jehoiachin's captivity, Ezekiel prophesied that Nebuchadnezzar
should have Egypt as wages for his service against Tyre (Ezek. 29[17]).

Then follows a *blank* of 9 years to the end of the reign of Nebuchadnezzar,
very noteworthy as the period containing the 7 years of Nebuchadnezzar's
madness, after which we read in Jer. 52[31] that on the 25th day of the 12th

month of the 37th year of Johoiachin's captivity (B.C. 561), Evil-merodach, the son and successor of Nebuchadnezzar, in the year in which he came to the throne, brought Jehoiachin out of prison, and in 2 Kings 25[27] that on the 27th day of the same month he showed him further kindness out of prison.

The Bible contains no record of the events of the succeeding 19 years, but we learn from Dan. 7[1] that in the 1st year of Belshazzar (B.C. 541), Daniel had his vision of the four beasts symbolizing Babylon, Medo-Persia, Greece and Rome, and throwing further light upon the course of the future history of the world, as revealed in the previous vision of Nebuchadnezzar's great image.

Two years later (B.C. 539), in the 3rd year of Belshazzar, Daniel had his vision of the ram and the he-goat, foreshadowing the coming conflict between Persia and Greece (Dan. 8[1]).

Daniel 5 gives a picture of the fall of Babylon in the year B.C. 538, and the transfer of the Empire of the world from Babylon to Medo-Persia. The accounts of this event are very divergent. One of them represents Cyrus as the nephew and son-in-law of Darius the Mede, but he was more probably his cousin and his brother-in-law, having married the sister of Darius the Mede (Astyages). See Vol. II, Chronological Tables, p. 54.

"In that night," we read (Dan. 5[30. 31]), "was Belshazzar the King of the Chaldeans slain. And Darius the Median received the Kingdom, being about 62 years old." There was no battle. Belshazzar was slain in the palace, Cyrus was the conqueror of Babylon, and he handed it over to Darius, who "received" it from him as his Co-Partner in the Empire of the world.

The length of the reign of Darius the Median is not stated in Scripture, nor is Darius himself mentioned in profane literature under that name, except in Josephus, but it is clear from Dan. 6[28] that he was succeeded by Cyrus, and from 2 Chron. 36[20-23] that the 1st year of Cyrus was the 70th and last of the 70 years' captivity which began in the 3rd year of Jehoiakim, B.C. 605. Hence, whatever may be the number and the names of the monarchs between Nebuchadnezzar and Cyrus, and whatever the number of years that each monarch reigned, we know that the 1st year of Cyrus was the year B.C. 536, and we may provisionally accept the received dates derived from secular history as given by E. A. W. Budge in the British Museum Guide :—

561. Evil-merodach.
559. Nergal-sharezer (Neriglissar).
556. Labashi-marduk.
555. Nabonidus.
538. Conquest of Babylon by Cyrus,

adding thereto the name of Belshazzar as Co-Rex with his father Nabonidus, B.C. 541–539, and the name of Darius the Mede as Rex B.C. 538 and 537, with Cyrus as Co-Rex during these two years, and making Cyrus sole King on the death of Darius the Mede, B.C. 536.

The Chronology of the first 20 years of the 70 years' servitude down to the 11th year of Zedekiah, has already been given in the present chapter. The remaining 50 years is divided into two equal parts of 25 years each. The Chronology of the period is as follows :—

The Seventy Years of Daniel's Captivity,
or
The Seventy Years of Servitude to Babylon.

AN. HOM.

3539. 11th Zedekiah = 19th Nebuchadnezzar (2 Kings 25 [8]) = 12th
Jehoiachin's captivity = 20th of the 70 years' servitude.
See above (present chapter), and Vol. II, Chronological
Tables, p. 30, AN. HOM. 3539.

Add 25 years from 12th to 37th year of Jehoiachin's captivity
= 45th year of the 70 years' servitude (2 Kings 25 [27]).
See Vol. II, Chronological Tables, pp. 30-32, AN. HOM. 3539–

25.   3564.

3564. Evil-merodach.

Add 25 years from 45th to 70th of the 70 years' servitude,
Dan. 1 [1], Jer. 25 [1-26].

25. See Vol. II, Chronological Tables, p. 32, AN. HOM. 3564–3589.

3589. Cyrus (1st year of sole Kingship).

CHAPTER XXV. THE RETURN.

(AN. HOM. 3589–3637.)

The Persian Period.

WE now reach the most difficult period in the whole realm of Bible Chronology, the period of Ezra, Nehemiah and Esther.

Our sole authority for this period is the Books of Ezra, Nehemiah and Esther. There are cuneiform Inscriptions by Cyrus, by Darius Hystaspes, and by each of the succeeding Persian monarchs down to the last King of Persia, who was slain by Alexander the Great, and the Behistun Inscription by Darius Hystaspes contains some very valuable information, but none of these Inscriptions give us any help in fixing the Chronology of the period.

Neither do we obtain any help in this direction from Jewish, Persian or Greek literature. The Jewish and the Persian traditions make the period of the Persian Empire a period of about 52 years. There are no contemporary chronological records whatever to fix the dates of any of the Persian Monarch after Darius Hystaspes. The clay tablets of Babylon fix the Chronology for the reigns of Cyrus, Cambyses, Pseudo-Smerdis and Darius Hystaspes, but they do not determine the date of any subsequent Persian King.

The dates that have reached us, and which are now generally received as historical, are a late compilation made in the 2nd Century A.D., and found in Ptolemy's Canon. They rest upon the calculations or guesses made by Eratosthenes and certain vague, floating traditions, in accordance with which the period of the Persian Empire was mapped out as a period of 205 years.

The count of the years is now lost, but if we may assume the correctness of the Greek Chronology from the period of Alexander the Great (B.C. 331) onward, this would leave a period of 123 years for the duration of the Persian Empire according to the prophecy of Daniel.

The received Chronology is as follows :—

The Received Chronology of the Persian Empire.

Cyrus, as Co-Rex with Darius the Mede .. B.C.	538.
,, as sole King	536.
Cambyses	529.
(Pseudo-Smerdis, 7 mos.)	
Darius Hystaspes	521.
Xerxes	485.
(Artabanus, 7 mos.)	
Artaxerxes Longimanus	464.
(Xerxes II, 2 mos.)	
(Sogdianus, 7 mos.)	
Darius II, Nothus	423.
Artaxerxes II, Mnemon	404.
Artaxerxes III, Ochus..	358.
Arogus or Arses	337.
Darius III, Codomannus, reigned 335–331, slain ..	330.

The generally received opinion is that Cambyses and Pseudo-Smerdis are not mentioned in Scripture, that Xerxes is the Ahasuerus of Esther, and that Artaxerxes Longimanus is the Artaxerxes of Ezra 7 [1] and Nehemiah 2 [1], 5 [14] and 13 [6].

As our sole authority for the dating of this period is the contemporary Hebrew Record contained in Chronicles, Ezra, Nehemiah and Esther, we shall, in this chapter, confine ourselves to an exposition of the statements made in these Books, from which we think we shall be able to prove conclusively that the identifications of the received Chronology are quite impossible.

Amended Chronology of the Persian Empire.

Cambyses is the Ahasuerus of Ez. 4 [6].

Pseudo-Smerdis is the Artaxerxes of Ez. 4 [7–23].

Darius Hystaspes is at once both

(1) Darius of Ezra 4 [5. 24], 5 [5. 6], 6 [1. 12. 14. 15];

(2) Artaxerxes of Ezra 6 [14], 7 [1–26], Neh. 2 [1], 5 [14] and 13 [6], and

(3) Ahasuerus of the Book of Esther.

The whole of the Chronology of this period depends entirely upon the correct identification of the monarchs mentioned in Ezra, Nehemiah and Esther. The present condition of the Chronology of the period is one of hopeless confusion. It is easy to expose the contradictions it contains, but what is really required is the construction of a positive system which shall prove its truth by embracing and explaining all the facts contained in the above-named sources.

For the accomplishment of this end, there must be close and scrupulous attention to the sources themselves, a good deal of long and patient thinking, and a wholesome disregard for the many idle hypotheses, rash conjectures, and fanciful conclusions which have brought the true science of Chronology into undeserved disrepute.

The three rules which must be observed by every Chronologer whose investigations are to lead him into the truth are—(1) Never adopt any date which is inconsistent with any other date. (2) Never frame any hypothesis, or entertain any conjecture, which cannot be verified or supported by positive evidence. And (3) never identify different persons bearing the same name, and never fail to identify the same person bearing different names.

We now turn to our sources, which we will cross-question and examine, taking each statement contained therein in chronological order. We begin with a reference to the last chapter of 2 Chronicles, which brings us down to the end of the 70 years' servitude in Babylon.

The four Books, 1 and 2 Chronicles, Ezra and Nehemiah are one work, on one subject, by one author, containing one connected, continuous narrative throughout, to which the Book of Esther is a picture, an illustration or an appendix, related to the Book of Chronicles-Ezra-Nehemiah in precisely the same way as the Book of Ruth is related to Judges 1–16.

The Book of Daniel is an independent narrative of events which slightly overlap the events of the last chapter of 2 Chronicles, and the first chapter of Ezra.

In 2 Chron. $36^{20,21}$, we read that the King of the Chaldees carried away them that escaped the sword at the destruction of Jerusalem to Babylon, where they were servants to him and his sons until the reign of the Kingdom of Persia, to fulfil the word of the Lord by the mouth of Jeremiah, until the Land had enjoyed her sabbaths, for as long as she lay desolate she kept sabbath, to fulfil threescore and ten years.

The prophecy here referred to is the prophecy of Jeremiah. The only 70 years referred to by the prophet Jeremiah is the 70 years from the 3rd year of Jehoiakim, B.C. 605. This prophecy of seventy years' servitude to the King of Babylon was made in the following year, the 4th of Jehoiakim, which was the 1st year of Nebuchadnezzar. It was made in the most solemn and impressive manner, as described in Jer. 25^{1-26}, and especially in verses 11 and 12 :—

> " And this whole land shall be a desolation, and an astonishment ; and these nations shall serve the King of Babylon 70 years.
> " And it shall come to pass, when seventy years are accomplished, that I will punish the King of Babylon, and that nation, saith the Lord, for their iniquity, and will make it perpetual desolations.

This period of 70 years' servitude in Babylon is referred to again in a letter which Jeremiah sent from Jerusalem to the people whom Nebuchadnezzar had carried away captive from Jerusalem to Babylon, after the captivity of Jehoiachin. In this letter (Jer. 29^{1-14}), Jeremiah tells them to build, to plant, to take wives and to beget children, and not to be deceived by the false prophets who prophesied a short captivity and a speedy return.

" For thus saith the Lord That after 70 years be accomplished at Babylon I will visit you, and perform my good word toward you, in causing you to return to this place."

This same period, is the period of 70 years referred to by the prophet Daniel, in Daniel 9^2, when in the first year of the reign of Darius the Mede, the 68th of the 70 years, he says :—

" I Daniel understood by books (i.e. from the Scriptures), the number of the years whereof the word of the Lord came to Jeremiah the prophet, that He would accomplish 70 years in the desolations of Jerusalem."

These are the only references to this period of 70 years in the Old Testament. That it begins with the 3rd year of Jehoiakim is clear from Jer. 25^{1-12} with Dan. 1^1. That it ends with the 1st year of Cyrus is clear from 2 Chron. 36^{22}.

" Now in the first year of Cyrus King of Persia, that the word of the Lord by the mouth of Jeremiah might be accomplished, the Lord stirred up the spirit of Cyrus King of Persia, that he made a proclamation," that whoever was willing should go up to Jerusalem and build the house of the Lord.

In issuing this proclamation, Cyrus says (Ezra 1^2) :—

" The Lord God of Heaven hath charged me to build Him a House at Jerusalem."

This is a reference to the prophecy of Is. 44^{28}–45^{13}.

" (Thus saith the Lord) . . . That saith of Cyrus, He is my shepherd, and shall perform all my pleasure : even saying to Jerusalem, Thou shalt be built ; and to the Temple, Thy foundation shall be laid. Thus saith the Lord to his anointed, to Cyrus, whose right hand I have holden, to subdue nations before him . . . I, the Lord, which call thee by thy name, am the God of Israel . . . I have surnamed thee though thou hast not known me . . . I have raised him (Cyrus) up in righteousness, and I will direct all his ways : he shall build my city, and he shall let go my captives, not for price nor reward, saith the Lord of hosts."

The whole of the prophecy is not quoted in Ezra 1^2, but enough is quoted to enable us to identify it, and to learn therefrom that the will of God concerning Cyrus had reference to the building of the city as well as the building of the Temple.

Also Daniel's prayer based on the prophecy of Jeremiah respecting this period of 70 years has reference to " thy city Jerusalem," as well as to " thy sanctuary that is desolate," and ends in the plea " for thy city and thy people are called by thy name " (Dan. 9^{16-19}).

We may therefore identify " the commandment to restore and to build Jerusalem " (Dan. 9^{25}) with the commandment issued two years later by Cyrus, in which mention is made of the House as the central feature of the city, but in a way that implies the restoration of the city as well as the rebuilding of the walls.

There is another period of 70 years, referred to in the Old Testament, quite distinct from the 70 years of the servitude, in part coinciding with it and in part going beyond it.

This is the period of the 70 years' indignation (B.C. 589–520) which begins with the epoch of the boiling cauldron so graphically described by Ezekiel (Ezek. 24[1-14]), dating from the 10th day of the 10th month of the 9th year of the captivity of Jehoiachin, on which day the Lord said to him,

> "Son of man, write thee the name of this day, even of this same day" (Ezek. 24[2]).

This period of 70 years is referred to in Zech. 1[7-12], from which we learn that it came to a close in the 2nd year of Darius.

> "Upon the 24th day of the 11th month . . . in the 2nd year of Darius . . . the angel of the Lord answered and said . . . how long wilt thou not have mercy on Jerusalem and on the cities of Judah, *against which thou hast had indignation these* 70 *years* ? "

To which enquiry the answer was (Zech. 1[16]), " I am returned to Jerusalem with mercies, my house shall be built in it."

Yet another period of 70 years, the 70 years of the fasts (B.C. 586–517) is referred to two years later in Zech. 7[5.] The foundation of the house of the Lord had been laid on the 24th day of the 9th month of the 2nd year of Darius (Hag. 2[10.15.18.20]). About two years later, on the 4th day of the 9th month of the 4th year of Darius (Zech. 7[1]), Bethel sent Sharezer and Regem-melech to enquire whether they should continue to fast on certain days now that the foundation of the House had been laid. In his answer to these men, Zechariah first asks (Zech. 7[5]),

> " When ye fasted and mourned in the 5th and 7th month, even *these* 70 *years*, did ye at all fast unto me, even to me ? "

He then goes on to direct (Zech. 8[19]), that

> " The fast of the 4th month (commemorating the city smitten on the 9th day of the 4th month of the 11th year of Zedekiah), and the fast of the 5th month (commemorating the burning of the Temple on the 7th day of the 5th month of the 11th year of Zedekiah), and the fast of the 7th month (commemorating the slaying of Gedaliah in the 7th month of the 11th year of Zedekiah), and the fast of the 10th month (commemorating the siege of the city on the 10th day of the 10th month of the 9th year of Zedekiah), shall be to the house of Judah joy and gladness and cheerful feasts."

These 70 years are not quite the same as the 70 years of the indignation referred to in Zech. 1[12.] They begin with the fall of the city of Jerusalem in the 11th year of Zedekiah, B.C. 586, and they end with the 5th year of Darius. The enquiry was made in the 9th, i.e. the last month of the 4th year of Darius (Zech. 7[1]), and the answer, though given immediately (in the 4th year) respecting two of the fasts, was delayed into the 5th year respecting the other two (Zech. 7 and 8).

We have therefore three periods of 70 years to help us in determining the Chronology of this period :—

1. The 70 years' servitude, from the 3rd year of Jehoiakim to the 1st year of Cyrus, B.C. 605–536.
2. The 70 years' indignation from the 9th year of Jehoiachin's captivity to the 2nd year of Darius, B.C. 589–520, and
3. The 70 years of the fasts, from the fall of Jerusalem to the 5th year of Darius, B.C. 586–517.

The first period of the 70 years' servitude enables us to bridge the gulf between the 1st year of Evil-merodach and the 1st year of Cyrus. Here we have the names of some of the monarchs who reigned during these years, Evil-merodach, Darius the Mede and Belshazzar, but not the number of the years they reigned, and consequently no connected, continuous Chronology. The Chronology, is however, given in the Babylonian clay tablets, the true interpretation of which is in entire agreement with the Chronology of the Old Testament.

The second period of the 70 years' indignation enables us to bridge the gulf between the 3rd year of Cyrus and the 2nd year of Darius.

The third period of the 70 years of the fasts duplicates and corroborates the Chronology of the second period of 70 years. Here again we have the names of the monarchs who reigned during these years, Cyrus, Ahasuerus and Artaxerxes, but not the number of the years they reigned, and consequently no continuous, connected Chronology.

In either case the gulf is bridged over and the chronological connection is maintained by means of these long numbers.

Cyrus.

We now resume the connected chronological study of the years from the 1st year of Cyrus, B.C. 536.

In this year, as we learn from Ezra 3 [1-3], Cyrus issued his proclamation. He was now the undisputed master of " all the Kingdoms of the earth." That implies that the joint sway of the Medes and Persians, or the Co-Rexship of Cyrus with Darius the Mede, was now over. This agrees with the date B.C. 536 as that of Cyrus' sole Kingship, and B.C. 538 as that of his conquest of Babylon and the beginning of the joint rule of Cyrus the military, and Darius the civil head of the Medo-Persian Empire, from B.C. 538 to B.C. 536.

It is clear from Ez. 1 [2] that Cyrus was acquainted with the prophecy of Is. 44 [28]–45 [13], which may have been pointed out to him by Daniel, since Daniel was in a position of high authority at Shushan, in the province of Elam, in the 3rd year of Belshazzar, B.C. 539 (Dan. 8 [1]), where he attended to the King's business (Dan. 8 [27]).

Again, when Belshazzar was slain, and Darius the Mede received the Kingdom, B.C. 538, Daniel was set over the three presidents who were set over the 120 princes of the whole Kingdom (Dan. 5 [30]–6 [2]). He continued to prosper, both in the reign of Darius, B.C. 538–536, and also *in the reign of Cyrus*, B.C. 536 (Dan. 1 [21] and 6 [28]). Finally, he lived on to the 3rd year of Cyrus, B.C. 534 (Dan. 10 [1]), in which he had his vision of the man clothed in white and the revelation of the " scripture of truth" (Dan. 10 [21]–12 [13]).

Further details respecting the proclamation or the decree of Cyrus are given in Ezra 5 [13-15] and Ezra 6 [3-5.] From these passages we learn that when he delivered the sacred vessels to Sheshbazzar he made him Pekah or governor of Judah, and that the foundations of the House were to be strongly laid, " the height thereof 60 cubits and the breadth thereof 60 cubits ; With three rows of great stones and a row of new timber : " at the King's expense.

From Ez. 5 [16] we learn that this same Sheshbazzar did actually lay the foundation of the House, and since the foundation of the House was laid by the hands of Zerubbabel (Zech. 4 [9]), this identifies Sheshbazzar with Zerubbabel, whilst the date of the foundation laying—the 24th day of the 9th month of the 2nd year of Darius—is given in Haggai 2 [10. 15. 18. 20.]

Thus the builders were hindered, and their plans thwarted, by the opposition of the Samaritans, for a period of 15 years from the 2nd year of Cyrus to the 2nd year of Darius.

In Ezra 2 [1-70] we have a list of the families of the 42,360 captives who returned with Zerubbabel. This list afterwards fell into the hands of Nehemiah, many details therein having been meanwhile revised and corrected, or brought up to date, whilst the total, 42,360, remained unaltered and unrevised. The revised list is given in Neh. 7 [5-73.]

Amongst the leaders of the people who returned with Zerubbabel and Jeshua in the 1st year of Cyrus, we find (Ezra 2 [2]) the names of Nehemiah, Seraiah (alternatively called Azariah, Neh. 7 [7,] and possibly identical with Ezra) and Mordecai.

There is no reason why these three should not be identified with the well known Nehemiah the Tirshatha (Neh. 8 [9]), Ezra the priest the scribe (Neh. 8 [9]), and Mordecai of the Book of Esther.

These three men take first rank. They stand at the very head of the list of the exiles who returned with Zerubbabel and Jeshua, and the prominence given to them in the narrative of Ezra, Nehemiah and Esther is quite in accord with the position assigned to them here.

It is only the mistaken identification of the Artaxerxes of Nehemiah with Artaxerxes Longimanus (B.C. 464–424) instead of with Darius Hystaspes (B.C. 521–485), and by consequence the mistaken date assigned to Nehemiah that has led to the distinguishing of the Nehemiah of the first year of Cyrus (Ezra 2 [2,] 7 [7]) from Nehemiah the cupbearer and the Tirshatha of Neh. 1 [11] and 8 [9].

And it is only the mistaken identification of the Ahasuerus of Esther with Xerxes (B.C. 485–465) instead of with Darius Hystaspes (B.C. 521–485), that has led to the distinguishing of the Mordecai of the first year of Cyrus (Ezra 2 [2] and Neh. 7 [7]), from the Mordecai of the Book of Esther, and the torturing of the passage in Esther 2 [5. 6] to make it mean that *Kish* was carried away with Jeconiah, instead of what it really does say, which is, that *Mordecai* was carried away with Jeconiah (B.C. 597).

From Ezra 3 [1-6] we learn that on the 1st day of the 7th month of the 1st year of Cyrus the people gathered together as one man, to Jerusalem. Zerubbabel and Jeshua built an altar and offered burnt offerings, *but the foundation of the House was not yet laid.*

Ezra 3 [7] proceeds to tell us how the materials were being prepared for the building of the Temple, in accordance with the grant of Cyrus.

From Ezra 3 [8, 9], we learn that in the 2nd year of their coming to the house of God at Jerusalem, which was the 2nd year of Cyrus, Zerubbabel and Jeshua began to set forward the work of the house of the Lord.

Then follows a paragraph, Ezra 3 [10-13], which needs careful scrutiny, for it is proleptic or anticipatory. The word "WHEN" at the beginning of verse 10 should be doubly underlined, and we should be careful to note that it is "WHEN" and not "THEN." It tells us that *when* the builders laid the foundation of the House, viz. not now in the 2nd year of Cyrus, B.C. 535, but 15 years later on, in the 2nd year of Darius, B.C. 520 (see Haggai 2 [10, 15, 18, 20], some "wept with a loud voice, and many shouted aloud for joy."

Then comes the explanation and the reason for this delay of 15 years, an explanation which occupies the whole of chapter 4.

The Samaritans troubled them, and hired counsellors to frustrate them all the days of Cyrus, and until the reign of Darius King of Persia (Darius Hystaspes).

The narrative then goes on to give a detailed account of this opposition, and to specify the names of the Kings between Cyrus and Darius, during whose reigns it was maintained. But before leaving the reign of Cyrus, one other event took place which must be inserted here in proper chronological order.

In the 3rd year of Cyrus (Dan. 10 [1]) Daniel, after 3 weeks' mourning (Dan. 10 [2]), perhaps on account of this Samaritan opposition to the building of the Temple for which he had so earnestly prayed (Dan. 9 [17]), had a vision of a man in white from whom he received the revelation contained in "the scripture of truth" (Dan. 10 [5-21]). "Behold there shall yet stand up three Kings in Persia" after the present King, (1) Cyrus, viz. (2) Ahasuerus (Cambyses), (3) Darius Hystaspes and (4) Xerxes ; and the fourth (Xerxes) "shall be far richer than they all ; and by his strength through his riches he shall stir up all against the realm of Grecia" (Dan. 11 [2]), a prediction which refers to the mighty host of 1,800,000 men, with which, as Herodotus tells us, Xerxes crossed the Hellespont, and which he led to disastrous defeat, at Thermopylæ and Salamis, in the year B.C. 480.

From this vision of Daniel in the 3rd year of Cyrus, we return to the story of the Samaritan opposition to the building of the Temple, detailed in Ezra 4 [6-24].

Ahasuerus = Cambyses.

From Ezra 4 [6] we learn that in the reign of Ahasuerus (Cambyses, B.C. 529–522, the son and successor of Cyrus), the Samaritans wrote an accusation against the inhabitants of Judah and Jerusalem.

Artaxerxes = Pseudo-Smerdis.

From Ezra 4 [7-24] we learn that in the days of Artaxerxes (Pseudo-Smerdis), Bishlam, Mithredath and Tabeel wrote to Artaxerxes, King of Persia (Pseudo-Smerdis), and also that Rehum and Shimshei wrote against Jerusalem to Artaxerxes the King (Pseudo-Smerdis).

This Pseudo-Smerdis was the usurper who seized upon the throne of Cambyses during his absence in Egypt, B.C. 522.   He was aided by his brother Patizithes.   The two brothers were called the Magi.   They occupied the throne for 7 months, after which they were slain by Darius Hystaspes.

In this letter they refer to " the Kings," Ezra 4^{13}, not to " the King," which agrees very well with the fact that the false Smerdis was really placed on the throne by his brother Patizithes, one of the chief of the Magians, whose authority was quite equal to that of Pseudo-Smerdis, whence the two are coupled together, and this reign or usurpation is often referred to as that of the two Magi or Magians, both being regarded as in a manner sharers of the same throne.

The word " Kings " occurs in the plural again in the King's reply, " Cause these men to cease.   Why should damage grow to the hurt of the *Kings?* " (Ezra 4^{22}).

On receiving the letter of King Artaxerxes (Pseudo-Smerdis), Rehum, Shimshei and their companions, went in haste to Jerusalem and made them cease by force and power (Ezra 4^{23}).   So it ceased until the second year of the reign of Darius King of Persia (Ezra 4^{24}).

This last verse cannot be torn from its immediate connection with the preceding verses respecting Artaxerxes.   It proves, therefore, that this Artaxerxes was King of Persia *before* Darius Hystaspes.

The passage Ezra 4$^{6-23}$ cannot, therefore, be an episodical illustration referring to a later opposition in the days of Xerxes and Artaxerxes Longimanus, though many modern scholars advocate that interpretation of it.

Nothing can be plainer than the fact that the writer of the passage represents Ahasuerus and Artaxerxes as Kings of Persia, who reigned between the time of Cyrus and that of Darius Hystaspes, and since no other Kings but Cambyses and the false Smerdis *did* reign between Cyrus and Darius Hystaspes, it must follow that none but Cambyses and the false Smerdis are intended.

Darius, Artaxerxes, or Ahasuerus = Darius Hystaspes.

We have now reached the 2nd year of Darius Hystaspes, B.C. 520.

The years of Darius are not reckoned on the Jewish and Assyrian method, from the 1st of Nisan, and not on the Egyptian method of Ptolemy's Canon, from the variable New Year's Day of the vague Egyptian year, but on the Aryan or English method, from the day of his accession, which was somewhere on or about the 25th day of the 9th month of the year B.C. 521.

Hence the 10th, 11th, and 12th months of the 2nd year of Darius precede the remaining months of the year, and the true beginning of the prophecies of Zechariah is Zech. 1^7, as anyone who reads the verse will see, whilst Zech. 1$^{1-6}$ is really later, and has been placed before Zech. 1^7 by mistake, because it was wrongly supposed that the 8th month of the year preceded the 11th month.   A comparison of all the dates of the reign of Darius will show this. It is also seen from a comparison of Neh. 1^1 with Neh. 2^1, where the 9th month

(Chisleu) precedes the 1st month (Nisan) of the same 20th year of this same Darius Hystaspes, who is there called Artaxerxes.

Following this, the true chronological order of the events, we reach next the prophecy of Zech. 1^{7-12}, from which we learn, that on the 24th day of the 11th month of the 2nd year of Darius, the angel enquires of Jehovah, " How long wilt thou not have mercy upon Jerusalem . . . against which thou hast had INDIGNATION THESE SEVENTY YEARS," to which Jehovah replies, " I am returned to Jerusalem with mercies, my house shall be built in it " (Zech. 1^{16}).

From Haggai $1^{1.14}$ and 2^{21}, we learn that Zerubbabel was still Pekah, or governor of Judah in this year ; from Ezra 5^1 and Hag. 1^{1-4}, that on the 1st day of the 6th month of the 2nd year of Darius, Haggai prophesied and reproached the people for living in ceiled houses whilst the house of God lay waste ; and from Ezra 5^2 and Hag. 1^{15}, that on the 24th day of the 6th month of the 2nd year of Darius, Zerubbabel and Jeshua bestirred themselves and did work in the house of God. But the house appeared insignificant, in comparison with the former Temple built by Solomon. " Who saw this house in its first glory ? " exclaims the prophet Haggai, on the 21st day of the 7th month of the 2nd year of Darius. He then declares that the glory of this latter house shall be greater than that of the former (Hag. 2^{1-9}).

Next, in order of time, comes the prophecy of Zech. 1^{1-6}, a prophecy of the 8th month of the 2nd year of Darius, in which Zechariah pleads with the people not to be as their fathers, who would not listen to the former Prophets, but to turn to the Lord of Hosts, Who would then turn to them.

It is at this juncture that the foundation of the Temple is laid, on the 24th day of the 9th month of the 2nd year of Darius (Hag. $2^{10.\,15.\,18.\,20}$), and WHEN the foundation of the house was laid, the ancient men that had seen the first house wept or sang for joy as we read in Ezra 3^{10-13}. That, however, was not in the 2nd year of Cyrus, but in the 2nd year of Darius.

In Zech. 4^{6-10} we read how Zechariah encouraged the people to persevere with the work in spite of the tremendous difficulties which they experienced in doing it. " Not by might, nor by power, but by my spirit saith the Lord. Who art thou, O great mountain ? Before Zerubbabel thou shalt become a plain, and he shall bring forth the headstone thereof with shoutings, crying Grace, Grace unto it . . . The hands of Zerubbabel have laid the foundation of this house, his hands shall also finish it."

Then comes the visit of Tatnai, the Pekah of the country west of the Euphrates, and Shetharboznai, and their enquiry, " Who commanded you to build this house and to make up this wall ? " from which we see that they were building both the house and the wall at the same time (Ezra 5^3).

" But the eye of God was on the elders, that they could not cause them to cease till the matter came to Darius " (Ezra 5^5). The same language is found in Zech. 3^9 and 4^{10}, " Upon one stone shall be seven eyes . . . they are the eyes of the Lord which run to and fro through the whole earth."

A copy of Tatnai and Shetharboznai's letter to Darius is given in Ezra 5^{6-17}. His reply follows in Ezra 6^{1-12}, Let the work of this house alone, and let the Pekah of the Jews build it.

That is all that belongs to the 2nd year of Darius. Our next note of time

Q

is found in the Book of Esther, " In the 3rd year of the reign of Ahasuerus." That the Ahasuerus of Esther is Darius Hystaspes and no other—although as Kitto says, " Almost every Medo-Persian King from Cyaxares I (B.C. 611-571) to Artaxerxes III Ochus (B.C. 358–338), has in turn been advanced as the Ahasuerus of Esther "—is abundantly clear, and would never have been doubted but for the misdating of the events of the Persian period, and the mistaken notion that the same Persian monarch could not be described by two or three different names.

" This is (that) Ahasuerus which reigned from India even unto Ethiopia over 127 provinces " (Esther 1 [1]). Darius Hystaspes invaded and conquered India B.C. 506 (Herodotus, Books 3 and 4). Darius inherited the conquests of his predecessor Cambyses, in Egypt and Ethiopia ; all Egypt submitted to Cambyses in the 5th year of his reign, B.C. 525, and he subdued the Ethiopians (Herodotus, Book 3).

" And King Ahasuerus laid a tribute upon the land and upon the Isles of the Sea " (Est. 10 [1]). The Fleet of Darius took Samos, Chios and Lesbos, and the rest of the Islands, in the year B.C. 496 (Herodotus, Book 6). Herodotus gives a list of the nations which paid tribute to Darius Hystaspes in his history, Book 3, Chapters 89–97. These include Egypt and India, the Island of Cyprus and the Islands of the Erythræan Sea. After adding up the total, Herodotus says, " Later on in his reign the sum was increased by the tribute of the Islands and of the nations of Europe as far as Thessaly " (Herodotus, Book 3, Chap. 96). Amongst the peoples who paid no settled tribute, but brought gifts to Darius Hystaspes, he mentions " The Ethiopians bordering upon Egypt, who were reduced by Cambyses " (Herodotus, Book 3, Chap. 97).

Susa or Shushan was built by Darius Hystaspes (Pliny vi, 27) or rather embellished with magnificent palaces by him (Elian, De Animal. xiii, 59). It was there that he resided and kept all his treasures (Herodotus, v, 49).

Thucydides (Book 1) and Plato (Menexenus) tell us that Darius Hystaspes subdued all the Islands in the Ægean Sea, and Diodorus Siculus (Book 12) tells us that they were all lost again by his son Xerxes *before the 12th year of his reign*, but it was after the 12th year of the reign of Ahasuerus that he imposed his tribute upon the Isles, and the successors of Xerxes held none of them except Clazomene and Cyprus (Xenophon, Hellenics, Book 5).

From all which it is clear that the Ahasuerus of Esther cannot be Xerxes, in fact that he can be none other than Darius Hystaspes, for his predecessors Cyrus and Cambyses never took *tribute* but only received *presents*. Polyenus (Stratagem, Book 7) says Darius was the first that ever imposed a tribute upon the people. For this reason Herodotus tells us (Book 3, Chap. 89) the Persians called Cyrus a father, and Cambyses a master, but Darius κάπηλον, a huckster, " for Darius looked to making a gain in everything."

Evidently Haman knew the weakness of his master, when he offered to pay him 10,000 talents of silver for his pogram or massacre of the Jews (Est. 3 [9]). Esther touches the same spring when she hints at the damage which the King's revenue would suffer if the pogram were carried into effect (Est. 7 [4]). And in Est. 10 [1] we have the direct mention of the fact that " he laid a tribute upon the land and upon the Isles of the Sea."

In the Apocryphal Books the Ahasuerus of Esther, and the Artaxerxes of Ezra 7[1], are both identified with Darius Hystaspes. In 1 Esdras 3[1, 2], we read, "Now when Darius reigned he made a great feast unto all his subjects and unto all his household, and unto all the princes of Media and Persia, and to all the governors and captains, and lieutenants that were under him, from India to Ethiopia, in the 127 provinces." This is word for word from Est. 1[1-3], with the name Ahasuerus, replaced by the name Darius who is afterwards identified with Darius Hystaspes, in whose sixth year the Temple was completed (1 Esdras 6[5], Ez. 6[15]).

In the Rest of the chapters of the Book of Esther, and in the LXX. throughout, Ahasuerus is everywhere called Artaxerxes. It was Artaxerxes whom Bigthan and Teresh sought to lay hands on (Rest of Esther 12[1, 2]). It was the great King Artaxerxes who wrote "to the princes and governors who were under him from India unto Ethiopia, in 127 provinces (Rest of Esther 13[1]).

Archbishop Ussher was a profoundly well read scholar, and he identifies Darius Hystaspes with Artaxerxes, and with Ahasuerus, and this is in entire agreement with everything contained in the Old Testament, and with all trustworthy ancient testimony.

But since Scaliger, the first modern Chronologer, introduced the new fangled notion that Ahasuerus must be Xerxes, most modern scholars have adopted his error, which rests on no more substantial ground than that of philological conjecture, and supposed congruity of character.

Having thus cleared the ground by removing those erroneous presuppositions which make the understanding of the Books of Ezra, Nehemiah and Esther impossible, for these never can be understood until we realize that Darius Hystaspes, the Artaxerxes of Ezra and Nehemiah, and the Ahasuerus of Esther are one and the same person, we proceed with the Chronology, which we have already brought down to the 3rd year of Darius Hystaspes, the Ahasuerus of the Book of Esther.

In Esther 1[1-5] we read that Ahasuerus, that is Darius Hystaspes, made a feast to all his princes, the power of Persia and Media, which lasted for six months, like the visit of the Colonial celebrities who attended Queen Victoria's Diamond Jubilee.

We note "Persia and Media" are coupled together in this order, now that the Persian Empire has been established. Before, in the time of Daniel, it was the "Medes and Persians." The feast of six months was followed by a feast of 7 days to the people of Shushan ; on the last day of this feast Vashti refused to appear before the King, and was divorced.

Next, we have two notices of events that took place in the 4th year of Darius Hystaspes.

In Zech. 7[1] we read that on the 4th day of the 9th month of the 4th year of Darius, Zechariah replied to the deputation from Bethel, Sharezer and Regem-melech, who wished to know whether they should continue to fast in the 5th and the 7th month as they would have done for a period of 70 years from the fall of Jerusalem, B.C. 586, in the ensuing year, B.C. 517.

It is not clear whether the deputation came from Bethel (translated in the A.V. house of God) on the border of Judea, or from a place or a person named Bethel living in Babylon.

Zechariah's reply was a challenge. Were they sincere when they fasted these 70 years ? (Zech. 7 [5]), and later on (Zech. 8 [19]) he declared that all their fasts should be joy and gladness and cheerful feasts.

Darius is believed to have executed the Behistun Inscription about the 5th year of his reign, though some portion of it was perhaps added a little later. In this wonderful rock Inscription he records the fact that during the first five or six years of his reign he reconquered all the revolted provinces of the Persian Empire (Elam, Susiana, Sagartia, Media, Babylonia, Parthia, Armenia, etc.), and overthrew all the nine pretenders to his throne, including (1) Gomates, the Pseudo-Smerdis, the Magian who claimed to be the brother of Cambyses, and who occupied the throne for a period of 7 months ; (2) a Nidinta-Bel, who called himself Nebuchadnezzar II, the son of Nabonidus, and claimed to be the King of Babylon ; (3) Phraortes, who said he was the son of Cyaxares, and claimed to be King of Media ; (4) a second pretender who claimed to be Bardis or Smerdis the brother of Cambyses, and several others.

He thus became " Arta-Xerxes " (Great Shah) (Ezra 6 [14, 7 1], etc.), " King of Assyria " (Ezra 6 [22]), " King of Kings " (Ezra 7 [12]), King of Babylon (Neh. 13 [6]), and master of the entire World-Empire of Persia.

This accounts for the change of name from Darius to Artaxerxes, which we note, when we pass from the events of his 4th to those of his 7th year in Ezra 6 [12] and 7 [1].

The change of name which is so puzzling to us, was perfectly well understood at the time when the Book of Ezra was written, and is thus a proof of the contemporaneity of the Record.

But in order that there might be no mistake about the matter, the writer tells us in the most distinct and explicit manner that this Darius is the King who was also called Artaxerxes. In Ezra 6 [14] he says, " They builded and finished it according to the commandment of Cyrus and Darius (*even* Artaxerxes), King of Persia. Two persons, and two only, are named here ; two decrees, and two only are specified, and the Hebrew *Vav* should be translated " Darius, *even* Artaxerxes," not " Darius *and* Artaxerxes," as though a reference were intended to some third decree by some third person, a reference which was not in the writer's mind at all.

The word Artaxerxes is an appellation like Pharaoh. The word Xerxes survives to this day. It is the ancient form of the modern " Shah." " Arta " signifies great or noble, and " Arta-Xerxes " is the exact equivalent of Darius the Great or Xerxes the Great. Similarly the son and successor of Darius Hystaspes, Xerxes in his Inscription at Persepolis, calls himself in one sentence " Xerxes the great King " and in the next " Darius the King."

Abraham Zacutus (15th Century A.D.), astronomer to Emanuel, King of Portugal, David Ganz of Prague (d. A.D. 1613) and the *Sedar Olam Zeuta* or the Lesser Chronicle of the Jews (Anonymous, A.D. 1123), all tell us that " Artaxerxes among the Persians was the common name of their Kings as that of Pharaoh was among the Egyptians."

It is one and the same Persian King throughout. In Ezra 4 ^{24} we have his 2nd year, in Ezra 6 ^{15} we have his sixth year, in Ezra 7 ^{1} his 7th year, in Nehemiah 1 ^{1} and 2 ^{1} his 20th year, and in Neh. 5 ^{14} and 13 ^{6} his 32nd year, whilst in the story of Esther, which is an appendix to the Ezra-Nehemiah narrative, we have mention of his 3rd, his 6th, his 7th and his 12th years. Haggai prophesied in his 2nd year.   Zechariah in his 2nd and in his 4th year.

We now reach the events of the 6th year of Darius Hystaspes, the year in which the Temple was finished, on the 3rd day of the 12th month, as we learn from Ezra 6 ^{15}.

In the same year Esther was brought to Shushan to the custody of Hegai (Est. 2 $^{8.12}$), and a year or so later she was taken to the royal apartments. A great feast, Esther's feast, was held in honour of the occasion of her marriage, in the 10th month of the 7th year of Ahasuerus, B.C. 515 (Est. 2 $^{16-18}$).

Turning now to Ezra 7 $^{8.9}$ we find that on the first day of the first month of this same 7th year of Darius, the Temple being now built, Ezra sets out from Babylon in order to be present at the ceremony of the opening, or the dedication, of the new building, taking with him the sacred vessels and a second band of 1,754 exiles.

Ezra mustered his company and kept a fast at " the river that runneth to Ahava," halting there from the 9th to the 11th day of the first month of the 7th year of Artaxerxes (Ez. 8 $^{15.21}$).   On the following day, the 12th day of the 1st month of the 7th year of Artaxerxes, Ezra left the river Ahava and started off on his 4 months' journey to Jerusalem (Ez. 8 ^{31}).

Meanwhile, the children of the captivity kept the Passover and the feast of unleavened bread at Jerusalem, from the 14th to the 21st day of the 1st month of the 7th year of Artaxerxes (Ez. 6 $^{19-21}$).

About four months later, on the 1st day of the 5th month of the 7th year of Artaxerxes, Ezra arrived at Jerusalem (Ez. 7 ^{8}, 8 ^{32}).

Three days later, on the 4th day of the 5th month of the 7th year of Artaxerxes, the sacred vessels were weighed and placed in the newly built house of God (Ez. 8 ^{33}).

Ezra was grieved at the number of heathen marriages that had been contracted, but he thanked God for the House set up, the desolations repaired, and the wall given in Judah and Jerusalem.   This shows that not only the Temple but also the wall had been rebuilt at this time (Ezra 9 ^{9}).

On the 20th day of the 9th month of the 7th year of Artaxerxes, all Judah and Jerusalem were gathered together at Jerusalem (Ezra 10 ^{9}). Ezra exhorted them to confess their sin and separate themselves from their heathen wives.

An Assize was held on the first day of the 10th month (Ez. 10 ^{16}), the matter was gone into, and the Assize was concluded on the 1st day of the 1st month (Ez. 10 ^{17}).   In neither case is the year mentioned, but if we are right in concluding that the years of the King are reckoned as commencing on his accession day, on or about the 25th day of the 9th month, these last two dates of the Assize would be in the 10th and the 1st months of the 8th year of Artaxerxes.

In the 1st month of the 12th year of Ahasuerus, Haman cast lots to find

a lucky day for his massacre of the Jews (Est. 3 [7]). On the 13th day of the
1st month the posts went out hastened by the King's commandment, with
the decree for Haman's Pogram (Est. 3 [12]).   On the 15th day of the 1st month
Esther touched the golden sceptre (Est. 5 [1. 2]).   At night the King could not
sleep (Est. 6 [1-14]). On the following day, the 16th day of the 1st month,
Esther gave her banquet.   Haman was accused and hanged, and Mordecai
was made Premier (Est. 5 [8], 7 [2-10]).

About two months later, on the 23rd day of the 3rd month, the scribes
were called and letters were sent by horse, mule, camel and dromedary, to
overtake the posts sent out by Haman, and to give the Jews liberty to defend
themselves if they were attacked (Est. 8 [9-14]).

Then follows an interval of about 9 months, during which the posts went
forward till they reached the uttermost limits of Ahasuerus' world-wide Empire.

On the 13th day of the 12th month, Pogram Day, the Jews defended themselves and slew 500 of their adversaries, who attacked them in Shushan, and
75,000 in the provinces (Est. 9 [1-12]).   On the following day, the 14th day of
the 12th month, the Jews slew 300 more in Shushan, whilst the Jews in the
provinces rested and observed this, the 14th day of Adar, as their day for keeping
the feast of Purim (Est. 9 [13-27]).   The day after this, the 15th day of the
12th month, the Jews in Shushan rested and observed this, the 15th day of
Adar, as their day for keeping the feast of Purim (Est. 9 [18-27]).

The next recorded event is found in the opening chapters of Nehemiah,
and belongs to the 20th year of Darius Hystaspes.   There is no record of the
events that occurred at Jerusalem between the 7th year of Artaxerxes and
the early months of the following year, except that which is contained in the
report which Hanani brought to Nehemiah 13 years later, in the month Chisleu,
the 9th month of the 20th year of Artaxerxes (Neh. 1 [1]).

From this we learn that, whilst nothing is reported respecting the Temple,
the *wall* of Jerusalem had been broken down, and the gates thereof burned
with fire (Neh. 1 [3]).

Ezra probably remained at Jerusalem during this interval of 13 years,
from the 7th to the 20th year of Artaxerxes, for we find him in active
co-operation with Nehemiah later on in this same 20th year (Neh. 8 [1. 4. 9],
12 [26. 36. 38]).

Josephus says that Jeshua the high priest died and was succeeded by his
son Joiakim, about the time that Ezra came to Jerusalem, in the 7th year
of the Persian monarch who is called *Artaxerxes* in Ezra, but whom Josephus
calls *Xerxes* (yet another name for Darius Hystaspes).   He adds, later on,
that Joiakim died, and was succeeded in the high priesthood by his son
Eliashib, about the time that Ezra died.

This is quite in accord with what we read in the Books of Ezra and
Nehemiah.   It is true that Eliashib is called the high priest in the 20th year
of Artaxerxes (Neh. 3 [1. 20]).   He may have been called " Eliashib the high
priest " without having been high priest *at that time*, but more probably
his father Joiakim was an aged man, and Eliashib was acting high priest
during his lifetime, just as Annas and Caiaphas were both high priests in
the time of our Lord (Luke 3 [2], " Annas and Caiaphas being the high priests ").

This is corroborated by the fact that Joiakim had a grandson Johanan, the son of Eliashib, old enough to have a chamber in the house of God in the 7th year of Artaxerxes, B.C. 515, when Ezra returned to Jerusalem (Ezra 10 [6]).

It is supported by the statement of Neh. 12 [26], which makes the days of Joiakim either immediately anterior to, or else contemporary with the days of Nehemiah the governor and of Ezra the priest the scribe.

It is also supported by the list of the men who were " priests, the chief of the fathers in the days of Joiakim " (Neh. 12 [12-21]).

Two lists are given here. The first is identical with the list of the priests who returned to Jerusalem with Zerubbabel (Neh 12 [1-7]) except that we have here only 21 names instead of 22, the name of Hattush, No. 6, being omitted. The second list is the list of their eldest sons who succeeded them, either on their death, or on their becoming too aged to discharge the duties of their office in the days of Joiakim, i.e. immediately before, or else during the days of Ezra and Nehemiah (Neh. 12 [26]), which of course carries us on to the 20th, or possibly to the 32nd year of Artaxerxes, B.C. 502–490. This list contains only 20 names, the eldest son of Miniamin, No. 13, being omitted.

The two lists are as follows :—

Fathers.	*Eldest sons.*
Priests who returned with Zerubbabel and Jeshua. Neh. 12 [1-7] *and* [12-21].	*Priests in the days of Joiakim the son of Jeshua. Neh.* 12 [12-21].
1. Seraiah.	Meraiah.
2. Jeremiah.	Hananiah.
3. Ezra.	Meshullam.
4. Amariah.	Jehohanan.
5. Melicu.	Jonathan.
6. Hattush (omitted Neh. 12 [12-27]).	———
7. Shebaniah.	Joseph.
8. Harim.	Adna.
9. Meraioth.	Helkai.
10. Iddo.	Zechariah.
11. Ginnethon.	Meshullam.
12. Abijah.	Zichri.
13. Miniamin.	———
14. Moadiah.	Piltai.
15. Bilgai.	Shammua.
16. Shemaiah.	Jehonathan.
17. Joiarib.	Mattenai.
18. Jedaiah.	Uzzi.
19. Sallai.	Kallai.
20. Amok.	Eber.
21. Hilkiah.	Hashabiah.
22. Jedaiah.	Nethaneel.

The 22 men in this first list returned to Jerusalem with Zerubbabel and Jeshua in the 1st year of Cyrus, B.C. 536 (Neh. 12 [1-7]). Fifteen of them sealed the covenant with Nehemiah in the 20th year of Artaxerxes, B.C. 502, the remaining 7 having probably died during the intervening 34 years. The 20 men in the second list succeeded them, " in the days of Joiakim " the son of Jeshua (Neh. 12 12-21), whose days are either identical with, or else immediately anterior to, the days of Ezra and Nehemiah, B.C. 502–490 (Neh. 12 26). See Vol. II, p. 53.

Nehemiah was grieved to hear Hanani's distressing report respecting the condition of affairs at Jerusalem (Neh. 1 4). He turned to God in prayer and waited his opportunity.

Four months later, in the month Nisan, the 1st month in the 20th year of Artaxerxes, that opportunity came.

But here arises one of the most perplexing problems in the Chronology of this period.

The Books of Ezra and Nehemiah are not two Books, but two parts of one and the same Book. They were never divided up into two, till this was done by Origen, the learned and distinguished *Textual* Critic, who was also unfortunately, the innovating *Higher* Critic, of the 3rd Century A.D.

The last note of time in Ezra is connected with the 7th year of Artaxerxes, and it is quite certain that the 20th year of the opening verse of Nehemiah refers to the 20th year of the reign of Artaxerxes. This was in Chisleu, the 9th month. But when we come to Neh. 2 1 we are still in the 20th year of Artaxerxes, although in the meantime we have passed over a New Year's Day.

The problem, then, is to ascertain from what point in the " sequence of the months " the years of the King's reign are reckoned, or on what day of the year the reckoning passes from the last day of one year to the New Year's Day of another.

The method of reckoning adopted is not the Hebrew method, for with them New Year's Day is always the 1st day of Nisan, and the first of Nisan following the 9th month of the 20th year of Artaxerxes would have been in the 21st year of Artaxerxes.

The method of reckoning adopted is not the Assyrian method, for with them also New Year's Day is always the 1st day of Nisan.

The method of reckoning adopted is not that of the vague Egyptian or Chaldean year of Ptolemy's Canon, the 365-day year, whose New Year's Day or 1st Thoth, or as we should say 1st January, fell back one day every 4 years, and travelled the entire circle of the four seasons in the course of the Sothic cycle of 1,460 years, for in the 20th of Artaxerxes, B.C. 502, the 1st Thoth or New Year's Day of the Egyptian or Chaldean year was on December 27th, and December was the 10th month, so that in passing from the 9th month Chisleu to the 1st month Nisan, a New Year would have been entered.

The same would hold good if this Artaxerxes were identified with Longimanus, for in his 20th year, B.C. 445, the 1st Thoth of the Egyptian or Chaldean year was December 12th.

The New Year did not begin with the summer solstice, about the 21st day of the 4th month, for the 1st day of the 1st month, and the 1st day of the 5th month of Artaxerxes, were both in the same 7th year of Artaxerxes (Ezra 7 7-9).

The New Year did not begin with the autumnal Equinox, about the 21st day of the 7th month, for the 6th, 7th and 9th months are all in the same 2nd year of Darius (Hag. 1^1, $2^{1.10}$).

The New Year did not begin at the winter solstice, about the 21st day of the 10th month, for some part of the 9th month, and the following 1st month were both in one and the same 20th year of Artaxerxes (Neh. 1^1, 2^1).

And it has already been shown that the New Year did not begin at the spring Equinox or about the 1st Nisan.

The solution probably lies in the fact that the Persians, being like ourselves, members of the Aryan or Japhetic, and not members of the Semitic race, reckoned as we do, and in that case the years of the King's reign would be reckoned not by calendar years, as with the Jews and the Assyrians, but from the day on which the King ascended the throne. Or, it may be that New Year's Day was immediately connected with the day on which the foundation of the Temple was laid, viz. the 24th day of the 9th month of the 2nd year of Darius (Haggai 2^{18}).

The data supplied by the Books of Ezra, Nehemiah, Esther, Haggai and Zechariah, require, and are satisfied with, a New Year's Day commencing sometime *after* the 24th day of the 9th month (about Nov. 24th), because the 24th day of the 9th month was in the same year as the 1st day of the sixth month (Hag. 1^1, 2^{10}), and sometime *before* the last day of the 9th month, (Nov. 30th) because some part of the 9th month was in the same 20th year of Artaxerxes as the succeeding 1st month.

The years of the reign of Darius Hystaspes, or Artaxerxes, or Ahasuerus, then, begin somewhere between the 24th and the 30th day of the 9th month of the year.

If this be so, then the 24th day of the 11th month of the 2nd year of Darius precedes the 8th month of the 2nd year of Darius, and the prophecy of Zech. 1^7, which reads as if it were the opening verse of the Book, precedes Zech. 1^1.

It is difficult to understand why the fact that Zechariah was the son of Berechiah, the son of Iddo, should be repeated in Zech. 1^7, if this verse were not originally the first verse of his Book of prophecy, the present arrangement being that of some critic who thought that the 8th month must necessarily precede the 11th month of the 2nd year of Darius.

The following is a complete list of the dated events of the reign of Darius Hystaspes = Artaxerxes = Ahasuerus, as given in the Books of Ezra, Nehemiah and Esther. His accession day is between the 25th and the 30th day of the 9th month.

Dated events of the Reign of Darius Hystaspes = Artaxerxes = Ahasuerus.

Day.	Month.	Year.	King.	Reference.	Event.
24	11	2	Darius	Zech. 1^7	70 years' indignation completed.
1	6	2	,,	Hag. 1^1	Zerubbabel, Pekah in Judah.
24	6	2	,,	Hag. 1^{15}	Zerubbabel bestirred himself.
21	7	2	,,	Hag. 2^1	The glory of the latter house.
—	8	2	,,	Zech. 1^1	Zechariah appeals for repentance.
24	9	2	,,	Hag. 2^{10}	Foundation of the House laid.
—	—	3	Ahasuerus	Est. $1^{1\text{-}6}$	Ahasuerus' feast. Vashti deposed.
4	9	4	Darius	Zech. 7^1	Zechariah on 70 years' fasts.
—	—	6	Ahasuerus	Est. $2^{8\text{-}16}$	Esther brought to Shushan.
3	12	6	Darius	Ezra 6^{15}	Temple finished.
14	1	—	,,	Ezra 6^{19}	Passover observed at Jerusalem.
—	10	7	Ahasuerus	Est. $2^{16\text{-}18}$	Esther's marriage and feast.
1	1	7	Artaxerxes	Ezra 7^9	Ezra left Babylon.
9	1	7	,,	$8^{15\text{-}21}$	Ezra halted 3 days at Ahava.
12	1	7	,,	8^{31}	Ezra left river of Ahava.
1	5	7	,,	7^9	Ezra arrived at Jerusalem.
4	5	7	,,	8^{33}	Vessels weighed in Temple.
20	9	—	,,	10^9	All Judah at Jerusalem.
1	10	—	,,	10^{16}	Assize (heathen wives) begun.
1	1	—	,,	10^{17}	Assize (heathen wives) ended.
—	1	12	Ahasuerus	Est. 3^7	Haman casts lots for Massacre.
13	1	—	,,	3^{12}	Haman's posts went out.
15	1	—	,,	$5^{1\text{-}8}$	Esther touches golden sceptre.
16	1	—	,,	5^8	Esther's banquet.
23	3	—	,,	$8^{9\text{-}14}$	Mordecai's posts went out.
13	12	—	,,	$9^{1\text{-}12}$	Massacre day, 500 +75,000 slain.
14	12	—	,,	$9^{15\text{-}27}$	300 slain, 14th Adar, 1st Purim.
15	12	—	,,	$9^{18\text{-}27}$	15th Adar, 2nd Purim.
—	9	20	Artaxerxes	Neh. 1^1	Hanani's report.
—	1	20	,,	2^1	Nehemiah sent to Jerusalem.
25	6	—	,,	6^{15}	Wall finished in 52 days.
1	7	—	,,	8^2	Ezra reads the Law.
2	7	—	,,	8^{13}	They read of dwelling in booths.
15	7	—	,,	$8^{14\text{-}18}$	1st day of feast of Tabernacles.
21	7	—	,,	8^{18}	7th day of feast of Tabernacles.
22	7	—	,,	8^{18}	Day of solemn assembly.
24	7	—	,,	$9^{1\text{-}2}$	Heathen wives put away.
—	—	32	Artaxerxes	5^{14}, 13^6	Nehemiah returned to Babylon.

These are the data supplied from the Old Testament. It would be interesting to compare them with information from other sources respecting the Persian method of reckoning the years of their Kings. The Behistun Inscription contains the days and the months, but not the years of Darius' reign, except in one place, and there the figure cannot be read. The other Persian Inscriptions give us no information on the subject.

There is a suggestive little touch in Neh. 2 [6] which favours the identification of Artaxerxes with Ahasuerus, the husband of Esther.   Nehemiah mentions in a parenthesis the fact that Artaxerxes' wife was sitting by him when he preferred his request.   This agrees very well with the fact that Esther was the wife of King Ahasuerus, otherwise Artaxerxes, otherwise Darius Hystaspes.

No doubt Nehemiah had already been in communication with her on the subject, and no doubt, also, she had something to do with the favour shown by Artaxerxes to the Jews in the 7th year of his reign, when he gave Ezra the liberal commission contained in his letter of Ezra 7 [12-26].

The building of the wall described so minutely in Neh. 3, was not the building of a *new* wall, but the repair of an old one.   It is so described throughout.   The wall was broken down, and the gates were burned with fire (Neh. 1 [3]), but parts of it were still standing, and it only needed *repair*. The word " *repaired* " occurs in almost every verse in Neh. 3.

It was a work that could be finished in 52 days (Neh. 6 [15]) and the Temple was still standing (Neh. 6 [10, 11]).

Nehemiah was appointed Pekah of the land of Judah from the 20th to the 32nd year of Artaxerxes.   Here we have another instance of the Aryan or English method of reckoning.   On the Semitic method of inclusive reckoning this period would have been called 13 years, but Nehemiah very emphatically points out that it was a period of 12 years.

In Neh. 7 [4] we read that the city was broad on both sides, and great, but the people were few and the houses were not builded.   This refers not to the material dwelling places, but to the people who dwelt in them—as the word is used in the phrase " the house and lineage " of David.

The remark that the houses were not builded leads on to the reproduction of the register of the genealogy of those who returned with Zerubbabel in the 1st year of Cyrus, some 34 years before (Neh. 7 [5-73]).

On the 1st day of the 7th month, doubtless of this same 20th year of Artaxerxes, though the year is not specified (Neh. 8 [1, 2]), the people assembled at Jerusalem, and sent for Ezra, who had probably been with them during the whole of the last 13 years, to bring the Book of the Law.

On the following day (Neh. 8 [13]) they read that they should dwell in booths in the 7th month (Neh. 8 [14]), which accordingly they did (Neh. 8 [15]).

On the 24th day of the 7th month the seed of Israel separated themselves from their heathen wives, they entered into a covenant that they would not intermarry with the heathen, nor trade on the Sabbath Day, that they would pay their tithes, " and we will not forsake the house of our God " (Neh. 10 [28-39]).

The last recorded event in the Old Testament is that contained in the paragraph, Neh. 13 [4-31].   In order to understand it we must first strike out the word " had " in the A.V., and in the R.V. translation of Neh. 13 [5]. Then we read   (Neh. 13 [4]), " Before this "—viz. before the revival of religion during Nehemiah's 12 years' residence in Jerusalem (B.C. 502–490), as described in the previous paragraph (Neh. 12 [43]–13 [3])—Eliashib was allied to Tobiah (Neh. 13 [4], 6 [17-18]).   Now, during the revival of religion, i.e. during Nehemiah's 12 years' residence in Jerusalem, Eliashib was appointed to the oversight of the Temple chambers (Neh. 12 [44]).   At this point in the

narrative, Nehemiah left Jerusalem in the 32nd year of Artaxerxes, and went
to Babylon, where he remained during an interval of "certain days,"
probably one year.   During this interval seven things happened :—

1. Eliashib, after Nehemiah had left Jerusalem, *desecrated* the Temple
   by preparing for Tobiah a great chamber in the courts of the Temple,
   "where aforetime," viz. during the revival of religion, i.e. during
   Nehemiah's 12 years' residence in Jerusalem, they kept the con-
   secrated things.
2. Tithes ceased to be paid (Neh. 13 ^{10}).
3. The house of God was forsaken (Neh. 13 ^{11}).
4. The Sabbath was profaned (Neh. 13 $^{15, 16}$).
5. Heathen marriages were contracted (Neh. 13 ^{23}).
6. The Jewish language was corrupted by the offspring arising therefrom
   (Neh. 13 ^{24}).
7. A son of Joiada, the son of the high priest Eliashib, married a daughter
   of Sanballat (Neh. 13 ^{28}).

At the end of this interval of "certain days," probably one year, the
following ten things happened :—

1. Nehemiah obtained leave of the King, and returned to Jerusalem,
   probably about 2 years after he left there, including the time occupied
   by the journey to Babylon and back, viz. in the year B.C. 488
   (Neh. 13 $^{6, 7}$).
2. He dealt summarily with Tobiah, putting his furniture into the street
   (Neh. 13 $^{6-8}$).
3. He restored the Temple services (Neh. 13 ^{11}, cp. Mal. 1 $^{7-14}$).
4. He restored the payment of tithes (Neh. 13 $^{12-14}$, cp. Mal. 3 ^{8}).
5. He restored the observance of the Sabbath (Neh. 13 $^{17-22}$).
6. He put a stop to heathen marriages (Neh. 13 $^{25-27}$, cp. Mal. 2 $^{11-16}$).
7. He chased the son of Joiada from him (Neh. 13 ^{28}).
8. He cleansed the priesthood (Neh. 13 ^{29}, cp. Mal. 2 $^{1-8}$).
9. He restored the covenant of the priests and Levites (Neh. 13 ^{29}).
10. He appointed the wards of the priests and Levites, everyone in his
    business, and for the offerings (Neh. 13 ^{30}).

Four of these items correspond so exactly with the tenor of the prophecy
of Malachi that we may probably conclude that his prophecy also belongs
to this period, viz. to the year B.C. 488, so that with the close of Old Testament
history we date also the close of Old Testament prophecy, viz. in the last year
of Daniel's seven sevens, B.C. 488, the time appointed for the sealing up of
vision and prophecy (Dan. 9 $^{24, 25}$). See Vol. II, Chronological Tables,
AN. HOM. 3637.

The phrase "after certain days" reads in the Hebrew "at the end of days,"
which probably means "at the end of a year," the word יָמִים, yâmim = days,
being frequently used to denote this period of time.   Compare the following
passages in which the word occurs :—

Gen. 4 ^{3}.   At the end of days (i.e. at the end of the year) Cain brought
    of the fruit of the land.

Gen. 27 [43, 44]. Flee thou to Laban and tarry with him one (cycle) of days (i.e. " one year," not as in A.V. and R.V. "a few days ").

Gen. 29 [20].   Jacob served 7 years for Rachel, and they seemed unto him as one (cycle) of days (i.e. " as one year," not as in A.V. and R.V. " but a few days ").

1 Sam. 2 [19]. The sacrifice of days (i.e. the sacrifice of the year = the yearly sacrifice).

1 Sam. 27 [7]. David abode in the city of the Philistines days (Heb.) and 4 months (i.e. a year and four months).

2 Sam. 14 [26]. Absalom polled his head from end of days to end of days (i.e. from year to year).

1 Kings 17 [7]. And it came to pass at the end of days (i.e. at the end of the year) that the brook dried up.

These passages show that the proper interpretation of the phrase " at the end of days " is " after one year."

If we allow 4 months for the journey each way, and a year for Nehemiah's residence in Babylon, this will bring the narrative of the paragraph, Neh. 13 [7-31], with which the Old Testament Record closes, down to the year B.C. 488.

Genealogical and other Lists of Names in 1 & 2 Chronicles, Ezra and Nehemiah.

Some valuable chronological information is contained in the genealogical and other lists in these Books. The list of those who sealed the covenant with Nehemiah, in the 20th year of Artaxerxes (Neh. 10 [1-13]) is almost identical with the list of those who returned to Jerusalem with Zerubbabel and Jeshua, given in Neh. 12 [1-9].

This is the crowning argument for the identification of the Artaxerxes of Nehemiah with Darius Hystaspes.

Between the 1st of Cyrus and the 20th of Darius Hystaspes was a space of 34 years, at the end of which time most of " the priests and Levites that went up with Zerubbabel " (Neh. 12 [1]) might still be living and able to seal the covenant with Nehemiah (Neh. 10 [1]).

But if the Artaxerxes of Nehemiah was Artaxerxes Longimanus, as all modern scholars maintain, the length of the time between the 1st of Cyrus and the 20th of Artaxerxes Longimanus is 91 years, after which space of time 20 out of the 30 priests and Levites who returned with Zerubbabel are still alive !

The argument is absolutely conclusive. It must convince every scholar who pays attention to it that the accepted Chronology is impossible. The Artaxerxes of Nehemiah reigned at least 32 years (Neh. 5 [14], 13 [6]), but no other Persian monarch except Darius Hystaspes reigned so long within such a space of time that 20 out of 30 men, who were old enough to be priests and Levites in the 1st of Cyrus, could still be alive in the 20th year of such other Persian monarch's reign.

The lists are as follows :—

Priests and Levites who returned with Zerubbabel in the 1st year of Cyrus, B.C. 536. Neh. 12 [1-9].	*Priests and Levites who sealed with Nehemiah in the 20th year of Artaxerxes, B.C. 502. Neh. 10 [1-10].*

1. *Priests.*

1. Seraiah	Seraiah.
2. Jeremiah	Jeremiah.
'. Ezra	(Azariah).
3. Amariah..	Amariah.
. Malluch (Melicu)	(Malchijah).
6. Hattush	Hattush.
7. Shechaniah (Shebaniah) ..	Shebaniah.
8. Rehum (Harim)	Harim.
9. Meremoth	Meremoth.
10. Iddo	—
11. Ginnetho	Ginnethon.
12. Abijah	Abijah.
13. Miamin	Mijamin.
14. Maadiah	(Maaziah).
15. Bilgah	Bilgai.
16. Shemaiah	Shemaiah.
17. Joiarib	—
18. Jedaiah	—
19. Sallu (Sallai)	—
20. Amok	—
21. Hilkiah	—
22. Jedaiah	—

Neh. 12 [7]. *" These were the chief of the priests and of their brethren in the days of Jeshua."*	*Neh.* 10 [8]. *" These" (with Zidkijah), Pashur, Malluch, Obadiah, Daniel, Baruch and Meshullam) " were the priests" that sealed with Nehemiah.*

2. *Levites.*

1. Jeshua.	Jeshua the son of Azaniah.
2. Binnui.	Binnui of the sons of Henadad.
3. Kadmiel.	Kadmiel.
4. Sherebiah.	(Shebaniah).
5. Judah.	(Hodijah, cp. Ezra 2 [40], 3 [9]).
6. Mattaniah (over the choirs). ..	
7. Bakbukiah (over the watches).	—
8. Unni. ,, ,,	—
	(and 12 others).

From these lists it will be seen that out of the 22 men who were the chief of the priests in the days of Zerubbabel and Jeshua, 15 were still chief of the priests 34 years later, and signed the covenant with Nehemiah.

Of the 8 Levites who are mentioned as returning with Zerubbabel, 5 are mentioned again as signing the covenant with Nehemiah.

It is quite natural that 20 out of these 30 men who returned with Zerubbabel in the first year of Cyrus (B.C. 536) should be alive 34 years later, in the 20th year of Darius Hystaspes (B.C. 502). But it is quite inconceivable that 20 of them should still be alive 91 years later, in the 20th year of Artaxerxes Longimanus (B.C. 445).

Therefore, the Artaxerxes of Neh. 2^1, 5^{14} and 13^6 cannot be Artaxerxes Longimanus, nor can he be any other Persian monarch of later date, and as the only Persian monarch of earlier date who reigned as long as 32 years (Neh. 5^{14}, 13^6) was Darius Hystaspes, the Artaxerxes of Nehemiah 2^1, 5^{14} and 13^6 can be no other than Darius Hystaspes himself.

The succession of the high priests was as follows (1 Chron. 6^{3-15}, Ezra 3^2, 7^{1-5}, Neh. $12^{10.11}$) :—

List of High Priests from Aaron to Jaddua.

1. Aaron.
2. Eleazer.
3. Phinehas.
4. Abishua.
5. Bukki.
6. Uzzi.
7. Zerahiah.
8. Meraioth.
9. Amariah I.
10. Ahitub I.
11. Zadok I.
12. Ahimaaz.
13. Azariah I.
14. Johanan.
15. Azariah II, contemporary with Solomon (1 Chron. 6^{10}) B.C. 1023-983.
16. Amariah II.
17. Ahitub II.
18. Zadok II.
19. Shallum.
20. Hilkiah, contemporary with Josiah (2 Chron. 34^9) B.C. 639-608.
21. Azariah III.
22. Seraiah. Slain by Nebuchadnezzar (2 Kings 25^{18-22}) B.C. 586.
23. Jehozadak, went into captivity (1 Chron. 6^{15}) B.C. 586.
24. Joshua, returned with Zerubbabel (Ezra 3^2) B.C. 536.
25. Joiakim, contemp. with Nehemiah and Ezra (Neh. 12^{26}) B.C. 515-490.
26. Eliashib, allied to Tobiah (Neh. 13^4, 6^{18}) younger contemporary of Nehemiah (Neh. 3^1, 13^{4-5}) B.C. 502-488.
27. Joiada.
28. Jonathan (Johanan).
29. Jaddua, contemporary with Darius, the last Persian King, who was slain by Alexander the Great B.C. 330.

These dates given above are the received Ptolemaic dates. All except the last (B.C. 330) are probably about 82 years higher than the truth.

Ezra B.C. (586–490), was the son of Seraiah (No. 22), and the brother of Jehozadak (No. 23). Josephus says he died an old man (*Antiquities* XI. 5.5.)

Johanan the son of Eliashib (Ezra 10⁶) cannot be certainly identified, but he may have been the son of the high priest Eliashib, No. 26 in the above list, and a younger contemporary of Ezra.

The unnamed son of Joiada (No. 27), who married the daughter of Sanballat, and was chased by Nehemiah (Neh. 13²⁸), was a younger contemporary of Nehemiah.

Jaddua was, no doubt, born at the time when his uncle married the daughter of Sanballat, and was chased by Nehemiah B.C. 488. This is the last recorded event in the history of the Old Testament.

Jaddua went out from Jerusalem to Sapha to meet Alexander the Great, B.C. 330. The fact must be accepted, but not the Chronology, which makes him 488–330 = 158 years old. If the Chronology of the period of the Persian Empire from the 1st year of Cyrus, B.C. 536, to the last year of the Darius who was slain by Alexander the Great, B.C. 330, is reduced from the 205 years of Ptolemy's Canon to the 123 years of Daniel's prophecy, Jaddua's age would be reduced by 205–123 = 82 years. This would make him 158–82 = 76 years of age when he went out to meet Alexander at Sapha. This is probably the true Chronology of the period between the last recorded date in the Old Testament history and the first reliable date in Greek history.

We are now in a position to give our final table of the Chronology of the Old Testament, viz. the Chronology of the period of the Return.

The Return.

AN. HOM.

3589. The return under Zerubbabel, in the 1st year of Cyrus, which was the 54th year of the 70 years' indignation (see Chapter 24 and Vol II, Chronological Tables, p. 32).

Add 16 years to complete the 70 years' indignation (see Zech. 1 [7. 12. 16] and Vol. II, Chronological Tables, pp. 30, 32, 34).

Within these years reigned the following Kings of Persia, but the length of their reigns is not given in the Old Testament :

Cyrus, Ezra 1 [1.]

Ahasuerus (Cambyses), Ezra 4 [6.]

Artaxerxes (Pseudo-Smerdis), Ezra 4 [7.]

Darius (Darius Hystaspes), Ezra 4 [5.]

16. (See Vol. II, Chronological Tables pp. 32, 34).

3605. Last of the 70 years' indignation = 2nd year of Darius.

Add 5 years to the return of Ezra in the 7th year of

5. Artaxerxes (Darius Hystaspes), Ezra 7 [8. 9.]

3610. Ezra returned to Jerusalem in the 7th year of Artaxerxes (Darius Hystaspes).

Add 13 years to the appointment of Nehemiah as Pekah of Judah in the 20th year of Artaxerxes (Darius Hystaspes),

13. Neh. 2 [1], 5 [14.]

3623. Nehemiah comes to Jerusalem.

Add 12 years' administration of Nehemiah from the 20th to the

12. 32nd year of Artaxerxes (Darius Hystaspes), Neh. 5 [14] 13 [6.]

3635. Nehemiah returns to Babylon in the 32nd year of Artaxerxes (Darius Hystaspes).

Add 2 years for Nehemiah's visit to Babylon, and his return to Jerusalem, after spending "certain days"

2. there, viz. 1 year, Neh. 13 [6.]

3637. Nehemiah's reforms. Close of the Old Testament Record.

CHAPTER XXVI. COMPARATIVE CHRONOLOGY.

The Captivity and the Return.

THE principal extra-Biblical sources for the Chronology of this period are, for the captivity, the Babylonian cuneiform Inscriptions, especially the Egibi Tablets, and for the return, the Persian cuneiform Inscriptions, especially the great Behistun Inscription of Darius Hystaspes. Also the history of Josephus in his *Antiquities*, Book x, Chaps. 9–11, for the captivity, and Book xi, for the return.

Herodotus (B.C. 484–424), Ctesias (fl. B.C. 401–384), and Xenophon (B.C. 430–357) are our chief classical authorities for this period. Nicolaus of Damascus (1st Century B.C.), Diodorus Siculus (1st Century A.D.) and Arrian (2nd Century

R

A.D.) are only late compilers. Ptolemy's Canon, to which modern scholarship attributes a species of quasi-infallibility, is also a compilation of the 2nd Century A.D.

The Egibi Tablets.

Table-case G in the Babylonian and Assyrian Room of the British Museum, contains a most important and valuable series of clay tablets, dating from the 1st year of Nebuchadnezzar to the 36th year of Darius. These are largely legal and commercial documents, many of them recording business transactions carried out by the members of the great mercantile house, founded by a wealthy merchant—a Babylonian Rothschild of the 7th Century B.C.— named Egibi or Sin-muballit.

These tablets include deeds respecting the sale of land, slaves, and houses, marriage contracts and dowries, loans of money and grain, payment of debts, divisions of property, accounts and receipts.

They are dated according to the year of the reign of the King of Babylon, and thus contribute to the fixing of the Chronology of the period. Transactions are recorded in every one of the 43 years of Nebuchadnezzar, from B.C. 604–562 ; the 2 years of Evil-merodach, B.C. 561–560 ; the 4 years of Neriglissar, B.C. 559–556 ; the accession year of Labashi-Marduk, B.C. 556 ; and the 17 years of Nabonidus, B.C. 555–539.

Transactions are recorded in each of the 9 years of Cyrus, B.C. 538–530, including the two years in which he was Co-Rex with Darius the Mede, B.C. 538–537, and the 7 years in which he was sole King, B.C. 536–530. Cyrus being regarded as King of Babylon during the whole of these 9 years, Darius the Mede, whose residence was at Ecbatana, is not mentioned.

Transactions are recorded in every one of the 8 years of Cambyses, B.C. 529–522, in the year of Smerdis, who is sometimes called Barzia (B.C. 521).

Transactions are recorded in about half the years of Darius Hystaspes, but tablets are wanting for 19 years of this reign. There is, however, a tablet dated as late as the 36th year of his reign, just two years beyond the close of the Old Testament Record and the period now under review.

The only tablets dated later than this in the Persian period are, one in the 2nd year of Xerxes, and one each in the 6th and the 13th years of Artaxerxes. Also one in the reign of Artaxerxes, but undated.

Possibly these also refer to Darius Hystaspes, for Xerxes calls himself Darius in the Persepolis Inscription, and Artaxerxes is clearly another name for Darius in the Book of Ezra.

This confirms the suspicion that, as there are no authentic records of this part of the Persian period, its duration may have been over-estimated by something like 82 years, by the late compilers Diodorus Siculus and Ptolemy.

The Nabonidus Cylinder.

There is a baked clay cylinder of Nabonidus (B.C. 555–539), No. 53, Table-case G, in the Babylonian and Assyrian Room of the British Museum.

It contains a prayer to the moon god on behalf of his eldest son Bel-shar-usur (the Belshazzar of Dan. 5, 7 [1], and 8 [1]). It runs as follows :—

" As for me, Nabonidus the King of Babylon, protect thou me from sinning against thine exalted godhead, and grant thou me graciously a long life ; and in the heart of Belshazzar my firstborn son, the offspring of my loins, set the fear of thine exalted godhead, so that he may commit no sin, and that he may be satisfied with the fulness of life."

The mention of Belshazzar in these terms is held to indicate that he was associated with his father as Co-Rex of Babylon.

This explains the curious offer of Belshazzar to Daniel, that if he could interpret the writing on the wall he should be " third ruler " in the Kingdom (Dan. 5$^{16.\ 29}$), there being already two supreme rulers, viz. Nabonidus and Belshazzar his son.

The most important Persian cuneiform Inscriptions are those of Cyrus and Darius Hystaspes.

The Cyrus Tablet and the Cyrus Cylinder.

Of the reign of Cyrus we have two important Inscriptions, the clay tablet of Cyrus and the clay cylinder of Cyrus. They were discovered and brought to England by Mr. Rassam.

The clay tablet of Cyrus (Case E, No. 122, in the Babylonian and Assyrian Room in the British Museum) contains the Annals of Nabonidus King of Babylon (B.C. 555–539). It records the defeat of Astyages the Mede by Cyrus, the capture and spoiling of Ecbatana the capital of Media, the taking of Babylon, and the downfall and death of Nabonidus.

From this we learn that Cyrus was King of Elam. He defeated Astyages and took Ecbatana in the 6th year of his reign, B.C. 550. In the 17th year, on the 14th day of the month Tammuz (June), Sippara was taken. Nabonidus fled. On the 16th Gobryas and the army of Cyrus entered Babylon without fighting. Nabonidus was put into fetters. On the 3rd of Marcheswan (October) Cyrus entered Babylon. On the 11th Gobryas was appointed over the other governors in Babylon, and Nabonidus died.

All this is perfectly compatible with the narrative in the 5th chapter of Daniel, but we must always remember that silence is not denial. It would, however, be difficult to reconcile the account of Cyrus with that of Herodotus or that of Xenophon.

The clay cylinder of Cyrus (Case G, No. 67, in the Babylonian and Assyrian Room of the British Museum) continues the history from the point at which the clay tablet of Cyrus leaves it. In this Inscription Cyrus glorifies himself and his son Cambyses.

" Marduk proclaimed Cyrus King of Anshan or Elam, by name, for the Sovereignty of the whole world (cp. Isaiah 44^{28}–45^{13}). Without fighting or battle he caused him to enter Babylon. Nabonidus the King he gave into his hand. I am Cyrus, the King of Legions, the great King, the powerful King, the King of Babylon, the King of Sumer and Accad, the King of the four zones ; the son of Cambyses the great King, the King of Elam ; the grandson of Cyrus, the great King, the King of Elam ; the great-grandson of Teispes, the great King, the King of Elam. Merodach the great lord graciously drew nigh unto me, Cyrus the King, his worshipper, and to Cambyses my son, the offspring of my heart. I restored the gods to their places, all their people I assembled, and I restored their lands " (cp. Ezra I [1- 3]).

Cyrus was originally King of Ansan, Anshan or Anzan. This was the native name of the country which the Assyrians, and the Hebrew Scriptures, called Elam. He became King of Persia between the 6th and the 9th years of Nabonidus, B.C. 549–546. The original capital of Cyrus was Susa or Shushan, which remained the principal city of the Persian Empire.

Cambyses has left us no Inscriptions but there are dated tablets for every year of his reign, and one dated in the fourth year of Cyrus, in which Cambyses is called the Crown Prince. He may, therefore, have been associated in the throne with his father Cyrus as early as the 2nd year of Cyrus' sole Kingship, B.C. 535.

The Great Behistun Inscription.

Darius Hystaspes has left us six Inscriptions, of which by far the most important is the Great Behistun Inscription. The three texts of the Inscription in the (1) Persian, (2) contemporary Elamite, and (3) Babylonian languages are published, with English translations, an introduction and photographic illustrations, by the Trustees of the British Museum, under the title *The Sculptures and Inscriptions of Darius the Great on the Rock of Behistun, in Persia* (1907).

Darius begins by giving his ancestry. This, when coupled with the information contained in the cylinder Inscription of Cyrus, yields the following table :—

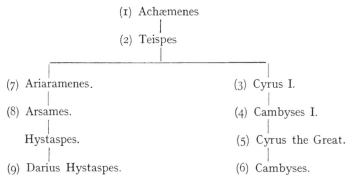

```
                    (1) Achæmenes
                          |
                    (2) Teispes
                          |
        _____
        |                                      |
(7) Ariaramenes.                        (3) Cyrus I.
        |                                      |
(8) Arsames.                            (4) Cambyses I.
        |                                      |
Hystaspes.                              (5) Cyrus the Great.
        |                                      |
(9) Darius Hystaspes.                   (6) Cambyses.
```

Darius says :—

" Eight of my family have been Kings before me. I am the 9th. In two branches have we been Kings."

Prof. E. G. Brown, in his *Literary History of Persia*, omits (3) Cyrus and includes Hystaspes, but Hystaspes is never called a King in any of the Inscriptions, and the addition of (3) Cyrus is necessitated by the cylinder Inscription of Cyrus.

The Behistun Inscription continues :—

" By the grace of Ormazd I became King of Persia, Elam (Susiana) Babylonia, Assyria, Arabia, Egypt, The Maritime Countries, Sepharad, Ionia, Media, Armenia, Cappadocia, Parthia, etc.
" A Magian, Gomates by name, said ' I am Bardes, son of Cyrus, the brother of Cambyses,' and seized the crown.   I killed this Gomates the Magian."

There is a sculptured figure of Gomates lying prostrate on the ground, a large figure of Darius Hystaspes standing with his foot upon him, and 9 other figures of men standing in a row with a rope round their necks.   These are the 9 Kings who rose up against him in various parts of the Empire, and whom Darius crushed in 19 battles, during the first five years of his reign. They are as follows :—

  1. Gomates the Magian, who claimed to be Bardes, son of Cyrus.
  2. Assina who claimed to be King of Susiana.
  3. Nidinta-Bel   ,,   ,,   Nebuchadnezzar, King of Babylon.
  4. Phraortes   ,,   ,,   Cyaxares, King of Media.
  5. Martiya   ,,   ,,   Immanes, King of Susiana.
  6. Chitratakhma ,,   ,,   King of Sagartia.
  7. Vahyazdates   ,,   ,,   Bardes, son of Cyrus.
  8. Arakha   ,,   ,,   Nebuchadnezzar, King of Babylon.
  9. Frâda   ,,   ,,   King of Margiana.
  10. Sakunka the Sakian.

Sir Henry Rawlinson, at the risk of his life, copied and obtained squeezes of the Inscription, mounting a ladder within a few inches of the edge of a projecting rock, with a precipice some 500 feet deep just in front.   Its decipherment was the romance of the 19th Century, and the key to the interpretation of the cuneiform Inscriptions of Assyria and Babylonia, which has enabled us to read so many Centuries of the past history of the race.

Later Persian Inscriptions.

There are other Inscriptions of Darius,—(1) on the walls of his magnificent palace at Persepolis, (2) round his tomb at Naksh-i-Rustam, and (3) on a granite slab on one of the rocky peaks of Mount Alwand, three miles to the south of Ecbatana, the modern Hamadan, but they throw no further light on the subject of Bible Chronology.

The Inscriptions of the succeeding monarchs of Persia do not belong to this period, but it will be convenient to complete our account of the Cuneiform Inscriptions of Persia at this point.

Xerxes has left five Inscriptions.   The Inscription of Xerxes at Persepolis reads as follows :—

" A great god is Ormazd, who created this earth, who created blessings for man, who has made Xerxes King, sole King of many Kings, sole lawgiver among many lawgivers."

" I am Xerxes the great King, the King of Kings, the King of the lands where many languages are spoken ; the King of this wide earth, far and near, the son of King Darius the Achæmenian."

" Says Xerxes the great King. By the grace of Ormazd, I have made this portal, which is sculptured with representations of all peoples. There are also many other beautiful buildings in Persia which I have made and which my father made. All such buildings as appear beautiful we have made by the grace of Ormazd."

" Says Darius the King. May Ormazd protect me and my Empire, and my work and my father's work. May Ormazd protect it all."

It will be noted that in the last paragraph Xerxes calls himself Darius. This proves that these Persian monarchs were sometimes called by different names.

There is another Inscription by Xerxes at Mount Alwand and also one at Van.

Of Artaxerxes Longimanus there is no Inscription except the words " Artaxerxes the great King " on a vase. This might equally well be an Inscription of Darius Hystaspes, who also bore the name Artaxerxes.

Of Darius II Nothus, there is only a short Inscription on the posts of the windows of the palace of Darius Hystaspes at Persepolis. It reads :—

" Summit of the palace of King Darius erected by a relative."

This also might equally well be an Inscription of Darius Hystaspes.

Of Artaxerxes II Mnemon, there is an Inscription at Susa (Shushan) which reads :—

" I am Artaxerxes, the great King, the King of Kings, the son of King Darius."

" Says Artaxerxes, the great King, the King of Kings, the King of the provinces, the King of this land, the son of King Darius."

" Darius was the son of King Artaxerxes, Artaxerxes was the son of King Xerxes, Xerxes was the son of King Darius, Darius was the son of Hystaspes, the Achæmenian."

" This temple my ancestor Darius built. Afterwards my grandfather Artaxerxes (restored it). I placed in it (the images of) Anahita, Tanaitis and Mithras. By the grace of Ormazd I built the temple. May Ormazd, Anahita and Mithras protect me."

Of Artaxerxes III Ochus, we have only this Inscription at Persepolis :—

" A great god is Ormazd, who created this earth, who created yonder sky, who created man, and above other animals created man, who made me Artaxerxes King, one King of many, one Ruler of many."

" Saith Artaxerxes the great King, the King of Kings, the King of the provinces, the King of this land. I am the son of King Artaxerxes. Artaxerxes was the son of King Darius, Darius was the son of King Artaxerxes, Artaxerxes was the son of King Xerxes, Xerxes was the son of King Darius, Darius was the son of Hystaspes, Hystaspes was the son of Arsames; Arsames was the son of Achæmenes."

" Saith Artaxerxes the King. This palace was built by me of stone. May Ormazd and Mithras protect me, and this region and that which I have built."

Of Arses we have only these words on the seal of Grotefend :—

" Arsaces a son of the race of Ahyabusanus."

" The Inscriptions of Xerxes and Artaxerxes," says Prof. A. V. Williams Jackson, in his excellent work on *Persia Past and Present* (1906), " are hardly more than reproductions of the minor tablets of Darius, formularic in their content and mechanical in their structure. The ring of the metal seems less true in these later Inscriptions, the language, like the style, shows signs of decadence."

In fact, what we have here is just what we should expect a dilettante tourist, with some knowledge of Persian, to carve on the ruins, if he had learned from Ptolemy and other late compilers the succession of the Persian monarchs and the relation between them. Standing alone, the Inscriptions of these later monarchs after Xerxes are not sufficient to authenticate the existence of the Kings whom they claim as their authors.

In any case we have here not the slightest confirmation of the *Chronology* of the Persian period such as we have for the Assyrian and the Babylonian periods which precede it, and the Greek period which succeeds it. The Chronology is amply authenticated down to the end of the reign of Darius Hystaspes, but further than that the Monumental evidence of the cuneiform Inscriptions does not go.

Josephus.

Josephus' history of the period of the captivity is contained in his *Antiquities*, Book x, Chapters 10, 11. It is derived partly from Scripture and partly from Berosus' *History of Chaldea*.

He agrees with the Babylonian clay tablets, with Ptolemy's Canon and with Scripture (Dan. 1 [1], Jer. 25 [1-3], 2 Kings 24 [12], 25 [27]), in ascribing 43 years to Nebuchadnezzar. He gives Evil-merodach 18 years, but Syncellus says Josephus followed Abydenus and Polyhistor in assigning 2 years to this reign. Neriglissar, whom he calls Neglissar, is credited with 40 years (possibly a copyist's error for 4 years). He gives 9 months to Labashi-Marduk, whom he calls Labosordacus ; and to Baltasar, called also Naboandelus, and in *Contra Apion* Nabonnedon, he ascribes 17 years, but he is mistaken in identifying Belshazzar, the son, with his father, Nabonidus. He says that the Queen mentioned in Dan. 5 [10] was Belshazzar's grandmother. She has been identified with the famous Nitocris, the wife of Nebuchadnezzar. He says that Babylon was taken by Darius, the son of Astyages of Media, and his kinsman Cyrus, King of Persia.

Josephus' history of the period of the return is contained in his *Antiquities*, Book xi, which brings his narrative down to the time of Alexander the Great. It will be convenient to consider his history down to that event in this chapter.

Josephus says that in the 70th year from the day that the Jews were removed out of their own Land, Cyrus, in the first year of his reign, gave them leave to return to Jerusalem *to rebuild their city* and the Temple of God. This was done in consequence of his reading the passage in the Book of Isaiah (44 ^{28}–45 ^{13}) in which he is mentioned by name.

Josephus follows Herodotus in making Cyrus die in the war against the Massagetæ, not Xenophon, who says he died a peaceful death in his own bed. Josephus identifies the Artaxerxes of Ezra 4 $^{7-23}$ with Cambyses, after whom he says the Magi attained the government of Persia for one year. Zerubbabel came from Jerusalem and obtained from Darius, the next King, permission to rebuild the Temple, and " all that Cyrus intended to do before him, relating to the restoration of Jerusalem, Darius also ordained should be done accordingly." Amongst the number of the distinguished men who returned with Zerubbabel (Ezra 2 ^{2}, Neh. 7 ^{7}), he mentions the name of the Mordecai of the Book of Esther.

It is very difficult to give an account of Josephus' view of the history of the Persian period. It is just the kind of history that would remain, if that of the Books of Ezra, Nehemiah and Esther were " emended," " corrected " and interpolated by some later copyist or editor with a view to bringing it into accord with some other version of the history. The result is just such a mixture of Scriptural events attributed to wrong persons as would follow from incorrect identifications of the persons named in the narrative. This may be due to Josephus himself, or more probably to some later hand.

Josephus tells us that on the death of Darius, " Xerxes his son " took the Kingdom. Perhaps this sentence is a late interpolation, and the name Xerxes throughout the succeding narrative may be a "·correction " by some late editor, supplanting the name Artaxerxes. For by Xerxes, Josephus always means the Artaxerxes of Ezra and Nehemiah. According to Josephus, it is this " Xerxes " who gives to Ezra the letter of Ezra 7 ^{12} beginning, " Xerxes King of Kings, unto Ezra the priest." On the 12th day of the 1st month of the 7th year of this " Xerxes " they set out to go to Jerusalem (cp. Ezra 8 ^{31}, 7 ^{9}). Then follow the rest of the events contained in Ezra 9 and 10.

Nehemiah is described as cupbearer to this " Xerxes." Nehemiah goes up to Jerusalem in the 25th year of this " Xerxes " and builds the walls in spite of the opposition of the Samaritans. The walls are completed in the 28th year of this " Xerxes," and the chapter concludes with the words " now this was done in the days of " Xerxes."

But the " Xerxes " of Ptolemy's Canon, the *son* of Darius, reigned only 20 years, and all the events ascribed to the reign of the " Xerxes " of Josephus, are attributed to the reign of " Artaxerxes " in Scripture.

Hence, we are compelled to say that either (1) Josephus used the word " Xerxes " as another name for the Artaxerxes whom modern scholars identify with Longimanus, in which case the words which make him the " son of Darius " are a late interpolation, or a mistake of Josephus himself; or else (2) Josephus is really referring under the name of " Xerxes " to Darius Hystaspes, and the opening sentence of the *Antiquities*, Book xi, Chap. v, which describes this " Xerxes " as a " son of Darius " is a late interpolation. In no case do the events which Josephus attributes to the reign of this

" Xerxes " belong to Xerxes the " son of Darius," the Xerxes of Ther-mopylæ and Salamis.

The confusion deepens as we pass into chapter 6. " After the death of Xerxes the Kingdom was transferred to his son Cyrus, whom the Greeks called Artaxerxes." The relationship here indicated points to Artaxerxes Longimanus (B.C. 464–424), but the sentence is probably either a late interpolation or an indication of Josephus' inability to understand the true meaning of the Ezra-Nehemiah-Esther narrative. For this " Artaxerxes " is immediately identified with the Ahasuerus of Esther, whom modern scholars identify with the " Xerxes " of Ptolemy's Canon. He reigns over 127 provinces from India to Ethiopia. In his 3rd year he makes a costly feast at Shushan. He divorces Vashti, and marries Esther the niece of Mordecai. Haman plots against the Jews, is accused by Esther and hanged, and his office is given to Mordecai. The massacre takes place on the appointed 13th day of Adar, but the Jews defend themselves, and the feast of Purim is instituted.

Here again we are compelled to say that either (1) Josephus used the word " Artaxerxes " as another name for Ahasuerus, whom modern scholars identify with the Xerxes of Ptolemy's Canon, in which case the words " Xerxes' son Cyrus, whom the Greeks called Artaxerxes," are a late interpola-tion, or a mistake of Josephus himself; or else (2) Josephus is really referring, under the name of " Artaxerxes," to Darius Hystaspes, and the opening sentence of the *Antiquities*, Book xi, Chap. vi, which describes this " Cyrus whom the Greeks called Artaxerxes " as a " son of Xerxes," is a late inter-polation. In no case do the events which Josephus attributes to the reign of this " Artaxerxes the son of Xerxes " belong to Artaxerxes Longimanus.

In chapter 7 we are introduced to Bagoses, the general of " another " Artaxerxes. This is said to indicate Artaxerxes II Mnemon (B.C. 404–359), the reign of Darius II Nothus (B.C. 424–404), being altogether omitted. But the word " another " is not in Josephus at all. The true reading is " Bagoses the general of the people of Artaxerxes " (τοῦ λαοῦ 'Αρταξέρξου). Vossius " emends " the text by what is really a pure conjecture to " Bagoses the general of another (or the other) Artaxerxes " (του ἄλλου' Αρταξέρξου) in order to manufacture another Persian King. He pleads Ruffinus's Latin Version of Josephus. But (1) the translation will not bear the construction put upon it, and (2) a long received reading of an ancient author ought not to be varied from, without the authority of some good manuscript to justify the emendation, and in this case there is none alleged.

In this connection Dr. Prideaux has well observed :—

" All that Vossius saith about it can amount to no more than a conjecture, which we can build nothing certain upon : and to alter old authors upon conjectures only is never to be allowed, especially where the context will bear the one reading as well as the other : for since the various fancies of men may lead to various conjectures, if there should be such a liberty allowed, whole books may be thus altered away and utterly defaced by such conjectural emendations ; and many good authors have already too much suffered by it."

" To change the text of an author where there is no internal evidence of corruption," says Canon Rawlinson, " merely on account of a chronological or historical difficulty, is contrary to all the principles of sound criticism."

The next King to this " Cyrus whom the Greeks call Artaxerxes " is " Darius the last King of Persia." He is mentioned in the following paragraph, and is described as a contemporary of Sanballat, the contemporary of Nehemiah on the one hand and Alexander the Great on the other. Josephus tells us that " about this time," Alexander the Great crossed the Hellespont, defeated the generals of Darius at Granicus (B.C. 334) and Issus (B.C. 333), took Tyre and Gaza (B.C. 332), and marched upon Jerusalem.

Jaddua the high priest was in an agony, but warned of God in a dream he went out to meet Alexander the Great as he reached Sapha, from which place there is a good view of Jerusalem and the Temple. When Alexander the Great saw the multitude in white garments, the priests in fine linen, and the high priest in purple and scarlet, with his mitre on his head, having the golden plate whereon the name of God was engraved, he fell down and adored the Name and saluted the high priest. With the date of this visit of Alexander to Jerusalem, in B.C. 332, Josephus connects the death of Sanballat.

The following reigns are all entirely omitted from Josephus :—

Darius II Nothus	..	..	..	..	423–404
Artaxerxes II Mnemon	..	..	..	..	404–358
Artaxerxes III Ochus	..	..	..	..	358–327
Arogus or Arses	..	..	..	..	337–335

This fact is not explained by Vossius and Dr. Hudson when they say Josephus was writing the history of the Jews, and only touched upon those Kings of Persia who had to do with the Jews.

As a matter of fact Josephus, or perhaps we should say his late revisers, represent Sanballat, the contemporary of Nehemiah in B.C. 445, as contemporary with Jaddua in B.C. 332, after an interval of 113 years, and transform the son of Joiada (Neh. 13 ^{28}) into his grandson. Modern advocates of the Ptolemaic dates endeavour to save the Chronology by inventing a second Sanballat.

A closer inspection of Josephus will show that, as in the case of the cuneiform Inscriptions, his works contain no authentic materials for any history of Persia for more than one or two generations beyond the end of the Old Testament Record, in the 34th year of Darius Hystaspes, B.C. 488. Josephus confirms the Daniel Chronology, which abridges the duration of the Persian Empire by 82 years.

His " Xerxes" is not the Xerxes of Ptolemy's Canon, but the Artaxerxes of Ezra 7 and Nehemiah, the Darius Hystaspes of Ptolemy's Canon. His " Artaxerxes " is not Artaxerxes Longimanus, and it is incorrect to say that, according to Josephus, Esther was married to Artaxerxes Longimanus. According to Josephus, the Artaxerxes who married Esther was simply Artaxerxes, and that was a name borne by several Persian monarchs, and certainly by Darius Hystaspes.

True he does say that this Artaxerxes who married Esther was the son of " Xerxes," but by " Xerxes " he means quite positively the Artaxerxes of

Ezra 7 and Nehemiah, who is identified by modern scholars with Artaxerxes Longimanus, but who is really Darius Hystaspes.

According to Josephus, Darius Hystaspes is succeeded by " Xerxes." To him is attributed the whole of the events of Ezra 7–Nehemiah 13. This " Xerxes " is succeeded by " Artaxerxes." To his reign is attributed the whole of the events of the Book of Esther, and nothing but those events, and they occurred for the most part in one and the same year. Beyond this, Josephus gives us information of no other Persian Kings except the Darius who was slain by Alexander the Great.

The Old Testament Apocrypha.

The Books of the Old Testament Apocrypha preserve certain traditional identifications that were current in the 1st and 2nd Centuries B.C.

In I ESDRAS 3 $^{1, 2}$ the Ahasuerus of Esther is identified with Darius Hystaspes.

In TOBIT it is Shalmaneser, " the father of Sennacherib," who carries Israel into captivity (not Sargon as the Monuments testify). Before he died Tobias heard of the destruction of Nineveh which was taken by Nabuchodonosor (Nabopolassar) and Assuerus (Ahasuerus = Cyaxares).

In the REST OF ESTHER, " Ahasuerus " is called " Artaxerxes " throughout.

In BEL AND THE DRAGON we read that King Astyages (viz. Darius the Mede) was gathered to his fathers, and Cyrus of Persia received the Kingdom.

Greek Writers.

Our chief classical authorities for the period of the captivity and the return are Herodotus, Ctesias and Xenophon.

Herodotus (B.C. 484–425) is an excellent authority for the period of the great Persian war, B.C. 490–485. The accounts which he gives of earlier and remoter periods, accounts which he received on trust, are not always to be relied upon. He gives us an exquisite picture of the first four Persian monarchs.

(1) " Cyrus, the simple, hardy, vigorous mountain chief, endowed with vast ambition, and with great military genius, changing as his Empire changed into the kind and friendly paternal monarch, clement, witty, polite, familiar with his people ; (2) Cambyses, the first form of the Eastern tyrant, inheriting his father's vigour and much of his talent, but violent, rash, headstrong, incapable of self-restraint, furious at opposition, not only cruel, but brutal ; (3) Darius Hystaspes, the model Oriental prince, brave, sagacious, astute, great in the arts of both war and peace, the organizer and consolidator as well as the extender of the Empire ; and (4) Xerxes, the second and inferior form of tyrant, weak and puerile as well as cruel and selfish, fickle, timid, licentious and luxurious " (Introduction to Rawlinson's *Herodotus*).

Herodotus' account of the earlier history of Assyria and Media, and his early history of Cyrus, cannot be regarded as authentic. His account of the taking of Babylon by Cyrus, (Herodotus i, 191) cannot be reconciled with the cylinder Inscription of Cyrus who says he took it " without fighting or battle." He appears to have inverted the order of the Kings of Media, Astyages and Cyaxares (Herodotus i, 73, 107, cp. Xenophon's *Cyropædia*, Books i and viii).

We have no authentic data for ascertaining the truth of the matter, but the Table given in Vol. II, Chronological Tables, p. 54, probably exhibits the relation of the families and the order of the succession of the Kings of Babylonia, Media and Persia, so far as they can be ascertained by unravelling the tangled skein of contradictory testimony gathered from all available sources, including Herodotus, Xenophon, Ctesias, Berosus, Josephus, Abydenus, Syncellus, the cylinder Inscription of Cyrus, and the Behistun Inscription of Darius Hystaspes.

Instead of the succession of Herodotus (Deioces, Phraortes, Cyaxares, Astyages), we adopt that of Xenophon, who makes Cyaxares (1) the son of Astyages I, (2) the brother of Mandane (Cyrus' mother), and (3) the father of Astyages II (Darius the Mede). Xenophon's order of succession is Deioces, Phraortes, Astyages I, Cyaxares, Astyages II (Darius the Mede), and this agrees best with Berosus, Josephus and the Books of Daniel, Tobit and Bel and the Dragon. Scholars find it hard to abandon so good an authority as Herodotus, but he must be rejected here.

Edouard Meyer unfortunately rejects the true statement of Herodotus that Cyrus was grandson of Astyages I, as legend (Encyclopædia Britannica, 11th Edition, article " Astyages ").

The accounts of the birth of Cyrus are likewise irreconcilable and perhaps, to some extent, mythical. His entire history is involved and crowded with legends. Herodotus gives one tradition, but tells us that he knew of four others. According to one account, he is the son of Mandane the daughter of Astyages, exposed on the mountains, suckled by a dog, and educated as a shepherd (Justin, Charon of Lampsacus, Ælian and Herodotus). In Herodotus' own account a woman, the wife of the shepherd, is substituted for the dog (Herodotus i, 95, 122).

The story as told by Ctesias makes Cyrus the son of a bandit. He enters the court of Astyages, becomes friendly with Œbares, who kills Astyages. The decisive battle is fought at Pasargadæ (Nicolaus of Damascus, Strabo, Justin, Photius).

Xenophon's is an ideal account based upon personal knowledge of later descendants of the royal Persian family, but he preserves in his historical romance the true order of the succession of the Kings of Media (Xenophon *Cyropædia*, Books i and viii).

The accounts of the death of Cyrus are just as contradictory as those of his birth and his life. He died fighting the Massagetæ (Herodotus), the Derbices (Ctesias), the Dahae (Berosus), a peaceful death in his own bed (Xenophon).

We have, therfore, no original sources containing authentic data for the history of Cyrus in classic literature.

Cambyses invaded and conquered Egypt in the year B.C. 525. Cambyses had a brother called Tanaoxares (Xenophon), Smerdis (Herodotus), Mergis (Justin), Bardis (the Behistun Inscription), whom he put to death.

In B.C. 522 he was personated by Gomates who was placed on the throne by his brother Patizithes, whom Cambyses had left in control of the Government of Asia during his absence in Egypt.

These brothers were Magians, and are hence often referred to as the Magi. Pseudo-Smerdis is also called Gomates (Behistun Inscription), Spendidates (Ctesias) and Orapastes (Justin), but in Ezra 4 $^{7-23}$ he is referred to under the name of Artaxerxes.

That Cambyses was the Ahasuerus of Ezra 4 ^{6}, and Pseudo-Smerdis the Artaxerxes of Ezra 4 ^{7}, is inferred from the fact that they are mentioned in that chapter as the Kings of Persia who reigned between Cyrus and Darius Hystaspes. The inference is confirmed by the use of the word " Kings " in Ezra 4 $^{13, 22}$ instead of " King," in reference to Pseudo-Smerdis and his brother, who was the power behind the throne and the real contriver of the whole plot. " The royal power was possessed by the Magi Patizithes and his brother " (Herodotus iii, 65).

Darius was a great conqueror. He conquered Asia Minor, Europe, India and the Isles of the Sea. In B.C. 494 he sent an expedition against Athens under his son-in-law Mardonius, but Mardonius was defeated and forced to return (Herodotus, Book vii). In B.C. 490 another expedition was fitted out by Datis and Artaphernes, and was utterly routed in the famous battle of Marathon. Darius now prepared to head an expedition in person.

He had three sons by his first wife, born before he became King, and four others by Atossa the daughter of Cyrus. There was some dispute about the succession which was settled by Darius, who appointed his son Xerxes to succeed him (Herodotus, Book vi). These circumstances throw some light upon the reference to " the realm of the King and his sons " in Ezra 7 ^{23}, and corroborate the identification of the Artaxerxes of Ezra 7 and Nehemiah, with Darius Hystaspes. Darius died suddenly, just as the expedition was ready to set out, B.C. 485.

Xerxes resolved to prosecute the war with Greece. He crossed the Hellespont with an army of nearly two million men, supported by 1,200 ships of the line of battle, and was utterly discomfited at Thermopylæ, Salamis and Platea, B.C. 480.

The remainder of the history of the Persian Empire is unknown, there being no authentic contemporary records until we reach the time of Alexander the Great.

Darius Hystaspes = Artaxerxes of Ezra 7 and Nehemiah.

We have now to prove that the identification of Darius Hystaspes with the Artaxerxes of Ezra 7 and Nehemiah is correct. Seven proofs are offered :—

1. The Continuity of the Narrative.

The Book of Ezra-Nehemiah is one Book, and the narrative is continuous throughout, except that in Ezra 3 $^{10-13}$ we have an anticipatory reference to the laying of the foundation of the Temple, introduced by the word *when*, indicating that the foundation of the Temple was not laid *then* (in the 2nd year of Cyrus), but as Haggai says, in the 2nd year of Darius (Hag. 2 $^{10. 15}$ $^{18. 20}$). Compare the following passages :—

The Continuity of the Ezra-Nehemiah Narrative.

Ezra 4^{24}.   2nd year of Darius—Temple begun.
6^{15}.   6th   ,,   ,,   Temple finished.
$7^{8.\ 9.}$ 7th   ,,   Artaxerxes—Ezra comes to Jerusalem.
Neh. 1^{1}.   20th   ,,   (Artaxerxes)—Hanani's Report.
2^{1}.   20th   ,,   Artaxerxes—Nehemiah goes to Jerusalem.
Neh. 5^{14}, 13^{6}.   32nd   ,,   ,,   Nehemiah returns to Babylon.

The transition is made in Ezra 6^{14} in which we are told that Artaxerxes was another name for Darius, " Darius *even* Artaxerxes."

2. The age of Ezra.

If the Artaxerxes of Ezra was Artaxerxes Longimanus (B.C. 464–424), then Ezra would be 128 years old when he came from Babylon in his 7th year (to be present at the dedication of the Temple).

For, as pointed out by *Lumen* in the *Prince of Judah*, Ezra was the brother of Jehozadak.

Genealogy of Jehozadak. 1 *Chron.* 6^{3-15}.				*Genealogy of Ezra.* *Ezra* 7^{1-5}.
1. Aaron	..	..	..	Aaron.
2. Eleazar ..	..	..	..	Eleazar.
3. Phinehas	..	..	..	Phinehas.
4. Abishua ..	..	..	..	Abishua.
5. Bukki	..	..	..	Bukki.
6. Uzzi	..	..	..	Uzzi.
7. Zerahiah	..	..	..	Zerahiah.
8. Meraioth	..	..	..	Meraioth.
9. Amariah I.	..	..	..	—
10. Ahitub I.	..	..	..	—
11. Zadok I.	..	..	..	—
12. Ahimaaz	..	..	..	—
13. Azariah I.	..	..	..	—
14. Johanan	..	..	..	—
15. Azariah II.	..	..	..	Azariah.
16. Amariah II.	..	..	..	Amariah.
17. Ahitub II.	..	..	..	Ahitub.
18. Zadok II.	..	..	..	Zadok.
19. Shallum	..	..	..	Shallum.
20. Hilkiah	..	..	..	Hilkiah.
21. Azariah III.	..	..	..	Azariah.
22. Seraiah	..	..	..	Seraiah.
JEHOZADAK ..	..	..	..	EZRA.

In Ezra 7 the genealogy is abridged, but it is sufficient for the purpose for which it is thus quoted. In 1 Chronicles it is given in full. Seraiah, the father of Jehozadak and Ezra, was slain by Nebuchadnezzar at Riblah in his 19th year, B.C. 586 (2 Kings 25 $^{8.\ 18-21}$). Therefore Ezra must have been born about or before B.C. 586. But the 7th year of Artaxerxes Longimanus was B.C. 458. Therefore, if the Artaxerxes of Ezra 7 was Artaxerxes Longimanus, Ezra must have been at least 128 years old when he came to Jerusalem in the 7th year of Artaxerxes Longimanus, and at least 141 when he walked in procession at the dedication of the wall with Nehemiah, in the 20th year of Artaxerxes Longimanus, which is absurd.

But the Artaxerxes of Ezra 7 is really Darius Hystaspes, whose 7th year was B.C. 515, in which year Ezra was (at least) 71 years old, and possibly more.

3. Twenty out of the thirty priests and Levites who returned with Zerubbabel in the 1st year of Cyrus, B.C. 536 (Neh. 12 $^{1-9}$), signed the covenant with Nehemiah (Neh 10 $^{2-10}$) in the 20th year of the Artaxerxes of Nehemiah. But the 20th year of Artaxerxes Longimanus was B.C. 445. Therefore, if the Artaxerxes of Nehemiah was Artaxerxes Longimanus, then twenty out of these thirty men were still alive 91 years after they came to Jerusalem, although they were all heads of their families then, which is absurd. But the Artaxerxes of Nehemiah was really Darius Hystaspes, and the interval between the return with Zerubbabel, B.C. 536, and the 20th year of Darius Hystaspes, B.C. 502, is only 34 years, during which time 10 of these 30 heads of families had died. See Vol. II, Chronological Tables, p. 53.

4. The Age of Nehemiah.

Nehemiah returned with Zerubbabel (B.C. 536), Ezra 2 ^{2}, Neh. 7 ^{7}. His name stands first on the list after Zerubbabel and Joshua. But the 32nd year of Artaxerxes Longimanus was B.C. 433. Therefore, if the Artaxerxes of Nehemiah was Artaxerxes Longimanus, Nehemiah must have been 103 years older when he returned to Babylon in the 32nd year of Artaxerxes Longimanus, than he was when he came to Jerusalem in the 1st year of Cyrus as one of the leaders of the people. But the Artaxerxes of Nehemiah is really Darius Hystaspes, and in the 32nd year of his reign (B.C. 490), Nehemiah was only 46 years older than he was when he came to Jerusalem with Zerubbabel in the 1st year of Cyrus.

5. The Artaxerxes of Nehemiah reigned 32 years.

Since the Artaxerxes of Ezra 7 and Nehemiah was not Artaxerxes Longimanus, and a fortiori not any Persian King who reigned after Artaxerxes Longimanus, he must have been Darius Hystaspes, for he reigned at least 32 years (Neh. 5 ^{14}, 13 ^{6}) which is what no other Persian King before Artaxerxes Longimanus except Darius Hystaspes did.

6. The Testimony of Josephus, the Old Testament Apocrypha, and the Jewish Tract, *Sedar Olam*.

Josephus identifies the Artaxerxexs of Ezra 7 with a Persian King (whom he calls Xerxes) who reigned at least 28 years. This cannot be the Xerxes of Ptolemy's Canon, for he only reigned 21 years. It must be Darius Hystaspes, and Josephus (or his late editors) must be in error in describing him as the " Son of Darius "(Hystaspes).

In 1 ESDRAS the Ahasuerus of Esther is identified with Darius Hystaspes, and in the REST OF ESTHER Ahasuerus is called " Artaxerxes " throughout. Jewish Tradition, as represented in the Jewish Tract *Sedar Olam*, also identifies the Artaxerxes of Nehemiah with Darius Hystaspes.

7. Corroborative Evidences.

The mention of the " King's sons " in Ezra 7 corroborates the identification of the Artaxerxes of Ezra 7 with Darius Hystaspes, for he had several sons before he became King, who disputed the succession with his sons by his second wife Atossa, the daughter of Cyrus, one of whom Darius Hystaspes appointed to succeed him, viz. Xerxes.

The parenthetic sentence in Neh. 2 [6], " the queen also sitting by him," is probably a reference to Esther, with whom Nehemiah may have had communications respecting the state of affairs at Jerusalem, and who may have encouraged him and influenced the King in his favour. But this King reigned at least 32 years (Neh. 13 [6]), and could not have been Xerxes, who only reigned 21 years, nor any other but Darius Hystaspes, who is frequently called both Artaxerxes and Ahasuerus in the Apocryphal literature and Josephus.

In Ezra 10 [44] we read " All these had taken strange wives, and some of them had wives by whom they had children." This corroborates the identification of the Artaxerxes to whose 7th year the remark applies, with some King of Persia, who lived nearer to the time of the return under Zerubbabel than Artaxerxes Longimanus.

The genealogical lists given in Ezra and Nehemiah corroborate the identification of the Artaxerxes of Ezra 7, and Nehemiah with Darius Hystaspes. The contrary view necessitates the hypothesis of two Ezras, two Nehemiahs, two Mordecais, two Sanballats, and so on.

On all these grounds we regard the identification of the Artaxerxes of Ezra 7 and Nehemiah with Darius Hystaspes as correct.

Darius Hystaspes = Ahasuerus of Esther.

Finally, we have to prove that the Ahasuerus of Esther was also Darius Hystaspes.

The Book of Esther is an appendix containing the record of an episode which took place in the time of Ezra and Nehemiah. The narrative itself occupies the space of one year, the 12th year of Ahasuerus, but there are also brief introductory references to his 3rd, 6th and 7th years. It is not a continuation of the Book of Ezra-Nehemiah, but an illustration of the times in which Ezra and Nehemiah lived.

We identify the Ahasuerus of Esther with Darius Hystaspes, and we offer the following five proofs :—

1. The Age of Mordecai.

Scaliger first suggested the identification of the Ahasuerus of Esther with the Xerxes of Ptolemy's Canon, and in this he has been followed by modern scholars almost universally. But Mordecai "was carried away from

Jerusalem with the captivity which had been carried away with Jeconiah King of Judah, whom Nebuchadnezzar King of Babylon carried away." B.C. 597 (Est. 2 5. 6). It is only by a forced construction that this sentence can be applied to his great grandfather Kish. Mordecai was Ahasuerus' premier in the 12th year of his reign. Therefore, if Ahasuerus was Xerxes, in his 12th year, B.C. 474, Mordecai would be *at least* 123 years old, at which rate Esther also must have been " an *aged* beauty ! "

2. Testimony of Josephus and the Old Testament Apocrypha.

Josephus tells the story of Esther at great length, but instead of speaking of Ahasuerus, it is " Artaxerxes " throughout. Now Artaxerxes was one of the names of Darius Hystaspes, as well as of several other Persian monarchs. True, Josephus speaks of this Artaxerxes as " Cyrus the son of Xerxes, whom the Greeks called Artaxerxes," but if the reference be to Artaxerxes Longimanus, that would raise the age of Mordecai to 143.

In 1 ESDRAS 3 1. 2 the Ahasuerus of Esther is identified with Darius Hystaspes, and in the REST OF ESTHER he is called "Artaxerxes " throughout.

3. Ahasuerus " reigned from India to Ethiopia, over 127 Provinces " (Est. 1 1).

Darius Hystaspes conquered India in B.C. 506. Herodotus says he " established 20 governments of the kind which the Persians call Satrapies, assigning to each its governor, and fixing the tribute which was to be paid him by the several nations " (iii, 89). These he proceeds to enumerate, a long list embracing nearly all the nations of the East—Asia Minor, Phœnicia Syria, Cyprus, Egypt, Libya, Cyrene, Susa, Babylon, Assyria, Media, Armenia, Parthia—these are all enumerated, with the amount of the tribute paid by each nation (iii, 90–94). " The Indians, who were more numerous than any other nation with which we are acquainted, paid a tribute exceeding that of any other people, to wit 360 talents of gold dust. This was the twentieth Satrapy " (iii, 95).

" The Ethiopians paid no settled tribute, but brought gifts to the King. Every third year the inhabitants of Egypt and Nubia brought 2 quarts of virgin gold, 200 logs of ebony, 5 Ethiopian boys, and 20 elephants' tusks " (iii, 97).

Darius the Mede set 120 Princes over his Kingdom (B.C. 538), Dan. 6 1. By the time of Darius Hystaspes (B.C. 521–485), the Empire had grown to 127 provinces, which he divided up into 20 Satrapies as stated above.

4. Ahasuerus " laid a tribute upon the land and upon the Isles of the Sea." (Est. 10 1).

After enumerating the 20 satrapies of the Empire and the amount of tribute paid by each satrapy, Herodotus concludes : " such was the revenue which Darius derived from Asia, and a small part of Libya. Later in his reign the sum was increased by the *tribute of the Islands* and of the nations of Europe as far as Thessaly " (Herodotus, Book iii, 96).

Thucydides says, " The Ionians had attained great prosperity when Cyrus

S

and the Persians, having overthrown Crœsus, and subdued the countries between them and the river Halys and the sea, made war against them and enslaved the cities of *the mainland*. Some time afterwards, Darius, strong in the possession of the Phœnician fleet, conquered *the Islands also*."

Herodotus (iii, 96), Thucydides (Book i), and Plato (*Menexenus*), all tell us that Darius Hystaspes subdued all the Islands of the Ægean sea, and Diodorus Siculus (Book xii) tells us that they were all lost again, by his son Xerxes, *before the 12th year of his reign*, (B.C. 474), which we can well believe after the humiliating defeat of his vast host of warriors by land and sea at Thermopylæ, Salamis and Platea, B.C. 480. The later Kings of Persia held none of these Islands except Clazomene and Cyprus (Xenophon, *Hellenica*, Book v). This is conclusive, both for the identification of the Ahasuerus of Esther with Darius Hystaspes, and against his identification with Xerxes, or with any later occupant of the Persian throne.

5. The dates and the events recorded in Esther, fit in exactly with the dates and the events of the reign of Darius Hystaspes.

Ahasuerus made his feast in the third year of his reign (B.C. 519). Darius Hystaspes was occupied during the first two years of his reign in overthrowing Gomates and the other pretenders to the throne of Persia. Babylon revolted twice from Darius, once in the first year of his reign and again in the fourth. On this second occasion the siege was a tedious affair, lasting nearly 2 years (Herodotus iii, 151). This brings us down to the 6th year of Darius, and explains how it was that although Vashti was divorced in his third year, he was not married to Esther until his 7th year (Est. 1^3, 2^{16}).

The chief argument relied upon by those who identify the Ahasuerus of Esther with Xerxes, is the congruity of the character of Ahasuerus with that of Xerxes as depicted by Herodotus, and other classic writers. But there is nothing in the character of Ahasuerus which does not agree equally well with all that we know from classic literature of Darius Hystaspes ; in fact the reference to the money matters, to the postal service, and above all the friendly disposition of Ahasuerus toward the Jews, agrees exactly with what we know of Darius the " huckster," the organizer of the Empire, and the " Darius even Artaxerxes " who issued the decrees of Ezra 6^{6-12} and Ezra 7^{12-26} for the rebuilding of the Temple, and the support of its services. The argument for the identification of Ahasuerus with Xerxes from the similarity between the old Persian name Khshayarsha, the Hebrew Achashverosh, and the Greek Xerxes, is of no force, for the word in any form, and however spelt, is simply the word " Shah," and might be applied to any monarch who sat upon the throne of Persia.

CONCLUSION.

CHAPTER XXVII. THE YEAR OF MESSIAH'S BIRTH ACCORDING TO THE PROPHECY OF DANIEL (AN. HOM. 4038).

"THE Epicureans are in error who cast providence out of human life, and do not believe that God takes care of the affairs of the world, nor that the universe is governed and continued in being by that blessed and immortal nature, but that the world is carried along of its own accord, without a ruler and a curator; which, were it destitute of a guide to conduct, as they imagine, it would be like ships without pilots, which we see drowned by the winds, or like chariots without drivers, which are overturned; so would the world be dashed to pieces by its being carried without a providence, and so perish and come to nought. Those men seem to me very much to err from the truth who determine that God exercises no providence over human affairs, for if it were the case that the world went on by mechanical necessity, we should not see all things come to pass according to the prophecy of Daniel." (Josephus, *Antiquities*, Book x, Chap. ii, 7).

We have now traced the dated events of the Old Testament step by step from the creation of Adam to the 1st year of Cyrus, and beyond it, to the end of the story of the return. Every step has been attested and proved. Every chasm has been bridged over. Every difficulty has been explained. Every problem has been solved.

The final test of truth is self-consistency. We have seen that every chronological statement in the Old Testament is consistent with every other chronological statement contained in it, consistent also with every chrono-logical statement contained in the *Cuneiform Inscriptions* of Assyria, Babylonia and Persia.

This should give us confidence in using the Scripture Chronology, as a standard with which to compare and by which to judge, the accuracy of statements and inferences obtained from other sources. It should also give us a measure of confidence in the great chronological predictions of Scripture.

For the realm in which we live is a realm of order, and order is a proof of intelligence and foresight and purpose.

The purpose of God in creation and redemption is made known to us in a revelation, in the light of which we are able to interpret the history of the past, to read the meaning of the present, and to anticipate the will and purpose of God with regard to the future.

If we believe in the universal sovereignty of God, in any real sense at all, we must admit that He retains in His own hands, and controls by His own power, the destiny of men and nations. If this be true of events in general, it must be true of the supreme event of all history, the advent of the Messiah, and the redemption of the race wrought out by Him.

Our scheme of Chronology, so far as we have yet gone, is incomplete. It ends in a *cul de sac*. It leads us nowhere. There remains one great final gulf or chasm which must be bridged over if we are to complete the cycle and read the meaning of the parts in the light of the whole.

This is done for us in the great 9th chapter of Daniel, which enables us to recover the lost count of the years and to connect the present with all the facts and the events of the past, and with the great central event of all history, the redemption of the race through the incarnation of the Messiah.

The revelation of the precise time of the Messiah's death is made in the last four verses of Daniel 9. It is made in the words of the angel Gabriel, the only angel of his rank whose name is known to us, the angel who made to Mary, " highly favoured," the announcement of the approach of Messiah's birth, as he made to Daniel, " greatly beloved," the announcement of the time of His death.

The expression " for thou art greatly beloved," כִּי חֲמוּדוֹת אָתָּה, is the exact equivalent of " thou art highly favoured," κεχαριτωμένη. It is used three times to Daniel, and never to anyone else except Mary, and Gabriel is the only angel employed to make known to men the revelation of the mystery of redemption through the incarnation of the Son of God.

Considering the singular nature of the revelation vouchsafed, we ought not to be surprised when we find that it contains not only the announcement of a great event, but also of the very time when it was ordained of God to come to pass.

The occasion of the prophecy was someting very extraordinary. It·is dated in the 1st year of Darius the Mede, the year of the passing of the great Babylonian World Empire in B.C. 538, the inaugural year of the second great World Empire of the Medes and Persians.

Daniel had been studying the 25th and the 29th chapters of the Book of Jeremiah, and there he had read the words, " after 70 years I will cause you to return." From the 3rd year of Jehoiakim—the year in which Daniel was carried away into captivity, B.C. 605, to the 1st year of Darius, B.C. 538, was a period of 68 years, inclusive reckoning. He knew, therefore, that he was standing on the threshold of the fulfilment of the prophecy. So he set his face unto the Lord God to seek by prayer and supplication to know His will. He prayed for Jerusalem, the city, the people, the holy mountain and the sanctuary that was desolate,. And while he was speaking the answer came.

Seventy sevens—not weeks, for that suggests a period of 7 *days*, and the word used means simply a septad, a *seven ;* the nature of the seven has to be discovered from the context. Here it is the seventy years of Jeremiah's prophecy, during which the Jews were to be in captivity, and the *seventy sevens* are therefore to be interpreted as years also. Seventy sevens are determined upon the holy city. God's dealings with the Jews and their city was to cover a period of 490 years.

" Know, therefore, and understand that from the going forth of the commandment to restore and to build Jerusalem unto the Messiah the Prince shall be seven sevens (49 years) and 62 sevens (434 years). The street shall be built again and the wall even in troublous times. And after the 62 sevens shall Messiah be cut off." Other events follow, and there is another seven years yet future to complete the whole period of God's dealings with His people in their own land, but the data we require for our Chronology are contained in the above words. From " the going forth of the commandment to restore and to build Jerusalem " to " the cutting off of the Messiah " is a period of 49+434 = 483 years.

The only point to be determined is the exact time at which the commandment went forth.

That commandment is unquestionably the proclamation of Cyrus in the 1st year of his sole reign, B.C. 536. This is proved conclusively from 2 Chron. 36 [20-23.] What Daniel had in his mind was the accomplishment of the 70 years' servitude in Babylon, and its termination by the issue of an edict by the King of Persia giving the Jews liberty to return.

" They were servants to him and his sons until the reign of the Kingdom of Persia," that is until the 1st of Cyrus, B.C. 536. " To fulfil the word of the Lord by the mouth of Jeremiah until the land had enjoyed her sabbaths : for as long as she lay desolate she kept sabbath, to fulfil threescore and ten years."

" Now in the 1st year of Cyrus, King of Persia, that the word of the Lord spoken by the mouth of Jeremiah might be fulfilled, the Lord stirred up the spirit of Cyrus, King of Persia, that he made a proclamation throughout all his Kingdom, and put it in writing, saying, Thus saith Cyrus, King of Persia, The Lord God of heaven hath given me all the Kingdoms of the earth ; and He hath charged me to build him a House at Jerusalem, which is in Judah."

The building of the Temple implies the building of the city and the wall. Cyrus obtained his knowledge of the " charge " to build a House from Is. 44 [28]-45 [13], which makes explicit what is implicit in the words of Cyrus. " Cyrus . . . shall perform all my pleasure : even saying to Jerusalem, Thou shalt be built ; and to the Temple, Thy foundation shall be laid . . . I have raised him (Cyrus) up in righteousness, and I will direct all his ways : he shall build my city, and he shall let go my captives."

The prophecy was not falsified. The people did return, the city was built, their enemies accused them, no doubt with perfect truth, of building what they called " the rebellious and the bad city," and of setting up the walls and joining the foundations thereof (Ezra 4 [12]). The people dwelt in " ceiled houses " (Hag. 1 [4]). Tatnai visited Jerusalem and asked them " Who hath commanded you to build this House and to make up this wall ? " (Ezra 5 [3]). Ezra returned to Jerusalem before Nehemiah received permission to return to Jerusalem to build the city, and he thanked God because the house of God was set up, the desolations were repaired, and a wall was given in Jerusalem as early as the 7th year of Darius Hystaspes, otherwise Artaxerxes (Ezra 9 [9]).

This is the simple, the obvious, and indeed the only possible interpretation of the prophecy. The words were spoken in the 1st year of Darius, B.C. 538, of a city then lying in ruins. The " street " was the broad, empty space where the houses were formerly built, the area enclosed by the circumventing wall. The wall was the enclosing and protecting defence of the city. Both were to be built again, even in troublous times.

" The commandment to restore and to build Jerusalem " was a commandment to build the houses and the wall, to re-people the city and to rebuild the Sanctuary.

The one great event, and the only one in the history of the Jews which corresponds with the prophecy, is the return of the 42,360 exiles under Zerubbabel and Joshua, the rebuilding of the city and the Sanctuary, and the securing of the safety of the same by the erection of the protecting wall.

None of the Chronologers have been able to adopt this interpretation, because, although they have seen its truth, they have been unable to shake off the tyranny of the Ptolemaic system of Chronology.

Thus, Prideaux says, " Jerusalem was rebuilt by virtue of the decree granted by Cyrus in the first year of his reign, and if the words of the prophecy " to restore and to build Jerusalem " are to be understood in a literal sense, they can be understood of no other restoring and building of that city than that which was accomplished by virtue of that decree, and the computation of the ,70 weeks must begin from the granting and going forth thereof." (Why not ?)

" But if the computation be begun so high, the 490 years of the said 70 weeks cannot come low enough to reach any of those events which are predicted by this prophecy."

He therefore rejects this interpretation of the prophecy, " because if the 490 years begin from the decree of Cyrus they cannot, by a great many years, reach the events predicted by this prophecy, and therefore none who understand this prophecy to relate either to the cutting off or the coming of the Messiah do begin from hence, for according to this computation no Chronology can ever reconcile these years to either the coming or the cutting off of the Messiah."

Benjamin Marshall follows in the same strain and makes the following calculation :—

$$7 \times 7 = 49 \text{ years.}$$
$$62 \times 7 = 434 \quad ,,$$
$$\text{Total} \quad 483 \quad ,,$$

But Cyrus' commandment was issued B.C. 536, and these 483 years bring us only to B.C. 53. Marshall places the death of Christ A.D. 33, and this makes the interval 86 years too long. If he had placed the death of Christ at A.D. 29 instead of A.D. 33, the interval would have been 82 years, which is just the exact number by which the Ptolemaic Chronology errs from the truth.

What Marshall and Prideaux say in effect is just this. Since the Messiah was not cut off till 82 years after the date expressed in the prophecy, reckoning from the going forth of the commandment of Cyrus according to the infallible Chronology of Ptolemy's Canon, therefore, the going forth of the commandment of Cyrus was not the event which the prophecy contemplated, and we must seek some other point to reckon from.

The truth is, it is not the starting point of the reckoning, but the Ptolemaic Chronology which is in error, and that by the space of just 82 years.

Other Chronologers take the same view with regard to the abandonment of the Decree of Cyrus, B.C. 536, as the starting point of the reckoning, but they disagree upon the choice of an alternative starting point.

Altogether *four* decrees are mentioned in the Books of Ezra and Nehemiah, each of which has found its advocates, except the Decree of Cyrus, which is the one to which the prophecy does really refer. These are :—

The four Decrees, one of which must be identified with " the commandment to restore and to build Jerusalem " (Dan. 9^{25}).

1. The decree of Cyrus to build the Temple.
   1st Cyrus to the Crucifixion = 536+32 = 568 years.
2. The decree of Darius to complete the Temple.
   2nd Darius to the Crucifixion = 520+32 = 552 years.
3. The decree of Artaxerxes to endow the Temple.
   7th Artaxerxes to the Crucifixion = 458+32 = 490 years.
4. The decree of Artaxerxes to build the city and the wall.
   20th Artaxerxes to the Crucifixion = 445+33 = 478 years = 483 Chaldean years of 360 days each.

The decree of Darius is that given in the 2nd, 3rd, or 4th years of Darius, Ezra 4^{24}, 6$^{1-12}$. It is rejected on the same ground as that of Cyrus—incompatibility with the received Ptolemaic Chronology.

Dr. Prideaux says—" The seventy weeks of this prophecy could not have their beginning from this decree, for the same reason that they could not begin from the decree of Cyrus, that is, because the 490 years, reckoning from the granting of this decree, cannot reach the chief events which are by this prophecy predicted to fall within the compass of them, that is, the coming and the cutting off of the Messiah."

Marshall calculates—Darius' decree was issued in his 2nd year, B.C. 520, and these 483 years bring us only to B.C. 37.

The decree of the 7th year of Artaxerxes is advocated by Dr. Prideaux. His starting point is the 7th year of Artaxerxes Longimanus = B.C. 458. His terminus is the death of Christ, which he puts at A.D. 33. He divides the 490 years as follows :—

Marshall's Interpretation of Daniel 9$^{24-27}$.

7 ×7 = 49 years to the reconstitution of the Jewish church and state in Jerusalem.

62 × 7 = 434 years to the first appearance of the Messiah in his forerunner, John the Baptist.

1 ×7 = 7 years, viz. 3½ years' ministry of John the Baptist and 3½ years' ministry of Jesus Christ.

Total seventy sevens, or 490 years.

According to Marshall, Artaxerxes' decree was issued in his 7th year—B.C. 458, and from this point, 483 years brings us to A.D. 21.

In all three cases the starting point is too early. It does not reach down to the date of the death of Christ, though Prideaux stretches the time by taking the word "after" to mean not *immediately* after, but *some little time* after the 62 sevens, "shall Messiah be cut off."

The decree of the 20th year of Artaxerxes is advocated by Petavius, Ussher, Lloyd, Marshall, and most present day students of Daniel's prophecy.

As the first three decrees all fall short of the assumed date of our Lord's death, A.D. 33, so this one falls beyond it. Accordingly, various expedients are adopted for computing the years in such a way as to make them fit the prophecy.

Petavius begins with the 20th of Artaxerxes, B.C. 454 (instead of B.C. 445), and so gets rid of 9 years by assuming that Artaxerxes began to reign as Co-Rex with his father Xerxes at that date. His excuse for this is the fact of the flight of Themistocles to the court of Artaxerxes Longimanus, which is dated by Thucydides and Charon of Lampsacus B.C. 471.

Ussher takes the same view, only he makes Xerxes die after a reign of 12 years instead of 21, and gives Artaxerxes Longimanus 50 years instead of 41. To get back 4 of these 9 years, both Ussher and Petavius assume that Christ's death, A.D. 33, took place in the middle of the last week of 7 years—hence they reckon $69\frac{1}{2} \times 7 = 486\frac{1}{2}$, or say 487 years from B.C. 454 to A.D. 33.

Lloyd adopts another expedient for getting rid of the superfluous 5 years over and above the 478 contained in the period from the 20th of Artaxerxes, B.C. 445, to the death of Christ, A.D. 33. He reckons that the 483 years of Daniel are Chaldean years of 360 days each, and as 69 ordinary Julian years of $365\frac{1}{4}$ days are equal to 70 Chaldean years of 360 days, Daniel's 483 Chaldean years = nearly 477 ordinary Julian years. Thus he gets rid of 6 years. Then he is one short. To get this back he explains that the 483 years of 360 days end May 18th, A.D. 32, and Christ's death took place, the following Passover.

Marshall agrees with Lloyd in all respects except that he applies the first $7 \times 7 = 49$ years to the period of the building of Jerusalem, whilst Lloyd applies it to the term of the continuance of prophecy, which accordingly ends with Malachi, 445 – 49 = 397 (inclusive reckoning); hence the date B.C. 397 in the A.V. margin of Malachi 1[1].

Ussher, Lloyd, Marshall. This represents the orthodox succession of Bible Chronologers. Ussher laid the foundation of Bible Chronology in his *Annals of the Old and New Testaments*. Lloyd adopted these with a few alterations, printed them for the first time in the margin of the A.V. in Lloyd' Bible, A.D. 1701, and explained them (1) in his Tables at the end of his Bible; (2) in his *Chronological Tables*, printed but never published (to be seen in the British Museum), and (3) in some private papers given to the world by his chaplain, Benjamin Marshall, in his *Chronological Tables* with an Appendix to Table 3, and the whole of Table 4, by Lloyd, Bishop of Worcester, published 1713. Bishop Lloyd published *An Exposition of the Prophecy of Seventy Weeks*, and Benjamin Marshall *A Chronological Treatise on the Seventy Weeks of Daniel*. These, with Prideaux's *Historical Connection of the Old and new Testaments*, are the standard works on the orthodox system of Bible Chronology. They all assume the infallibility of Ptolemy's Canon, and bend their interpretation of the Chronology of the Old Testament to make it agree therewith.

The Miraculous Element in the Book of Daniel.

The extraordinary character of the Book of Daniel, and in particular the dated prophecy of Daniel 9, is accounted for by the wonder and the marvel of its theme.   God is here revealing to men the central purpose, and the final goal, of human history, the redemption of the race through the incarnation and the death of His own beloved Son.

This involves a survey of the whole field of human history and a clear and convincing proof of the fact that God Himself is a real factor, and not merely *a* factor, but *the* supreme, the inclusive, the controlling factor.   Who, whilst He gives men perfect freedom of choice and will, always within limits, nevertheless Himself determines what those limits shall be, how long, how deep and how broad the stream of time shall flow, bearing upon its bosom the ships of the nations with their cargo of human affairs.

The world-wide survey of human history all down the stream of time is seen in Nebuchadnezzar's dream of the great image, and in Daniel's complementary vision of the four beasts, where the rise and fall of the Babylonian, the Medo-Persian, the Greek and the Roman Empires are in full view.   The more immediate contest between Persia and Greece is depicted in Daniel's vision of the ram and the he-goat, whilst further down the stream of time, the revelation of " the Scripture of Truth " presents us with the story of the conflict between Syria and Egypt, the persecution of Antiochus Epiphanes, and the appearance on the horizon of the mighty Empire of Rome.

But all this is but a prelude to the coming of the Son of Man and the establishment of the Kingdom of God.

So, too, the stories of Shadrach, Meshach and Abed-nego in the fiery furnace, and Daniel in the den of lions, are meant to convey the lesson that in the hands of God all material forces are frangible and ductile.   Events are produced by causes which appear to be utterly inadequate to account for them, because God is moving in the midst of them, directing, controlling, protecting and subordinating all the forces of nature, and co-ordinating the obedient and the refractory wills of men to the attainment of His own ends.

Thus we are led to see that we are in the hands of One Who is ever cherishing and ever executing a purpose of holy love, and Who has His way with us, not we our way with Him.

From this point of view the element of the extraordinary, the miraculous, the supernatural, which bulks so largely in the Book of Daniel, is seen to be quite consonant with the theme of the Book, producing an atmosphere in which the impressive revelation of the universal sovereignty and the immediate and miraculous, as well as the mediate and continuous, activity of God, is brought home to intellect and conscience, to heart and will.

The marvel of the prediction of the exact date of the Messiah's birth is made all the more easy of belief, because all the leading events of human history, all down the stream of time, are touched upon as the vision grows, and when at last the Messiah does appear He attests the prophetic character of the Book which contains the vision, and accompanies His exposition of the prophecy with the impressive counsel, " Whoso readeth, let him understand " (Matt. 24[15]).

We complete our Chronology of the Old Testament as follows :—

BIBLE DATES.

From the Return to the Messiah.

According to the Hebrew Text of the Old Testament.

3589. 1st year of Cyrus' sole Kingship (see Chapter 24).
Add 482 years to the crucifixion.
From 1st year of Cyrus to cutting off of Messiah = 483 years, Dan. 9[25].

$$7 \times 7 = 49$$
$$62 \times 7 = 434$$
$$\overline{483}$$

1 Deduct 1 for inclusive reckoning.

482. $\overline{482}$

482

4071. Messiah cut off.   Date of the crucifixion of Christ.
Deduct 33 years to date of actual birth of Christ.
Jesus was about 30 years old when He began His ministry (Luke 3[23]).
His ministry lasted about 3 years.

	1st Passover at which He began His ministry John 2[23].		
	2nd	,,	,, 5[1].
	3rd	.	,, 6[4].
33.	4th	,, at which He was crucified.	,, 12[1].

4038. Date of the actual birth of our Lord—Dec. 25th, B.C. 5 (see Andrews' *Life of our Lord*).
Add 4 years to the end of B.C. 1 and the commencement of
4.   the Christian Era, Anno Domini.

AN. HOM. 4042. = B.C. 1 ; and AN. HOM. 1 = B.C. 4042, according to the Chronology of the Old Testament.
N.B.—According to the received Ptolemaic Chronology, AN. HOM. 1 = 4124, a difference of 82 years.

The Messiah did appear at the appointed season, and was cut off 483 years after the going forth of the commandment of Cyrus to restore and to build Jerusalem in the 1st year of his sole reign, B.C. 536.

The Chronology of the Jews is indicated in the tenets of the Herodians, who knew that the time for the appearance of the Messiah was at hand, and who, in consonance with their gross and worldly conception of His Kingdom, regarded Herod himself, the builder of the Temple, as the Messiah (Epiphanius, Παναριαν, *The Drugchest, a Refutation of all Heresies.* Tertullian, *De præscriptione hæreticorum*).

They correctly reckoned the seventy sevens from the reign of Cyrus, and found that the term of the 490 years was approaching its completion in the time of Herod, in whose days the Messiah was born. But when the true Messiah was rejected, and the time for His coming had gone by, they corrupted their Chronology and shortened the duration of the Kingdom of Persia, so as to be able to apply the prophecy to Theudas and Judas of Galilee (Acts 5 $^{36. 37}$), and at length to Bar Cochab, and thus the count of the years was lost, until it was falsely restored by the heathen astrologer Ptolemy.

The wise men from the East were expecting the Messiah at this time, and their interpretation of the appearance of the star in the East may have been assisted by a knowledge through Daniel, or through some other member of the Jewish faith, who instructed them in the prophecies respecting the Star that was to come out of Jacob (Numb. 24 ^{17}), and the time of its appearance toward the end of Daniel's 70 weeks.

The general expectation of the Jews was that the Messiah was now at hand ; the time for His appearance had come. Hence the Jews sent priests and Levites to John the Baptist to ask him, Who art thou ? " And he confessed and denied not, but confessed I am not the Messiah " (John 1 $^{19. 20}$). Many of those who heard him and saw his works said " This is of a truth that prophet that should come into the world " (John 6 ^{14}, 7 ^{40}). John the Baptist understood the Chronology of Daniel's prophecy, and made it one of the bases of his appeal, " Repent ye, for the Kingdom of Heaven is at hand " (Matt. 3 ^{2}). Later on, when he heard in prison of the works of Christ, he sent two of his disciples and said unto Him, " Art thou He that should come, or do we look for another ? " (Matt. 11 ^{3}).

But the most definite and specific statement of the interval between the going forth of the commandment, and the appearance of the Messiah, is given in the opening message of Jesus Himself, in which He strikes the three great bell notes of the Gospel (Mark 1 ^{15}).

> " The time is fulfilled ..
> The Kingdom of God is at hand :
> Repent ye and believe the good news."

There is a most minute and exact correspondence between the other prophecies of Daniel and their fulfilment. Compare, for example, the prophecy of the four great Kings of Persia (Dan. 11 ^{2}), and the appearance of Cyrus, Cambyses, Darius and Xerxes ; the vision of the ram and the he-goat (Dan. 8), and its fulfilment in the conquest of Asia by Alexander the Great ; the prophecy of the mighty King (Dan. 11 ^{3}) and the appearance of Alexander the Great ; the prophecy of the conflict between the King of the North and the King of the South (Dan. 11 $^{5-19}$), and the wars between the Seleucids of Syria and the Ptolemys of Egypt ; the prophecy of the rise of the vile person (Dan. 11 ^{21}), and the persecution of Antiochus Epiphanes ; the prophecy of his checkmate by the arrival of ships of Chittim (Dan. 11 ^{30}), and the banner of Rome flung round the infant Ptolemy ; and then the closing vision of the time of trouble such as never was, seen through the haze that envelops the distant hills that fringe the borderland of eternity, where many of them that sleep in the dust awake, " some to everlasting life and some to shame and everlasting contempt " (Dan. 12 ^{2}.)

The perversion of this ancient prophecy into a *vaticinium post eventum et ex eventu* originated in the attack of Porphyry the deadly enemy of the Christian faith. It has sent its ringing echoes of unbelief all down the ages, and it is heard in our midst to-day, but those whose insight into the ways of God is clear and keen, and whose touch with God is close and sure, will see in these prophecies and their fulfilment a confirmation of their faith in the incorruptible integrity of the word of God.

The cutting off of the Messiah, at the precise moment at which it was foretold, has become the pivot of the world's history, and His birth the central epoch of its Chronology.

" Here I stand." *Athanasius contra mundum.* The received Chronology is false. The Chronology of the Old Testament is true.

CHAPTER XXVIII.   COMPARATIVE CHRONOLOGY.

The Year of Messiah's Birth according to the Canon of Ptolemy, AN. HOM. 4120.

CLAUDIUS PTOLEMÆUS, the originator of the Ptolemaic astronomy, superseded by the Copernican System, A.D. 1530, when Nicolas Copernicus (1473–1543) published his great epoch-making work, *De Orbium Revolutionibus*, flourished at Alexandria in Egypt in the 2nd Century A.D. He was both a learned man and a great man. He gripped the phenomena of the heavens, and welded them into such a comprehensive system, that the Ptolemaic astronomy maintained its hold on the mind of Europe for a period of 14 Centuries, in spite of the fact that the Copernican astronomy, which makes the sun the centre of the solar system, was taught in its essentials by Pythagoras (B.C. 582–c. 500), who explained the motions of the heavenly bodies in his *Harmony of the Spheres* some 600 years before Ptolemy was born.

The Ptolemaic Astronomy has gone. But the Ptolemaic Chronology remains. And since the actual count of the years of the Persian period, between Darius Hystaspes and Alexander the Great, has been lost, no one will ever be able to replace the erroneous Chronology of Ptolemy, by producing a positive Chronology of the period in harmony with the truth, unless the gap should be filled by the discovery of ancient Monuments of this period in the East.

One reason why Ptolemy's Canon has maintained its hold upon the modern mind is because there is no other system which bridges the gulf of time from the 8th Century B.C. to the 2nd Century A.D. All other systems fail at the same point. For the later Persian period Ptolemy is the only witness, his Canon the only strand connecting the events of antiquity with those of modern times.

His Canon exists in three forms. The genuine original is found in Theon, Ptolemy's successor in the chair of astronomy at Alexandria. Two other lists of reigns, based on Ptolemy's Canon, are preserved by Syncellus (A.D. 792), the one called *The Astronomical Canon*, the other *The*

Ecclesiastical Canon. In these the names and dates are corrected, interpolated and modified in such a way as to present, in tabular form, the chronological opinions of Syncellus.

Another reason for the high esteem in which Ptolemy's Canon is held is the quasi-infallibility which is attached to a mathematical demonstration, and which has been transferred by Ptolemy's readers to all the inferences and conclusions embodied in his Canon.

Ptolemy's method of determining dates is the astronomical method of the calculation of eclipses. He also had access to the information contained in Berosus, (B.C. 356–323). He based his Chronology upon the calculations of Eratosthenes (b. B.C. 276) and Apollodorus (2nd Century B.C.), and he had before him all the information contained in Diodorus Siculus (fl. A.D. 8), and all the literature of Greece and Rome and Alexandria.

The main thing to note is the fact that he is not an original authority, not a witness recording contemporary events, still less is he a standard by which to correct other witnesses. He is a late compiler, living in the 2nd Century A.D., and constructing a scheme of Chronology covering nearly 1,000 years, from B.C. 747 to A.D. 137.

Prideaux puts the authority of Ptolemy's Canon above that of every other human writer. He says :—

" Ptolemy's Canon being fixed by the eclipses, the truth of it may at any time be demonstrated by astronomical calculations, and no one hath ever calculated those eclipses but hath found them fall in the times where placed ; and, therefore, this being the surest guide which we have in Chronology, and it being also verified by its agreement everywhere with the Holy Scripture, it is not for the authority of any other human writer whatsoever to be receded from."

Lloyd and Marshall speak of it in similar terms. Halma regards it as " the most precious monument of antiquity."

An examination of the table of eclipses, gathered from the works of Ptolemy by M. Halma, shows that whilst there are eclipses recorded in the 1st and 2nd years of Merodach-baladan (Mar. 19, 720, Mar. 8, 719 and Sep. 1, 719), the 5th year of Nabopolassar (Apl. 22, 600), the 7th of Cambyses (July 16, 522), and the 20th and 31st years of Darius Hystaspes (Nov. 19, 501 and Ap. 25, 490), as soon as we reach this point, at which the narrative of the Old Testament closes, and the late Persian period begins, there is from the 31st year of Darius to the Archonship of Phanostratus, no eclipse whatever on record, and consequently no astronomical data by which to fix the duration of the reigns of the Kings of the later Persian period.

Apart from three eclipses recorded by the Chaldees on Dec. 23, 381, and June 18, 380, in the Archonship of Phanostratus, and on Dec. 10, 380, in the Archonship of Evander, there is not a single eclipse on record from the 31st year of Darius to the death of Alexander the Great.

Ptolemy's Canon is compiled from Chaldean records in which eclipses of the moon alone are registered, the Chaldean astronomers not being able to calculate the eclipses of the sun.

So that for the construction of that part of Ptolemy's Canon which covers the interval of 109 years between B.C. 490 and 381, eclipses are entirely wanting, and Ptolemy has to fall back upon the same materials as other Chronologers. At the very point at which the Old Testament, the Apocryphal literature, Josephus, the classics, the *Cuneiform Inscriptions* of Persia and the tablets of Babylonia all fail, *Ptolemy fails also.* These 82 years are years that never existed except in the constructive imagination of the Chronologer. They are years in which the sun never set, and on which the light never shone.

Of course, if one could be quite sure of the exact date of an eclipse, like the Eclipse of Thales, and could identify it with an event like the Battle of Halys, such an eclipse would measure the lapse of time between that event and the present day, and also between that event and every other event connected with it by a chain of continuous, contemporary historical records.

But the date of the Eclipse of Thales and the Battle of Halys is quite unknown to us. All that we know of it is what we are told in Herodotus, Book i, Chap. 74, where he says :—

" War broke out between Cyaxares the Mede and Alyattes the Lydian, and continued for five years with various success. In the course of it the Medes gained many victories over the Lydians, and the Lydians also gained many victories over the Medes. A combat took place in the 6th year, in the course of which, just as the battle was growing warm, *day was in a sudden changed into night.* This event had been foretold by Thales the Milesian, who forewarned the Ionians of it, fixing for it the very year in which it actually took place."

The date of this eclipse as fixed by Volney was B.C. 625. Clinton made it B.C. 603. Ideler said no eclipse fulfilled the conditions except that of B.C. 610. Later still, Mr. Hind and Prof. Airy brought it down to B.C. 585. The Eclipse of Thales has been placed in 607 (Calvisius), 603 (Costard, Montucla and Kennedy), 601 (Ussher), 597 (Petavius, Marsham, Bouhier and Larcher), and 585 (Pliny, Scaliger, Newton, Ferguson, Vignoles and Jackson). George Rawlinson concludes a paragraph on the subject by saying, " It may be doubted whether astronomical science has yet attained to such exactness with respect to the *line* of solar eclipses as to justify the adoption of its results as the basis of a chronological system. All astronomical calculations are uncertain since they assume the uniformity of the moon's motion which is a very doubtful point, and since Professor Airy made his calculations for Mr. Bosanquet, which brought the date of the Eclipse of Thales down to B.C. 585, certain irregularities in the moon's movements have been discovered."

In any case, since there are never less than 2 eclipses in any year, usually 4, and sometimes as many as 7, and since an eclipse repeats itself more or less completely every 18 years and a few days, and much more completely every 54 years and a month, there will always be an eclipse available within a reasonable number of years with which to identify any recorded eclipse, the date of which we desire to fix ; apart from which, it is a perfect paradox to contemplate the fixing of the current of the history of the entire world by the motions of the moon, the very type and symbol of instability.

The method of astronomical calculation is, therefore, by no means an infallible guide to Chronology, but even if it were an infallible guide, Ptolemy could make no use of it, for he had no recorded eclipses to work the method with, during the later Persian period, the only part of his Chronology which is in dispute.

We have seen that the received Chronology and the received dating of the Books of Ezra and Nehemiah, which identifies the Artaxerxes of Ezra 7 and Nehemiah with Artaxerxes Longimanus, lands us in the absurdity of making the leading men of the period live to an impossible age,

> Ezra, 141 in the 20th year of Artaxerxes Longimanus.
>
> Nehemiah, 103 years older in the 32nd year of Artaxerxes Longimanus than when he returned to Jerusalem in the 1st year of Cyrus.
>
> Mordecai 123 in the 12th year of Xerxes.

Now, if the great and improbable age of these Biblical characters is due simply to an error in the Chronology of the period, it will follow that other men, belonging to profane history, but living in the same period, will also be represented as living to a similarly great and improbable age, and if such aged men are found in the history of the period, it will be a confirmation of the fact that some error has found its ways into the received Chronology.

The Kings will be represented as reigning for an extraordinary number of years, or fictitious Kings will be invented, the Jewish high priests will hold office for very long periods, and some men mentioned by the same name at great intervals apart will appear to be too old to be identical, and will be split up into two, an earlier and a later, both bearing the same name and title, and appearing in many respects as if they were one and the same person.

And this is exactly what we find. First, take the case of Josephus. Here we have Sanballat old enough to be Pekah of Samaria in the 20th year of Arta-xerxes Longimanus, B.C. 445, and still living when Alexander besieges Gaza, B.C. 332, at the age of 113 *plus* however old he was when he opposed Nehemiah in B.C. 445, at the building of the wall, when he was Governor of Samaria. The alternative is to split him up and say there were two Sanballats.

Again, during this period, the Jewish high priests hold office for long terms, and the contemporary Kings appear to have unusually long reigns. Thus :—

JEWISH HIGH PRIESTS.		KINGS OF PERSIA.	
Joshua	56	Darius I	36
Joiakim	36	Xerxes	21
Eliashib	34	Artaxerxes I..	41
Joiada	36	Darius II	19
Johanan	34	Artaxerxes II..	46
Jaddua	17	Artaxerxes III	21
Average 35.		*Average* 30.	

KINGS OF MACEDON.			KINGS OF SPARTA.		
Æropas	..	.. 26	Agasicles	..	.. 41
Alectus	..	.. 29	Ariston	..	.. 38
Amyntas I	..	.. 50	Demaratus	..	.. 35
Alexander	..	.. 43	Leotychides	..	.. 22
Perdiccas II	..	.. 41	Archidamus II		.. 42
Archelaus	..	.. 14	Agis II	..	.. 30
Amyntas II	..	.. 19	Agesilaus II	..	.. 36
Alorites	..	.. 4	Archidamus III		.. 23
Perdiccas III	..	6	Agis III	..	.. 8
Philip	..	.. 24	Eudamidas I		.. 33
Alexander the Great		12			
Average 25.			*Average* 30.		

The following aged men are mentioned in the history of Greece for this period :—

Xenophanes	..	.. 141.	Timæus, Plutarch.
Pythagoras	..	.. 99.	Aristogenus, Jamblicus.
Æschylus (69 or)	..	154.	Author of Life of Æschylus.
Isocrates	..	.. 99.	Corsini.
Cratinus	..	.. 97.	Lucian.
Sophocles	..	.. 95.	Lucian.
Democritus	..	.. 104.	Lucian.
,,	..	.. 109.	Laertius.
Hippocrates	..	.. 109.	Suidas.
Timotheus	..	.. 97.	Suidas.

The following have very long productive periods or *floruits*.

Plato (comic poet)	..	63 years,	Scholiast apud Plutarch.
Parmenides	..	68 ,,	Laertius.
Gorgias (ambassador)		79 ,,	Suidas with Pausanias.
Antiphanes (comic poet)		71 ,,	Suidas with Athenæus.
Aristophanes (comic poet)		53 ,,	Internal evidence.
Aristophon (ambassador)		63 ,,	Demosthenes.

The following contradictions, variations or discrepancies, emerge between the Chronology of Ptolemy's Canon and other sources for this period :—

B.C. 480. Birth of Euripides, (Plutarch, Eratosthenes).
But the Parian Marble says B.C. 485.

B.C. 475. Cimon took Scyros (Plutarch).
Bentley alters the date to B.C. 469, as " otherwise it would be 7 years before the oracle would be obeyed."

B.C. 471. Flight of Themistocles, who had been banished from Athens, to the Persian court of King Artaxerxes Longimanus (Thucydides, Charon of Lampsacus).
But, according to Ptolemy's Canon, Artaxerxes did not come to the throne till 7 years after this, in B.C. 464.

B.C. 464. Charon of Lampsacus (born B.C. 554) still writing history. Creuzer rejects the date of his birth, " because it would make him 90 years old."

B.C. 439. Pindar completes his 80th year (Scholiast apud Thomas Magister). But Thomas Magister makes him 66 and Suidas 65.

B.C. 424. Death of Artaxerxes Longimanus, who reigned 40 years (Thucydides Diodorus), 41 including the odd months of Xerxes II and Sogdianus (Ptolemy's Canon), 42 (Ctesias).

B.C. 404. Artaxerxes II Mnemon reigned 40 years (Eusebius, Alexandrine Chronicle), 42 years (Clement of Alexandria), 43 years (Diodorus), 46 years (Ptolemy's Canon), 62 years (Plutarch). The cuneiform tablets say he began to reign B.C. 395, which, according to A. H. Sayce, gives Darius II Nothus, 29 years instead of 19 as in Ptolemy's Canon.

B.C. 358. Artaxerxes III Ochus (Ptolemy's Canon), B.C. 361 (Diodorus). Reigned 21 years (Ptolemy's Canon), 23 (Diodorus).

B.C. 356. Death of Alexander of Pheræ (Diodorus). But his death is mentioned by Xenophon, who died 3 years before.

B.C. 340. Aristophanes *floruit* B.C. 403, i.e. 63 years before this date, and was ambassador B.C. 411, i.e. 71 years before this. Clinton says, " the consideration of dates proves that he was not the same man," and that " the text of Demosthenes, who gives the facts, must be corrupt."

From these facts it will be seen that the testimony of Ptolemy's Canon is contradicted at various points by many competent witnesses. The facts also suggest the possibility that the extraordinary ages and long *floruits* of many distinguished men, may be due to an error, by which the Chronology of the period may have been unduly extended some 50 or 60 years.

Clinton says, " The government of Pisistratus at Athens (B.C. 560) is marked as being the first date in Grecian history from which an unbroken series of dates can be deduced in regular succession," and he gives a list of the Archons of Athens which practically fills each year of the whole period.

It is not denied that such a list was compiled by the early Chronologers of Greece about 100 years after the death of Alexander the Great, but it is affirmed that they were not derived from authentic contemporary sources.

Respecting the period in question, the later Persian Empire, from Xerxes to Alexander the Great, Clinton says, " From B.C. 480 to B.C. 303 we have an unbroken series (of Archons) by the combined assistance of Diodorus, A.D. 8, and Dionysius of Halicarnassus, B.C. 70 – 6." But these are not contemporary witnesses. They are late compilers, constructing a scheme of Chronology, dependent upon the conjectural results of Eratosthenes (B.C. 276) and Apollodorus (2nd century B.C.).

The celebrated Parian marble was purchased by Mr. William Petty for Thomas, Earl of Arundel, in the year A.D. 1624. It was brought to England and placed in the gardens of Arundel House, Strand, A.D. 1627. It appears to have been found in the Island of Paros. The Chronicle is engraved on a marble slab 3ft. 7 by 2ft. 7 and 5 inches thick. It gives the principal events of Greek history from its legendary beginnings to the year B.C. 264, in which it was executed.   It gives the date of the reign of Cecrops, the flood of Deucalion, the trial between the gods Mars and Neptune, the planting of corn by Ceres, the *floruits* of Hesiod and Homer, the reign of Cyrus, Darius (Marathon), and Xerxes (Thermopylæ), the dates of the poets Æschylus, Sophocles and Euripides.

Touching the late Persian period, the only Kings of Persia which it mentions after Xerxes are (1) The brother of Cyrus the younger (Artaxerxes Mnemon), who died B.C. 357, and (2) his son Artaxerxes III Ochus.   This is remarkable in itself, but when compared with (1) the history of this period in Josephus and (2) the tenor of the Jewish and Persian tradition of the Chronology of this period, it suggests very forcibly that the Chronology of the latter part of the Persian period from Xerxes to Alexander the Great has been exaggerated, and that the 5 Kings who fill this period :—

Artaxerxes I	..	..	..	..	41 years.
Darius II	..	..	..	..	19 ,,
Artaxerxes II	..	..	..	..	46 ,,
Artaxerxes III	..	..	..	..	21 ,,
Darius III	..	..	..	..	4 ,,

were perhaps in fact only 2 or 3 multiplied into five in order to fill the gap made by the artificial enlargenent of the Chronology by some 82 years more or less.

The marble gives the dates of the Annual Archons for the following years :—

I. Before the death of Xerxes, B.C. 465.

B.C.	B.C.	B.C.	B.C.
682	582	508	472
645	561	495	470.
605	556	489	468
594	537	486	—
591	512	481	—

II. After the death of Xerxes, B.C. 465.

B.C.

463 ⎫
457 ⎬ Artaxerxes I Longimanus.
442 ⎪
420 ⎭

408—Darius II Nothus.

403 ⎫
400 ⎪
380 ⎪
377 ⎬ Artaxerxes II Mnemon.
373 ⎪
371 ⎪
368 ⎪
358 ⎭

355—Artaxerxes III Ochus.

264—Ptolemy Philadelphus.

It will be seen that only 15 Archons are given for the period of 134 years from the death of Xerxes, B.C. 465 to the 1st year of Alexander the Great.

The gaps were filled in by Dionysius of Halicarnassus, and Diodorus, who flourished some 300 years afterwards.

Clinton accepts the testimony of Diodorus for this period, although elsewhere he truly points out that Diodorus is not an independent witness, but merely a reproducer of the approximate computations of the conjectural Chronologers Eratosthenes and Apollodorus.

The truth is, there are no authentic records of the late Persian period in existence. The method of measuring time by means of Olympiads was not adopted till more than 60 years after the death of Alexander the Great. It was not used in the Parian Chronicle. A Chronology was framed by Eratosthenes and Apollodorus, and all the known facts of past history were made to fit into it. Hence discrimination is needed to enable us to separate what is really certain from what is mere matter of opinion and conjecture.

The period of the later Persian Empire from Xerxes to Alexander the Great, is the great gap or blank in the Chronology of the world's history. For this period Thucydides is our only authority.

Herodotus is the historian of the Persian war which ended B.C. 479. Thucydides is the historian of the Peloponnesian war, which commenced B.C. 432.

The history of the interval between B.C. 479 and B.C. 432 has never been written.

" I have gone out of my way," says Thucydides, " to speak of this period, because the writers who have preceded me treat either of Hellenic affairs previous to the Persian invasion or of that invasion itself. The intervening portion of history has been omitted by all of them, with the exception of Hellanicus, and he, where he has touched upon it, in his Attic history, is very brief and inaccurate in his Chronology."

The one event which Thucydides does mention in his brief and hurried summary of this unwritten period, is the flight of Themistocles, and just here, at the very point which he does touch the Chronology of the period, he is in flat contradiction to Ptolemy's Canon. Writing of the year B.C. 471, Thucydides says, Themistocles had been ostracised and was living at Argos. Lacedæmonians and Athenians sent officers to arrest him. He fled to the Corcyreans. They conveyed him to the neighbouring continent. The officers constantly enquired in which direction he had gone, and pursued him every-where. He stopped at the house of Admetus the King of the Molossians, who protected him and would not give him up to his pursuers, though they pressed him do so. And as Themistocles wanted to go to the King (of Persia), Admetus sent him on foot across the country to the sea at Pydna (which was in the Kingdom of Alexander). There he found a merchant vessel sailing to Ionia, in which he embarked. It was driven by a storm to Naxos, but at length he arrived at Ephesus. Themistocles then went up the country with one of the Persians who dwelt on the coast, and sent a letter to *Artaxerxes the son of Xerxes, who had just succeeded to the throne.*

According to Ptolemy's Canon, Artaxerxes the son of Xerxes is Artaxerxes

Longimanus. In 471 Xerxes was in the 15th year of his reign, and he reigned 21 years, after which Artabanus reigned 7 months, and Artaxerxes Longimanus, who was now, on the arrival of Themistocles, only a boy of 14, did not come to the throne till 7 years later, in B.C. 464.

The case then stands thus. For the period from Xerxes to Alexander the Great we have no authentic contemporary record of the Chronology of the Persian Kings. The only strand that continues the Chronology throughout this period is Ptolemy's Canon, a late compilation put together 600 or 700 years after the events it tabulates, the absence of authentic data being made good by the estimates of the early Chronologers, who planned the scheme of the Chronology, and filled in the intervals as best they could, using where necessary what Clinton calls, " the method of conjecture."

Thucydides, the most accurate and reliable of all the early writers on the subject, gives a brief summary of the leading events of a period, the history of which has never been written (except by Hellanicus, whose Chronology is inaccurate), and mentions one dated event which happened in the year B.C. 471. This event is dated in Ptolemy's Canon 7 years later than the time at which it occurred.

No blame attaches to Ptolemy for this. He did the best he could with the materials at his disposal. But real blame does attach to the modern scholar, who refuses to recognise a proved error, and continues to regard as an infallible chronological guide, a table of reigns, which, as regards this part of the Persian period, is incapable of verification, suspect as to its source and false in its facts.

The reconstruction of the true Chronology of the late Persian and the Greek period, from the close of the Old Testament Records, B.C. 488, to the Christian Era, does not come within the scope of the present work. It must be left over for investigation by other workers in this department. It is enough for our purpose that the received Ptolemaic Chronology of this period has been shown to be false and cannot therefore be resorted to as a court of final appeal, nor even regarded as a trustworthy witness against the historical data, testimony, evidence or proof, of the Chronology of the Old Testament.

PTOLEMAIC DATES.

From the Return to the Messiah.

According to Clinton and modern Chronologers generally.

AN. HOM
   3589 = 1st year of Cyrus' sole Kingship (see Chapter 24).
   535. Add 535 years to B.C. I. (B.C. 536–535 = B.C. I.
   4124 = B.C. I ; and AN. HOM. I – B.C. 4124.

Clinton's dates are based on Ptolemy's Canon.
Ptolemy's Canon is based on the conjectural Greek Chronology
of Eratosthenes, the father of Chronology.

The Chronology of Eratosthenes is based, not upon historical data, testimony, evidence or proof, but upon his own subjective estimate of the probable length of the reigns, generations and successions of Kings, Ephors and Priestesses in early Greek history.

In any case it is only an approximate and an uncertain estimate.

According to the prophecy of Daniel it is 82 years longer than the truth.

According to Ptolemy AN. HOM. I = B.C. 4124
According to Daniel AN. HOM. I = B.C. 4042
_____

A difference of   ..   .. 82 years.

The present year of the world (A.D. 1913) is,

According to Ptolemy 4124 + 1913 = 6037.
According to Daniel 4042 + 1913 = 5955.

Yet 45 years, and the sixth millennium of the world's history will be fulfilled, and the seventh millennium ushered in.

" Surely I come quickly, Amen.   Even so, come, Lord Jesus."—REV. 22 [20].

INDEX.

SCRIPTURE REFERENCES.

Judges—cont.

11^{14-28}	149.
11^{26}	139, 140, 146.
12^{7}	143, 148.
12^{8}	143.
12^{9}	148.
12^{11}	143, 148.
12^{13}	143.
12^{14}	148.
$13^{1}-16^{31}$	143.
13^{1}	149.
15^{20}	139, 141, 148.
16^{31}	140, 141, 148.
$17-21$	140, 141, 143.
20^{28}	137.

1 Samuel.

$1-7$	141, 145, 151.
1^{20}	72.
1^{21-23}	116.
2^{19}	253.
4^{18}	149.
7^{2-12}	150, 151.
7^{2}	67, 149, 150.
7^{9}	159.
7^{13-17}	149, 150, 151.
8^{4}	151.
8^{6}	159.
10^{17-27}	164.
10^{25}	111.
11^{14}	158.
12^{19-23}	159.
13^{1}	164.
14^{47-52}	150, 164.
15^{11}	159.
27^{11}	253.

2 Samuel.

2^{11}	165.
$5^{4\cdot5}$	165, 169.
7^{12-16}	68.
14^{26}	253.
$15^{1-6\cdot7}$	166.
$21-24$	140, 166.
21	166.
22	166.
23^{1-7}	166.
23^{8-39}	166.
24	166.

1 Kings.

2^{1-3}	111.
6^{1}	152, 154-160, 166, 167, 169.
$6^{37\cdot38}$	167.
7^{1}	167.
9^{10}	167.
11^{40}	191.
11^{42}	167, 169.
11^{43}	227.
12^{20}	228.
14^{20}	177, 228.
14^{21}	227.
$14^{25\cdot26}$	191.
$15^{1\cdot2}$	177, 227.
15^{9}	177, 178, 227.
15^{25-33}	177, 178, 228.
16^{8}	178, 228.
16^{10-15}	178.
16^{16-22}	178.
16^{22-28}	178, 194, 228.
16^{29}	178, 229.
17^{7}	253.
22^{1-40}	179.
$22^{1\cdot2}$	199.
$22^{41\cdot42}$	173, 178, 227.
22^{50}	227.
22^{51}	170, 173, 180, 229.

2 Kings.

1^{1}	194.
1^{2}	176.
1^{17}	170, 173, 176, 179, 180, 227, 229.
3^{1}	173, 176, 180, 227, 229.
$3^{4\cdot5}$	194.
3^{6-25}	194.
3^{26-27}	194.
$8^{16\cdot17}$	170, 173, 174. 180, 227.
8^{20}	195.
$8^{25\cdot26}$	180, 181, 227.
$9^{13\cdot24\cdot27\cdot33}$	229.
9^{29}	227.
9^{37}	186.
$10^{19\cdot25\cdot28}$	182.
10^{35}	229.
10^{36}	183, 229.
$11^{1\cdot3\cdot4}$	183, 227.
11^{4-21}	182.
$11^{16\cdot21}$	183, 227.
$12^{1\cdot21}$	183, 227.
13^{1}	183, 229.
13^{7}	183.
$13^{9\cdot10}$	173, 174, 183, 229.
$14^{1\cdot2}$	183, 227.
14^{16}	229.
14^{17-22}	183, 184, 227.
14^{21}	184, 228.
14^{23}	183, 184, 229.
$14^{25\cdot26\cdot27}$	185.
14^{29}	184, 229.
15^{1}	174, 184, 185.
$15^{1\cdot2}$	228.
15^{2}	185.
15^{8}	184.
15^{8-10}	185, 229.
$15^{13\cdot14}$	185, 229.
15^{17}	229.
15^{18-22}	255.
15^{19}	200.
$15^{23\cdot24}$	185, 229.
15^{25-27}	185, 204, 229.
15^{29}	203.
15^{30}	170, 173, 186, 204.
$15^{32\cdot33}$	185, 228.
15^{33}	173, 185.
15^{38}	228.
16^{1}	173.
$16^{1\cdot2}$	186, 228.
16^{2}	186, 187.
16^{8}	204.
16^{9-16}	203.
16^{20}	228.
17^{1-23}	229.
17^{1}	186, 203, 229.
17^{4}	191, 205, 207.
17^{24}	15.
18^{1}	186.
$18^{1\cdot2}$	187, 212, 228.
18^{4}	187.
$18^{9\cdot10}$	186, 188.
$18^{13}-19^{37}$	188, 212, 214.
18^{13-16}	214.
18^{13}	212, 213, 214.
18^{17}	210.
$18^{30}-20^{19}$	214.
19^{37}	215.
$20^{1\cdot6\cdot11\cdot12}$	188, 212, 214.
20^{12-21}	188.
20^{21}	228.
21^{1}	189, 228.
$21^{13\cdot14}$	216, 219.
$21^{18\cdot19}$	189, 228.
21^{23-26}	228.
22^{1}	189, 228.
23^{36}	228.
$24^{1\cdot2}$	223.
24^{6-8}	223, 228.
24^{7}	223.
24^{8-16}	188, 223.
24^{12}	263.
$24^{17\cdot18}$	228.
25^{1-21}	228.
25^{1-4}	227,
25^{1}	226, 230.
25^{2-8}	188, 227, 232.
25^{18-21}	227, 271.
25^{23}	203.
25^{25}	227.
25^{27}	231, 232, 263.

1 Chronicles.

1^{18-24}	85, 86.
1^{28}	68.
$5^{6\cdot26}$	200, 203.
6^{1-15}	227, 255, 270.
7^{14-20}	122.
26^{31}	167.
29^{27}	165, 166, 169.

2 Chronicles.

3^{2}	167.
8^{1}	167.
9^{30}	167, 169.
12^{2-9}	191.
13^{20}	170.
16^{1-3}	173, 174, 224.
16^{1}	170, 181.
17^{7-9}	111.
18^{1}	179.
20^{36}	179.
21	176.
21^{1}	170.
21^{3}	180.
21^{4}	179.
21^{11}	179.

WS - #0053 - 030820 - C0 - 229/152/16 - PB - 9780282495343